The Pen Confronts the Sword

The Pen Confronts the Sword
Exiled German Scholars Challenge Nazism

AVIHU ZAKAI

Cover photo from iStock by Getty Images.

Published by State University of New York Press, Albany

© 2018 State University of New York

All rights reserved

No part of this book may be used or reproduced in any manner whatsoever without written permission. No part of this book may be stored in a retrieval system or transmitted in any form or by any means including electronic, electrostatic, magnetic tape, mechanical, photocopying, recording, or otherwise without the prior permission in writing of the publisher.

For information, contact State University of New York Press, Albany, NY
www.sunypress.edu

Library of Congress Cataloging-in-Publication Data

Names: Zakai, Avihu, author.
Title: The pen confronts the sword : exiled German scholars challenge Nazism / Avihu Zakai.
Description: Albany : State University of New York Press, [2018] | Includes bibliographical references and index.
Identifiers: LCCN 2017056059 | ISBN 9781438471631 (hardcover) | ISBN 9781438471648 (pbk. : alk. paper) | ISBN 9781438471655 (ebook)
Subjects: LCSH: Exiles' writings, German—History and criticism. | German literature—20th century—History and criticism. | Authors, German—20th century—Political and social views. | Philosophy, German—20th century.
Classification: LCC PT3808 .Z35 2018 | DDC 830.9/00914—dc23
LC record available at https://lccn.loc.gov/2017056059

10 9 8 7 6 5 4 3 2 1

And the divisions on the central front, under Field Marshall von Bock,
Had already sighted through their binoculars the battlements of
    Moscow.
Luckily for the Russians, the autumn rains fell unrelentingly,
Turning the approaches to Smolensk into the usual quagmire.
Then, in October, the snow began falling in cruel abundance,
Recalling, a spark of hope, what befell Napoleon's Grande Armée
On the deadly white expanse.
We feared what spring would bring,
Dreaded, too, the forces of Field Marshal von Rundstedt,
Which, having taken Rostov, were pressing on toward
The Caucasus and the oilfields of Iraq.
And we feared the Panzer divisions of Field Marshall Rommel,
On their way to Mersa Matruh, and from there to—
Why not?—Tel Aviv, Ein Harod, and Jerusalem.

—Haim Gouri, "And the Divisions—1942,"
translated by Michael Swirsky

Contents

Acknowledgments — ix

Introduction: The Age of Catastrophe: Exile and the Struggle for the Humanist Soul of Europe — 1

I. Apocalypse and Eschatology in Thomas Mann's *Doctor Faustus*: The "Secret Union of the German Spirit with the Demonic" — 23

II. Ernst Cassirer and *The Myth of the State*: Portrait of the Disillusioned Philosopher — 83

III. Erich Auerbach's Book of Books and the Rational Representation of Reality in Western Literature
WITH DAVID WEINSTEIN — 167

IV. Enlightenment and Its Enemies: Max Horkheimer, Theodor Adorno, and the Dialectic of *Dialectic of Enlightenment* — 243

Conclusion: Exile, Trauma, and Interpretation — 307

Bibliography — 323

Index — 349

Acknowledgments

Several colleagues and friends read all or part of my work and offered valuable comments and criticism, among them, Martin Vialon, Stephen G. Nichols, the late William Calin, Martin Elsky, James Porter, Paul Mendes-Flohr, the late Menachem Brinker, David Weinstein, Stephen Whitfield, Walter Nugent, Alexander Yakobson, David Heyd, and Avraham Shapira (Patchi). I owe special thanks to my longtime editor Julie Edelson, who once again made my work shine in a new light. Finally, special thanks to Rafael Chaiken at State University of New York Press, who never ceased to believe in the worth of this study and followed it closely until its final production.

Chapter 3, "Erich Auerbach's Book of Books and the Rational Representation of Reality in Western Literature," appeared previously under different titles in David Weinstein and Avihu Zakai, *Jewish Exiles and European Thought in the Shadow of the Third Reich: Baron, Popper, Strauss, Auerbach* (Cambridge: Cambridge University Press, 2017) © David Weinstein and Avihu Zakai 2017. Reprinted with permission. The author would like to thank the Israeli poet Haim Gouri for permission to reprint his poem "And the Divisions—1942."

Introduction

The Age of Catastrophe

Exile and the Struggle for the Humanist Soul of Europe

Scribere est agere (to write is to act).

—Sir William Blackstone, *Commentaries on the Laws of England*, 1765–1769

On February 22, 1942, Stefan Zweig, the exiled Austrian Jewish novelist, playwright, journalist, and biographer, committed suicide in Brazil. As he explained in his suicide letter, "the world of my own language sank and was lost to me and my spiritual homeland, Europe, destroyed itself."[1] Days later, Klaus Mann, another exile and Thomas Mann's son, explained that Zweig "could not bear the gruesome spectacle of a world bursting asunder."[2]

"The decades from the outbreak of the First World War to the aftermath of the Second," wrote Eric Hobsbawm, "was an Age of Catastrophe," or *historia calamitatum*. "For forty years it stumbles from one calamity to

---

1. See Matti Friedman, "70 years later, a handwritten note recalls the end of a literary life," http://www.haaretz.com/jewish-world/israeli-library-uploads-suicide-letter-of-jewish-writer-stefan-zweig-1.414312.

2. Klaus Mann, *The Turning Point* (New York: L. B. Fischer, 1942), 356–57. Note Christopher Browning's use of 1942 as the transition point of the Holocaust in his book *Ordinary Men: Reserve Police Battalion 101 and the Final Solution in Poland* (New York: HarperCollins, 1992), xiii: "In mid-March 1942 some 75 to 80 percent of all victims of the Holocaust were still alive, while 20 to 25 percent had perished. A mere eleven months later, in mid-February 1943, the percentages were exactly the reverse."

another. There were times when even intelligent conservatives would not take bets on its survival. . . . While the economy tottered, the institutions of liberal democracy virtually disappeared between 1917 and 1942 from all but a fringe of Europe and parts of North America and Australia."[3] In Hannah Arendt's summation, "two world wars" took place "in one generation, separated by an uninterrupted chain of local wars and revolutions"; hence, the "subterranean stream of Western history has finally come to the surface and usurped the dignity of that tradition."[4] According to Ernst Cassirer, "In the last thirty years, in the period between the first and second World Wars, we have . . . passed through a severe crisis of our political and social life." His generation experienced "a radical change in the form of political thought . . . the appearance of a new power: the power of mythical thought."[5] Another exile from Nazi Germany, the philosopher Karl Löwith argued that "the world is still as it was in the time of Alaric,"[6] the first king of the barbaric Germans who led to the sack of Rome in 410. Georg Lukács called it "the age of absolute sinfulness."[7] By the same token, the English philosopher and historian R. G. Collingwood wrote in 1942 about "the incessant tempests through which we have precariously lived for close to thirty years."[8] English poet, novelist, and essayist Stephen Spender wrote in 1945 that these years, especially World War II, "brought nearly all those things which we hold firm and sacred into danger and collapse: truth and humanity, reason and right. We lived in a possessed world. For many of us the result was not unexpected when the insanity of a day broke out into delirium in which this poor European humanity

---

3. Eric Hobsbawm, *The Age of Extremes: History of the World, 1914–1991* (New York: Pantheon, 1994), 6–7.

4. Hannah Arendt, "Preface to the First Edition" (1950), *The Origins of Totalitarianism* (New York: Harvest Books, 1976), vii, ix.

5. Ernst Cassirer, *The Myth of the State* (New Haven: Yale University Press, 1967 [1946]), 3.

6. Karl Löwith, *Meaning in History* (Chicago: Chicago University Press, 1949), 191.

7. Georg Lukács, "Preface" (1962), *The Theory of the Novel: A Historic-Philosophical Essay on the Forms of Great Epic Literature* (London: Merlin, 1971 [1920]), 18.

8. R. G. Collingwood, *The New Leviathan: Or Man, Society, Civilization, and Barbarism* (Oxford: Clarendon Press, 1942), lx.

sank back, fanatical, stupefied and mad."⁹ French Jewish historian Marc Bloch (1886–1944), cofounder of the highly influential Annales School of French social history, joined the French Resistance in 1942 in "a world assailed by the most appalling barbarism"¹⁰ and died fighting in 1944. A year after the end of the war, young Albert Camus sailed to the United States in 1946, watching from the deck of the *S.S. Oregon* "the very edge of a wounded" Europe. The topic of his lecture at Columbia University was "The Crisis of Humankind."¹¹ Indeed World War II was an epistemological watershed in modern Western humanist civilization.

If 1942 appeared to be the nadir of civilization, that cultural low point was made flesh by what was happening on the battlefield. It was the year of the Battle of Stalingrad, the most crucial struggle of World War II, a great epistemological watershed in which European humanist civilization faced its gravest existential moment. Many contemporaries shared "a general conviction that *Stalingrad* signifies a *turning-point* in the war."¹²

In the eyes of contemporaries as well as historians, 1942 was the most crucial year of World War II because of three decisive battles on three different fronts. The Battle of Midway in the Pacific took place between June 4 and June 7, the First Battle of El Alamein in Egypt from July 1 to July 27, and the Battle of Stalingrad, Russia, between August 1942 and February 1943. These battles eventually turned the tide of the war in favor of the Allies, but in Istanbul, Auerbach could not know what the outcome would be, let alone whether the German army would reach Turkey from the south via Egypt or the north after conquering Russia. On May 8, 1942, for instance, the German army withstood a Soviet counteroffensive near Kharkov and inflicted heavy losses. The Wehrmacht was on the move and winning in Russia: it reached the Donets, recaptured the Crimea, and took Sevastopol by mid-June. Voronezh was taken while the bulk of the German forces moved toward the oil fields and the Caucasus. At the same time, Friedrich Paulus's Sixth Army advanced along the Don

---

9. Stephen Spender, *European Witness* (New York: Renal & Hitchcock, 1946), 231.

10. Marc Bloch, *Strange Defeat: A Statement of Evidence Written in 1940* (New York: Octagon, 1969 [1949]), 177–78.

11. Camus as quoted in Elizabeth Zerofsky, "Camus Again," *The New Yorker*, May 16, 2016, 36.

12. Richard J. Evans, *The Third Reich at War, 1939–1945* (New York: Allen Lane, 2008), 421, emphasis original.

in the direction of Stalingrad. The German army clearly had the upper hand.[13]

It also seemed invincible in North Africa. Panzer Army Africa (Panzerarmee Afrika) under Field Marshal Erwin Rommel (1891–1944) started the second phase of its advance toward Egypt, and from February to May 1942, the front line settled down near Tobruk. Rommel thought his army would soon "secure the oilfields of the Middle East, Persia, and even Baku on the Caspian Sea."[14] He attacked in June, defeating the Allies and reaching the El Alamein line just one hundred kilometers from Alexandria and the vital Suez Canal. The British army prepared to make its last stand.[15]

The year 1942 brought European humanist civilization to the brink of extinction. Wehrmacht victories in Russia and North Africa portended disaster, yet they also prompted German intellectual exiles to conceive works that took aim at Nazi barbarism and profoundly transformed the content and form of modern intellectual history. In clear contrast to Zweig, these authors stood up against the horrors of Nazi Germany, and their *Kulturkampf* changed the subject matter, methods, and analysis of political, economic, sociological, anthropological, literary, philosophical, and ethical discourse.

~

The Pen Confronts the Sword draws attention, for the first time, to the shared motives behind four remarkable texts, all begun in 1942 by exiled scholars

---

13. See Saul Friedländer, *The Years of Extermination: Nazi Germany and the Jews, 1939–1945* (New York: HarperCollins, 2007), 331. For a description of the atrocities the German army inflicted on Russia, see Evans, *Third Reich at War*; and Jonathan Littell, *The Kindly Ones* ([*Les Bienveillantes*, 2006]; New York: Harper, 2009). For terrible eyewitness accounts, see Ilya Ehrenburg and Vasily Grossman, *The Black Book: The Ruthless Murder of Jews by German-Fascist Invaders throughout the Temporarily-Occupied Regions of the Soviet Union and in the Death Camps of Poland during the War of 1941–1945*, trans. John Glad and James S. Levine (New York: Holocaust Publications, 1981); and Timothy Snyder, *Bloodlands: Europe between Hitler and Stalin* (New York: Basic Books, 2012). On the atrocities in Poland, see Göran Rosenberg, *A Short Stop on the Road from Auschwitz* (Stockholm: Albert Bonniers Förlag, 2012).

14. Evans, *Third Reich at War*, 467.

15. See Andrew Roberts, *The Storm of War: A New History of the Second World War* (London: Allen Lane, 2009), chaps. 4 and 9; and Rick Atkinson, *An Army at Dawn: The War in North Africa, 1942–1943* (New York: Henry Holt, 2002).

confronting Nazi barbarism.¹⁶ The list is impressive: Thomas Mann, *Doctor Faustus* (1947); Ernst Cassirer, *The Myth of the State* (1946); Erich Auerbach, *Mimesis: The Representation of Reality in Western Literature* (1946); and Max Horkheimer and Theodor W. Adorno, *Dialectic of Enlightenment* (1944).¹⁷ Each identified a specific danger in Nazi ideology and mustered new theories, new approaches, new sources, and a new energy to combat it. While scholars have examined these authors' individual legacies, no one has drawn them together for comparative analysis or isolated this watershed moment in their careers. The sense of urgency in their works demands attention. They all raised their pen against Nazi barbarism, believing exactly like Sir William Blackstone, the English jurist and judge, who wrote in his *Commentaries on the Laws of England* (1765–1769), "*Scribere est agere*" (to write is to act).

A book's title reveals intention and meaning. Change the title, and you've wrested it from the history that bore it; you're drifting away from the author's understanding of its intention, content, and form. Accordingly, the titles of these books reflect, directly or indirectly, the trauma the authors experienced as their culture turned toward myth and unreason. In literature, Thomas Mann's *Doctor Faustus* renders Nazi Germany as the new incarnation of the old German legend of amoral arrogance and ambition, equating Germany's covenant with Nazism with a contract with the devil

---

16. To this list one should add other works written against Nazi barbarism, such as R. G. Collingwood's *The New Leviathan: Or Man, Society, Civilization, and Barbarism* (1942), Franz Neumann's *Behemoth: The Structure and Practice of National Socialism* (1942), Karl Popper, *The Open Society and Its Enemies* (1945), Leo Strauss, *Natural Right and History* (1950), Hannah Arendt, *The Origins of Totalitarianism* (1951), and Hans Baron, *The Crisis of the Early Italian Renaissance* (1955), to name only a few.

17. Another important work, which is not included in my study, is *From Caligari to Hitler: A Psychological History of the German Film* (1947), by Siegfried Kracauer (1889–1966), the German writer, journalist, sociologist, cultural critic, and film theorist, who has sometimes been associated with the Frankfurt School of critical theory. In 1942 Kracauer began his study, which traces the birth of Nazism from the cinema of the Weimar Republic. In this work he argued that *The Cabinet of Dr. Caligari*, a 1920 German silent horror film about an insane hypnotist who uses a somnambulist (sleepwalker) to commit murders, can be considered as an allegory for German social attitudes in the period following World War I. More specifically, he maintained that the character of Caligari represents a tyrannical figure, to whom the only alternative is social chaos represented by the fairground. The author would like to thank Dr. Ofer Ashkenazi for this important information about Kracauer.

and predicting the same apocalyptic destruction.[18] In political philosophy, Cassirer denounced the Aryan racist mythos of *Blut und Boden* (blood and soil)—the major slogan of Nazi racial ideology, which grounded ethnicity in a toxic mythology of blood, folk, and homeland (*Heimat*)—which led to systematic terrorization and extermination of people deemed alien and condemned philosophers, such as Oswald Spengler (1880–1936) and Martin Heidegger (1889–1976), for supporting the German culture of pessimism, fatalism, and paranoia, or the destructive "myth of the state." In philology, Auerbach struggled against the rejection of the Old Testament and Jewish influence on European humanist civilization, history, and culture, taking up the ancient Greek debate about the value of art that imitates or reproduces reality to elevate *mimesis* over myth and ordinary human dignity over specious superheroes. Finally, in sociology, Horkheimer and Adorno illuminated how the "dialectic of enlightenment" was driven by a myth of power, first over nature, then over other people, and led to the subjugation—indeed, destruction—of the powerless by the powerful.

Times of crisis, great danger, and risk always elicit responses that are later canonized. As Leopold von Ranke (1795–1886) wrote: "War, Heraclitus tells us, is the father of all things. Out of the conflict of opposing forces, in the great moment of danger, disaster, resurgence, and deliverance, new developments proceed most decisively."[19] Thus, Saint Augustine's *City of God* was written as a defense of, and apologia for, the Christians and Christianity, at a moment of great crisis when they were blamed for the Visigoths' destruction of Rome in 410. Dante Alighieri's *Divine Comedy* (1308–1320) bears the scars of its author's sad, devastating experience of exile; in it, he fought many who drove him from his beloved Florence, condemning some to eternal damnation. Crisis and interpretation, exile and interpretation, are inextricable in Western intellectual history.

The Pen Confronts the Sword asks readers to attend far more sensitively to the shared motives running under the remarkable texts I examine. Trauma always scars the texts it leaves behind, and unprecedented political trauma scars them deeply—however skillfully their authors bury the scars beneath layers of erudition. Deeply scarred by unprecedented political trauma, they wrote a defense of Western civilization that would outlast the "Thousand-Year Reich."

---

18. I use the German title, *Doktor Faustus*, throughout to reference the old German legend; in Mann's novel, Nazi Germany is the new incarnation of this legend.

19. Leopold von Ranke, "Universal Tendencies" (1833), in *Leopold von Ranke, The Secret of World History: Selected Writings on the Art and Science of History*, ed. Roger Wines (New York: Fordham University Press, 1981), 150.

I chose these five refugee intellectuals not only because of their impact, but because the works they wrote in exile during this critical year were intended for polemical uses contemporary readers scarcely imagine. They represent their best efforts to wage *Kulturkampf*, cultural war, against Nazi lies, distortions, tyranny, and barbarism. In Horkheimer and Adorno's words, they all took up "the cause of the remnant of freedom, of tendencies toward real humanity, even though they seem powerless in face of the great historical trend."[20] Of course, not everyone who wrote against Nazism in 1942 was an exile. For example, R. G. Collingwood's *The New Leviathan* also reacted to World War II and the Nazi and fascist threat to Western civilization. However, exilic displacement is the obvious common denominator among the authors considered here. Had they not gone into exile, their outspoken critique would not have been loud or lasting, as they were born into Jewish families and/or married to Jews. From a distance, they witnessed the destruction of family, friends, their whole cultural milieu, their values, their world. They could not keep silent.

Pessimism about the fate of humanist civilization in Western Europe pervades the books they began in 1942, when *no one could predict the war's outcome*. Their writings all support the *crisis mode of historical thought*, the view that harrowing moments, or major turning points, direct the course of history—and not toward progress, but decline. Walter Benjamin expressed this idea beautifully in "Theses on the Philosophy of History," describing thus the "Angel of History": "His face is turned toward the past. Where we perceive a chain of events, he sees one single catastrophe which keeps piling wreckage upon wreckage and hurls it in front of his feet."[21]

Above all, they were united in struggle against the atavistic Nazi *Kultur* of myths, heroes, and legends, which glorified the racist, chauvinistic, homophobic "Community of Blood and Fate of the German people" and rejected European civilization. Its exiled guardians were appalled by their society's flight from reason and reality. They shared Mann's intrinsic connection of Nazi Germany to Satanism and Horkheimer and Adorno's assertion that "despite the fascist lies," the "concept of homeland is opposed to myth."[22]

Given their agonizing times, all contested Nazi distortion and the return of myth and irrationalism in modern history. Mann's apocalyptic

---

20. Max Horkheimer and Theodor W. Adorno, *Dialectic of Enlightenment: Philosophical Fragments*, ed. Gunzelin Schmid Noerr and trans. Edmund Jephcott (Stanford: Stanford University Press, 2002 [1944]), xi.
21. Walter Benjamin, "Theses on the Philosophy of History," in *Illuminations*, trans. Harry Zohn (New York: Schocken, 1969), 257–58.
22. Horkheimer and Adorno, *Dialectic of Enlightenment*, 60.

reading of German history connected Luther and the Reformation to the smoking ruins of German cities and the gates of the concentration camps: "What was found there and elsewhere surpassed in frightfulness all expectation and all conception. In Germany," he adds crisply, this hell "was called 'the National State.'"[23] Cassirer traced the rise of nineteenth-century political myths to modern totalitarianism: "In the last thirty years, in the period between the first and second World Wars.... We experienced a radical change in the form of political thought... the appearance of a new power: the power of mythical thought."[24] Auerbach championed the rise of the rational representation of reality, starting with the Old Testament, as a flight from irrationalism and mythic thought, yet he discerned a decline in early twentieth-century works by Virginia Woolf, Marcel Proust, and James Joyce. These modern writers' work, he argued, constituted "a mirror of the decline of our world."[25] Horkheimer and Adorno looked to the failure of the Enlightenment. Their ultimate goal was to reveal why humanity is sinking into "a new kind of barbarism" and to demonstrate a cultural progress turned "into its opposite."[26] In sum, all these exiled writers viewed history as a Golgotha of hope, or "hope for the hopeless," in Walter Benjamin's ironic words.[27]

Elective Affinities

Apart from the overarching common theme of *Kulturkampf* against Nazi barbarism, or the chauvinist, racist, and anti-Semitic premises of Aryan philology, based on *völkisch* mysticism and Nazi historiography, the works of Mann, Cassirer, Auerbach, Horkheimer, and Adorno share

---

23. Thomas Mann, *The Story of a Novel: The Genesis of Doctor Faustus* (New York: Knopf, 1961 [1949]), 115.

24. Cassirer, *Myth of the State*, 3.

25. Auerbach, *Mimesis*, 551.

26. Horkheimer and Adorno, *Dialectic of Enlightenment*, xiv, viii.

27. "Only for the sake of the hopeless ones have we been given hope," in Walter Benjamin, *Selected Writings*, I, *1913-1926* (Cambridge: Belknap Press, 1996), 356. It is the concluding sentence of his essay on "Goethe's Elective Affinities," in the translation by Stanley Corngold. Herbert Marcuse translated it as "It is only for the sake of those without hope that hope is given to us" in *One-Dimensional Man* (Boston: Beacon Press, 1964), 257. The original reads: "Nur um der Hoffnungslosen willen ist uns die Hoffnung gegeben."

other important themes, giving them unity and coherence as a group. Ultimately, these men all read Western intellectual history with German eyes in terms of the crisis of German ideology[28] in their times, and each responded in his field of expertise. Mann attacked the barbarization of German literature and historiography. Cassirer delineated the rise the of modern myth of the state, which led to the modern Nazi totalitarian state. Auerbach connected the decline of the West to the dissolution of the realist representation of reality, and Horkheimer and Adorno explained how the Enlightenment's enslavement of nature led to the enslavement and, worse, murder of human beings in the Holocaust and Nazi concentration camps.

Except for Mann, who traced the singular course of German history from the Protestant Reformation to Nazi barbarism and pointed to the intrinsic and inseparable connections between these two periods, the other authors deal with the whole of Western civilization, from classical Greece to Nazi barbarism in the twentieth century. Cassirer begins with the golden age of political thought, from the pre-Socratic Greek philosophers who inaugurated the rational theory of the state to Plato's concept of the Legal State, or the state as the administrator of justice. Auerbach begins *Mimesis* with a chapter, "Odysseus' Scar," in which he opposes reality to myth, rationality to the flight from reason, or the "Jewish-Israelitish realm of reality" to "Homer's realism" and classical Greek myths, legends, and heroes.[29] In contrast to Cassirer, his aim is to undermine the unique status Greek culture enjoyed in Nazi and Aryan Germany, instead claiming the Old Testament's superiority and priority in creating and forming Western culture's understanding of reality and humanity in a head-on attack.[30] Horkheimer and Adorno also begin with Odysseus, but they count the *Odyssey* as "bourgeois prehistory" and boldly argue that "the hero of the adventures turns out to be *the prototype of the bourgeois individual.*" In contrast to Auerbach's identification of Homeric poems with myths and the barbaric age, Horkheimer and Adorno claim that until Homer, "true humanity has flourished only in conjunction with the barbaric element," but his epics reflect "a world charged with meaning" that "reveals itself as

---

28. George L. Mosse, *The Crisis of German Ideology: Intellectual Origins of the Third Reich* (New York: Grosset & Dunlap, 1964).

29. Auerbach, *Mimesis*, 16, 23.

30. See Avihu Zakai, *Erich Auerbach and the Crisis of German Philology: The Humanist Tradition in Peril* (Dordrecht: Springer, 2016), especially the chapter "Odysseus' Scar," 96–106.

an achievement of *classifying reason, which destroys myth by virtue of the same rational order which is used to reflect it.*"[31]

They all adhered to the crisis mode of historical thought, or crisis history, the view that history proceeds in a series of crises, or well-defined, decisive turning points. Mann claimed that "the themes of the book" *Doctor Faustus* are "crisis themes," the "whole cultural crisis in addition to the crisis of music." In form, it "was to be some demonic intoxication and its liberating, but catastrophic effects."[32] Mann's reading of German history traces a path from Luther to Nazi barbarism, and his *Doctor Faustus* is a great apocalyptic, eschatological novel, directed and structured by Satan's prophecy, in which Faust's rise and fall are aligned with, and inextricable from, the Nazi catastrophe.

Cassirer's *The Myth of the State* traces the rise and triumph of the myth of the state during the nineteenth century and its full-blown expression in Nazi Germany, where "[m]ythical thought . . . starts to rise again and to pervade the whole of man's cultural and social life."[33] In politics, Cassirer wrote, "we are always living on a volcanic soil and must be prepared for sudden convulsions and eruptions." The eruption took place during his lifetime. Hence, in the "Conclusions," he comes to a sad recognition: "What we have learned in the hard school of our modern political life is the fact that human culture is by no means the firmly established thing that we once supposed it to be."[34]

Auerbach wrote in *Mimesis* that the dissolution of the representation of reality prefigured "the decline of our world."[35] More specifically, as he wrote to Benjamin in 1937: "the contemporary world situation is nothing other than the cunning of providence to lead us along a bloody and circuitous route," which, he thought, was evident "already in Germany and Italy, especially in the horrifying inauthencity of 'Bluebopropaganda' [*Blut und Boden*—Blood and Soil, the major slogan of Nazi racialist propaganda]."[36]

---

31. Horkheimer and Adorno, *Dialectic of Enlightenment*, 46, 35, 59, 35–36, emphasis added.

32. Mann, *Story of a Novel*, 55, 64, 17.

33. Cassirer, *Myth of the State*, 297–98.

34. Ibid., 280.

35. Auerbach, *Mimesis*, 551.

36. Auerbach to Benjamin, 3 January 1937, in Martin Elsky, Martin Vialon, and Robert Stein, eds., "Scholarship in Times of Extremes: Letters of Erich Auerbach (1933–46) on the Fiftieth Anniversary of His Death," *PMLA* 122 (January 2007): 751.

In the same vein of pessimism and despair, Horkheimer and Adorno wrote, "The present time is without turning points. A turn of events is always for the better. But when, as today, calamity is at its height, the heavens open and hurl their fire on those who are lost in any case."[37] They argue that the origins of fascism and Nazism, symbolized by the flight from reason, should be located in the Enlightenment and capitalist, bourgeois society. For them all, crisis, not progress, or the glorious Enlightenment vision of human advance, is the marrow of the historical process.

Given that the works begun in 1942 are based on the crisis mode of historical thought, no wonder they are all very pessimistic and emphasize the decline of Western humanist civilization. *Doctor Faustus* ends with the protagonist's death and the destruction of Nazi Germany. Cassirer gloomily acknowledges the "disintegration and the sudden collapse of our social and political life in the last decades" or "these last thirty years," which "have been a period of continuous war."[38] *Mimesis*'s final chapter comments on the dissolution of realism in modern literature with Virginia Woolf, Marcel Proust, and James Joyce, or the "the complicated *process of dissolution* which led to fragmentation of the exterior action, to reflection of consciousness, and to stratification of time," and aligns it with the decline of the West.[39] Horkheimer and Adorno, who lost all confidence in human rationality and modernity during the dark years of World War II, sadly lament that their *Dialectic of Enlightenment* "demonstrates tendencies which turn cultural progress into its opposite"; hence, their goal was "to explain why humanity instead of entering a truly human state, is sinking into a new kind of barbarism."[40]

---

37. Horkheimer and Adorno, *Dialectic of Enlightenment*, 182. Compare Karl Löwith, another exile from Nazi Germany, who wrote: "The problem of history as a whole is unanswerable within its own perspective. Historical processes as such do not bear the least evidence of a comprehensive and ultimate meaning. History as such has no outcome. There never has been and never will be an immanent solution to the problem of history, for man's historical experience is one of steady failure. . . . *The world is still as it was in the time of Alaric*; only our means of opposing and destruction (as well as of reconstruction) are considerably improved and are adorned with hypocrisy." See Löwith, *Meaning in History*, 191.

38. Ernst Cassirer, "Judaism and the Modern Political Myth" (1944), in *Symbol, Myth, and Culture: Essays and Lectures of Ernst Cassirer, 1935-1945*, ed. Donald Philip Verene (New Haven: Yale University Press, 1979), 240-41.

39. Auerbach, *Mimesis*, 552-53, emphasis original.

40. Horkheimer and Adorno, *Dialectic of Enlightenment*, xiii, xiv.

Another important theme closely connecting these works is the mutual acknowledgment and affirmation of Jewish life and culture. Except for Mann, they all belonged to what George L. Mosse calls "German Jews beyond Judaism," people who searched "for a personal identity beyond religion and nationality."[41] Because the trauma of Nazism, forced exile, and the rising knowledge of Holocaust atrocities radically transformed their views, they came to the defense of Judaism directly or indirectly. Since the Aryan myth of blood was inextricable from anti-Semitism, they all came to the defense of Judaism and Jewish history and rejected anti-Semitism. The Judaic turn in their works may be attributed, in part, to the fact that at the end of 1941 and in the summer of 1942 the terrible news of the massacre of European Jews, later termed the Holocaust, reached England and the United States.

In his address at the Library of Congress on November 17, 1942, Mann told the audience: "some people were inclined to regard" his book *Joseph and His Brothers* (*Joseph und seine Brüder*), a four-part novel written over the course of sixteen years (1926–1943), "as a Jewish book, even merely a novel for the Jews." In response, he pointed to "the growing vulgar anti-Semitism which is an essential part of the Fascist mob-myth, and which commits the brutish denial of the fact that Judaism and Hellenism are the two principal pillars upon which our occidental civilization rests. To write a novel of the Jewish spirit was timely, just because it seems untimely."[42]

Cassirer turned to Jewish issues late in his life. He first dealt with them briefly in *An Essay on Man* (1944), where he provided a strong defense of Jewish thought and praised the Old Testament as one source of Western humanism, freedom, and the rise of the ethical standpoint of religious consciousness. Writing about "our own European civilization," he stressed that "the great prophets of Israel no longer spoke merely to their nations. Their God was a god of Justice and His message was not restricted to a special group." The ultimate message of this "prophetic religion" was "its ethical meaning."[43] Later, in the face of the growing awareness of the

---

41. George L. Mosse, *German Jews beyond Judaism* (Bloomington: Indiana University Press, 1985), 2.

42. Mann, "The Theme of the Joseph Novels," 1942, in *Thomas Mann's Addresses Delivered at the Library of Congress, 1942–1949* (Washington: Library of Congress, 1963), 11–12. See also Hermann Kurzke, *Thomas Mann: Life as a Work of Art. A Biography* (Princeton: Princeton University Press, 2002 [1999]), 414.

43. Ernst Cassirer, *An Essay on Man: An Introduction to A Philosophy of Human Culture* (New Haven: Yale University Press, 1944), 103.

Holocaust, he wrote: "What the *modern Jew* had to defend in this combat [against Nazism] was not only his physical existence or the preservation of the Jewish race. Much more was at stake. *We had to represent all those ethical ideals that had been brought into being by Judaism and found their way into general human culture, into the life of all civilized nations.*"[44]

Cassirer's essay "Judaism and the Modern Political Myth" (1944) addressed head-on Germany's unique anti-Semitism and its fatal consequences. It entangles a clear defense of Judaism with his longtime theory of myth, or the struggle between myth and reason. In the context of the political crisis that ushered in the Nazi Revolution's "devilization" of German state and society,[45] Cassirer referred directly in the essay's last paragraphs to the tragic fate of Jews in the Nazis' haunted, possessed imagination, which associated them with Satan: "In the mythical pandemonium we always find maleficent spirits that are opposed to the beneficent spirits. There is always a secret or open revolt of Satan against God. In the German pandemonium this role was assigned to the Jew." However, the "German form of persecution was something that never had existed before," he argued. "What was proclaimed here was a mortal combat—a life and death struggle which could only end with the complete extermination of the Jews."[46]

Auerbach turned to Jewish issues only after the Nazi Revolution, when he strove to provide an *apologia* for the Old Testament's validity and credibility. It draws on the Christian figural interpretation of history—the view that Old Testament events and persons are *figures*, or prefigurations, of events and persons in the New Testament—to prove that the Old Testament is inseparable from the New Testament and inextricably linked to Western culture and civilization as a whole, contrary to the racist and anti-Semitic claims of Aryan philology, *völkisch* mysticism, and Nazi historiography. This contention serves as the cornerstone of his discussion in *Mimesis* of "the representation of reality in Western literature" in an impressive array of literary works spanning three thousand years: "figural interpretation" serves "as the basis on which the world could be ordered, interpreted, and represented as a reality and as a whole"; hence, "the picture of man living in reality which the Christian" figural interpretation "had produced."[47] Auerbach argues that with its rise in the first century, Christianity's adoption

---

44. Cassirer, "Judaism and the Modern Political Myth," 241, emphasis added.
45. Ibid., 238.
46. Ibid., 239.
47. Auerbach, *Mimesis*, 231, 248.

of the figural interpretation was made "within the Jewish religious frame." In this broad interpretative context, he asserts that "Paul and the Church Fathers reinterpreted the entire Jewish tradition as a succession of figures prognosticating the appearance of Christ, and assigned the Roman Empire its proper place in the divine plan of salvation." Figural interpretation led to the utmost historicization of the Old Testament. Auerbach concludes: "the reality of the Old Testament presents itself as complete truth with a claim to sole authority," which forces it "to a constant interpretative change in its own content; for millennia it undergoes an incessant and active development with the life of man in Europe."[48] Thus asserting the Old Testament's authority, validity, and credibility against the premises of Aryan philology.

Finally, Horkheimer and Adorno devote their last chapter to anti-Semitism and the Jewish problem, which, they contend, reveals the central significance of the "ambivalent relationship of enlightenment to power." Examined in these terms, they boldly claim that "only the liberation of thought from power, the abolition of violence, could realize the idea which has been unrealized until now: the Jew is a human being." In the transformation from an anti-Semitic to a human society, "the Jewish question would indeed prove the turning-point of history."[49]

They first address Judaism in chapter 3, "Juliette, Or Enlightenment and Morality," where they praise it for leading to the flight from myth: "The demise of idolatry follows necessarily from the ban on mythology pronounced by Jewish monotheism."[50] Like Auerbach and Cassirer, Horkheimer and Adorno believe Jewish culture and thought were crucial for the civilizing process that abandoned myth and embraced rational thought. They reiterate much of Mann, Cassirer, and Auerbach's arguments in defense of Judaism and accept and defend its universal humanist message as a crucial contribution to European civilization. For example, they argue that its prohibitions were a vehicle for enlightenment and progress because religious sacrifice became rational. Most important for our concerns here, they saw the "Jewish Question" and anti-Semitism as embodiments of the dialectical intertwining of enlightenment and power, or the myth of power.

The marrow of *Dialectic of Enlightenment* is the contention that the overall humanization process, based on flight from myth, power, and domination toward rationalism, is inextricable from the "Jewish Ques-

---

48. Ibid., 16.

49. Horkheimer and Adorno, *Dialectic of Enlightenment*, 36, 165.

50. Ibid., 89.

tion." The Jewish question and anti-Semitism are inextricable from history: "Only the *liberating of thought from power*, the abolition of violence, could realize the idea which has been unrealized until now: *that the Jew is a human being*. This would be a step away from the anti-Semitic society, which drives both Jews and others into sickness, and toward the human one. Such a step would fulfill the fascist lie by contradicting it: *the Jewish question would indeed prove the turning point of history*."[51]

The reform of society is a precondition for any possible solution of the Jewish question; abolishing the quest for power and control inherent in enlightenment will *ipso facto* transform attitudes toward the Jews and lead to a more just society. Horkheimer and Adorno provide an important modification of Marx's dictum—"the emancipation of the Jews is the emancipation of mankind from Judaism"[52]—claiming rather that emancipation from enlightenment's myth of power will emancipate the Jews and everyone else. Marx emphasized "the emancipation of mankind from Judaism," while Horkheimer and Adorno stressed the emancipation of society from power and dominance.

Elective Aversions

Along with the essential convergences between the four books, such as the myth of blood and the crisis mode of historical thought, the authors differed on such significant subjects as historicism, the Enlightenment, and Hegel, to name only a few. Auerbach embraced historicism enthusiastically, declaring it "the Copernican discovery in the cultural sciences."[53] Fellow exile Hans Baron, historian of the early Italian Renaissance, agreed. He was taught by the luminaries of German historicism at the University of Berlin, Ernst Troeltsch (1865–1923) and Friedrich Meinecke (1862–1954), and rejected, like Auerbach, the Nazi ideology of history based on *Blutsgemeinschaft*, *Volksseele*, and *Volksgeist*, to emphasize "the percepts of historicism which had re-established the Judeo-Christian foundations of European culture in Greek and Roman antiquity as well as the Near East."[54] In Baron's words:

---

51. Ibid., 165, emphasis original.
52. See https://en.wikipedia.org/wiki/On_the_Jewish_Question.
53. Eric Auerbach, *Literary Language and Its Public in Late Latin Antiquity and the Middle Ages*, trans. Ralph Manheim (Princeton: Princeton University Press, 1993 [1965]), 10.
54. Kay Schiller, "Hans Baron's Humanism," *Storia della storiografia* 34 (1998): 55.

"Unless we know exactly when, where and under what conditions a work was written . . . we cannot judge the author's intention" or "the relationship of his work to the actual life of his time."[55]

In clear contrast, Walter Benjamin's "catastrophic antihistoricism explicitly challenged the nineteenth century's triumphant philosophy of progress" and "redemption."[56] Ernst Cassirer, too, denounced "our historicism," blaming it for misreading, among others, Machiavelli and Machiavellianism: "Since the time of Herder and Hegel we have been told that it was a mistake to regard Machiavelli's *Prince* as a systematic book—as a *theory* of politics." Many German idealist philosophers followed Hegel, including Johann Gottlieb Fichte (1762–1814), who "praised Machiavelli's political realism and tried to exculpate him from all moral blame." In sum, if, "in the literature of the seventeenth century Machiavelli has been described as an incarnation of the devil; and then, in a curious hyperbole, the devil himself was sometimes styled a Machiavellian and tinged with Machiavelism," then, two hundred years later, "there was the complete reversal of this judgment. The devilization of Machiavelli was superseded by a sort of deification," especially in Germany.[57]

The same negative views of historicism pervaded Popper's thought. He declared that Hegel's historicism "encouraged" and "contributed to" totalitarian philosophizing and political practice, and almost "all the more important ideas of modern totalitarianism are directly inherited from Hegel." Hence, he advocated "harsh words" for counterfeit Hegel as well as Plato and Marx, if our "civilization is to survive."[58] For Leo Strauss, totalitarianism was rooted, in part, in historicism, which reduced "our ultimate principles" to "arbitrary" and "blind preference," amounting to a kind of "madness."[59]

---

55. Hans Baron, *From Petrarch to Leonardo Bruni: Studies in Humanistic and Political Literature* (Chicago: Chicago University Press, 1968), 2. On Baron's life and work, see David Weinstein and Avihu Zakai, *Jewish Exiles and European Thought in the Shadow of the Third Reich: Baron, Popper, Strauss, Auerbach* (Cambridge: Cambridge University Press, 2017).

56. Anson Rabinbach, *In the Shadow of Catastrophe: German Intellectuals between Apocalypse and Enlightenment* (Berkeley: University of California Press, 1997), 8.

57. Cassirer, *Myth of the State*, 123–24, emphasis original.

58. Karl Popper, *The Open Society and Its Enemies* (London and New York: Routledge, 2002 [1945]), 584–87, 315, xxxiii. On Popper's life and thought, see Weinstein and Zakai, *Jewish Exiles*.

59. Leo Strauss, *Natural Right and History* (Chicago: University of Chicago Press, 1953), 4. On Strauss's life and work, see Weinstein and Zakai, *Jewish Exiles*.

Our authors also held contrasting views of the Enlightenment. Cassirer highly praised it as the revival of Stoic ideas about natural rights and human equality and dignity, a principle that "proved to be *a turning point* in the history of ethical, political and religious thought"; namely, "the conception of the *fundamental equality of men*."[60] Horkheimer and Adorno saw in it the source or foundation of social domination realized in fascism and Nazism, boldly claiming that "[w]ith the spread of the bourgeois commodity economy the dark horizon of myth is illuminated by the sun of calculating reason, beneath whose ice rays the seeds of the new barbarism are germinating."[61] Against Cassirer, who believed that Enlightenment rationalism was a bulwark against myth, Horkheimer and Adorno held that "[m]yth is already enlightenment, and enlightenment reverts to mythology"; hence, the "Enlightenment's mythic terror springs from a horror of myth."[62]

Auerbach was also suspicious about the Enlightenment, claiming, for example, that "Voltaire's style in propaganda,"[63] which consists "in overilluminating one small part of an extensive complex, while everything else which might explain, derive, and possibly counterbalance the thing emphasized is left in the dark,"[64] resembled Nazi propaganda against the Jews. Whenever "a specific form of life or a social group has run its course, or has only lost favor and support, every injustice which the propagandists perpetrate against it is half consciously felt to be what it actually is, yet people welcome it with sadistic delight," and the result is "an ocean of filth and blood."[65]

There is also a great divide about Hegel. Auerbach was greatly influenced by his historicism, aesthetics, and philosophy of history[66] and closely followed his view that reality is knowable, in clear contrast to Kant. This belief is the cornerstone of *Mimesis*; namely, that writers in different periods describe the historical reality in which they live. He believed,

---

60. Cassirer, *Myth of the State*, 100, emphasis original.
61. Horkheimer and Adorno, *Dialectic of Enlightenment*, 25.
62. Ibid., xviii, 22.
63. Auerbach, *Mimesis*, 411.
64. Ibid., 402–03.
65. Ibid., 404.
66. See Avihu Zakai, "Constructing and Representing Reality: Hegel and the Making of Erich Auerbach's *Mimesis*" *Digital Philology: A Journal of Medieval Cultures* 4, 1 (Spring 2015): 106–33.

following Hegel, that a word or concept (*Begriff*) is the source of realism because "on the basis of its semantic development a word may grow into a historical situation and give rise to structures that will be effective for many centuries."[67]

In the realm of aesthetics, more specifically, Auerbach wrote that "Dante's inhabitants of the three realms" in the *Divine Comedy* lead "a 'changeless existence.'" He deems Hegel's "expression in his *Lectures on Aesthetics* [*Vorlesungen über die Ästhetik*, published posthumously in 1835] . . . one of the most beautiful passages ever written on Dante." Dante, Hegel wrote, "plunges the living world of human action and endurance and more specifically of individual deeds and destinies" into this "changeless existence."[68]

Cassirer, Popper, and Strauss, on the other hand, blame Hegel for much of the twentieth century's miseries. Cassirer claimed that the Hegelian worship of the state "is an entirely new type of absolutism"[69] with tremendous implications for the rise of the myth of the state and, concomitantly, the totalitarian regimes of the twentieth century. Given that the Hegelian system is "the firmest stronghold of political reaction," he calls Hegel "*the most dangerous enemy of all democratic ideals*"[70] and advocated abandonment of "the Hegelian view of history" as determined by *Idee* and a return to the belief that "human action again has an open opportunity to determine itself by its own power and through its own answer, knowing full well that the direction and future of civilization are dependent upon this kind of determination."[71] Like Popper, Cassirer raised his pen against Hegelian historical determinism in favor of human freedom, human autonomy, and the self-direction of human actions in time and history.

Popper claimed the "responsibility of Hegel and the Hegelians for much of what happened in [Nazi] Germany." He felt obliged "as a philosopher" to expose this politically perilous "pseudo-philosophy."[72] Hegel's

---

67. Erich Auerbach, "Figura," in *Scenes from the Drama of European Literature* (Gloucester: Peter Smith, 1973), 76.

68. Auerbach, *Mimesis*, 191. For Hegel's expression, see G. W. F. Hegel, *Aesthetics: Lectures on Fine Art*, 2 vols., trans. T. M. Knox (Oxford: Clarendon, 1998), 2: 1103.

69. Cassirer, *Myth of the State*, 263.

70. Ibid., 251, emphasis added.

71. Ernst Cassirer, *The Logic of the Humanities* (New Haven: Yale University Press, 1961), 37–38.

72. Popper, *Open Society*, 584–56.

historicism "encouraged" and "contributed to" totalitarian philosophizing and political practice.[73] For Strauss, the political crises of modernity, especially the rise of fascism, were, to a significant extent, a philosophical crisis brought on by historicism. He saw historicism as the single greatest threat to intellectual freedom because, in rejecting "natural right" or "right by nature," it denies any attempt to address injustice. With regard to Hegel, Strauss argued: "Transcendental standards can be dispensed with if the standard is inherent in the process: 'the actual and the present is the rational,'"[74] referring to Hegel's famous saying: "*What is rational is actual and what is actual is rational*,"[75] meaning that "reason is an actual (*wirklich*) power in the world working to create the institutions of freedom."[76]

These differences apply to views of Marx. While Auerbach, Horkheimer, and Adorno, as well as Walter Benjamin, were greatly influenced by the founder of dialectic materialism, Cassirer and Popper strongly denounced him. Auerbach called dialectic materialism the "most inspired and influential attempt to apprehend modern history as a whole in terms of laws."[77] Hence, his ultimate goal in *Mimesis* was to describe "the rise of more extensive and socially inferior human groups to the position of subject matter for problematic-existential representation."[78] According to Geoffrey H. Hartman, another exile from Nazi Germany and Auerbach's colleague at Yale, "practicing an urban, undogmatic Marxism," Auerbach "took the pattern of a unified development characterizing European history more from social and economic realities."[79] Consequently, according to Auerbach, some readers thought that the book's "tendency was socialist."[80]

Horkheimer and Adorno belonged to the Frankfurt School of social theory and philosophy associated with the Institute for Social Research

---

73. Ibid., 586–87.

74. Strauss, *Natural Right*, 319.

75. G. W. F. Hegel, *Outlines of the Philosophy of Right*, trans. T. N. Knox (Oxford: Oxford University Press, 2008 [1821]), 14, emphasis original.

76. Ibid., 326–27; see also editor's "Explanatory Notes," 14.

77. Auerbach, in "Introduction: Purpose and Method," in *Literary Language*, 21.

78. Auerbach, *Mimesis*, 491.

79. Geoffrey H. Hartman, *A Scholar's Tale: Intellectual Journey of a Displaced Child of Europe* (New York: Fordham University Press, 2007), 169. Marx's philosophy of history, or historical materialism, is also based on Hegel's philosophy of history; for him, history is embodied within a larger project, namely, class struggle.

80. See Auerbach, "Appendix: 'Epilegomena to *Mimesis*,'" in *Mimesis*, 570.

at the Goethe University Frankfurt. The institute was the first Marxist-oriented research center affiliated with a major German university. Following Marx, they were concerned with the conditions that allow social change and the establishment of rational institutions. Though their texts do not directly mention Marx, their theories clearly draw great inspiration from his thought. The same can be said about Walter Benjamin, who used Marxist terms, concepts, and explanations, which greatly irritated his friend Gershom Scholem.[81]

In clear contrast, Cassirer argued that we must understand how and why Hegelian philosophy became "one of the greatest *revolutionary* forces in modern political thought"; the philosopher of "the Prussian State became the teacher of Marx and Lenin—the champion of 'dialectic Marxism'"; and the "Hegelian system" became "one of the explosive forces in the development of political thought during the nineteenth century."[82] Likewise, in *The Open Society and Its Enemies*, Popper traced three "events"—Plato, Hegel, and Marx—in historicism's "pernicious influence" on philosophy and politics. Both Cassirer and Popper condemned historicism for justifying totalitarianism. Since historicism encouraged political fatalism, it tended to excuse totalitarianism's evils: "Harsh words" must be spoken about counterfeit liberals, like Hegel, and antiliberals like Plato and Marx, if our "civilization is to survive."[83] These "harsh words" must be said in "memory of the countless" victims of belief in the "Inexorable Laws of Historical Destiny."[84]

Finally, there is strong difference between the purely humanist ideals of Mann and Cassirer and the socialist, Marxist approach of Auerbach, Horkheimer, and Adorno. Particularly for the latter two there is a strong critique of humanist thought. While Auerbach used the Marxist approach in order to emphasize "the rise" of "socially inferior human groups" to be the subject in modern Western literature,[85] Horkheimer and Adorno rather employed Thomas Hobbes's views that might is right, claiming that as in Hobbes, self-preservation is the source and final drive of all human action;

---

81. See Walter Benjamin, *The Correspondence of Walter Benjamin and Gershom Scholem, 1932-1940*, ed. Anson Rabinbach et al. (Cambridge: Harvard University Press, 1992); specifically, a 1934 exchange: Scholem to Benjamin, April 19, 107; Benjamin to Scholem, 26 April 26, 108-09; and Benjamin to Scholem, May 6, 110.

82. Cassirer, *Myth of the State*, 251, 253, emphasis original.

83. Popper, *Open Society*, xxxiii.

84. Karl Popper, *The Poverty of Historicism* (London and New York: Routledge, 1997 [1957]), dedication.

85. Auerbach, *Mimesis*, 491.

"Spinoza's proposition: 'the endeavor of preserving oneself is the first and only basis of virtue,' contains the true maxim of all Western civilization," the authors agreed.[86]

Despite their various differences, Mann, Auerbach, Cassirer, Horkheimer, and Adorno shared one important view: fear about the dangerous consequences of the mythos of blood, the source of Nazi barbarism, or the mythical turn in Nazi Germany, which ruined their lives and those of many millions all over the world.

Trauma caused by Nazism and fascism led to the writing of many works that transformed modern intellectual history, many of the most prominent begun in 1942, the nadir of European humanist civilization. Though previously analyzed separately, these works should be analyzed together, since they constitute a collective *Kulturkampf* against Nazi barbarism and all identify the Aryan mythos of blood as its trigger.

∽

Three years after the end of World War II, on March 8, 1948, the American weekly newsmagazine *Time* celebrated its twenty-fifth birthday. Featured on the cover of the anniversary edition was a picture of the famous American Protestant theologian Reinhold Niebuhr, captioned "Man's Story Is Not a Success Story."[87] The authors and works discussed here are full proof of this deep pessimism and provide a prismatic glimpse into the dark labyrinth of modern history.

Their works written in 1942 are indeed small solace to the vicissitudes of history's grief and agony, but they are crucial for them to set the record straight.

---

86. Horkheimer and Adorno, *Dialectic of Enlightenment*, 22.

87. See Avihu Zakai, "The Irony of American History: Reinhold Niebuhr and the American Experience." *La Revue LISA/ LISA e-journal*, World War II Thematic dossier, 2008, 1–21, http://www.unicaen.fr/mrsh/lisa/publicationsGb.php?p=2&numId=1&it=inTheWar.

I

Apocalypse and Eschatology in Thomas Mann's *Doctor Faustus*

The "Secret Union of the German Spirit with the Demonic"

[The Nazis] entered the arena of history proclaiming themselves bearers of a barbarism that, while wallowing in ruthlessness, was to rejuvenate the world.

. . .

[T]he very definition of Germanness [is] a psychological state threatened by the poison of loneliness, by eccentricity, provincial standoffishness, neurotic involution, unspoken Satanism.

—Thomas Mann, *Doctor Faustus*, 1947

A secret union of the German spirit with the Demonic.

—Thomas Mann, "Germany and the Germans," May 29, 1945

Paul Thomas Mann was born in Lübeck in 1875, the second son of a merchant and senator of the Free City, Johann Heinrich Mann, and his wife Júlia da Silva Bruhns. Mann's father died in 1891, and Mann moved to Munich, where he lived until 1933, with the exception of a year in Palestrina, Italy, with his novelist elder brother Heinrich. Thomas worked with the South German Fire Insurance Company in 1894–1895. His career as a writer began when he wrote for *Simplicissimus*, a satirical weekly. Mann's first short story, "Little Mr. Friedemann" ("Der Kleine Herr Friedemann"), was published in 1898. In 1905, Mann married Katharina Hedwig Pringsheim, daughter of a wealthy, secular Jewish industrialist family. She later joined the Lutheran church. The couple had six children.

After perfunctory work in an insurance office and on the editorial staff of *Simplicissimus*, Mann devoted himself to writing, as his elder brother Heinrich had already done. His early works were influenced by the philosophers Arthur Schopenhauer and Friedrich Wilhelm Nietzsche and the composer Wilhelm Richard Wagner. Most of Mann's first stories center in the problem of the creative artist, who in his devotion to form contests the meaninglessness of existence, an antithesis that Mann enlarged into that between spirit (*Geist*) and life (*Leben*). This ambivalence found full expression in his first novel, *Buddenbrooks*, a 1900 novel chronicling the decline of a wealthy north German merchant family over the course of four generations. Mann's early novels—*Buddenbrooks* (1900), *Der Tod in Venedig* (1912; *Death in Venice*), and *Der Zauberberg* (1924; *The Magic Mountain*)—earned him the Nobel Prize for Literature in 1929.

The outbreak of World War I evoked Mann's ardent patriotism and awoke, too, an awareness of the artist's social commitment. His brother Heinrich was one of the few German writers to question German war aims, and his criticism of German authoritarianism stung Thomas to a bitter attack on cosmopolitan litterateurs. In 1918 Thomas Mann published a large political treatise, the infamous *Reflections of an Unpolitical Man*, in which all his ingenuity of mind was summoned to justify the authoritarian state as against democracy, creative irrationalism as against "flat" rationalism, and inward culture as against moralistic civilization. This work belongs to the tradition of "revolutionary conservatism" that leads from the nineteenth-century German nationalistic and antidemocratic thinkers Paul Anton de Lagarde and Houston Stewart Chamberlain, the apostle of the superiority of the "Germanic" race, toward National Socialism. Later Mann repudiated these ideas.

With the establishment of the German (Weimar) Republic in 1919, Mann slowly revised his outlook, becoming defender of the fragile Weimar Republic after the assassination in 1922 of Walther Rathenau, who served as foreign minister during the Weimar Republic. The essays "Goethe und Tolstoi" and "Von deutscher Republik" ("The German Republic") show his somewhat hesitant espousal of democratic principles. Later, with the rise of the National Socialists he gave in 1930 a courageous address in Berlin, "Ein Appell an die Vernunft" ("An Appeal to Reason"), appealing for the formation of a common front of the cultural bourgeoisie and the Socialist working class against the inhuman fanaticism of the Nazi.

When the Nazi Revolution took place on January 30, 1933, and Hitler rose to power, Thomas Mann (1875–1955) and his Jewish wife Katia were on holiday in Switzerland.[1] Mann had stridently denounced Nazi policies, and on the advice of their children, the couple did not return to Germany. In retaliation, the Nazis began a campaign of abuse. In 1936, Mann's German citizenship was revoked, and in 1937, the University of Bonn deprived the 1929 Nobel laureate in literature of his honorary doctorate (conferred 1919, restored 1946). In fall 1938, Mann and his family left for the United States of America, first, to Princeton University, where Mann became lecturer in the humanities; in 1941, they moved to Pacific Palisades, California, in the Los Angeles area. Mann continued to combat Nazism and fascism in pamphlets, talks, and radio speeches. His bibliography lists "over three hundred nonliterary contributions from 1937 to 1945."[2] Exile provided no escape from politics. To the contrary, the history of his times demanded that he "help stop civilization sliding into the fascist abyss." Mann returned to Switzerland in 1952; he lived his remaining years in Kilchberg and "as far as the world would let him, from history."[3]

Mann's exilic displacement had a crucial mission: it "created a situation in which he could speak the words 'Wo ich bin ist die deutsche Kultur' (where I am is German culture), not as an arrogant personal claim but as

---

1. For a wonderful literary reconstruction of Mann's life in Switzerland in 1936 and his decision at that year to openly denounce the Nazi regime, see Britta Böhler, *The Decision*, trans. Jeannette K. Ringold (Chicago: University of Chicago Press, 2015). This intriguing novel follows German author Thomas Mann during three crucial days in 1936. Away in Switzerland and fearing arrest by the Nazis upon his return to Germany, Mann must choose whether to travel back to Munich. Eventually he decides to release an open letter to the Nazi regime to a Swiss newspaper. On life in Nazi Germany during the 1930s, see Irmgard Keun, *Nect Mitternach* (*After Midnight*) (London: Melville House, 2011 [1937]).

2. Kurzke, *Thomas Mann*, 417. On Mann's struggle in America against National Socialism and his abhorrence of Hitler, see 415–58. See also Wolfgang Beutin, et al., *A History of German Literature: From the Beginning to the Present Day* (London: Routledge, 1993), 521. On German exile culture in Los Angeles during World War II, see Ehrhard Bahr, *Weimar on the Pacific: German Exile Culture in Los Angeles and the Crisis of Modernism* (Berkeley: University of California Press, 2007). See also James Schmidt, "Mephistopels in Hollywood: Adorno, Mann, and Schoenberg," *Cambridge Companion to Adorno*, ed. Tom Huhn (Cambridge: Cambridge University Press, 2004), 148–80.

3. T. J. Reed, "Mann and History," in *The Cambridge Companion to Thomas Mann*, ed. Ritchie Robertson (Cambridge: Cambridge University Press, 2001), 15, 19.

a necessary political act. For the Nazis had narrowed the definition of what was German and what was culture to something crude and chauvinist."[4] One proof of this mission is *Doctor Faustus* (1949),[5] which attempts the impossible: "to encompass and explain the German catastrophe,"[6] or the cultural roots of Nazi Germany.

Selection of the Faust legend was not an offhanded whim but a much-deliberated decision:

> [T]he choice of the Faust theme was not arbitrary or facile. It was not a case of the most eminent German writer taking up the most prestigious German myth. Nor was it a case of hasty recourse to a diabolic explanation for the rise of forces Mann hated. This was a possible reaction in minds accustomed to analysis but stunned by the catastrophe of Nazism. Meinecke, for example, called Hitler's doings a 'breakthrough of the satanic principle in world history.' Mann's satanic idea had roots further back, in time and in his characteristic themes.[7]

Mann wrote that "the themes of the book" are "crisis themes," the "whole cultural crisis in addition to the crisis of music." In form, it "was to be some demonic intoxication and its liberating, but catastrophic effects."[8] Given the urgency to oppose Nazi Germany's breakneck war on humanist civilization in Europe, Mann compared his role as a writer to that of soldiers on a battlefield or sailors in a storm: "A difficult work of art, like

---

4. T. J. Reed, *Thomas Mann: The Uses of Tradition* (Oxford: Clarendon, 1996 [1973]), 1. According to Hans Vaget in a letter to the author, February 27, 2014, "these famous words"—"Wo ich bin, ist die deutsche Kultur"—appear in Heinrich Mann's autobiography, *Ein Zeitalter wird besichtigt*, but he knew them only by hearsay. Many commentators have erroneously taken this as their source. What Thomas Mann actually said in a press conference upon his arrival in New York in February of 1938 is this: "Where I am, there is Germany." This seems to be the correct version because in the German text on which his statement appears to be based he writes: "Wo ich bin, ist Deutschland."

5. Thomas Mann, *Doctor Faustus: The Life of the German Composer Adrian Leverkühn as Told by a Friend*, trans. John E. Wood (New York: Vintage, 1999). All references in the text are to this edition.

6. Reed, *Thomas Mann*, 360.

7. Ibid., 360–61.

8. Mann, *Story of a Novel*, 55, 64, 17.

battle, peril at sea, or danger to life, brings us close to God in that it fosters a religious mood, and makes us raise our eyes reverently in appeal for blessing, help, grace."[9]

Times of great peril demanded nothing less than a novel of Faustian ambition. Mann would hold a mirror to German abomination, figuring the terrifying consequences of its pact with Hitler in Faust's covenant with Mephistopheles. The constant incorporation of historical events in the novel transformed legend into indictment: *Doctor Faustus* dealt with "the long roots of Nazism in German culture and society"[10] and "created what is at once an autobiographical novel of exemplary forthrightness and a historical document" of great "import."[11] As "a historical document," it "is the greatest of Thomas Mann's works."[12]

Doctor Faustus is ultimately a great apocalyptic, eschatological novel, based on the unfolding of Satanic revelation, in which Faust's existential condition and eventual collapse are closely described as parallel to, and inextricable from, the German catastrophe of Nazism. The novel is directed, structured, and organized from beginning to end (*primo capite libri ad ultimum caput*) by Satanic prophecy, Satan's Apocalypse, culminating in imminent judgment, destruction, and collapse. A doomsday atmosphere pervades the book, from the first-page reference to "Fortress Europe" (*Festung Europa*)—the Nazi military propaganda slogan for the occupied areas of the continent—to the very end of the epilogue, where the Nazi "monster state that had at that time held this continent, and more besides, in its tentacles has celebrated its last orgies" (528). Mann describes it "as a book about endings and the final end."[13] His Frankenstein strategy releases the diabolic from German history and charges the legend with new life. He places the Faust legend at the crossroads of historical time and German cultural history from the Protestant Reformation to the rise and fall of Nazism.

However, the old German tale and Mann's novel have a radical difference. In the early Faustus tales, the fate of the hero is an object lesson:

---

9. Ibid., 64.

10. Reed, "Mann and History," 1.

11. Hans Rudolf Vaget, "'German' Music and German Catastrophe: A Re-Reading of *Doktor Faustus*," in *A Companion to the Works of Thomas Mann*, ed. H. Lehnert and E. Wessell (Rochester: Camden House, 2004), 239.

12. Reed, *Thomas Mann*, 378, 402.

13. Susan von Rohr Scaff, "Doctor Faustus," in *Cambridge Companion*, 170.

irrevocably corrupted, his sins cannot be forgiven, and when payment is due the devil, he is carried off to the abyss. In Mann's rendering of Nazi Germany's covenant with Satan, his Faust surrogate goes nowhere: as Mephistopheles remarks in Marlowe's *Doctor Faustus*, "Why, this is hell, nor am I out of it."[14] In literary terms, the diabolic erupts into history in the "hellish laughter" and "triumphant laughter of hell" (397) of Leverkühn's "apocalyptic oratorio" (374), *Apocalypsis cum Figuris*, with its Satanic vision of the end right here and now. Mann clearly sees Nazi concentration camps and other atrocities as hell on Earth, ramifications of the regime's pact with the devil: "What was found there and elsewhere surpassed in frightfulness all expectation and all conception." "In Germany," he adds crisply, this hell "was called 'the National State.'"[15]

Without grasping the singular apocalyptic and eschatological context of *Doctor Faustus*, its unique content and form, its meaning and implications, cannot be understood. Mann's apocalyptic reading of German history traces a path from "Luther and the Reformation to the smoking ruins of the German cities and the gates of the concentration camps."[16] Apocalypse and eschatology are intrinsic to this story and the wider culture and literature, not only because Luther and Leverkühn were obsessed with the

---

14. Christopher Marlowe, *Doctor Faustus* (Cambridge: Harvard Classics, 1909–1914), lines 74–78.

> Mephistopheles: Why, this is hell, nor am I out of it.
> Think'st thou that I, who saw the face of God
> And tasted the eternal joys of heaven,
> Am not tormented with ten thousand hells
> In being deprived of everlasting bliss?

15. Mann, *Story of a Novel*, 115. The Nazi concentration camps provided an additional clear evidence of the Nazi flight from reason and reality. "Nazism taught the Germans to see themselves as a beleaguered nation, constantly set upon by enemies external and internal. Metaphors of infection and disease, of betrayal and stabs in the back, were central to Nazi discourse. The concentration camp became the place where those metaphorical evils could be rendered concrete and visible. Here, behind the barbed wire, were the traitors, Bolsheviks, parasites, and Jews who were intent on destroying the Fatherland." See Adam Kirsch, "The System: Two New Histories Show How the Nazi Concentration Camps Worked," *The New Yorker*, April 6, 2015, 80–81.

16. Todd Kontje, *Thomas Mann's World: Empire, Race, and the Jewish Question* (Ann Arbor: University of Michigan Press, 2011), 153.

devil and his minions.[17] Accordingly, along with the contextualization and historicization of the novel, or Mann's close association between historical events and apocalyptic visions, the work must be seen as Satan's apocalypse and eschatology, leading to Leverkühn's insanity and to Nazi Germany's destruction. In Mann's hands, Nazi Germany is the new incarnation of the old German legend of amoral hubris and ambition. He confessed that *Doctor Faustus* was "his most radically autobiographical novel as well as his most unsparing reckoning with German's past."[18]

Exile and Literary Mission

Due to the Nazi rise, "there were several thousand German émigrés who found refuge in southern California, and it may well have been that never before in history had there been more German musicians, writers, actors and other artists collected together in one area at the same time." In this community of about ten thousand exiles, about half of them Jews, Thomas Mann was called "Der Kaiser." He "played the role of 'emperor' of the German émigrés in southern California: 'Everything was expected from him, everything was owed to him, and he was held responsible for everything.'"[19] Mann himself referred to this community as the "German colony."[20] Among them, Theodor W. Adorno (1903–1969) played a crucial role in the making of *Doctor Faustus* based on his wide knowledge of

---

17. For Luther's apocalyptic and eschatological thought, as well as his demonology, see Robin B. Barnes, *Prophecy and Gnosis: Apocalypticism in the Wake of the Lutheran Reformation* (Redwood City: Stanford University Press, 1988); Mark U. Edwards Jr., *Luther's Last Battles: Politics and Polemics, 1531–46* (Ithaca: Cornell University Press, 1983); Avihu Zakai, "Reformation, History and Eschatology in English Protestantism," *History and Theory* 26 (October 1987): 300–18, and "The Poetics of History and the Destiny of Israel: The Role of the Jews in English Apocalyptic Thought during the Sixteenth and Seventeen Centuries" *Journal of Jewish Thought and Philosophy* 5 (1996): 313–50.

18. Vaget, "'German' Music," 221.

19. Jarrell C. Jackman, "Exiles in Paradise: German Émigrés in Southern California, 1933–1950," *Southern California Quarterly* 61 (Summer 1979): 183–205. The quotes are from 197.

20. Mann, *Story of a Novel*, 54.

musical theory.[21] He wrote *On the Philosophy of Modern Music* (1949) and many studies on Gustav Mahler, Alban Berg, Ludwig van Beethoven, and others. Mann conceived *Doctor Faustus* as a "novel of music"; after reading Adorno's manuscript *On the Philosophy of Modern Music*, he claimed that it had "the strangest affinity to the idea of my book."[22] What Adorno's manuscript offered him was nothing less than "the key to deciphering the process by which culture had collapsed into barbarism."[23] "Would you be willing," Mann consequently asked Adorno, "to think through with me how the work—I mean Leverkühn's work—might look; how you would do it if you were the Devil?"[24] Adorno thus became "the most important adviser for the Faust novel."[25] Exile has its rewards.

Washed up on the Pacific Coast, uprooted from his homeland, trying to piece together what remained of his shattered life, Mann wrote to Adorno about his agonizing exilic experience: for exiles "homeland . . . has

---

21. Thomas Mann and Adorno first met in California in 1942 or 1943 at the home of Max Horkheimer. See Theodor W. Adorno and Thomas Mann, *Theodor Adorno and Thomas Mann: Correspondence, 1943–1955*, 3–4n1. On Adorno's life in Los Angeles and his complex relationship with Mann, see Bahr, *Weimar on the Pacific*, 56–78, and Lorenz Jäger, *Adorno: A Political Biography* (New Haven: Yale University Press, 2004), 128–32. According to Jäger, 131, many writers have pointed out "the similarity between Adorno and the modern musical devil around whom the novel revolves." Adorno wrote in 1943 that he is "acting as a manner of musical advisor" for "Thomas Mann's new novel, about a musician." See Theodor W. Adorno, *Letters to His Parents: 1939–1951* (Cambridge: Polity, 2006), 154, 165.

22. Mann, *Story of a Novel*, 42–43. According to Lorenz Jäger, "Adorno provided sketches for Leverkühn's chamber music and his cantata *The Lamentation of Dr. Faustus*, which interprets Faust's final meeting with his pupil as a 'negative communion.'" See Jäger, *Adorno: A Political Biography*, 129.

23. Schmidt, "Mephistopheles in Hollywood: Adorno, Mann, and Schoenberg," 158.

24. Stefan Müller-Doohm, *Adorno: A Biography* (Malden: Polity, 2005), 316.

25. Kurzke, *Thomas Mann*, 417. According to Kurzke, Adorno "lends the Devil" in Mann's book "not only many of his thoughts but also in passing his appearance as a bespectacled music intellectual" (473). An analysis of the image of the Jew in Mann's works can be seen in Ruth Angress-Klüger, "Jewish Characters in Thomas Mann's Fiction," *Horizonte: Festschrift für Herbert Lehner zum 65. Geburstag*, ed. H. Mundt et al. (Tübingen: Niemeyer, 1990), 161–72; and Todd Kontje, "Doctor Faustus and the Jewish Question," in Kontje, *Thomas Mann's World*, 168–73. See also Müller-Doohm, "*The Privy Conccillor*: Adorno and Thomas Mann," in *Adorno: A Biography*, 311–21.

become foreign," and "here in the foreign land that has become home we cannot help feeling we are in the wrong place, something which robs our own existence of a certain moral authority."[26] Mann's daughter Monica saw the situation differently:

> Let me only hint at my belief that the odd elegance of that distant shore, with its almost intangible beauty and worldly barrenness, which surrounded my father for twelve years had a great influence on him and his work. It drove him from his own tradition to stylistic daring and gave him the courage for those linguistic experiments in *The Holy Sinner* and the thoroughly polemic major confession of *Dr. Faustus*.[27]

The German Jewish novelist and playwright Lion Feuchtwanger wrote about the meaning of exilic experience for a writer: "The landscape around him changed the landscape within him. . . . A vast abundance of new material and new ideas pour in upon him, he is confronted with a variety of impressions he would never have known at home."[28]

Adorno praised Mann for his rootedness: "Who after all, one may ask, has ever stayed more faithful to the utopia of youth, to the dream of a world unspoilt by ends and purposes, for all your unremitting emphasis upon maturity and responsibility?" Adorno further claimed that after meeting Mann on "this remote western coast," "I only now, for the first time, actually encountered that German tradition from which I have received everything—including the strength to resist the tradition." For him, the meeting with Mann in California was "a moment of realized utopia."[29] Thus, Mann was the best example of German humanist tradition, according not only to himself ("Wo ich bin ist die deutsche Kultur") but to Adorno and many other German exiles.

Many of his compatriots strove to make sense of their exilic displacement. For example, the German poet, playwright, and theater director Bertolt Brecht (1898–1956) wrote that refugees became "refugees as a result of

---

26. Mann to Adorno, January 9, 1950, in *Theodor W. Adorno and Thomas Mann: Correspondence*, 41.

27. Monica Mann, quoted in Jackman, "Exiles in Paradise," 192.

28. Lion Feuchtwanger, quoted in ibid., 187.

29. Adorno to Mann, June 3, 1945, in *Theodor W. Adorno and Thomas Mann: Correspondence*, 9–10.

changes which they were forced to study all about them."[30] Mann's *Doctor Faustus* is a clear and important example of this contention: "This time [in exile] . . . in this work of my old age . . . I knew what I was setting out to do and what task I was imposing upon myself: to write nothing less than the novel of my era, disguised as the story of an artist's life."[31]

Mann's Criticism of Fascism and Nazism

Mann had anticipated and warned against the rise of Nazism during the Weimar Republic (1919-1933). To him, it meant "what is impure, what is unvirtuous, the babbling foolishness of Baal, irrationality abiding in dark fertility."[32] In a 1930 public address in Berlin, "An Appeal to Reason," he strongly denounced National Socialism's flight from reason. Numerous essays and lectures attacking the Nazis followed. More specifically, in 1932, he spoke out directly and forcefully against the rising tide, claiming "National Socialism," this "falsification of renewal," which is "brainless and aimless confusion in itself," would never be able "to create anything but confusion and misfortune." It is "incomparably a fraud against the people and a spoiler of youth without equal that covers itself with revolution and with a tissue of lies."[33] Tirelessly struggling against fascist and Nazi political irrationalism, between 1922 and 1933, he published "375 journalistic contributions, some of them in numerous printings." He became "the decisive defendant of the Weimar democracy."[34]

Mann's firm opposition to fascism can be seen for example in his novella *Mario and the Magician* (1929). Likewise, his lecture on Richard Wagner, "which provided a subtle and critical analysis of Wagner and his work, obliquely attacking the Nazi view of Wagner as a prophet of German nationalism and indeed of National Socialism," became the grounds for his emigration to Switzerland following Hitler's rise to power in 1933.[35]

---

30. Brecht, quoted by Jackman, "Exiles in Paradise," 186.

31. Mann, *Story of a Novel*, 37-38.

32. Kurzke, *Thomas Mann*, 414.

33. Ibid., 330.

34. Ibid., 328.

35. See James Joll, "Mann and the Magician," *New York Review of Books*, March 27, 1986. In February 1933, two weeks after Hitler's appointment as German chancellor, "Thomas Mann delivered a lecture in Munich to commemorate the

The novella *Mario and the Magician* prefigures the political emphasis of *Doctor Faustus*. The sorcerer, diabolical magician, and controller-of-wills Cavalier Cipolla is analogous to the fascist dictators of the era with their fiery speeches and rhetoric; he is a "dreadful being" who seems to represent "all the peculiar evilness" of the time.³⁶ Alan Bance explicitly associates the character with Benito Mussolini, Il Duce (the leader) of fascist Italy: "Cipolla-like in hating to be laughed at, [Mussolini] similarly prided himself on his great intelligence, iron will and perfect sense of timing. Like Cipolla, Mussolini was initially not taken seriously, and resorted to sadistic measures to intimidate the opposition." Both "treat the masses of ordinary people like children."³⁷

As a hypnotist—"this self-confident cripple was the most powerful hypnotist"³⁸—Cipolla represents contemporary European authoritarian leaders' use of their mental powers to control audiences. He artificially boosts his self-confidence through autocratic misuse of power to counterbalance his inferiority complex. At once offensive and intriguing, the dynamic and diabolical Cipolla repulses and captivates the audience. At the end of the story, during a show, he convinces a waiter, Mario, to kiss him on the cheek; Mario has been induced to believe the magician is the female object of his desire. Here, the novella demonstrates the interplay of "Volk

---

fiftieth anniversary of Wagner's death; and he went on to repeat it in Amsterdam, Brussels, and Paris. It is indeed a masterpiece of criticism and remains one of the best things ever written about Wagner. But because it provided a subtle and critical analysis of Wagner and his work, obliquely attacking the Nazi view of Wagner as a prophet of German nationalism and indeed of National Socialism, and especially because it had been delivered to foreign audiences, it was at once the object of a violent public attack organized by the conductor Hans Knappertsbusch and signed by the composers Richard Strauss and Hans Pfitzner as well as an array of Munich notables: 'We are not disposed to tolerate such disparaging treatment of our great German musical genius from anyone—and most certainly not from Herr Thomas Mann.' Nor did it stop there. Mann, on holiday in the Swiss Alps after his lecture tour, was warned by friends that he would be in personal danger if he returned to Germany. It was the start of his sixteen years of exile." See http://www.nybooks.com/articles/1986/03/27/mann-and-the-magician/.

36. Thomas Mann, *Mario and the Magician* (New York: Knopf, 1931), 3.

37. Alan Bance, "The Political Becomes Personal: *Disorder and Early Sorrow* and *Mario and the Magician*," in *Cambridge Companion*, 112.

38. Mann, *Mario and the Magician*, 59.

34 / The Pen Confronts the Sword

and Führer" (people and leader)[39]: humiliation based on deception. The audience's silent reaction is broken by the sound of two gunshots, leveled from the slender hands of Mario. The demonic magician lies crumpled on the stage, his subjects falling still. His assassination is hardly a tragedy: "An end of horror, a fatal end. And yet, a liberation."[40]

Mann had no illusions about Nazi Germany; in 1940, he wrote:

> Where there is Nazism, there is to be found the denial of every decent human attribute and a reversion to the pagan and barbaric state of life in which murder, corruption, and intrigue are not merely condoned but advocated. Truth, justice, dignity have been ideals cherished by free men through the ages, but under Hitlerism they are simply empty words.[41]

He struggled against Hitler in particular. Writing "Bruder [Brother] Hitler" in the spring of 1938,[42] Mann fiercely denounced Hitler's character as well as his political and social policies: "The fellow is a catastrophe. But that is no reason why we should not find him interesting, as a character and an event. Consider the circumstances. Here is a man possessed of a bottomless resentment and a festering desire for revenge; a man ten times a failure, extremely lazy, incapable of steady work; a man who has spent long periods in institutions; a disappointed bohemian artist; a total good-for-nothing." Politically, Mann continues, "with masterly adroitness he exploits the weariness of the continent, its agony of fear, its dread of war. He knows how to stir up the peoples over the heads of their rulers and win large sections of opinion to himself. Fortune is his slave; all walls fall before him. The one-time melancholic ne'er-do-well, simply because he has learned—for aught he knows, out of patriotism—to be a political animal now bids fair to subjugate Europe, or, God knows, maybe the whole

---

39. Manfred Dierks, "Thomas Mann's Late Politics," in *Companion to the Works of Thomas Mann*, 221.

40. Mann, *Mario and the Magician*, 81.

41. Mann to Edward Edwards, June 23, 1940, in *Letters of Thomas Mann, 1889-1955*, sel. and trans. Richard and Clara Winston (New York: Knopf, 1971), 340.

42. According to Hans Vaget in a letter to the author, February 27, 2014, "Bruder Hitler" was written in the spring (April 4–21) of 1938, in Los Angeles. Both the English and the German versions were published in March of 1939.

world."⁴³ In 1945, Mann confessed, the "years of struggle against" Hitler "had been morally a good era."⁴⁴

In military and political terms, Mann fully understood that the subjugation of Europe was no fantasy but a real and feasible aim for Hitler. "In launching a war to be fought on a European scale," his ultimate goal was "world domination."⁴⁵ All during the 1930s, popular songs of the Nazi youth movement (Hitler-Jugend) revealed unmistakably chauvinist and imperialist goals:

> The rotten bones of the world
> are trembling before the coming war . . .
> we'll go on marching forever,
> even if everything falls to pieces,
> For today, Germany belongs to us—
> And tomorrow the whole world.⁴⁶

In 1940, Mann vehemently denounced Nazi anti-Semitism as a means to this end in a radio speech: "The anti-Semitism of today, the efficient though artificial anti-Semitism of our technical age, is no object in itself. It is nothing but a wrench to unscrew, bit by bit, the whole machinery of our civilization. Or, to use an up-to-date simile, anti-Semitism is like a hand grenade tossed over the wall to work havoc and confusion in the camp of democracy. That is its real and main purpose."⁴⁷ Thus, following the outbreak of World War II, Mann began to conceive the fight against Hitler and Nazi Germany in Manichean, eschatological, and apocalyptic

---

43. Thomas Mann, "Bruder Hitler." See also Thomas Mann, "A Brother," 298.

44. Mann, *Story of a Novel*, 163.

45. Evans, *Third Reich at War*, 760. For earlier German striving toward European domination, see Roderick R. McLean, "Dreams of German Europe: Wilhelm II and the Treaty of Björkö of 1905," in *The Kaiser: New Research on Wilhelm II's Role in Imperial Germany*, ed. A. Mombauer and W. Deist (Cambridge: Cambridge University Press, 2003), 119–42.

46. Annette Dumbach and Jud Newborn, *Sophie Scholl and the White Rose* (Oxford: Oneworld, 2006), 28–29.

47. See "Rare 1940 Audio: Thomas Mann Explains the Nazis' Ulterior Motive for Spreading Anti-Semitism," at http://www.openculture.com/2013/06/rare_1940_audio_thomas_mann_explains_the_nazis_ulterior_motive_for_spreading_anti-semitism.html.

terms. It was the "struggle against the enemy of mankind."[48] In a revealing passage, he admits, "[when I wrote] *Faustus*, I was greatly drawn to Dostoevsky's grotesque, apocalyptic realm of suffering, in contrast to my usual preference for Tolstoy's Homeric, primal strength."[49]

Living in exile, Mann asked himself many times how he could best fight Nazi barbarism apart from writing political essays and making anti-Nazi radio speeches. Obviously, the best way for him would be in a novel, yet at the time, he was finishing his biblical tetralogy *Joseph and His Brothers* (1933–1943).[50] The last book, *Joseph the Provider (Joseph, der Ernährer)*, was completed only in 1943. Mann wrote with great irony: "I got finished with Joseph sooner than the world did with fascism."[51]

These historical biblical novels were directed against the prevailing ills in German life and culture after World War I and the premises of Aryan ideology and Nazi historiography, based on overtly chauvinist, *völkisch*, nationalist, racist, and anti-Semitic ideas. These forces strove to eliminate the Hebrew Bible, or Old Testament, from German culture in particular and Western culture and civilization in general, and with the Nazi Revolution of 1933, they triumphed. As Mann told the audience in an address at the Library of Congress on November 17, 1942, "some people were inclined to regard *Joseph and His Brothers* as a Jewish book, even merely a novel for the Jews." He agreed that

> the selection of the old testamental subject was certainly not mere accident; most certainly there were hidden defiantly polemic connections between it and certain tendencies of our time which I always found repulsive from the bottom of my soul; the growing vulgar anti-Semitism which is an essential part of the Fascist mob-myth, and which commits the brut-

---

48. Mann, *Story of a Novel*, 96. At about the same time, in the summer of 1944, Herrmann Karl Robert "Henning" von Tresckow (1901–1944), a major general in the Wehrmacht, who was one of the organizers of the Valkyrie plan to assassinate Hitler, wrote before he committed suicide on the Eastern Front following the plot's failure: "Hitler is the arch-enemy not only of Germany but of the whole world." See Evans, *Third Reich at War*, 642.

49. Mann, *Story of a Novel*, 125.

50. These volumes include—1933, *The Tales of Jacob (Die Geschichten Jaakobs)*; 1934, *The Young Joseph (Der junge Joseph)*; 1936, *Joseph in Egypt (Joseph in Ägypten)*; and, 1943, *Joseph the Provider (Joseph, der Ernährer)*.

51. Kurzke, *Thomas Mann*, 391.

ish denial of the fact that Judaism and Hellenism are the two principal pillars upon which our occidental civilization rests. To write a novel of the Jewish spirit was timely, just because it seems untimely.[52]

Finishing *Joseph the Provider* took place "amid the thunder of the battles for burning Stalingrad."[53] This crucial and heroic battle for the humanist soul of Europe was probably the last trigger for Mann's decision to embark on a new political, historical novel,[54] which aimed to reveal not only that the Nazis "entered the arena of history proclaiming themselves bearers of a barbarism that, while wallowing in ruthlessness, was to rejuvenate the world" (184) but also to fully expose the dark, Satanic abyss of the German soul. The goal, in other words, was to show that the "very definition of Germanness [is] a psychological state threatened by the poison of loneliness, by eccentricity, provincial standoffishness, neurotic involution, unspoken Satanism" (326). The outcome would be *Doctor Faustus*, conceived in 1942 and begun in 1943, which mercilessly exposes the barbaric, intoxicated, "secret union of the German spirit with the Demonic."[55]

"The Tables of the Law"

Before turning to *Doctor Faustus*, however, Mann took eight weeks to rush out "The Tables of the Law" ("Das Gesetz"), a dramatic retelling of the biblical story of Moses. Mann's diaries note that "he started writing on January 18, two days after an entry about the fighting in Stalingrad." As in *Joseph and His Brothers*, his "artistic intention" was to bring "these far and legendary figures close to the modern in an intimate, natural and

---

52. Mann, "Theme of the Joseph Novels," 11–12. See also Kurzke, *Thomas Mann*, 414.

53. Mann, *Story of a Novel*, 7.

54. According to Scaff, Mann's intention to write the Faustus novel in early 1942 was expressed in a letter "to Agnes E. Meyer, 21 February 1942." See Scaff, "Doctor Faustus," 168.

55. Mann, "Germany and the Germans," May 29, 1945, in *Thomas Mann's Addresses Delivered at the Library of Congress, 1942–1949*, 51. Hermann Kurzke poses a rhetorical question: "Thomas Faust?" (*Thomas Mann*, 462) and answers it on 484: "The Devil of Thomas Mann and Germany are one. . . . Thomas Mann is looking for fascism in himself."

convincing manner."[56] In opposing Aryan ideology and Nazi desecration of the Mosaic Decalogue, Mann defends it as the very foundation of civilization and morality.

This novella, the last of his "whole mythological-oriental materials," was commissioned for "an antifascist book on the Ten Commandments."[57] It was the first in the collection *The Ten Commandments: Ten Short Novels of Hitler's War Against the Moral Code* (1943), written by ten authors, one on each commandment. The collection was a response to Hitler's vehement attacks on Judaism and Christianity: "Historically speaking," Hitler said, "the Christian religion is nothing but a Jewish sect. It has always been and it will always remain just that, as long as it will exist." He added: "After the destruction of Judaism, the extinction of Christian slave morals must follow logically. I shall know the moment when to confront, for the sake of the German people and the world, their Asiatic slave morals with our picture of the free man, the god-like man." Hitler continues:

> We are fighting against the most ancient curse that humanity has brought upon itself. We are fighting against the perversion of our soundest instinct. Ah, the God of the deserts, that crazed, stupid, vengeful Asiatic despot with his powers to make laws! The slavekeeper's whip . . . It's got to get out of our blood, that curse from Mount Sinai.[58]

Nazi barbarism, anti-Semitism, and antihumanism could not be better articulated. Nor the blind contradictory irrationality of the absolute dictator excoriating "the crazed, stupid, vengeful . . . despot with his powers to make laws."

Now, Mann wrote: "The question was whether the hour had come for this task [*Doctor Faustus*] so long ago though so dimly sighted." He knew

---

56. Marion Faber and Stephen Lehmann, "Introduction," in Thomas Mann, *The Tables of the Law* (Philadelphia: Paul Day Books, 2010 [1944]), vii–viii.

57. Kurzke, *Thomas Mann*, 391, 417.

58. Hitler as quoted in Michael Wood, "Afterword," in Mann, *Tables of the Law*, 114. Wood took these words of Hitler from Herman Rauschning, "Preface" to *The Ten Commandments: Ten Short Novels of Hitler's War Against the Moral Code*, ed. Armin L. Robinson (New York: Simon & Schuster, 1943), xi–xii. According to Wood in a letter to the author, December 29, 2013, "Rauschning's preface" to the "book reports the conversation verbatim. As I say, there is some skepticism about its authenticity."

that writing the book would "cost heart's blood, a great deal of it, to whip it into shape" and clearly understood "how everything in it would have to be carried to extremes." He considered another idea that might save him from this hard work: "Let me try something else first." Sheer historical urgency and the fate of humanist culture as well as the need to explain Germany's struggle against humanity carried the day. The "War in North Africa, where Montgomery had brought Rommel to a standstill, held me in suspense." The advance "of the Russians in the Crimea" foreshadowed the Allied "imminent invasion of Europe."[59] With the tide of the war turning and, for the first time, the end of Nazi barbarism in sight, though still very far away, Mann could turn to the Faust novel.

He did so after the Casablanca Conference (January 14–24, 1943). Convened to plan the Allied strategy for the next phase of World War II, its result, the Casablanca Declaration, stipulated "unconditional surrender," perhaps its most historically provocative statement of purpose. This doctrine came to represent the unified voice of implacable Allied will—the determination that the Axis powers would be fought to utter defeat and annihilation. The war's end seemed feasible and in sight and the defeat of Nazi Germany more than probable. Moreover, in the eyes of the world, there existed "only one Germany" and that "single Germany would be held accountable for the evil perpetrated, supposedly, in the name of its people." "Mann himself had come to embrace" this position: "ridding the world of Nazism."[60]

The Year 1942, an Epistemological Watershed

Mann conceived *Doctor Faustus* in 1942 because civilization appeared to be at its nadir. That year, the Wehrmacht seemed invincible in Russia and North Africa. On February 22, Stefan Zweig, Austrian Jewish novelist, playwright, journalist, and biographer, committed suicide in Brazil. His letter explained, "the world of my own language sank and was lost to me and my spiritual homeland, Europe, destroyed itself."[61] Days later, Klaus Mann, Thomas Mann's son, also in exile, explained that Zweig "could not

---

59. Mann, *Story of a Novel*, 20, 23, 22. For the Nazi invasion of Russia and their terrible, horrifying atrocities there, see Snyder, *Bloodlands*.

60. Vaget, "'German' Music," 221–22.

61. See Friedman, "70 years later, a handwritten note recalls the end of a literary life."

bear the gruesome spectacle of a world bursting asunder."[62] British historian Eric Hobsbawm wrote: "The decades from the outbreak of the First World War to the aftermath of the Second were an Age of Catastrophe." Hobsbawm continues:

> For forty years it stumbles from one calamity to another. There were times when even intelligent conservatives would not take bets on its survival. . . . While the economy tottered, the institutions of liberal democracy virtually disappeared between 1917 and 1942 from all but a fringe of Europe and parts of North America and Australia.[63]

In this "Age of Catastrophe," or "the age of absolute sinfulness,"[64] in the words of Georg Lukács (1885–1971), the Hungarian Marxist philosopher, aesthetician, literary historian, and critic, the year 1942 signified more than any other that European humanist culture and civilization were under siege and faced extinction.

Like other exiled intellectuals, Thomas Mann followed the terrible and terrifying news from Stalingrad and El Alamein very closely. Readers of *Doctor Faustus* must see its inextricable connection to the war. Stalingrad and the "news of the war in North Africa"[65] in the Egyptian coastal city of El Alamein (October 23–November 11, 1942) would spark "a daring new artist's tale that might, he believed, be the most bizarre and outlandish he had ever produced."[66] Mann actually began writing "on 23 May 1943" (5), which is crucial since to use the Satanic apocalypse and eschatology of the Faustian theme, he had to be convinced that Germany's defeat and collapse were imminent. Only then could the Faustus legend and the fate of Nazi Germany become intelligible and inseparable. Similarly, Mann wrote that during the great Red Army offensive of early 1944, with "the hysterical declamations of the German radio announcer about the 'holy struggle for freedom against the soulless [Russian] hordes' ringing in my ear, I wrote the pages on hell, which are probably the most powerful thing" in

---

62. Mann, *The Turning Point*, 356–57.

63. Hobsbawm, *Age of Extremes*, 6–7.

64. Lukács, *Theory of the Novel*, 18. These words are taken from the preface, written in 1962.

65. Mann, *Story of a Novel*, 7.

66. Scaff, "Doctor Faustus," 168.

chapter 25, when Leverkühn and the devil make their pact. "Inconceivable, incidentally, without the psychological experience of Gestapo cellars." This chapter, Mann felt, was "the most effective part of the book."[67]

Given that Mann "fought fascist Germany passionately" for many years, in "1945 he spoke of the Devil's pact of Hitler's Germany and saw it in the image of Faust, the lonely thinker in his seclusion, who, out of longing for the pleasures of the world and dominion over the world, sells his soul to the Devil and then in 1945 is literally fetched by the Devil." Mann wrote about the connection of the German mind with the demonic but, conversely, related it to the inner, cultural, and psychological dimension: "Where the arrogance of intellect mates with spiritual antiquatedness [sic] and bondage, there the Devil is."[68]

Literary Antecedents

Mann's *Faustus* is based on three important literary moments: first, the old German legend, the Faustian moment, when a pact with Satan only defers judgment and destruction, which extended into the Goethean moment, the collision of Enlightenment and Romantic hubris that, in part 2 of Goethe's *Faust II* (1832), drifts into historical, social, political, and scientific commentary, Goethe simply *as* Faust, trying to cram everything into his remaining days; second, the Miltonian moment, when Satan, the fallen Angel, becomes one of the heroes of *Paradise Lost*; finally, the Dantean moment, when an epic journey to the very bottom of hell is required before ascent. While Mann was aware of these grand apocalyptic and eschatological structures, he changed them considerably.

Doctor Faustus is the history of the origin and eventual realization of hell on Earth, the result of a pact with Satan and his minions. As Leverkühn tells Satan, without love, the devil prepared him to live in "hell" on "earth" (265). By drawing close parallels between the composer's apocalypse and imminent doom and Nazi Germany's eschatological, impending destruction and defeat, Mann establishes the nexus between the Faustus legend and German history and culture: "the downfall of Germany is counterpointed by the catastrophe [of Adrian Leverkühn] that draws ever and more balefully closer."[69] In literary, historical terms, only the terrifying legend of Faustus

---

67. Mann, *Story of a Novel*, 108.
68. Kurzke, *Thomas Mann*, 484.
69. Mann, *Story of a Novel*, 131.

could expose the true nature and horrors of Nazi Germany because, Mann believed, with "National Socialism, and its revival of Germanic pagan cults, the German disposition for nationalism and barbarism gains an overwhelming preeminence,"[70] raising the sleeping monster.

A covenant with Mephistopheles determines Doctor Faustus's and Nazi Germany's doom. Satan prophesies: "German I am, German to the core" and "German I shall be" (242), leaving no doubt of his deep roots in German identity. The novel is the terrible revelation of Satan's Apocalypse and its ensuing "devilish time" (250) in contrast to God's divine Apocalypse, as portrayed in the book of Revelation, based on salvific time. Satanic time is limited: sin, imminent judgment, and final destruction; divine time expands through grace, love, mercy, and hope.

In preparing to write his Faustus novel, Mann read many works on witchcraft and the legend to enhance his understanding of Germany's union with the demonic and to define the apocalyptic and eschatological dimensions of his work. He studied *Malleus Maleficarum* (*Hammer of the Witches*), a 1486 treatise on prosecuting witches by the German churchman and inquisitor Heinrich Kramer (1430–1505). Its main purpose was to systematically refute arguments that deny the existence of witchcraft, to discredit skepticism about its reality, to show that witches are more often women than men, and, finally, to teach magistrates how to identify and convict them. In the context of witches and sorcerers, Mann emphasized that his novel would reveal "the cold breath of inhumanity."[71]

Mann also read Christopher Marlowe's play *The Tragical History of the Life and Death of Doctor Faustus* (1604, but probably written circa 1592). Using Mephistopheles as a messenger, Faustus strikes a deal with Lucifer: he is to be allotted twenty-four years of life on Earth, a year for each hour of the day, and Mephistopheles will be his personal servant. At the end, he will give his soul to Lucifer in payment and be damned to hell eternally. The idea of selling the soul to the devil for power and knowledge is an old motif in German folklore. It became attached to the historical persona of Johannes Faustus, a disreputable astrologer who lived in Germany sometime in the early 1500s. The immediate source for Marlowe's play seems to be *Historia von D. Iohan Fausten*, the first "Faust book," a chapbook of stories by an anonymous German author published by Johann Spies (1540–1623) in Frankfurt am Main in 1587. In 1592, the book was translated into English,

---

70. Hannelore Mundt, *Understanding Thomas Mann* (Columbia: University of South Carolina Press, 2004), 178.

71. Mann, *Story of a Novel*, 27.

and from it, Marlowe lifted the bulk of his plot. His play was the first dramatized version of the story. It opposes intellect and faith: Marlowe's Faust will not burn his books or repent to evade his fate.

As the self-proclaimed embodiment of German culture, Mann would have to be acutely aware of Goethe's *Faust I* (1808) and *Faust II* (1832), if not the *Urfaust* (1772–1775, but the manuscript was lost, and only in 1886 did a copy surface). The first two are considered by some the apotheosis of German literature. Goethe was clearly obsessed with the tale throughout his life, perhaps as an energetic polymath who lived to the full—what deals with what devils contributed to his success, or did he aspire to more at any cost? Mann's debt to Goethe is more implicit than explicit.

Mann notes *The Black Spider* (1842), a tale by Swiss writer Jeremias Gotthelf (*né* Albert Bitzius [1797–1854]), as a source. This highly dramatic, moving, vivid Christian tale portrays a village ruled by the cruel Teutonic knight Hans von Stoffeln. He oppresses and intimidates the village farmers ruthlessly, forcing them to complete increasingly pointless tasks. At this hopeless juncture, the devil appears as the "tall and gaunt figure of a green huntsman" with "a little red beard" and offers to assist the farmers in exchange for an unbaptized child.[72] After initially refusing, the farmers accept the bargain but do not intend to fulfill their part. In retaliation, the devil terrorizes the valley, killing animals and people, including von Stoffeln and his knights. The cruelly overbearing lord of the manor, the oppressed villagers who must render him service, and the morality of collective guilt combine in a parable of evil in the heart or evil at large in society. Mann saw it as foretelling the advent of Nazism and wrote that he admired it "almost more than anything else in world literature."[73] Elsewhere, he claimed that *The Black Spider* was the model for his *Doctor Faustus*: "To be in contact with great narrative literature, more or less to bathe forces in it, is advisable if you are yourself striving for serious narrative: This is how I came to read Jeremias Gotthelf's 'Black Spider.' There is scarcely a work in world literature that I admire more."[74] Even today, the book is read with fear and trembling.

Mann confessed that the devil is "the secret hero of the book,"[75] defining *ipso facto* its unique apocalyptic and eschatological time-dimension.

---

72. Jeremias Gotthelf, *The Black Spider* (London: Knightscross Books, 1992), 44.

73. Mann, *Story of a Novel*, 63.

74. Mann's words appeared in Gotthelf, *The Black Spider*, 5.

75. Mann, *Story of a Novel*, 71.

Mann was not the first to portray the Devil as a superhero in apocalyptic and eschatological terms. Satan (Lucifer) is one of the main protagonists, along with Adam and Eve, in *Paradise Lost* (1658-1664), the *magnum opus* of English poet John Milton (1608-1674). Milton's story has two narrative arcs: one for Satan, the other for Adam and Eve. Likewise, Mann's novel has two overarching narratives, one relating composer Leverkühn's covenant with the devil and the other Germany's pact with Hitler and Nazism. However, Milton's Adam and Eve are excluded from Eden but inherit the Earth and may regain God's salvation, as revealed in his *Paradise Regained* (1671). Milton ends his epic with these remarkable lines:

> The world was all before them, where to choose
> Their place of rest, and Providence their guide . . .[76]

Not so for Adrian Leverkühn or Nazi Germany.

That *Doctor Faustus* is an apocalyptic and eschatological novel can be seen in the motto Mann chose for it. Taken from the opening of the second canto of Dante Alighieri's *Inferno*, these lines depict the narrator beginning his sad, painful, and pitiful journey through hell. Dante's hell is an imaginative space shared with poets, but Mann's is earthly and contemporary—Nazi Germany's concentration camps and death factories. The Dantean moment fulfills a mission. Just before embarking on his journey, *il Sommo Poeta* prays to the Muses and memory for help in recording his dreadful visions for posterity:

> Day was now fading, and the dusky air
> Released the creatures dwelling here on earth
> From tiring tasks, while I, the only one,
>
> Readied myself to endure the battle
> Both of the journey and the pathos,
> Which flawless memory shall here record.
>
> O Muses, O high genius, aid me now!
> O memory that noted what I saw,
> Now shall your true nobility be seen!

---

76. John Milton, *Complete Poems* (Cambridge: Harvard Classics, 1909-1914), 646-47.

Dante's long journey into the Inferno represents the beginning of the soul's journey toward God. Here, sin is recognized and rejected for the later rise through *Purgatorio* to reach *Paradiso*.

The *Divine Comedy* is based on a grand teleological theology, or the sacred, providential order embedded in the system and structure of the universe, as promulgated by the Doktor Angelicus, Doktor Communis, or Doktor Universalis Thomas Aquinas in his *Summa Theologica* (1265–1274).[77] The famous philologist Erich Auerbach wrote, "The *Comedy* represented the physical, ethical, and political unity of the Scholastic Christian cosmos."[78] The title is "[i]n line with the scholastic view, based on fragmentary recollections of antiquity, which prescribed a happy beginning and an unhappy end for tragedy and the opposite for comedy." For Dante, wrote Auerbach, "the meaning of every life has its place in the providential history of the world, the general lines of which are laid down in Revelation which has been given to every Christian, and which is interpreted for him in the vision of the *Comedy*."[79] Such a grand, sacred, providential plan is based on God's Apocalypse of grace, His plan for the redemption and salvation of humankind.

In clear contrast, Mann's novel is based on Satan's Apocalypse—a terrible, eternal judgment and fall. While Dante's story begins in hell and reaches the promised heaven, where the godly sit on God's right side, Doctor Faustus wanders only through the savage wilderness of an earthly hell, and Leverkühn's and Germany's "adventures of drunkenly intense subjective feeling and super-greatness" lead "to mental collapse and spiritual death, and soon to physical death."[80] Dante writes a *Divine Comedy*; Mann, a ghastly secular tragedy. These two grand pilgrimages stand in radical opposition. If Dante's mission is to describe the way to heaven, Mann's is to blast Germany's fall into imperialist, *völkisch*, murderous, mindless nationalism, according to which "the world was to be renewed under the emblem of Germany, under the emblem of a militaristic socialism" (318).

---

77. In his book on Dante, *Dante: Poet of the Secular World*, Auerbach argues that the title, *Comedy*, is based on the scholastic view: "In line with the scholastic view, based on fragmentary recollections of antiquity, which prescribed a happy beginning and an unhappy end for tragedy and the opposite for comedy," Dante "called it a comedy." See Erich Auerbach, *Dante: Poet of the Secular World*, trans. Ralph Manheim (New York: New York Review of Books, 2007 [1929]), 92.

78. Auerbach, *Dante: Poet of the Secular World*, 175.

79. Auerbach, "Figura," 70–71.

80. Mann as quote by Reed, *Thomas Mann*, 365.

Mann chose Dante's words for his epigraph to reflect his goal: in the midst of the battles and atrocities of World War II, the writer's portion is to appeal to intellect and moral sensitivity with the help of the Muses Erato, the Greek Muse of lyric and love poetry who inspires literature, and Mnemosyne, memory and mother of all the Muses. Like Dante, Mann's narrator needs all the help he can get from literary reflection and memory. However, unlike Dante, who writes in the first line of the *Divine Comedy*, "Midway upon the journey of our life," Dr. Serenus Zeitblom, the narrator, is "sixty years of age" (5), adding urgency to his appeal to inspiration and memory.

In another salient difference, Dante has the Roman poet Virgil (70 BCE–19 BCE) as his guide through the dark labyrinth, and Beatrice becomes his guide in the last four cantos of the *Purgatory* and all through *Heaven* because, as the incarnation of love, she can lead him to the beatific vision (*visio beatifica*), which is God's direct self-communication to the individual. In contrast, Leverkühn is a sinner who sells his soul to Satan; he has no humanist authority to guide him in the abysses of the earthly hell. He is not a simple victim of Nazism's diabolic creation of hell on Earth; his "apocalyptic oratorio" swells "to a dreadful mayhem of yowls, yelps, screeches, bleats, bellows, howls, and whinnies, to the mocking, triumphant laughter of hell" (397). Such laughter can be clearly recognized as "something of the uncanny, an element of religious diabolism."[81] As for love, Leverkühn's love for "Esmeralda" (*Hetaera Esmeralda*) results in incurable syphilis and strengthened his pact with the devil.[82] The hell of German culture and history is seductive and offers no way out.

Both Dante and Mann start their sad journeys in hell. Both are very mindful that, in Dante's words, "to endure the battle" of both "the journey and the pathos" will serve as an example for generations to come: for Dante, of the power of grace and love; for Mann, the need to resist Nazi inhumanity. Both are literary contributions to *Kulturkampf*, Dante's based on "the general lines . . . laid down in Revelation . . . given to every Christian, and which is interpreted for him in the vision of the *Comedy*," and Mann's on Satan's Apocalypse unfolding through German history and culture. Literature is the writer's weapon: in Dante's case, against sin, in Mann's, against German infatuation with the demonic. In sum, *Doctor Faustus* represents the best way Mann knew to fight against fascism and

---

81. Mann, *Story of a Novel*, 70.

82. *Hetaera Esmeralda*; Hetaera—an ancient Greek courtesan or concubine, especially one who was highly educated or refined. Esmeralda—the Latin name of a butterfly whose pink and violet wings resemble the prostitute's garish makeup.

Nazism. His close affinity with Dante resides in their use of literature and memory to fight present evils and to teach future generations.

History: Time and Place

Like apocalypse and eschatology, history played an enormous and crucial role in shaping the content and form of *Doctor Faustus*. In 1906, Leverkühn makes his pact with the devil, and in 1930, he loses his sanity and consciousness as it expires. Mann did not explain why he chose these two years, but they are very significant in German history.

The year 1906 saw the barbarization of the German soul in the Herero and Namaqua genocides in German Southwest Africa, present-day Namibia. The conflict (1904–1907) "escalated into one of the most brutal colonial wars in history, and the first German genocide." Termed "race war" by the Germans, it was "a war of annihilation. Women and children were seen as legitimate targets, too. Race war is war without limit, a life-or-death struggle against an 'absolute enemy.'" The Namibian War was not only "the first genocide of the twentieth century" but also "the first genocide in German history." The native "Herero resisted as a group, a 'tribe,' a 'race' "; hence, "they must be annihilated as such."[83]

"The last years of my hero's intellectual life, the two years of 1929 and 1930," correspond "in fact to the ascent and spread of that usurping power now perishing in blood and flames" (507), Nazism and fascism in Germany, and marked the end of the Golden Age of the Weimar Republic. The 1929 depression in the United States sent shock waves through Germany, and liberal democracy collapsed in 1930, when President Hindenburg assumed emergency dictatorial powers. Article 48 of the Weimar Republic Constitution allowed the president to take emergency measures, including the promulgation of "emergency decrees" (*Notverordnungen*), without prior consent of the Reichstag under certain circumstances. In September 1930, the Nazi Party (NSDAP) entered the Reichstag with 19 percent of the popular vote. The convergence between Leverkühn's personal crisis and the crisis of German politics reached its culmination; literature and history are intertwined in Mann's hands, and diabolic apocalypse spread from literary works into history,

---

83. Jürgen Zimmerer, "Annihilation in Africa: The 'Race War' in German Southwest Africa (1904–1908) and Its Significance for a Global History of Genocide," *GHI Bulletin* 37 (Fall 2005): 51–53.

The historical parallel between Leverkühn's apocalypse and German apocalypse can be seen in the fact that Leverkühn dies at the age of fifty-five, ten years after losing his sanity in 1930. Hitler took power in 1933, and the writing of *Doctor Faustus* began in 1943, ten years after the Nazi Revolution in which Germany lost its sanity. In Mann's apocalyptic and eschatological novel, structured according to Satan's prophecy, events in Leverkühn's tragic life—his pact with the devil, his insanity—are not symbols but omens that are realized in German history. The personal and the national are inextricably connected; the composer, the author, and Germany are bedeviled for the same span of time. The historic events of World War II conflate directly with Leverkühn's story.

The physical location and time of the writing also reveal its apocalyptic and eschatological dimension. In beginning in 1943 in Germany, Zeitblom admits that chances are slim that he will see the work published: "there is still not the slightest prospect that my manuscript will ever see the light of the public day, unless by some miracle it were to leave our beleaguered Fortress Europe and share the whispered secrets of our isolation with those outside" (5). He needs a miracle, given his opposition to Nazism. Further, if insanity means hiding from the light of truth and rationality, then it finds its proper home in Fortress Europe, seat of Nazi Germany's deep-seated paranoia. The narrator's aim is clear: *Doctor Faustus* will present ample evidence of the deterioration of German sanity in parallel with Leverkühn's. It can be seen as an urgent, subversive message, hidden in a bottle, to be flung outside the walls in hope of warning the humanist world outside of the dark, irrational, and inhumane life within. However, only at the end of the book, with the final defeat of the "monster state," can the author muse that "it might be possible to think of the publication" of "these memoires, this biography of Adrian Leverkühn" (528). Only in 1944–1945, when "the career of the Third Reich was speeding to its conclusion," and the "struggle had ceased to be for 'Fortress Europe' and was only concentrating upon 'Fortress Germany,'" could the work see the light of the day.[84]

Doctor Faustus

Doctor Faustus: Das Leben des deutschen Tonsetzers Adrian Leverkühn, erzählt von einem Freunde (*Doctor Faustus: The Life of the German Composer Adrian Leverkühn, Told by a Friend*), was published in 1947. Depicting

---

84. Mann, *Story of a Novel*, 97.

Satan's Apocalypse, it is almost devoid of love, grace, and mercy, in contrast to God's Apocalypse, His providential plan for human salvation and redemption. The Faust apocalypse is the anti-Apocalypse; directed by Satan, it ends with doom and terrible destruction. There is no New Heaven or New Earth, no New Jerusalem descending from heaven, as in the book of Revelation. In the broad context of "endings and the final end,"[85] the Faust novel is eschatology, bodying forth the imminent doom of Nazi Germany in the composer's pact with the devil.

The view of *Doctor Faustus* as a prophetic Satanic apocalypse is easily supported by the prevalence of apocalyptic and eschatological themes. During Leverkühn's university studies in Halle, the historical center of German Pietism, theology becomes demonology: "the infiltration of theological thought by irrational currents within philosophy, in whose domain the nontheoretical, the vital, the will of instinct—in short once again, the demonic" (99). In this fervid atmosphere, Leverkühn "was abandoning his career as a scholar, 'shoving Holy Writ under the bench,' to use his own expression, and flinging himself totally into the arms of music" (147). The narrator explains that the relation of "the German to the world is abstract and mystical, that is, musical," with "a touch of demonism."[86] Leverkühn's decision to abandon theology for music "was . . . uniquely stamped with destiny" (147). In his final confession, Leverkühn testifies that in his youth, his soul "was upon the road to Satan." "I was born to hell," he continues before he loses his sanity, and his theological studies in his youth were "not for God's sake, but for the sake of that Other," or Satan (523).

This apocalyptic and eschatological scenario reaches a climax with Leverkühn's "apocalyptic oratorio" (374) *Apocalypsis cum Figuris* (*Apocalypse with Pictures*), a musical work based on his pact with, and stimulated by, the devil. It references the work of another German artist, Albrecht Dürer (1471–1528), whose *Apocalypsis cum Figuris* (1498) comprises fifteen woodcuts of scenes from the book of Revelation. The progress of the novel explores the close association of the era of the Protestant Reformation and Nazism; if the events of the Christian Apocalypse are prophesied and proceed according to God's plan for the world to turn from alienation to reconciliation with its creator, events in Nazi apocalypse are directed solely according to Satan's whim and lead only to destruction.

Leverkühn's apocalyptic oratorio originates "at the age of thirty-five," when he experiences "a first wave of euphoric inspiration." It is "his chief

---

85. Scaff, "Doctor Faustus," 170.
86. Mann, "Germany and the Germans," 51.

work, or his first principal work,"[87] fruit of his covenant with the devil. Mann constantly emphasizes its compression of apocalyptic and eschatological traditions "into a menacing latter-day artistic synthesis." He aims to hold "the mirror of revelation up to humanity's eyes, so that it may see what is approaching and near at hand," but his vision is radically different from God's Apocalypse as told by Saint John of Patmos. Leverkühn uses text from Ezekiel 7: 6-7, "An end is come, the end is come; it watcheth for thee: behold, it is come. The morning is come to thee, O thou that dwellest in the land" (376-77), and it ends with a terrible apocalyptic vision and horrified eschatological expectation: "the time is come, the day of trouble is near." Clearly, as the narrator is quick to point out, these "words do not belong to the Apocalypse of John at all." Leverkühn's musical "creation is tantamount to a new apocalypse of his own" (376-77). Christian Apocalypse transforms the world into the Kingdom of God, while Leverkühn focuses on decadence and death, the transformation of the world into the Kingdom of Satan. As the devil promises him, "you will break through the age itself, the cultural epoch," and "dare a barbarism, a double barbarism, because it comes after humanitarianism" (259).

For Mann, the Protestant Reformation "leads not only out of the Scholastic period into our world of free thinking, but at the same time deep into the Middle Ages as well" (10), or barbarism. This view stands in clear contrast to those of a long series of distinguished German scholars, most prominently Max Weber (1864-1920). In *The Protestant Ethic and the Spirit of Capitalism* (1905), Weber argues that the Protestant Reformation inaugurated the modern world. For Mann, the Protestant Reformation signals the beginning of "a secret union of the German spirit with the Demonic,"[88] as can be seen for example in the works of Dürer, such as *Apocalypsis cum Figuris* (1498) and *Knight, Death and the Devil* (*Ritter, Tod und Teufel*, 1513),[89] or in the works of Martin Luther (1483-1546).[90] The

---

87. Mann, *Story of a Novel*, 151. Compare Dante's first line in the *Inferno*: "Midway upon the journey of our life."

88. Mann, "Germany and the Germans," 51.

89. For the demonic strain in Dürer's works, see Andrew Butterfield, "Dürer's Devil Within," at http://www.nybooks.com/blogs/nyrblog/2013/may/20/durer-devil-within/.

90. An analysis of Luther's demonology can be found in Heiko A. Oberman, *Luther: Man Between God and the Devil*, and Barnes, *Prophecy and Gnosis*. See also Benjamin Mayes, "Quotes and Paraphrases from Lutheran Pastoral Handbooks of the 16th and 17th Centuries on the Topic of Demon Possession," at http://www.angelfire.com/ny4/djw/lutherantheology.demonpossession.html.

crisis of Nazism thus led Mann to a radically different reading of German history, a Satanic interpretation of the regression of German culture.

According to Mann, his Faustian apocalypse deals with "the flight from the difficulties of a cultural crisis into the pact with the devil; the craving of a proud mind, threatened by sterility, for an unblocking of inhibitions at any cost; and the parallel between pernicious euphoria ending in collapse with the nationalistic frenzy of Fascism."[91] Myth, culture, history, and psychology are inextricably bound. Given that Mann witnessed two world wars, many revolutions, and the rise of fascism and Nazism, no wonder he considered Satanic apocalypse the appropriate literary form. Rhetorically, he asks, "How much *Faustus* contains of the atmosphere of my life?" and answers that the "book contained too much of my life, too many of my secrets."[92] One of his biographers observes that the work is "full of his own experience like none other . . . closer to him than any other."[93] This observation applies to both his private and public realms.

Mann's mission in exile is to unveil the irrationality, antihumanism, the flight from reason and reality, and the culture of sadomasochistic myths, legends, and heroes embedded in the German spirit, which found horrible expression in Nazi Germany and World War II. To wage his *Kulturkampf* against these forces, no other literary model was left but *Doctor Faustus*, perhaps to deliberately rattle the bones of Goethe, avatar of German greatness, as "the sordid abuse and cheap peddling of what was old and genuine, faithful and familiar, of what was fundamentally German, from which liars and frauds then prepared a stupefying poisonous home-brew" (186).

The end determined the means by which Mann would wage his literary war. Only "through a glass darkly"[94]—a deeply rooted German legend—could Mann reflect the depth and reach of Nazi evil. The Revelation of Saint John the Divine was written toward the end of the first century on the Greek island of Patmos to help God's people understand their flight and persecution in the context of final victory and transformation of the world into the Kingdom of God. Mann's anti-Apocalypse was also written in exile, but it describes only decline and fall, destruction and defeat. Redemption and salvation were unimaginable.

Doctor Faustus is based on a demonic, prophetic, apocalyptical, and eschatological dimension of time in which the tragedy and imminent death

---

91. Mann, *Story of a Novel*, 30.
92. Ibid., 154, 229–30.
93. Kurzke, *Thomas Mann*, 463.
94. 1 Corinthians 13: 12.

of Adrian Leverkühn unfolds in parallel with Nazi Germany's decline and eventual collapse in 1945. Both the cultural and the political pact with Satanic ideology constitute, for Mann, the German catastrophe. Apocalypse and eschatology are inseparable from the book because the progress of Satan's revelation in time and history determines its content and form.

The work is constructed as a long series of prophetic binary contradictions within an overarching eschatological context: God's revelation of His mercy versus Satan's revelation of judgment and death; the coming of God's Kingdom on Earth versus Satan's Kingdom on Earth; "devilish time" (250) versus divine, salvific time; the Son of God versus. Leverkühn as the "Son of Hell" (509) or "the Devil's own monk" (525); Leverkühn's movement from theology to music to demonism; Friedrich Schiller's "Ode to Joy" ("Ode an die Freude," 1785) versus Leverkühn's "Ode of Sorrow," *The Lamentation of Dr. Faustus*; Beethoven's Ninth Symphony, which concludes with the "Ode to Joy,"[95] versus Leverkühn's Satanic oratorio *Apocalypsis cum Figuris*, in which harmony is used "to represent the infernal, the apocalyptic; dissonance conveys the pious";[96] and love, mercy, and salvation versus lust, syphilis, and death, or "love and poison," which become "mythological unity" (165) in Wagner's *Tristan und Isolde* (1865). Leverkühn's oratorio (374) with its "hellish laughter" (397) is created in 1919, the same year as the Weimar Republic, the city that was during the eighteenth century the cradle of German Enlightenment, center of Weimar Classicism (Weimarer Klassik) with its new humanism, and near Buchenwald concentration camp, an enactment of Nazi abomination.[97]

Through Leverkühn, who intentionally contracts syphilis to deepen his artistic inspiration through madness, Mann's goal is to depict:

---

95. According to Schiller's "Ode to Joy," 1785:
    Joy is called the strong motivation
    In eternal nature.
    Joy, joy moves the wheels
    In the universal time machine.
See http://www.raptusassociation.org/ode1785.html.

96. Mundt, *Understanding Thomas Mann*, 188.

97. "Jedem das Seine" was the sign on Buchenwald's gate facing the inside of the camp, so that it could be easily read by the prisoners. This sign can be translated as "To each his own" or as "Everyone gets what he deserves." Auschwitz had a sign on the entrance gatehouse facing the outside of the camp that read "Arbeit Macht Frei"—"Work sets you free."

> ... the bursting of social bonds, which occurs as a disintegration by infectious disease, at the same time *political*. Intellectual-spiritual fascism, throwing off of human principle, recourse to violence, blood-lust, irrationalism, cruelty, Dionysiac denial of truth and justice, self-abandonment to the instincts and unrestrained 'Life,' which in fact is *death* and, insofar as it is life, only the *devil's work, product of infection*. Fascism as a Devil-given departure from bourgeois society which leads through adventures of drunkenly intense subjective feeling and super-greatness to mental collapse and spiritual death, and soon to physical death: the *reckoning is presented*.[98]

Mann talked about "*the cold breath of inhumanity* that blows through the book at the end."[99] He found out the inevitable: that writing about inhumanity and irrationalism in a diabolic apocalyptic novel will end up siding with the "blasphemers of humanity."[100]

Doctor Faustus's aim is not only to relate the life of a German composer but also "to portray the whole cultural crisis." This larger goal, Mann wrote, "was the fundamental motif of my book: the closeness of sterility, the innate despair that prepares the ground for" Leverkühn's or Germany's "pact with the devil."[101] Mann felt that since the "themes of the book, crisis themes, had an extremely German coloration, I must attempt, as much as possible, to fuse them in the universalities of the era and of Europe."[102] He places them in the first half of the twentieth century, *ipso facto* the crisis of Western civilization as a whole, and asks rhetorically, "A novel of music? Yes. But it was also conceived as a novel of the culture of the era," whose "main idea" is "ill-gotten inspiration, whose ecstasy carries it beyond itself."[103] Ecstasy and irrationalism thus merge with apocalypse and eschatology. Further, Mann sees Leverkühn as "a kind of ideal figure, a 'hero of our time,' a person who bore the suffering of the epoch," or German

---

98. Mann, quoted by Reed, *Thomas Mann*, 365. It should be noted that the quotation is from a work note for the novel.
99. Mann, *Story of a Novel*, 27, emphasis added.
100. Ibid., 117.
101. Ibid., 64.
102. Ibid., 55.
103. Ibid., 42–43.

barbarism. Only the Faustus tale can convey the life and sad fate of this "hero." Frankly, Mann added, "I shared good Serenus' feeling for him."[104]

Doctor Faustus addresses Germany's demonic strain of thought and actions, its devilish modes of persuasion and conduct. From the outset, the narrator finds it necessary to disassociate himself. "Scarcely presuming to deny the influence of the demonic on human life," he writes, "I have always found it a force totally foreign to my nature and have instinctively excluded it from my worldview" (6), although his "humanist worldview" (10) forces him to make some "sacrifices" in Nazi Germany. Since he "could not be reconciled with the spirit and claims of our historical developments," or the triumph of Nazism, Professor Zeitblom "did not hesitate prematurely to retire from the teaching profession," which he "loved" (6), because his "teaching position" has "fallen away under the thunder of history" (529). He discovers a new humanist mission in the form of a literary work that will illuminate the union of Germany with the demonic through the quintessentially German legend of Faust.

Mann went into exile; Zeitblom resorts to "inner emigration," a position among artists and intellectuals who remained in Nazi Germany that Mann vociferously opposed. Zeitblom avoids taking part in the Satanic culture and irrational ideas as a criticism of Aryan ideology and Nazi historiography and disapproves of his friend's musical work *Apocalypsis cum Figuris* with its "mocking, triumphant laughter of hell" (397). As Satan's proxy, "the Devil's own monk" or the "Son of Hell" (509), Leverkühn spreads hell on Earth; in his music, the devil is "invisibly present."[105]

Beginning in 1943, the turning point of the war, Zeitblom is sure that the "time will . . . come when our prison [Germany], which though extensive is nonetheless cramped and filled with suffocatingly stale air, has opened—that is, when the war raging at present has come to an end." Now, "we are profoundly aware of the crushing consequences, in all their irrevocable horror, of a German defeat, so that we cannot help fearing it more than anything else in the world" (33). Because Germany lives "under the rule of the most brazen despotism" (110), its portion and "the fate of our whole nation, always excepting cases of oversize stupidity and base self-interest," will eventually lead Germany to "unparalleled tragedy" (34).

The narrator knows too well that Nazism spells nightmare not only for Germany but for humanist civilization as a whole. The Hitler "regime that led us into this war and has indeed laid the entire continent at our

---

104. Ibid., 88–89.

105. Mann, *Story of a Novel*, 70–71.

feet" replaced "the intellectual dream of a European Germany with the albeit rather terrifying, rather flawed, and as the world sees it, so it would seem, quite intolerable reality of a German Europe" (183). Melita Maschmann, who before and during the war worked in the high echelons of press and propaganda of the Bund Deutscher Mädel, the girls' Nazi youth organization, wrote: "For us," Hitler "embodied the unprecedented effort that had made the German nation take over the government of the continent."[106] Such a gamble proved a sheer disaster of magnifying proportions, she admitted: "we have played *va banque* [a chemin-de-fer or baccarat player's willingness to bet against the banker's whole stake] that the failure of our plans to conquer the world is of necessity equivalent to a national catastrophe of the first order" (184).

In the fight against Hitlerism, Mann supported the "student uprising in Munich," which was "quelled in a ghastly bloodbath" (183–84). The reference is to the actions of the White Rose, 1942–1943, a nonviolent student resistance group in Nazi Germany, which in its first leaflet, June 1942, foresaw the downfall of Hitler and Nazism, quoting from Goethe's *The Awakening of Epimenides* (1814), act 2, scene 4:

> SPIRITS:
> Though he who has boldly risen from the abyss
> Through an iron will and cunning
> May conquer half the world,
> Yet to the abyss he must return.
> Already a terrible fear has seized him;
> In vain he will resist!
> And all who still stand with him
> Must perish in his fall.
>
> HOPE:
> Now I find my good men
> Are gathered in the night,
> To wait in silence, not to sleep.
> And the glorious word of liberty
> They whisper and murmur,

---

106. Evans, *Third Reich at War*, 679. Based on this Nazi plan of subduing Europe, Maschmann supervised the eviction of Polish farmers and the resettlement of ethnic Germans on their farms. Arrested in 1945 at the age of twenty-seven, she completed a mandatory de-Nazification course and became a freelance journalist.

> Till in unaccustomed strangeness,
> On the steps of our temple
> Once again in delight they cry:
> Freedom! Freedom!¹⁰⁷

Mann was deeply moved by the actions of the White Rose. In his broadcast from exile in the radio series "German Listeners," June 27, 1943, he told the audience: "Good splendid young people! You shall not have died in vain; you shall not be forgotten." Their actions, he announced on the air, are a proof that "a new faith in freedom and honor [in Germany] is dawning."¹⁰⁸

The intermingling of the story of Faustus with German history in 1943 is nowhere clearer than in chapter 21, in which the narrator turns to the reader to explain the German catastrophe:

> I am saying all this to remind the reader of the historical circumstances under which this account of Leverkühn's life is being written, and to make him realize how the agitated state that is part of my work is constantly fused beyond recognition with that caused by the convulsion of our day. (184)

In response to rising voices in Germany against the Allied air bombardment of German cities, the narrator sadly reminds his readers about the "barbaric turn" of German history and asks ironically: "How strange that lament for culture, raised now against crimes that we called down upon ourselves, sounds in the mouths of those who entered the arena of history proclaiming themselves bearers of a barbarism that, while wallowing in ruthlessness, was to rejuvenate the world" (184). He ridicules German historians' defense of Germany's "special path," or *Sonderweg*,¹⁰⁹ claiming: "Yes, we are a completely different nation, one that is a contradiction to sobriety and common sense and whose soul is powerfully tragic; our love belongs to fate, any fate, if only it is one, even doom that sets the heavens

---

107. Dumbach and Newborn, *Sophie Scholl*, 188. See also http://educate-yourself.org/cn/whiteroseleaflet1942germany.shtml.

108. Dumbach and Newborn, *Sophie Scholl*, ii.

109. Ernst Schulin, "German and American Historiography in the Nineteenth and Twentieth Centuries," in *An Interrupted Past: German-Speaking Refugee Historians in the United States after 1933*, ed. Hartmut Lehmann and James J. Sheehan (Cambridge: Cambridge University Press, 1991), 19.

afire with the red twilight of the gods" (185). *The Twilight of the Gods* (*Götterdämmerung*) is the last of the four operas of Wagner's *Ring of the Nibelung* cycle. It is based on a Norse myth prophesying a war with the gods that ends with their consumption by flames.

The belief in *Sonderweg* stipulated that the "German nation-state was different from and superior to the West European nation-states on several accounts," especially "the Prussian idea of the state standing above society and party politics."[110] Gerhard Ritter's influential *Machtstaat und Utopia* (*National Power and Utopia* [1940]) was "an elaborate justification of the German path" and "placed state authority and military needs higher than liberal principles."[111] Ritter (1888–1967), like so many of his colleagues, "justified the expansionist eastward aims of the Nazis by seeking to demonstrate the cultural superiority of Germans over Slavs."[112] A product of Wilhelmine Germany and its Prussian traditions, Ritter claimed that the nation is a living organism with a right to life, namely, territorial expansion.

It was during the Franco-Prussian War (1870–1871) that the Germans were first called "the Huns," referring to a barbaric tribe and its leader Attila (d. 453), one of the most fearful enemies of the Western and Eastern Roman Empires.[113] At the turn of the century, on July 27, 1900, Kaiser Wilhelm II plainly identified Germany with the Huns when he bade farewell to the expeditionary corps sailing off to China to defeat the Boxers (1899–1901):

> When you meet the enemy, he will be defeated! No quarter will be given! No prisoners will be taken! Those who fall into your hands are forfeit to you! Just as a thousand years ago, the Huns under their King Etzel [Attila] made a name for themselves which shows them as mighty in tradition and myth, so

---

110. Stefan Berger, *The Search for Normality: National Identity and Historical Consciousness in Germany since 1800* (Oxford: Berghahn Books, 1997), 37.

111. Wolfgang J. Mommsen, "German Historiography during the Weimar Republic and the Émigré Historians," in *An Interrupted Past: German-Speaking Refugee Historians in the United States after 1933*, ed. Hartmut Lehmann and James J. Sheehan (Cambridge: Cambridge University Press, 1991), 37.

112. Georg G. Iggers, "The German Professors in the Third Reich," *Central European History* 25 (1992), 447.

113. On the place of Attila the Hun in history, see John Man, *Attila the Hun: A Barbarian King and the Fall of Rome* (New York: Random House, 2006).

shall you establish the name of Germans in China for 1000 years, in such a way that a Chinese will never again dare to look askance at a German.[114]

The Kaiser's speech was widely reported in the European press and became the basis for characterizing the Germans during World War I as barbarians and savages with no respect for European humanitarian values. Ferdinand August Bebel (1840–1913), a Marxist and one of the founders of the Social Democratic Party of Germany (SDP), gave a speech to the Reichstag on the cruelty of the German expedition to China taken from soldiers' letters home, styled the *Hunnen-Briefe* (letters from the Huns). "No," he declared, "this is no crusade, no holy war; it is a very ordinary war of conquest . . . a campaign of revenge. A campaign of revenge as barbaric as has never been seen in the last centuries, and not often at all in history . . . not even with the Huns, not even with the Vandals."[115]

The identification of Germany with the barbaric Hun intensified during the first year of World War I with "The Rape of Belgium," from August to September 1914, when "Germany had provoked and begun hostilities, had flouted morality and broken international law by invading France via neutral Belgium, and was now committing atrocities."[116] In response, Rudyard Kipling (1865–1936) wrote the poem "For All We Have and Are" in 1914:

> For all we have and are,
> For all our children's fate,
> Stand up and take the war.
> *The Hun is at the gate!*[117]

When *Doctor Faustus* begins in 1943, the Russians were winning the battle of Stalingrad, a turning point in the European theater of war and the struggle over European humanist culture. Even Germany noted "a

---

114. See http://en.wikipedia.org/wiki/List_of_terms_used_for_Germans#Hun.

115. Bebel, quoted in Annika Mombauer, "Wilhelm, Waldersee, and the Boxer Rebellion," in *The Kaiser: New Research on Wilhelm II's Role in Imperial Germany*, ed. A. Mombauer and W. Deist (Cambridge: Cambridge University Press, 2003), 97.

116. Reed, "Mann and History," 7.

117. See http://www.poetryloverspage.com/poets/kipling/for_all_we_have_and_are.html, emphasis added; and A. Michal Matin, "'The Hun is at the Gate!': Historicizing Kipling's Militaristic Rhetoric," 432–70.

general conviction that *Stalingrad* signifies a *turning-point* in the war."[118] On January 28, during the battle, the German Army issued a horrible order stipulating that "the sick and wounded should be starved to death." German troops were "in effect suffering the same fate that Hitler had planned for the Slavs."[119] When Mann wrote chapter 21, the Russians had defeated the Germans in the Battle of Kursk, July to August 1943, considered "the greatest land battle in history."[120]

At this crucial moment and in the face of the Wehrmacht's spectacular failures, Zeitblom writes: "We are lost. Which is to say: the war is lost, and that means more than a lost campaign, it means that *we* in fact are lost—lost, our cause and soul, our faith and our history" (186, emphasis original). Such testing times called for a German reckoning:

> . . . when I think back ten years to its awakening and blind fervor, to the uprising that broke forth to break open and break down, to the new beginning that was to purify everything, to our popular and national rebirth, to that specious holy ecstasy, in which, to be sure, were mixed, as warning signs of its treachery, so much savage brutality and hulking vulgarity, so much obscene lust to violate, torture, humiliate, and which, as every sensible person knew, already bore war, the entire war within it. . . . out of hatred for the wanton contempt for reason, the sinful ignoring of truth, the vulgar voluptuous cult of a trashy myth, the culpable confounding of something that has run to seed with what it once was, the sordid abuse and cheap peddling of what was old and genuine, faithful and familiar, of what was fundamentally German, from which liars and frauds then prepared a stupefying poisonous home-brew. (186)

Constantly yearning "to be intoxicated, we drank freely, and under that illusory euphoria we have for years committed a plethora of disgraceful deeds" for which they now had to pay (186).

In chapter 25, Adrian Leverkühn makes his contract with the devil. The scene in which he "wed with Satan" (521) takes place while he is vacationing in the small town of Palestrina, east of Rome, in 1906. Mann emphasizes that the city is "mentioned by Dante in Canto XXVII of the

---

118. Evans, *Third Reich at War*, 421, emphasis original.
119. Ibid., 417.
120. Ibid., 486.

Inferno" (226), confirming Dante's enormous influence on the novel, and clearly situating it in the infernal dimension of time and history. Dante's hell is located in the center of the earth, underneath the city of Jerusalem, which is at the center of the northern hemisphere. Opposite Jerusalem, at the center of the southern hemisphere, is the mountain of Purgatory. Lucifer is immobilized at the bottom of hell after the defeat of his rebellion against God.

In Mann's novel, the devil's sphere of action and center of influence is Germany, so Leverkühn is astonished when the devil appears to him in Italy, the birthplace of Renaissance humanist culture and civic humanism. He tells him, "In Wittenberg or on the Wartburg, even in Leipzig I would have thought you credible," but "in Italy of all places, where you are quite out of your realm and enjoy not the least popularity? What an absurd want of fashion." The devil replies without the slightest hesitation: "German I shall be," and "German I am, German to the core" (242). He enjoys "foremost German popularity" (242), noting that "this world wherein we are together" is "[g]ood times, devilish German times" (247).

Their pact is very clear—Adrian Leverkühn's soul in exchange for twenty-four years of genius, of *ingenium*: "years, decades of lovely, nigromantic [sic] time, a whole hour-glass of devilish time, of genius time" (250). As for the fruits of this "genius time":

> A veritably gladding, ravishing, undoubtful, and believing inspiration, an inspiration for which there can be no choosing, no bettering, no mending, in which everything is received as blessed decree, which trips up and tumbles, ruffling sublime shudder from pate to tiptoe over him whom it visits and causing him to burst into streaming tears of happiness—that comes not from God, who leaves to reason all too much to do, but is possible solely with the Devil, the true Lord of Enthusiasm. (253)

Further, continues Satan, glory and fame are awaiting Leverkühn:

> We pledge to you the vital efficacy needed for what you will accomplish with our help. You will lead, you will set the march for the future, lads will swear by your name, who thanks to your madness will no longer need to be mad. In their health they will gnaw at your madness, and you will become healthy in them. Do you understand? It is not merely that you will break through the laming difficulties of the age—you will break through the age itself, the cultural epoch, which is to say, the

epoch of this culture and its cult, and dare a barbarism, a double barbarism, because it comes after humanitarianism, after every conceivable root-canal work and bourgeois refinement. (258–59)

At the end of the twenty-four years and on the verge of losing his sanity, Leverkühn confesses his covenant with the devil to his close friends:

I have already since my twenty-first year been wed with Satan, and in full knowledge of the peril and with duly considered valor, pride, and presumption, I did, out of a wish to find fame in this world, make a bond and league with Him, in such wish that what I would [ac]complish within the term of four and twenty years and what men would rightly regard with distrust, would come to pass solely by His help and is Devil's work, poured out of the Angel of Poison. (521)

The exact terms of the pact are very clear: "From us you have taken time, genius time, high-flying time, a full twenty-four years *ab dato recessi* [from today], which we set as your bound. And when they are over and their course run, the which cannot be foreseen, and such a time is likewise an eternity—you shall be fetched" (264). Leverkühn gets to enjoy the "work-filled eternity of a human life" (265). As for the devil and his minions, "we will meanwhile be subject and obedient to you in all things, and hell shall profit you, if you but renounce all who live, all the heavenly host and all men, for that must be" (264). The pact also stipulates: "Love is forbidden you insofar as it warms. Your life shall be cold—hence you may love no human" (264). Leverkühn perfectly understands that being "the Devil's own monk," he "might love no human creature" (525). Deviation from this condition will have tragic consequences; his deep love for his angelic nephew Nepomuk (Echo) Schneidewein leads to the child's sad death.

"Peculiar Intertwining of Time's Course"

In "the autumn of 1912, twenty-two months prior to the outbreak" of World War I (267), "the war that will end war,"[121] according to English

---

121. Herbert George Wells, *The War That Will End War* (Whitefish: Kessinger, 2009 [1914]). See also Jill Lepore, "The Tug of War: Woodrow Wilson and the Power of the Presidency," *The New Yorker*, September 9, 2013, 84.

writer H. G. Wells (1866–1946), Leverkühn "returned to Munich from Palestrina" (267). In one of the first manifestations of his covenant with the devil, he is about to begin his eighteen year stay in the farm house of "Frau [Else] Schweigestill and Clementina, her daughter" in Pfeiffering outside Munich (271–72). On the day of his arrival, both women stand at the gate of the house, their greetings totally lost in the wild barking of the watchdog. They cannot calm his "rage," and Leverkühn steps forward. As a result of his "surprise tone of admonishment," the dog "calmed down almost immediately and let the wizard stretch out a hand and pat his old battle-scarred skull—and there was deep seriousness in those yellow eyes gazing up at him." Frau Elsa tells Leverkühn that most "people are afraid of the beast, and when it carries on like that you can't blame a body either" (271). Leverkühn now has the demonic power which the English playwright and poet William Congreve (1670–1729) attributed to music: "to soothe a savage breast."[122]

The narrator remarks on the difference between the time of the story, fall 1912, and the time of the narration, April 1944, exposing the unique time frame and structure of the novel. He feels "compelled to call attention to it" because the constant "double-entry account of time intrigues me" (267). Mann points to the "peculiar intertwining of time's course," or the "time in which the narrator moves and that in which his narrative took place," which should "be bound up with yet a third—that is, with the time the reader will one day take for receptive reading of what is told here, so that he will be dealing with threefold ordering of time: his own time, that of the chronicler, and that of history." To avoid any confusion, the narrator specifies that the word "'history' . . . applies with far more dire vehemence to *the time in which, rather than to that about which, I write*" (267, emphasis added), forging the inextricable link between the composer's and Nazi Germany's doom (267). Leverkühn's life is based on the Satanic apocalypse and eschatology fulfilled by Nazi Germany. The explicit distinction between the novel's time frames clearly illuminates the Dantean moment, or the crucial role assigned to the narrator as a witness for posterity. The threefold refraction of time connects Leverkühn's story to the witness in Nazi Germany to the future reader evaluating the aftermath of its destruction.

---

122. William Congreve, *The Mourning Bride*, 1697:
    Musick has charms to sooth a savage breast,
    To soften rocks, or bend a knotted oak.
See https://archive.org/stream/mourningbrideat00conggoog#page/n25/mode/2up, 13.

Thus, as Leverkühn moves to the farm, the narrator moves to the Russian front, April 10, 1944: "In the last few days the battle for Odessa raged with heavy losses, but in the end that famous city on the Black Sea fell into the hands of the Russians." In Germany, on the other hand, "the terror of almost daily air raids on our nicely encircled Fortress Europe increases to dimensions beyond conceiving." Thousands of Allied airplanes "darken the skies of this brashly united continent, and more and more of our cities collapse in ruin" (267). Clear doom awaits both Leverkühn and Germany: an "attack on our European castello [sic]—or should I say our prison, or perhaps our madhouse?—is expected from all sides, with superior arms and millions of soldiers" (268). For both protagonists, the pact with the devil leads to madness, departure or severance from the civilized, rational world. The narrator ponders the meaning of this moment: "Certainly the time in which I write has disproportionally greater historical momentum than that about which I write: Adrian time, which led him only to the threshold of our incredible epoch." He calls Leverkühn "lucky you" because in losing his sanity in 1930 and dying in 1940, he escaped "the terror of our time in which I live on" (268).

With the war's end in sight, the narrator hardens his attacks on the content and form of German barbarism. He relentlessly denounces the German claim that the national rage for power is based on a "new breakthrough . . . that would make us a dominant world power—which, to be sure, could not be effected by moral framework. War then, and if need be, against everyone, in order to convince everyone, to win them over, that was the 'destiny' (how German the word 'Schicksal' sounds—primal, pre-Christian, a tragical-mythological motif from a music drama!) that had been assigned to us." *Schicksal* sounds barbaric. Like *Sonderweg*, the belief in Germany's unique destiny is "filled with the certainty that the hour of Germany's era had come, that history was holding its hands over us, that after Spain, France and England it was now our turn to put our stamp upon the world and lead it, that the twentieth century belonged to us." In sum, "the world was to be renewed under the emblem of Germany, under the emblem of a militaristic socialism yet to be completely defined" (318). These overt militaristic, imperialistic views and chauvinistic nationalist beliefs "formed the high emotion of our ordeal, of our calling, of the great moment, of sacred necessity." They also constitute a clear military threat to other nations, exemplified in two world wars: "The nations out there might consider us disturbers of peace and justice, intolerable enemies of life—we had the means to bang the world over the head until it formed another opinion of us, and not only admire us, but love us as well" (318). Barbarism, then, is Germany's singular role and fate.

Such a bold criticism of the sources of German militarism and "the mythic emergence of national character" (321) could be levied only from elsewhere—for example, from the United States, where Mann lived. It articulates the deep, agonizing search by a German writer tracing the innermost abysses of the German soul and its union with the demonic to explain the "German catastrophe." In psychological terms, "the very definition of Germanness" is "a psychological state threatened by the poison of loneliness, by eccentricity, provincial standoffishness, neurotic involution, unspoken Satanism" (326).

The narrator argues that the end of World War II bodes terrible judgment on Nazi Germany. He is more than sure that the coming disaster will be bigger and much more tragic than the crisis after World War I. "For us Germans, the period *about* which I am writing," or after the Great War, "was an era of governmental collapse, capitulation, revolts born of exhaustion, and helpless surrender into the hands of strangers." However, it will be nothing compared to the terrible impending crisis soon to befall Nazi Germany with its inevitable and unmistakable defeat in the Second World War: "The period *in* which I write," 1944, "and which must serve to help me here in my silent seclusion to put these memories to paper, bears within its horrible swollen belly a national catastrophe compared with which our former defeat now looks like a mild mishap, a sensible liquidation of a failed enterprise" (354, emphasis in original). In the narrator's mind, it recalls nothing else but apocalyptic divine judgment of terrifying proportions and enormous magnitude: "An ignominious ending will always be more normal, something quite other than the divine judgment that hangs over us at present, just as it once descended upon Sodom and Gomorrah—a judgment that we did not, after all, call down upon ourselves that first time" (354); that is, the defeat in the Great War (354). No one can "have the slightest doubt" that this terrible judgment is "drawing near" and that "there [has been] no holding it back for some time now." The "horror grows absolute," and "each man reads the truth in the furtive or anxious stare of his fellows" (354). These words were written after D-Day, the Allied invasion of Normandy on June 6, 1944.

In the summer of 1944, the Third Reich was fighting on three fronts—Russia, Italy, and France—without any chance of stopping the Allied forces' progress. "No stopping them! Oh my soul, do not think it through to the end! Do not venture to measure what it would mean if in our extreme, singularly awful situation the dams were to break—as they are about to do—and there is no stopping the immeasurable hatred that we were adept at fanning against us in the nations roundabout" (356). As the battles approached German borders, German propaganda warned the Allies "against incursion upon our soil, our sacred German soil." The narrator is astonished, "as if that would be some grisly atrocity," as "if anything were still sacred about it, as if it had not long ago been desecrated again and again by the immensity of our rape of justice and did not lie naked, both morally and in fact, before the power of divine judgment." Invasion of German soil is only due justice against the Nazi regime, which "does not understand even now" in 1944 "that it has been condemned, that it must vanish, laden with the curse of having made itself intolerable to the world—no, of having made us, Germany, the Reich, let me go further and say, Germanness, everything German, intolerable to the world." Zeitblom curtly defines the Nazi government as "the rule of scum" (356). These words—"our rape of justice," which will bring down "the power of divine judgment" as well as Sodom and Gomorrah—are one of the very rare instances in which the novel invokes divine judgment rather than Satan's.

The novel's "peculiar intertwining of time's course" is further seen in Leverkühn's sickness after the Great War. When Zeitblom tells his friend his thoughts on the anarchy in Germany after World War I, he notices that Leverkühn "was extraordinarily ill at the time," but claims, "As impossible as it was to find an emotional correlation between his deteriorating health and our national calamity, my inclination to see some objective connection or symbolic parallel between the two," the basis of the novel's content and form, "was not vanquished by his remoteness from outside events" (360). Needless to say, the reader is left to make the connection between the pact with Satan and the catastrophe of German history and to carry this insight into the future.

Apocalypsis cum Figuris and the Rebarbarization of German Culture

With the establishment of the Weimar Republic, its first *Reichspräsident*, Friedrich Ebert (1871-1925) of the Social Democratic Party of Germany (SPD), and first president of Germany (1919-1925) signed the new constitution into law on August 11, 1919, the "burden of illness was removed" from Leverkühn "as if by a miracle and his mind soared phoenix-like to the most sublime freedom and astonishing power in a period of unrestrained, if not to say, uninhibited, or at least unstoppable and onrushing, almost breathless productivity." The proof is "the birth of a work that did not lack certain bold and prophetic connections" (372) to the cultural discussions that took place in Schwabing, a borough in the northern part of Munich, "in the apartment of Herr Sixtus Kridwiss," a "graphic artist, an ornamentor of books, and collector of East Asian color woodcuts and ceramics" (381). The work is an "apocalyptic oratorio" (374) called *Apocalypsis cum Figuris* (*Apocalypse with Pictures*), which Leverkühn finishes in "early August 1919" after "four and a half months," or overall "six months" (380).

The discussion of the content and form of *Apocalypsis cum Figuris* and of the Kridwiss circle is the marrow of *Doctor Faustus*; hence, it expands over three long sections gathered under chapter 34. They focus on the future of German culture and, most important, the rebarbarization of German culture as a precursor of Nazism, the inextricable relationship between aestheticism and barbarism, and, finally, the view of aestheticism as precursor of barbarism. The decline of individualism and the old liberal bourgeois concepts of culture, Enlightenment, humanism, and progress is evident in these debates.

The people who participate in these discussions represent the *Bildungsbürgertum* (cultured middle-class intellectuals) "among whom contempt for the Weimar Republic was normal and flirtation with the extra right-wing ideas common." Their beliefs "involve the abandonment of cultural achievements for the sake of simplification or 're-barbarization'" based on their "total rejection of truth," which the narrator sums up as "the German Will to Legend in full flower after 1933."[123] In this context, Leverkühn's *Apocalypsis cum Figuris* firmly links intellectualism, aestheticism, and barbarism. D. H. Lawrence's remarkable *Letter from Germany* (written in 1928 and published 1934) notes the barbaric turn during the Weimar Republic, time "whirling to the ghost of the old Middle Ages of Germany, then to the Roman days, then to the days of the silent forest and the dangerous, lurking barbarians." In sum, "Something about the Germanic races is unalterable. White-skinned, elemental, and dangerous."[124] In the same vein, Georg Lukács saw the "danger of a barbaric underworld latent in German civilization as its necessary complementary product."[125]

If *Doctor Faustus* is based on the three time structures, it is also based on three apocalyptic dimensions: first, literary apocalypse, based on the old Faust legend; second, historical revelation of the imminent judgment falling on Nazi Germany because of its covenant with Satan; and, third,

---

123. Reed, *Thomas Mann*, 375, 377–78.

124. Quoted in ibid., 399n88. See also, "D. H. Lawrence: A Letter from Germany," at http://www.newstatesman.com/europe/2013/07/d-h-lawrence-letter-germany.

125. Quoted in Reed, *Thomas Mann*, 385.

a musical apocalypse, Leverkühn's *Apocalypsis cum Figuris*. All three are intertwined: individual conduct, history, and art conduce together toward apocalypse. Leverkühn's illness and eventual completion of his apocalyptic oratorio lead the narrator to conclude: "Genius is a form of the life force that is deeply versed in illness, that both draws creatively from it and creates through it" (374). German philosopher Arthur Schopenhauer (1788–1860) developed the concept "life force" in *The World as Will and Representation* (*Die Welt als Wille und Vorstellung* [1818; 1844]), where he argues that our world is driven by blind will, continually seeking satisfaction. It spurs the individual to fulfill successive goals, none of which provide permanent satisfaction. These words can apply not only to Leverkühn but also to the German spirit. At the time of his sickness and Germany's crisis after the Great War, the composer devotes himself to writing a musical work about "a menacing latter-day" apocalypse, which holds "the mirror of revelation up to humanity's eyes, so that it may see what is approaching and near at hand" (376). Like Mann, he transforms the Apocalypse of Saint John into a Satanic apocalypse that mirrors the Nazi apocalypse.

The birth of *Apocalypsis cum Figuris* prompts the narrator to consider "how close aestheticism and barbarism are to each other" (392). One of the members of the Kridwiss circle, the literary historian Georg Vogler, advances the racist, Aryan thesis that "the history of German literature" should be viewed "from the perspective of tribal membership, whereby each writer" should be "treated and valued not as a writer *per se*, not as a universally trained mind, but as the genuine, blood-and-soil product of a real, concrete, specific corner of the world, hour of which he was born and to which he bore witness" (383, emphasis original). *Blut und Boden*—Blood and Soil—was a major slogan of Nazi racialist propaganda.

Another guest at these meetings is the nationalist, chauvinist, imperialist, and fascist young poet Daniel Zur Höhe, who "loved to cross his arms over his chest or to hide one Napoleonic hand in his bosom" (383), a clear reference to the posture of Adenoid Hynkel (Hitler) in Charlie Chaplin's *The Great Dictator* (1940).[126] His "poetic dreams told of a world that bloody crusade had made subject to pure Spirit and that was kept in fear by the Spirit's sublime discipline." He produces only one poem, "Proclamations," which is "a lyrico-rhetorical outburst of voluptuous terrorism," supported by the signature of "an entity named *Christus Imperator*

---

126. Chaplin was a friend of Mann, and they met frequently in the United States. "I have unlimited admiration for well-aimed parody," wrote Mann. "I greet Charlie Chaplin at a party." See *Story of a Novel*, 207.

Maximus, an Energy who enlisted and commanded troops prepared to die in the cause of subjugation of the globe." Clearly, this poet is the forerunner of Nazism: "Proclamations" concludes, "Soldiers! I entrust to you the plundering—of the world" (383). For the humanist narrator of *Doctor Faustus*, Zur Höhe's poem is "the sheerest aesthetic mischief I have ever encountered" (383). Höhe recalls Ernst Jünger (1895–1998), who developed an aesthetics of industrial war in his works.[127] Toward the end of the novel, in the midst of the Battle of Berlin in 1945, with Leverkühn's sanity fading, the narrator recalls again "Zur Höhe's bizarre poetical mischief about obedience, violence, blood, and the plundering of the world" (523). No one can escape the great historical irony reading these words at the final collapse of Nazi Germany.

The meetings of the Kridwiss circle in 1919 naturally dealt with the horrors of the Great War, or the "four-year bloody circus" (384). Based on his humanist persuasion, the narrator tends not to take part in them because of their overt militaristic, totalitarian, and barbaric tone. Instead, he reflects that "the world that was coming" would be an "old-new, revolutionary atavistic world, in which values linked to the idea of the individual (such as, let us say, truth, freedom, justice, reason) were sapped of every strength and cast aside." The cultural crisis in Germany following World War I created a whole new system of alternative values to Renaissance humanism, individualism, civic humanism, Enlightenment humanism, liberal democracy, freedom, and human rights. The new values cherished "violence, authority, the dictatorship of belief." Such a radical medieval, barbaric turn was "tantamount to humanity's being transferred" back "to the theocratic situations and conditions of the Middle Ages" (387) or what Mann calls in *The Magic Mountain* the "iron allegiance, discipline, denial of the individual, violation of the personality" and "the revolution of antihuman backlash."[128]

In this desperate and deteriorating intellectual, cultural, and ideological atmosphere, the narrator can only lament: "Oh yes, force gave one firm footing" (388). The coming age will be

---

127. According to Jünger, "Death for a conviction is the highest accomplishment. It is proclamation, deed, fulfillment, faith, love, hope and goal; it is, in this imperfect world, a perfect thing, absolute perfection. In this the cause is nothing and the conviction everything. One can die stubbornly for an indubitable error: that is the greatest thing there is." See http://thedisorderofthings.com/2013/10/23/junger-meaning-on-the-industrial-battlefield/.

128. Reed, "Mann and History," 12.

a matter of mankind instinctively getting into shape for hard and dark times that would scoff at humanity, for an age of great wars and sweeping revolution, presumably leading far back beyond the Christian civilization of the Middle Ages and restoring the Dark Ages that preceded its birth and had followed the collapse of the culture of antiquity. (389)

Such gloomy prospects were fully affirmed in Nazi Germany, based on racism, chauvinism, and the mythologies of *Blut, Volk, und Boden*, or the Community of Blood and Fate, glorifying a concept of *culture* that has more to do with appetite than art, and rejecting the very civility of European civilization. "No one can follow my argument here," writes the narrator, "who has not experienced as I have how close aestheticism and barbarism are to each other, or who has not felt how aestheticism prepares the way for barbarism" (392).

Doctor Faustus is thus a historical, cultural analysis of the sources and causes of the German catastrophe. "Mann confronted the Germans with the painful truth that National Socialism was not totally alien to them; that Nazism was not without roots in their nature as a people; that it was prefigured in the traits of their great men; and that it was not brought about by small elite of perpetrators but rather by hundreds of thousands of Germans."[129] *Apocalypsis cum Figuris* represents the highest synthesis of intellectualism and barbarism, or "the most hidden things, from the beast in man to his most sublime emotions—incurred reproaches both of bloody barbarism and bloodless intellectuality" (393). In it, the narrator finds "something anticultural, indeed anti-human, even demonic" (393). In particular, the "sardonic *gaudium* of Gehenna" that progresses, "beginning with the giggle of a single voice, only to spread rapidly and seize choir and orchestra, then, amid rhythmic upheavals and counterblows and jettisons, to swell to a horrible *fortissimo tutti* [all together as loud as possible] to a dreadful mayhem of yowls, yelps, screeches, bleats, bellows, howls, and whinnies, to the mocking, triumphant laughter of hell" (397). This laughter is not only the main characteristic of the musical work but "Adrian Leverkühn in his entirety" (398).

Leverkühn's apocalyptic oratorio is an aesthetic image of Nazi apocalypse during World War II, or the creation of a new Satanic world order. It brings "the tradition of the demonic music squarely into the twentieth

---

129. Vaget, "'German' Music," 239.

century"[130] and foretells the fall of the Third Reich: "Oh Germany, You are perishing," Zeitblom cries, due to "the monstrous untrustworthiness, eccentricity, and virulent sans-culottism of our deportment since 1933 and especially since 1939" (408). Weimar hoped for "an age of psychological recovery, of social progress in peace and freedom, of mature and forward-looking cultural endeavor, of a well-intentioned accommodation of our emotions and thoughts to what the world considers normal." That was "the purpose, the hope of the German republic, in the sense of Europeanizing or even 'democratizing'" Germany and thus "incorporate it in the social life of nations" (408–09). This great hope was shattered with the Nazi Revolution of 1933, which inaugurated the Age of Nazi Barbarism. Hence, when "the first complete production of Adrian Leverkühn's apocalyptic oratorio took place" in Frankfurt (409) in February 1926 (475), the seeds of the Nazi Revolution were firmly planted.

The narrator parallels the first complete performance of *Apocalypsis cum Figuris* with the terrifying end of World War II: "Ruin masses above Germany, rats grown fat on corpses inhabit the rubble of our cities, the thunder of the Russian cannons rolls on toward Berlin." In historical terms, during February and March of 1945, the Soviets invaded Silesia and Pomerania, and "for the Anglo-Saxons the crossing of the Rhine was child's play." The apocalyptic oratorio and Germany's destruction sound together. The sheer magnitude of the Nazi fall summons biblical apocalyptic and eschatological language: "An end is come, the end is come, it watched for thee and is come unto thee, O thou that dwellest in the land" (455), citing Ezekiel 7: 7 and his prophecy of doom: "Your doom has come to you, O inhabitant of the land. The time has come, the day is near—tumult rather than joyful shouting on the mountains" (*New American Standard Version*, 1995).

Mann wrote that he composed *Doctor Faustus* as a musical work. The novel ends in a great crescendo. Chapter 36 and those that follow are the fulfillment of Satanic prophecy about Nazi Germany. The sense of ending dominates:

> My tale hastens toward its end—as thus everything. Everything is pushing and plummeting toward the end, the world stands in the sign of the end, at least it stands in it for us Germans,

---

130. Susan von Rohr Scaff, *History, Myth, and Music: Thomas Mann's Timely Fiction* (Rochester: Camden House, 1998), 112: "Mann himself viewed the oratorio as the *particular* issue of the devil's contract."

whose thousand-year history—confounded, carried to absurdity, proven by its outcome to have gone fatally amiss and demonstrably astray—is rushing into the void, into despair, into unparalleled bankruptcy, is descending into amid the dance of thundering flames.

The identification of Nazi Germany with hell on Earth is more than clear; the Nazi dream of a Thousand-Year Reich is proved a great sin. The narrator's words turn prophetic: "one must admit that the path that led to this doom—I used the word in its strictest most religious sense—was doomed at every point, at every turn, however bitter love may find it to endorse this logic." Evidently, this "ineluctable recognition of hopeless doom" leaves nothing but to await "our fate, beyond whose calamity no man can surmise" (474).

Satan's Apocalypse

Entering his "hermit's cell" in Freising to avoid "the sight of our hideously battered Munich," the narrator's ultimate goal is now to finish *Doctor Faustus* "amidst the destruction" of Germany (474). It is his duty, his Dantean moment, to record for posterity the course of Leverkühn's and Germany's path in hell. He bears witness to the sad history of both in accordance with Dante's words: "O Muses, O high genius, aid me now! / O memory that noted what I saw, / Now shall your true nobility be seen!"[131] This is Thomas Mann's exhortation to himself at the outset of writing the novel.

The Dantean task is most urgent because the Nazi apocalypse is reaching its end; from the summer of 1944 onward, the air attacks on Munich greatly intensified, and conditions of life there worsen. In July alone, the US Air Force dropped one million incendiary bombs. However, the narrator's sorrow over civilian deaths is tempered by admonition: "My heart falters when I think in pity of my foolish sons, who believed with the nation's masses, believed, exulted, sacrificed, and struggled with them, and for a good while now, like blankly staring millions of their kind, have tasted the disillusion that is certain to become final helplessness, all embracing despair" (474–75). In this time of despair and destruction, "The prophecy of the end entitled *Apocalypsis cum Figuris* resounded fiercely and grandly" not only "at Frankfurt am Main in February 1926" (475) but also in Germany

---

131. See http://www.italianstudies.org/comedy/Inferno2.htm.

in 1944. Doom is unavoidable; musical and historical crescendo are inextricable. History becomes the realization of Satanic prophecy.

The time has now come to relate "events that our unhappy nation, sapped by misfortune and dread, is incapable of grasping and endures with apathetic fatalism." In "the year of destiny 1945," its last hour, Germany's "defenses in the west have plainly been in total disarray." Now "surrender on all sides, everything scattering. Our shattered and devastated cities fall like ripe plums." Among them most notoriously is "Nuremberg—the city of state ceremonials for the uplifting of unwise hearts. Among the regime's great men, who wallowed in power, riches, and injustice, suicide rages, passing its sentence" (504). Most important, in the east, the invincible "Russian troops, a million-man army," advances "against the Reich's capital city," soon to reach "the core of the city" (505).

In this last hour, the Nazi "freedom movement" was created—a unit of "berserk boys" who plan to wreak maximum havoc on the Allied forces invading the "fatherland territories" (505). They named themselves after the Hermann Löns novel *Der Wehrwolf* (1910), set in Lower Saxony during the Thirty Years' War (1618–1648). In it, the peasant Harm Wulf organizes a militia, *die Wehrwölfe*, to pursue and execute the marauding soldiers who killed his family. The name plays on *wehr* (defense) and *Werwolf* (werewolf), as the pack comes to enjoy killing. Zeitblom says of the contemporary commandos' pathetic reach into folklore, "And so, to the bitter end, the crudest fairy tale, that grim substratum of saga deep in the soul of the nation, is still invoked—not without finding a familiar echo" (505). The desperate conceit of the thoroughly impotent werewolves at the very end of the war is clear evidence of "the German Will to Legend in full flower after 1933."[132]

Völkisch ideology itself led to an apocalyptic, eschatological reading of history. During the Weimar Republic and increasingly after the triumph of National Socialism in 1933, believing "themselves involved in a permanent crisis of nationhood and ideology," Germans saw themselves "as knights riding bravely between death and the devil," recalling Dürer's woodcut *Knight, Death and the Devil*. Not only in Germany but all over Europe, fascism "exhibited a flight from reality into the realm of emotional and mystical ideology." Fascist movements "were all part of the 'displaced revolution' which moved from a rejection of reality to glorification of ideology."[133]

In mid-April 1945, US troops liberated Buchenwald concentration camp near Weimar. General George Patton was so shocked that he ordered

---

132. Reed, *Thomas Mann*, 377–78.
133. Mosse, *Crisis of German Ideology*, 203.

"the inhabitants of Weimar" to see the crematoria. He declared that they as "citizens who went about their business in seeming honest and tried to know nothing, though at times the wind blew the stench of burned human flesh up to their noses," shared "the guilt for these horrors that are now laid bare and to which he forced them to direct their eyes." Zeitblom laments: "Let them look—I shall look with them, in my mind's eyes I let myself be jostled along in those same apathetic, or perhaps shuddering, lines" (505).[134] Flight from reason, rationality, and reality led inevitably to the denial and rejection of human values and basic ethics.

The city of Weimar was once the home of the German Enlightenment and its intellectual leaders, such as Goethe and Schiller, whose Weimar Classicism (*Weimarer Klassik*) proposed a new humanism synthesizing Classical, Enlightenment, and Romantic ideas.[135] In stark contrast, in July 1937, the Nazis built one of the first and largest concentration camps on German soil close to Weimar. Mann wrote: "What was found there and elsewhere surpassed in frightfulness all expectation and all conception," but he concluded that for people like him, "who had early understood the nature of what in Germany was called 'the National State,'" it was "nothing surprising and nothing incredible."[136] The millions murdered in concentration camps knew the diabolic character of Nazism; witness the apocalyptic poem "We, the Dead, Accuse!" by an anonymous Czech Jewish writer in Auschwitz. It evokes "an apocalyptic scene of endless columns of the dead, all bones and ashes, a vast host ever multiplying within the bowels of the earth":[137]

---

134. "General Patton was so angry at what he found at Buchenwald that he ordered the Military Police to go to Weimar, four miles away, and bring back 1,000 civilians to see what their leaders had done, to witness what some human beings could do to others. The MPs were so outraged they brought back 2,000. Some turned away. Some fainted. Even veteran, battle-scarred correspondents were struck dumb." See https://www.jewishvirtuallibrary.org/jsource/Holocaust/usarmy_holo.html.

135. On the importance of Weimar Classicism in Mann's thought, see Paul Bishop, "The Intellectual World of Thomas Mann," in *Cambridge Companion to Thomas Mann*, ed. Ritchie Robertson (Cambridge: Cambridge University Press, 2001), 36–41.

136. Mann, *Story of a Novel*, 115.

137. Otto Dov Kulka, *Landscapes of the Metropolis of Death: Reflections on Memory and Imagination* (London: Allan Lane, 2013), 51. The author spent some years in Auschwitz as a child. It should be noted, as Kulka wrote in a personal letter to the author on March 10, 2015, that the "privilege" of dying in Auschwitz's gas chamber was reserved only for Jews.

> And then we'll emerge, in awful ranks,
> a skull on our skulls and bony shanks;
> and we'll roar in the faces of all the people
> We, the dead, accuse![138]

Another poem from the hell called Auschwitz, "Alien Grave," by the same anonymous Czech Jewish writer, expresses "a crescendo of mourning and protest at the pointless mass murder in the two world wars that felled successive generations of Europe's young men":[139]

> A leaning cross and a cracked helmet;
> the rain will not water the parched earth.
> In that tomb beneath the collapsed tower
> like aliens in an alien grave lie
> Europe's slaughtered youth . . .
>
> But when the storm blows over
> who will understand, who will understand
> that here in an alien grave there rots
> (who will say for whose utopia)
> Europe's betrayed youth?[140]

Mann was writing the novel as the horrors of the camps were exposed, and Zeitblom seizes the time. He sees the torture cells in Buchenwald as a microcosm of the torture state: "Our thick-walled torture chamber, into which Germany was transformed by a vile regime of conspirators sworn to nihilism from the very start, has been burst open, and our ignominy lies naked before the eyes of the world." Such a horror "exceeds anything that human imagination can conceive." In light of "these incredible scenes," it seems that "all that is German" shares "in the disgrace of such revelations and is plunged into profound doubt" (505). The only question left is: "How can 'Germany,' whichever of its forms it may be allowed to take in the future" be able "to speak of mankind's concern" ever again. It must admit that "in fact tens of thousands, hundreds of thousands of Germans . . . committed the acts before which humanity shuddered, and whatever lived as German stands now as an abomination and the epitome

---

138. Ibid., 52.
139. Ibid., 51.
140. Ibid., 53.

of evil." To belong to Germany now meant to be part of "a nation whose history bore this gruesome fiasco within it, a nation that has driven itself mad, gone psychologically bankrupt," hence, "a nation that cannot show its face" to the civilized world (506).

With the discoveries at the Nazi concentration camps, the three narrative times—protagonist's, narrator's, author's—twist into a hangman's knot. "Damn, damn those who taught their lessons in evil to originally honest, law-abiding" people. "Those [Nazi] corruptors" have led the German spirit astray, creating "a patriotism" based on "untold crimes, a state whose bellowing proclamations and announcements cancelling human rights swept the masses up into enraptured frenzy, and under whose garish banners our youth marched with flashing eyes, brazenly proud and firm in their faith." Now "this defeated nation," this "bloody state whose gasping agonies we are now experiencing" stands "wild-eyed before the abyss, because its final and most extreme attempt to find its own political form is perishing in such ghastly failure" (506).

Zeitblom cannot but wonder: "How singularly the years in which I write now close ranks with those that frame this biography." Based on the Satanic "prophetic connections" (372) between the composer's life and German history, "the last years of my hero's intellectual life, the two years of 1929 and 1930"—"the collapse of his marriage plans, the loss of his friend," and others—correspond "in fact to the ascent and spread of that usurping power now perishing in blood and flames" (507).

Typology in Christian theology is a figural interpretation of history in which features in the Old Testament are fulfilled in the New Testament. Apocalyptic and eschatological thought speaks of *type* and *antitype* and, at its most extreme, views the Old Testament's sole purpose as providing types that Christ, the antitype, fulfills. The theory arose with the Early Church and was most influential in the High Middle Ages, although it remained popular after the Protestant Reformation, especially among Calvinists.[141] In this context, Leverkühn's intellectual decline serves as the type of the rise

---

141. On typology, or the figural interpretation of history, see Auerbach, "Figura," 11–76; Avihu Zakai, *Jonathan Edwards's Philosophy of History: The Re-Enchantment of the World in the Age of Enlightenment* (Princeton: Princeton University Press, 2003), "Reformation, History, and Eschatology in English Protestantism," *History and Theory* 16 (October 1987): 300–18, and "The Poetics of History and the Destiny of Israel: The Role of the Jews in English Apocalyptic Thought during the Sixteenth and Seventeenth Centuries," *The Journal of Jewish Thought and Philosophy* 5 (1996): 313–50.

of Nazism and fascism in Germany, which is its antitype. Not based on the fulfillment of God's divine providence, however, it reveals a Satanic typology of crushing failure. The dark cloud that spreads through the composer's mind and soul in 1930 prefigures the smoke of the Reichstag fire in 1933, which brings the Nazi Party to power and occludes Germany's sanity. Further, while the narrator is writing about Leverkühn's struggles in 1930, the Battle of Berlin is raging. The unique three-dimensional narrative posits the composer's collapse, the collapse of order with the rise of Nazi Germany, and the final collapse of Nazi Germany in one apocalyptic moment.

As for the composer, the plot has a very interesting twist. In the last years before losing sanity, he is writing "his last and indeed in a historical sense somehow final and ultimate work: the symphonic cantata, *The Lamentation of Dr. Faustus*" (*Dr. Fausti Weheklag*). Being "deprived of happiness in life, for having been denied permission to love," Leverkühn fully immerses himself in it (507), and the narrator uses it to expose the rebarbarization of Germany by comparing it to the reception of works by Beethoven. In the past, he writes, "we children of the dungeon dreamt of a song of joy—*Fidelio*, the Ninth Symphony—with which to celebrate Germany liberation, its liberation of itself." Now, during the spring of 1945, only *The Lamentation of Dr. Faustus* "can be of any use, and it will be sung from our soul: the lamentation of the son of hell, the most awful lament of man and God ever intoned on this earth, which begins with its central character," Doctor Faustus, "but steadily expanding, encompasses, as it were, the cosmos" (509). Schiller's "Ode to Joy" is replaced by the "Ode of Sorrow," signifying the whole pitiful course of German history.

However, sorrow can point toward salvation. Deviating from the original Faustus tale, Mann suggests possible redemption for the composer. In the midst of the fall of Nazi Germany at the end of the novel, the identification with Leverkühn breaks down. Earlier Mann referred "to the substantial identity of what is most blessed and most heinous, to the inner sameness of its children's angelic chorus and hell's laughter" in *Apocalypsis cum Figuris* (511). Now, the symphonic cantata, the "Ode to Sorrow," is presented as an antitype of Schiller's "Ode to Joy," celebrating the brotherhood and unity of all mankind and devoid of Satanic form and content. This work is based on "the spirit and infection of Monteverdi's 'Lamento'" (512) from the opera *L'Arianna* composed in 1607–1608. In it Ariadne laments her lost love, Theseus, who abandoned her on the island of Naxos to found Athens. Most important, Leverkühn's "monumental work of lamentation . . . sought to express liberation" (510); hence, "music is liberated as language" (512), rather than laughter. Leverkühn writes it after the death of his beloved angelic nephew Echo, so the work is based on love and clearly defies his contract with the devil. Redemption is suggested because "Leverkühn's final composition lifts our vision from hell toward heaven and reinfuses music with meaning," as salvation.[142]

Conclusion: *Doctor Faustus*'s Reckoning and Germany's Abomination

No one who reads *Doctor Faustus* can forget the very moving epilogue, depicting Leverkühn's gradual loss of sanity, the emotional, speechless meeting with his mother in the "private mental clinic" in Munich (530), and, finally, his return to his mother's house, to his old room, where he dies. "One cannot imagine anything more horribly touching and pitiful then when a spirit that has boldly and defiantly emancipated itself from its origins, that has traced a dizzying arch above the world, returns broken to its mother's care" (530). When the composer's mother, Elsbeth Leverkühn, comes to see him for the first time after he has gone mad, "[s]he came . . . her white hair pulled back tight, determined to fetch her lost child back to his childhood. At their first meeting, Adrian lay trembling for a long while on the breasts of this woman" (532). The image brings to mind Michelangelo's *Pietà*. Again, the devil's curse, that Leverkühn be permitted no love, proves wrong as in the case of Echo.

Love, rising from the abyss of the protagonist's soul, finally transforms his existential condition. His love for the child and his mother change Leverkühn and may save him. In Dante's *Comedy*, his love Beatrice guides him; Mann's hero has no guide, but the Christian concept of love, *agape*, selfless love, especially spiritual love, reigns. In fact, motherly love is the final reward for both the Son of God and the "Son of Hell" (509). In proposing possible salvation and redemption for Leverkühn, in contrast to the Faustus legend, Mann clearly adopts Goethe's solution in the second part of *Faust* (1831), where the protagonist ascends to heaven, and angels, messengers of divine mercy, greet him, declaring at the end of act 5: "He who strives on and lives to strive / Can earn redemption still."[143]

> He's escaped, this noble member
> Of the spirit world, from evil,
> Whoever strives, in his endeavour,

---

142. Scaff, *History, Myth, and Music*, 114.
143. See http://en.wikipedia.org/wiki/Goethe%27s_Faust.

> We can rescue from the devil.
> And if he has Love within,
> Granted from above,
> The sacred crowd will meet him,
> With welcome, and with love. (5: 11934–41)[144]

The destruction of the devilish state brings the possible salvation of the European humanist culture. Nazi Germany's collapse is the composer's and Europe's liberation.

The narrator is also saved. He returns with great pride to his Dantean mission. His duty to his friend and his mission for posterity are finished: "The task" to which he was "called by love, loyalty, and my role as an eyewitness. . . . has been accomplished." The composer's and Nazi Germany's final moments are fully merged as "its matadors have been themselves poisoned by their doctors, then drenched in gasoline and set on fire that nothing whatever might remain of them." With the final liberation of Germany, the "memoires, this biography of Adrian Leverkühn" can be published (528). On the opening page in 1943, Zeitblom predicts, "there is still not the slightest prospect that my manuscript will ever see the light of the public day, unless by some miracle it were to leave our beleaguered Fortress Europe and share the whispered secrets of our isolation with those outside" (5). This miracle is fulfilled, and the collapse of the Satanic state makes it possible to claim once again that "Germany is free" (529) and to entertain once more "the cultural ideal" of "the ethical cult of Olympian reason and clarity" after "the savage decade" (529). Leverkühn dies on August 25, 1940, but:

> In those days Germany, a hectic flush on its cheeks, was reeling at the height of its savage triumphs, about to win the world on the strength the fact that it was intended to keep and signed with its blood. Today, in the embrace of demons, a hand over one eye, the other staring into the horror, it plummets from despair to despair. When will it reach the bottom of the abyss? When, out of this final hopelessness, will a miracle that goes beyond faith bear the light of hope? A lonely man folds his hands and says: 'May God have mercy on your poor soul, my friend, my fatherland.' (534)

---

144. See http://www.poetryintranslation.com/PITBR/German/Fausthome.htm.

Thus ends *Doctor Faustus* with a grand politicization of literature. In a time of horrifying prospects for the humanist soul of Germany and the urgent need to fight Nazism, a German writer in exile mingles history and literature, apocalypse and eschatology, to wage a *Kulturkampf* against Nazi Germany. *Doctor Faustus* is not only about the composer's soul but Germany's. What was discovered in Buchenwald and other camps was hell on Earth, released, directed, and structured by devilish ideology.

Ironically, in emphasizing the close, intrinsic connections between himself and his work and its Satanic apocalyptic and eschatological dimension, Mann did not only revive an old German myth but, like Dürer, Luther, and many other Germans, succumbed to it. Turn to Mann's address "Germany and the Germans" (1945), which can be regarded as the marrow of the Faustus novel. He gave this lecture in the year Nazi Germany was defeated and, in the language of *Doctor Faustus*, "this vast canvas, this cathedral of a book, this woven tapestry of symbolism," was almost completed.[145] First, he was old, "a man of seventy."[146] Likewise, in the epilogue, Zeitblom describes himself as an "old man, bent, almost broken by the horrors of the time in which he wrote and those that are the subject of what he has written" (528), Second, in the address as in the novel, Mann's goal is to deal with "the German problem, the enigma in the character and destiny of this people which undeniably has given humanity much that is great and beautiful, and yet has time and again imposed fatal burdens upon the world." Furthermore, "Germany's terrible fate, the tremendous catastrophe in which her modern history now culminates, compels our interest." Given that the German spirit has "a quality of secret demonism," continues Mann, "I am trying to suggest a secret union of German spirit with the Demonic."[147]

Mann cites Luther's obsession with the devil and "Goethe's' Faust," who "stands at the dividing line between the Middle Ages and Humanism, a man of God who, out of a presumptuous urge for knowledge, surrenders to magic, to the Devil." Wherever "arrogance of the intellect mates with the spiritual obsolete and archaic, there is the Devil's domain." In sum, "the Devil, Luther's Devil, Faust's Devil, strikes me as a very German figure, and the pact with him, the Satanic covenant, to win all treasures and powers on earth for a time at the cost of the soul's salvation, strikes me as something exceedingly typical of German nature." And if "Faust is to be

---

145. See: http://en.wikipedia.org/wiki/Doctor_Faustus_%28novel%29.
146. Mann, "Germany and the Germans," 47.
147. Ibid., 48–49, 51.

the representative of the German soul, he would have to be musical, for the relation of the German to the world is abstract and mystical, that is, musical,—the relation of a professor with a touch of demonism, awkward and at the same time filled with arrogant knowledge that he surpasses the world in 'depth.' "[148] All Germany stood on trial in 1945; Mann asked his audiences, "[I]sn't this the right moment to see Germany in this picture, the moment in which Germany is literally being carried off by the Devil?"[149]

There could be no better summary of the unique Satanic apocalyptic and eschatological content and form of Mann's *Doctor Faustus*. He shows that the pact with the devil does not reside in the Dark Ages but in the core of modern German history. Ironically, however, the novel too is an integral part of the German demonic tradition, of the "secret union of German spirit with the Demonic," for it not only criticizes but embraces the diabolic reading of German history and culture. As Bruno Latour writes, "we are always prisoners of language;"[150] that is, we are always prisoners of our culture, our ideologies. By using the Satanic Faustus legend to fight the horrors of Nazi Germany, Mann made the demonic one of the crucial dimensions of the German spirit, which he denounced and abhorred.[151] A book about the devil must bear his mark.[152] Kurzke writes, "The Devil

---

148. Ibid., 51. On the centrality of magic in Mann's *Doctor Faustus*, see Benjamin Bennett, "Magic and History: The Roots and Branches of Dr. Faustus," in *The Dark Side of Literacy: Literature and Learning Not to Read* (New York: Fordham University Press, 2008), 185–220.

149. Ibid., 51.

150. Bruno Latour, "Why Has Critique Run Out of Steam? From Matters of Fact to Matters of Concern," *Critical Inquiry* 30 (Winter 2004): 227.

151. According to Susan Scaff in a letter to the author, March 6, 2014, we should make a distinction between "the Satanic (or diabolic), which is solely destructive, and the demonic, which goes back at least to Goethe and functions as a creative as well as a destructive force. In my mind Zeitblom moves from technical brilliance in the appalling vision of the *Apocalypsis cum Figuris* (the breakthrough granted by his contract with the devil) to demonic inspiration at the end of the Faust cantata, possibly (just maybe) inspired by God." See also Scaff, *History, Myth, and Music*, 108.

152. In a letter to the author, February 24, 2014, Herman Rapaport wrote: "The problem with a novel like Faustus is that it has to risk allegorizing history. Maybe that could be defended by [Walter] Benjamin. But it's always a problem when one sets up a metaphysical conceit to ground historical realities. Mann risked installing something very acceptable to Nazism, namely, the passion play. When you establish plays about the devil, you're establishing medieval mystery and passion plays. In Germany those were anti-Semitic by definition. The genre is contaminated. I don't see how Mann could take that up without having reservations."

of Thomas Mann and Germany are one. . . . Thomas Mann is looking for fascism in himself."[153] In the end, if the devil assisted Adrian Leverkühn in composing the musical works that made him famous, perhaps he also helped Mann in writing *Doctor Faustus*, where his signature is evident in the sad history of the composer, of Germany and Europe.

---

153. Kurzke, *Thomas Mann*, 484.

II

Ernst Cassirer and *The Myth of the State*

Portrait of the Disillusioned Philosopher

> We are always living on a volcanic soil and must be prepared for sudden convulsions and eruptions. In the critical moments of man's political and social life myth regains its old strength. It was always lurking in the background, waiting for its hour of opportunity. This hour comes if the other binding forces of our social life, for one reason or another, lose their influence; if they can no longer counterbalance the demonic power of myth.
>
> —Ernst Cassirer, "The Technique of
> Our Modern Political Myths," 1945

> In the last thirty years, in the period between the first and second World Wars, we have not only passed through a severe crisis of our political and social life but have also been confronted with quite new theoretical problems. We experienced a radical change in the form of political thought . . . the appearance of a new power: the power of mythical thought.
>
> —Ernst Cassirer, *The Myth of the State*, 1946

Ernst Cassirer's *The Myth of the State: A Portrait of the Disillusioned Philosopher* explores the last book by the German Jewish philosopher[1] in light of the agonies initiated by Nazi Germany's political myths based on worship of heroes, "race," and state. It analyzes the work's content and form in light of Cassirer's intellectual biography. For most of his career, he focused on the role of myth in epistemological terms, striving to "sketch . . . a

---

1. Ernst Cassirer, *The Myth of the State* (New Haven: Yale University Press, 1967 [1946]), 3. All references in the text are to this edition.

phenomenology of mythical and religious thinking."[2] He regarded myth as part of human "Symbolic Forms" and our " 'understanding' of the world."[3] How ironic and sad that his important philosophical and epistemological subject became his worst, most dangerous enemy and eventually drove him into exile. During his lifetime, fascists and Nazis transformed myth from an abstract problem into a vital, concrete historical force able to destroy the foundations of humanist civilization of Europe.

At the end of the book, Cassirer asks, "What can philosophy do to help us in this struggle against the political myth?" (295). His answer is emphatically negative: "It is beyond the power of philosophy to destroy the political myths," or the Nazi worship of heroes, race, and the state, yet it could do an important service: "In order to fight an enemy you must know him." He urges his reader: "We should see the adversary face to face in order to know how to combat him" (296). The sad lessons of his life are engraved in these words. In America, the old exile took on a grand mission to combat the political myths of his times; the young scholar who completed his doctorate in 1899 would never have thought he would have to minimize the power of his philosophical discipline, nor the famous scholar that he would have to attack his longtime subject in fear for his life and the life of European humanist civilization. Such was Cassirer's unique and tragic fate: to attack what he had built to preserve what he valued with his back to the grave.

The Myth of the State should be examined not only in light of Nazi history but also in relation to other cultural battles, or *Kulturkampfen*, against Nazism, fascism, and totalitarianism by fellow expatriates from Germany and Europe: Karl Popper's political philosophy in *The Open Society and Its Enemies*; Erich Auerbach's *Mimesis*, which counters Aryan philology with new, sharp tools of literary analysis; Hans Baron's *The Crisis of the Early Italian Renaissance*, which opposes Nazi *völkisch* historiography; Horkheimer and Adorno's sociological enterprise in *Dialectic of Enlightenment*; Leo Strauss's consideration of justice in *Natural Right and History*, and, not least, Thomas Mann's apocalyptic eschatology of Nazi Germany, *Doctor Faustus*.

---

2. Ernst Cassirer, *The Philosophy of Symbolic Forms*, vol. 1, *Language* (New Haven: Yale University Press, 1953), 69.

3. Ernst Cassirer, *Philosophy of Symbolic Forms*, vol. 2, *Mythical Thought* (New Haven: Yale University Press, 1955 [1925]), 69. For a study of Cassirer's philosophy of symbolic forms in the context of contemporary continental philosophy, especially structuralism, see S. G. Lofts, *Ernst Cassirer: A "Repetition" of Modernity* (Albany: State University of New York Press, 2000).

Cassirer's exilic displacement was not unusual; many German intellectuals, Jewish and otherwise, shared the ordeal. As a result, common themes appear in their works. Cassirer and Auerbach fought against the Nazi and Aryan culture of heroes, legends, and myths. Cassirer, Horkheimer, and Adorno shared the view that fascism and Nazism signified the regression of reason and found answers in Homer's *Odyssey*: Cassirer compared the episode on the island of Circe, the beautiful witch-goddess who enchanted Odysseus's men and turned them into pigs, to events in Nazi Germany, and Horkheimer and Adorno drew similar parallels with the Sirens, the beautiful yet dangerous creatures, portrayed as *femmes fatales* whose enchanting voices lured sailors to shipwreck on the rocky coast of their island. But if for Horkheimer and Adorno Odysseus's story signified "the retreat of the individual from the mythic powers," hence tracing "the path of the subject's flight from the mythical powers," and thus revealing "Homer's antimythological, enlightened character" and claiming it represents a concentrated expression of rationality,[4] then for Auerbach in contrast the story of Odysseus as all of Homer's stories is rather based on myths and legends—"all this is only legend, 'make-believe.'"[5]

On the other hand, Cassirer and Horkheimer and Adorno considered the contributions of the Enlightenment, but while Cassirer praised it as the revival of Stoic ideas about natural rights and human equality and dignity, Horkheimer and Adorno saw it as the source or foundation of social domination realized in fascism and Nazism, boldly claiming that with "the spread of the bourgeois commodity economy the dark horizon of myth is illuminated by the sun of calculating reason, beneath whose ice rays the seeds of the new barbarism are germinating."[6] And against Cassirer, who believed that Enlightenment rationalism worked against myth, Horkheimer and Adorno held that "[m]yth is already enlightenment, and enlightenment reverts to mythology"; consequently, the "Enlightenment's mythic terror springs from a horror of myth."[7]

Both Popper and Cassirer denounced German historicism and Hegel as promoting totalitarianism. For Popper, Plato was the forerunner of

---

4. Horkheimer and Adorno, *Dialectic of Enlightenment*, 37.

5. Auerbach, *Mimesis*, 13.

6. Horkheimer and Adorno, *Dialectic of Enlightenment*, 25.

7. Ibid., xviii, 22. For an analysis of these statements, see Jürgen Habermas, "The Entwinement of Myth and Enlightenment: Max Horkheimer and Theodor Adorno," in *The Philosophical Discourse of Modernity* (Cambridge: MIT Press, 1987 [1985]), 106–30.

Hegel and Marx, while Cassirer proposed Machiavelli and attributed the introduction of rationalism in politics to Plato; each read Plato or Machiavelli in the distorting light of Nazism. All these exiled intellectuals shared Thomas Mann's view, elaborated in his novel *Doctor Faustus*, connecting Nazi Germany with Satanism and demonism.

In what follows, one of my goals is to show the similarities and dissimilarities between Cassirer's thought and that of his fellow exiled intellectuals. I believe that *The Myth of the State* constitutes only one chapter in the *Kulturkampf* that many intellectual expatriates levied against Nazi Germany from their new abodes; Cassirer's book is only intelligible in this context.

Sudden Convulsions

Cassirer's prominent place in twentieth-century philosophy is well secured:

> Ernst Cassirer occupies a unique place in twentieth-century philosophy. His work pays equal attention to foundational and epistemological issues in the philosophy of mathematics and natural science and to aesthetics, the philosophy of history, and other issues in the "cultural sciences" broadly conceived. More than any other German philosopher since Kant, Cassirer thus aims to devote equal philosophical attention both to the (mathematical and) natural sciences (*Naturwissenschaften*) and to the more humanistic disciplines (*Geisteswissenschaften*). In this way, Cassirer, more than any other twentieth-century philosopher, plays a fundamental mediating role between C. P. Snow's famous "two cultures."[8]

As far as it goes, this description is correct about Cassirer's philosophical works, yet it overlooks the *Kulturkampf* he waged against the evils of his time, most prominently in *The Myth of the State*, "his final, belated counterblast to Nazism."[9] Like many other German Jewish intellectuals

---

8. Michael Friedman, "Ernst Cassirer," in *The Stanford Encyclopedia of Philosophy*, ed. Edward N. Zalta (Spring 2011), http://plato.stanford.edu/archives/spr2011/entries/cassirer/.

9. Edward Skidelsky, *Ernst Cassirer: The Last Philosopher of Culture* (Princeton: Princeton University Press, 2008), 4.

who waged their idiosyncratic attacks on the destructive, inhuman forces of Nazism and totalitarianism from various seats of exilic displacement, Cassirer drafted a radical view of the history of political thought and philosophy based on the agonizing triumph of Aryanism, racism, and the Nazi state. *Blut und Boden*, blood and soil, the major slogan of Nazi racial ideology, grounded ethnicity in a toxic mythology that reserved homeland (*Heimat*) for one group and ultimately entitled it to everything.[10] One of Cassirer's closest friends and colleagues at Yale wrote, "No man of his high caliber could live through these last twenty-five years [1920–1945] without giving profound thought to the whole flight of humanity in all nations of the world. He knew what adversity meant close at home."[11]

These twenty-five years, encompassing not only the rise and fall of the Weimar Republic but the rise, triumph, and fall of National Socialism, left an indelible mark on the content and form of Cassirer's thought. Implicit in *The Philosophy of Enlightenment* (1932), it is most explicit in *The Myth of the State*, a study closely derived from his generation's failure to keep National Socialism at bay as well as his own lifetime study of myth. A few examples show the evolution of Cassirer's thought. In 1925, he firmly believed that "the history of philosophy as a scientific discipline may be regarded as a single continuous struggle to effect a separation and liberation from myth. The form of this struggle varies according to the stage of theoretical self-consciousness, but the general trend stands out plainly."[12]

---

10. For an analysis of other works by German-speaking Jewish intellectual exiles, see Avihu Zakai and David Weinstein, *Exile and Interpretation: The Shaping of Modern Intellectual History in the Age of Nazism and German Barbarism* (Tel Aviv: Resling Publishing House, 2014, Hebrew); Weinstein and Zakai, *Jewish Exiles and European Thought*, "Exile and Interpretation: Popper's Re-Invention of the History of European Political Thought," and "Leo Strauss: The Exile of Interpretation," *New Trends in the Study of German Jewry*, Leo Baeck Institute, 13 (2009): 3–31 (Hebrew); and Avihu Zakai and David Weinstein, "Erich Auerbach and His 'Figura': An Apology for the Old Testament in an Age of Aryan Philology," *Religions* 3 (2012): 320–38, http://www.mdpi.com/journal/religions/special_issues/jewish-emigres/. See also Avihu Zakai, "Professor of Exile: Edward Said's Misreading of Erich Auerbach," *Moment Magazine* 14, 8 (2014): http://www.momentmag.com/edward-said-erich-auerbach/.

11. Charles W. Hendel, "Ernst Cassirer," in *The Philosophy of Ernst Cassirer*, ed. Paul A. Schilpp (Evanston: The Library of Living Philosophers, 1949), 58. The same essay appeared earlier under another title, "Ernst Cassirer, Man and Teacher," *Philosophy and Phenomenological Research* 5 (1944–1945): 156–59.

12. Cassirer, *Mythical Thought*, xiii.

However, this belief in the unavoidable separation of reason and myth began to be shaken in 1932. Written in part against the threatening myths of Blood, Folk, and Soil, or the Community of Blood and Fate of the German people, *The Philosophy of Enlightenment* attempted, in part, to refute "the verdict of the Romantic Movement on the Enlightenment." Its slogan, the "shallow Enlightenment" was "in vogue" during the Weimar Republic. Instead, Cassirer proclaimed, "[m]ore than ever before, it seems to me, the time is again ripe for applying such self-criticism to the present age, for holding up to it that bright clear mirror fashioned by the Enlightenment."[13]

As we know, presenting the "bright clear mirror" of Enlightenment ideas to the German mind did not prevent the Nazi Revolution of 1933. As the Nazi party became the largest party in the Reichstag in 1932, Max Horkheimer (1895–1973), the leader of the Frankfurt School, a group of philosophers and social scientists associated with the Institut für Sozialforschung (Institute for Social Research) in Frankfurt am Main, who was the director of the institute and Professor of Social Philosophy at the University of Frankfurt, wrote: "Only one thing is certain, the irrationality of society has reached a point where only the gloomiest predictions have any plausibility."[14] As for Cassirer, by the 1940s he had no more illusions about the power of reason and the Enlightenment's universal, liberal, and humanist ideas to keep myths at bay. His longtime thesis about the struggle to separate and to liberate the history of philosophy from myth proved dead wrong.

In *The Myth of the State*, Cassirer radically revised this contention and replaced it with a thorough and direct analysis of the various causes that led to the nightmare victory of Nazism and fascism throughout Europe. Tragically, Cassirer admitted, myth had won the struggle with reason, at least in Nazi Germany, and he turned to a new study of political philosophy: a highly idiosyncratic history of political thought based on the agonizing lesson of his time:

> In the last thirty years, in the period between the first and second World Wars, we have not only passed through a severe crisis of our political and social life but have also been confronted with quite new theoretical problems. We experienced a radical change in the form of political thought . . . the appearance of a new power: the power of mythical thought. (3)

---

13. Ernst Cassirer, *Philosophy of the Enlightenment* (Princeton: Princeton University Press 1979 [1951]), xi.

14. Horkheimer as quoted by Müller-Doohm, *Adorno*, 175.

Like many other German Jewish exiles, Cassirer now adopted the crisis mode of historical thought—the view that crisis, not progress, decline, not advance, drive the course of history. For a scholar who had dedicated much of his life to showing how the history of philosophy transformed mythical thought to reason, this recognition must obviously be very painful.

Here, I aim to make sense of *The Myth of the State* in light of his intellectual "long Odyssey,"[15] as he termed it, and to contextualize it. More specifically, I will examine the pure philosophical questions he wrestled with in the context of "the Age of Catastrophe," or *historia calamitatum*, the "decades from the outbreak of the First World War to the aftermath of the Second," when European civilization "stumble[d] from one calamity to another. And there were even times when even intelligent conservatives would not take bets on its survival."[16] It was marked by "the incessant tempests through which we have precariously lived for close to thirty years," or since 1914, as R. G. Collingwood wrote in 1942.[17] World War II, poet and novelist Stephen Spender wrote in 1945,

> brought nearly all those things which we hold firm and sacred into danger and collapse: truth and humanity, reason and right. We lived in a possessed world. For many of us the result was not unexpected when the insanity of a day broke out into delirium in which this poor European humanity sank back, fanatical, stupefied and mad.[18]

In *The Myth of the State*, Cassirer responded to "the incessant tempests" by working to salvage the humanist values of Western civilization.

The immediate circumstances that led to the book are well known. In the early 1940s, colleagues in the Yale philosophy department asked

---

15. In a 1944 speech at Yale's Philosophical Club, Cassirer described his "long academic life" as "a long Odyssey. It was a short pilgrimage that led me from one university to the other, from one country to the other, and, at the end, from one hemisphere to the other." In contrast to Odysseus, who fought in Troy and eventually returned to his home in Ithaca, Cassirer's Odyssey "was rich in experiences—in human and intellectual adventures," or "a sentimental journey," but he did not return to Germany. See Hendel, "Ernst Cassirer," 56; and Donald P. Verene, "Introduction," in *Symbol, Myth, and Culture: Essays and Lectures of Ernst Cassirer, 1935-1945* (New Haven: Yale University Press, 1979), 7.

16. Hobsbawm, *Age of Extremes*, 6-7.

17. Collingwood, *New Leviathan*, lx.

18. Spender, *European Witness*, 231.

Cassirer to explain "the dark, troubled times in which we were living" and "the meaning of what is happening *today*, instead of writing about past history, science and culture."[19] The timing was crucial: the year 1942 marked the nadir of civilization, exemplified by the Battle of Stalingrad and Wehrmacht victories in Russia and North Africa. To understand these horrifying events, signifying the seemingly invincible power of Nazi Germany, the Americans turned to a German scholar to guide their understanding of the ideological origins of World War II.

Obviously, Cassirer was very invested in, and anxious about, the outcome of the struggle; he accepted the challenge and devoted his last book to a grand historical and political exposition of the battle between reason and myth and, in the third part, analyzing the evil consequences of myth in political and social life. German history turned his whole thesis upside down; the struggle to separate philosophy from myth had been a total failure. *The Myth of the State* was not only a sad explanation but also an agonizing personal acknowledgment of "the appearance of a new power: the power of mythical thought" (3).

The year 1942–1943 was an epistemological watershed that marked a major intellectual transformation. Scholars and artists exiled from Nazi Germany seized the moment to begin works whose goal was to salvage Western civilization's humanist tradition against Nazi historiography based on *völkisch*, chauvinist, racist, and anti-Semitic premises. Baron's *The Crisis of the Early Italian Renaissance*, Auerbach's *Mimesis*, Horkheimer and Adorno's *Dialectic of Enlightenment*, Mann's *Doctor Faustus*, and Cassirer's *The Myth of the State* were conceived at this time and constituted a comprehensive *Kulturkampf* against Nazi barbarism.

Early Life and Works

> Cassirer's philosophy was indeed an attempt—a characteristically Jewish attempt—to preserve the liberal ideal of culture under increasingly hostile conditions. It was a reargued action on behalf of a vanishing civilization.
>
> —Edward Skidelsky, *Ernst Cassirer: The Last Philosopher of Culture*

---

19. Hendel, "Foreword," in Cassirer, *Myth of the State*, x.

In 1874, Cassirer was born into a prosperous Jewish family in the German city of Breslau, now Wroclaw, Poland.[20] His cousin Bruno, a distinguished publisher in Berlin, would bring out most of his works. Cassirer entered the University of Berlin in 1892, studying literature and philosophy. From 1896 to 1899, he studied with Hermann Cohen (1842–1918) at Marburg. Cohen later remarked, "as a young student Cassirer was able to quote by heart whole pages of almost all the classical poets and philosophers. . . . Even all modern poets, like Nietzsche and Stefan George, he could quote you by heart for hours!"[21] Cassirer's dissertation, "Descartes' Kritik der mathematischen und wissenschaftlichen Grundlagen" (*Descartes's Critique of Mathematics and Natural Scientific Knowledge*), obtained the highest possible mark, *opus eximum*.[22] It became the introduction to his first book, *Leibniz' System in seinen wissenschaftlichen Grundlagen* (*Leibniz' System in Its Scientific Foundations* [Marburg: Elwert, 1902]). In the same year, he married Toni, his first cousin from Vienna, and over time, they had three children.

The family moved to Berlin in 1903 and there, Cassirer worked on his monumental interpretation of the development of modern philosophy and science from Descartes to Kant. He produced a three-volume edition of *Leibniz' Philosophische Werke* (1906) and ten volumes of Kant's works (*Immanuel Kants Werke* [Berlin: Bruno Cassirer, vols. 1, 2, 1912]).

Hermann Cohen was the leader of the Marburg School of Neo-Kantianism, which included Paul Gerhard Natorp (1854–1924) and Ernst Cassirer. By its broadest definition, the term "Neo-Kantianism" names any thinkers after Kant who both engage substantively with the basic

---

20. The following intellectual biography of Cassirer is based, in part, on Dimitri Gawronsky, "Cassirer: His Life and His Works," in Schilpp, *Philosophy of Ernst Cassirer*, 3–37; Skidelsky, *Ernst Cassirer*; S. G. Lofts and A. Calcagno, "Translators' Introduction," in Ernst Cassirer, *The Warburg Years (1919–1933): Essays on Language, Art, Myth, and Technology* (New Haven: Yale University Press, 2013), ix–xxxiii; S. G. Lofts, "Translator's Introduction," in Ernst Cassirer, *The Logic of Cultural Sciences: Five Studies* (New Haven: Yale University Press, 2000), xiii–xliii; Verene, "Introduction," *Symbol, Myth, and Culture*, 1–48, and Friedman, "Ernst Cassirer."

21. Gawronsky, "Cassirer," in Schilpp, *Philosophy of Ernst Cassirer*, 9.

22. Ibid., 12.

ramifications of his transcendental idealism[23] and cast their own project at least roughly within his terminological framework. Along with the Marburg School, the Southwest School (or Baden School, in southwestern Germany), included Wilhelm Windelband (1848–1915), Heinrich John Rickert (1863–1936), and Ernst Troeltsch (1865–1923). The Southwest School emphasized culture and values, epistemology and logic, and believed that Kant's transcendental method began with a "fact of science" and argued regressively from its presuppositions or the conditions that would support its possibility. In Cohen's hands the nature of philosophical investigation becomes an exposition of the a priori rules that alone make possible any and every judgment. The world itself is the measure of all possible experience. Accordingly, those of the Marburg School read Kant as epistemologists (*Erkenntniskritikers*) or adherents of the scientific method rather than the metaphysicians supported by the post-Kantian tradition of German idealism.

Initially, Cassirer followed his mentor Cohen in proposing an idealistic philosophy of science in the two volumes of *The Problem of Knowledge in the Philosophy and Science of Modern Times* (*Das Erkenntnisproblem in der Philosophie und Wissenschaft der neueren Zeit* [Berlin: Bruno Cassirer, 1906, 1907]), tracing the development of knowledge theory from Nicholas of Cusa (1401–1464) to Kant. Philosophy students all over the world quickly recognized the quality of these volumes, which became "the standard work on the history of human thought."[24] Another work of the period, *Substanzbegriff und Funktionsbegriff: Untersuchungen über die Grundfragen der Erkenntniskritik* (Berlin: Bruno Cassirer, 1910; translated as *Substance and Function* [Chicago: Open Court, 1923]), "brought the most renown to Cassirer as a thinker in his own right."[25] It analyzed the influence of mathematical science on the natural sciences.

---

23. In the *Critique of Pure Reason*, 1781, Kant argues that space and time are merely formal features of how we perceive objects, not things in themselves that exist independently of us, or properties or relations among them. Objects in space and time are said to be "appearances," and he argues that we know nothing of substance about the things in themselves of which they are appearances. Kant calls this doctrine (or set of doctrines) "transcendental idealism." In other words, Kant held that the human self, or transcendental ego, constructs knowledge out of sense impressions and from universal concepts called categories that it imposes upon them.

24. Ibid., 14.

25. Lofts and Calcagno, "Translators' Introduction," x.

Cassirer was drafted for civil service in World War I, assigned to read foreign newspapers, which involved, typically, for censors of this period, creatively defining the context in summaries and clacking out aspects of texts to be published. In sum, he was a censor, effectively but apparently a very good one. In 1916, he published *Freiheit und Form: Studien zur deutschen Geistesgeschichte* (*Freedom and Form: Studies of German Intellectual History*), in which he explored the humanistic ideals of German culture. The final volume of his edition of Kant's works, *Kant's Leben and Lehre*, came out in 1918.

After working for thirteen years as an instructor, or *Privatdozent*, at Friedrich Wilhelm University in Berlin, in 1919, Cassirer was finally offered professorships at two newly founded universities under the auspices of the Weimar Republic. He accepted the Philosophy Chair at the University of Hamburg and lectured there until 1933, supervising the doctoral thesis of Leo Strauss (1899–1973), the German American political philosopher and classist, among others.

This period was "the most productive" of his career, not least because of his close collaboration with the members of the Warburg Library for Science and Culture.[26] Seeing its resources and treasures for the first time, he said, "The library is dangerous. I shall either have to avoid it altogether or imprison myself here for years."[27] In 1924, he wrote, "Here I found abundant and almost incomparable material in the field of mythology and general history of religion, and its arrangement and selection."[28] Several of his works, such as *The Individual and the Cosmos in Renaissance Philosophy* (1927) and *The Platonic Renaissance in England* (1932), were published in the series Studien der Bibliothek Warburg.[29] Completing *Zur Einsteinschen Relativitätstheorie: Erkenntnistheoretische Betrachtungen* (Berlin: Bruno Cassirer, 1921; translated as *Einstein's Theory of Relativity* [Chicago: Open Court, 1923]), he embarked on a vast new project.

Cassirer developed a theory of symbolism and used it to expand the phenomenology of knowledge into a more general philosophy of culture in

---

26. Ibid., ix. See also Emily Levine, *Dreamland of Humanists: Warburg, Cassirer, Panofsky, and the Hamburg School* (Chicago: University of Chicago Press, 2013).

27. Quoted in F. Saxl, "Ernst Cassirer," *Philosophy of Ernst Cassirer*, 48. See also Hendel, "Preface," in Cassirer, *Mythical Thought*, ix.

28. Cassirer, *Mythical Thought*, xviii.

29. See Ernst Cassirer, "Critical Idealism as a Philosophy of Culture" (1936), in Verene, *Symbol, Myth, and Culture*, 91n26.

Philosophy of Symbolic Forms (Berlin: Bruno Cassirer, 1923, 1925, 1929). The first volume was on language (*Die Sprache*); the second, mythical thinking (*Das mythische Denken*); and the third, on the phenomenology of knowledge (*Phänomenologie der Erkenntnis*), is considered "truly the central work of Cassirer's genius."[30] A fourth volume, *The Metaphysics of Symbolic Forms*, was written in exile and appeared after his death in 1996. These studies were based on the contention that human reason is the only path to understanding reality. In Cassirer's words, the "true concept of reality cannot be pressed in a plain and abstract form of being, it rather contains the whole manifold and wealth of spiritual life." What bridges the human soul and reality is "the intuitive world of art or myth or language," which "represents—according to the saying of Goethe's—a revelation directed from the inside toward the outside, a 'synthesis of world and mind.' "[31] Reality can be grasped only with the help of mental images or symbolic forms. This epistemology led to Cassirer's understanding of "symbolic forms as a system of fundamental functions of the human mind underlying basic human tendencies of human culture and explaining the particular nature of any of them," or the view that the "whole of human culture is reflected in our mind in an endless row of symbolic forms."[32]

The central concern of *Philosophy of Symbolic Forms*, wrote Cassirer, is "the problem of knowledge, the structure and articulation of a theoretical world view," or, more specifically, "the structure of mathematical and scientific thought." As such, it broke fundamental new ground, beyond the Neo-Kantianism of the Marburg School, and articulated Cassirer's original attempt to unite scientific and nonscientific modes of thought (" 'symbolic forms'") within a single philosophical vision. As he wrote in the preface to the first volume, his goal was to broaden "the program of epistemology" to include "the cultural sciences" and "to differentiate the various fundamental forms of man's 'understanding' of the world and apprehend each one of them as sharply as possible in its specific direction and characteristic spiritual form." By way of "a 'morphology' of the human spirit," he hoped "to develop the plan of a general theory of cultural forms." The first volume conducts "an analysis of linguistic form"; the second provides a "sketch of a phenomenology of mythical and religious thinking"; and the third deals

---

30. Hendel, "Introductory Note," in Cassirer, *Phenomenology of Knowledge*, ix.
31. Quoted in Gawronsky, "Cassirer," in Schilpp, *Philosophy of Ernst Cassirer*, 25.
32. Ibid., 26.

with "epistemology proper," or "the morphology of scientific thinking."[33] In contrast to Kant, who argued that "the way to a transcendental order could be gained only through an analysis of the forms and methods of human thought," Cassirer's epistemology included "the methodology of history and moreover of all forms of creative civilization, finally encompassing even the expressions of pre-scientific human thought and imagination as revealed in language and myth."[34]

For our purposes, note that, early on, Cassirer was preoccupied with the problem of myth. In volume 2, *Mythical Thought*, he wrote that he followed "Kant's 'Copernican Revolution'" in philosophy but strove "to broaden it."[35] He provided an overview of the nature and meaning of the philosophical discipline: "the history of philosophy as a scientific discipline may be regarded as a single continuous struggle to effect a separation and liberation from myth. The form of this struggle varies according to the stage of theoretical self-consciousness, but the general trend stands out plainly."[36] In his last book, *The Myth of the State*, he returned to this theme, sadly acknowledging the triumph of myth over reason and rationalism.

Allied works include *Language and Myth* (*Sprache und Mythos: Ein Beitrag zum Problem der Götternamen* [Leipzig: Teubner, 1925]) and *Zur Logik der Kulturwissenschaften* (translated as *The Logic of the Humanities*).[37] He wrote as well important studies on early modern intellectual history, such as *The Individual and the Cosmos in Renaissance Philosophy* (1927) and *The Case of Jacques Rousseau* (1931). The summer of 1931 he spent in the Bibliothèque National de Paris working on his famous study *The Philosophy of the Enlightenment* (1932). Clearly, entering the 1930s, Cassirer had reached "the pinnacle of his academic career in Germany."[38]

Soon his life—and Germany—turned upside down. As a Jew, he early recognized "the great danger" of the Nazi movement; "he never listened

---

33. Cassirer, *Language*, 69.
34. Hajo Holborn, "Ernst Cassirer," in Schilpp, *Philosophy of Ernst Cassirer*, 43.
35. Cassirer, *Mythical Thought*, 29.
36. Ibid., xiii, emphasis added.
37. Göteborg: Göteborgs Högskolas Årsskrift 47, 1942; New Haven: Yale University Press, 1961.
38. Lofts and Calcagno, "Translators' Introduction," xv. To Cassirer's *The Philosophy of the Enlightenment* (1932), should be added also his essay "Enlightenment" in the first edition of the *Encyclopedia of the Social Sciences*, 1931, 547–52.

to the speeches of Hitler or his henchmen; he never read their books and pamphlets; yet seemed to know with uncanny foresight what Nazism was about to do to Germany and the rest of the world." When he first heard the notorious slogan, "Right is what serves our Fuehrer," he said, "This is the end of Germany."[39] After Hitler became chancellor on January 30, 1933, Cassirer wasted no time, immediately requesting a leave of absence from his university for the next academic year. Compare his reaction to that of the philosopher Martin Heidegger (1889–1976), who, at the same time, told students: "Let not propositions and 'ideas' be the rules of your Being [*Sein*]. The Führer alone is the present and future German reality and its law."[40]

By March, Cassirer, his wife, and two children had left Hamburg. In July, the University of Hamburg "officially informed Cassirer that he had been 'retired' from his post."[41] He spent the last twelve years in exile; from 1933–1935, he taught at All Souls College in Oxford and the next six years at the University of Gothenburg in Sweden (1935–1941).[42] Cassirer described "the Gothenburg years" as a memorable part of the "long Odyssey" of his academic life.[43] In 1941, considering Sweden unsafe, he moved to the United States, teaching at Yale from 1941 to 1944 and at Columbia in 1944–1945.[44]

Cassirer published *Determinism and Indeterminism in Modern Physics: Historical and Systematic Studies of the Problem of Causality* (*Determinismus und Indeterminismus in der modernen Physik* [Göteborg: Göteborgs Högskolas Årsskrift 42, 1936]) in Sweden. He regarded it as "one of his most important achievements."[45] Another book, *The Problem of Knowledge: Philosophy, Science, and History since Hegel*, 1950, was, in a sense, "a sequel

---

39. Gawronsky, "Cassirer," in Schilpp, *Philosophy of Ernst Cassirer*, 28.

40. Peter E. Gordon, "Heidegger in Black," *New York Review of Books*, October 9, 2014, http://www.nybooks.com/articles/archives/2014/oct/09/heidegger-in-black/.

41. Lofts and Calcagno, "Translators' Introduction," xvi.

42. On Cassirer's life in Sweden, see Jonas Hansson and Svante Nordin, *Ernst Cassirer: The Swedish Years* (Bern: Peter Lang, 2006).

43. Hendel, "Preface," in Cassirer, *Problem of Knowledge*, viii.

44. See Kay Schiller, "Paul Oskar Kristeller, Ernst Cassirer and the 'Humanistic Turn' in American Emigration," in *Exile, Science and Bildung: The Contested Legacies of German Emigre Intellectuals*, ed. David Kettler and Gerhard Lauer (London: Palgrave Macmillan, 2005), 125–138.

45. Hendel, "Preface," in Cassirer, *Problem of Knowledge*, viii.

to the Determinismus but it was above all the completion of a long program whose execution covered the whole period from 1902 to 1940." Cassirer finished the manuscript while in Sweden and left it behind when in May 1942, he emigrated yet again: "the ship on which he traveled was the last one the German Government permitted to come from Sweden to the United States, and it was stopped and searched." Cassirer's wife recovered it only after his death "on a visit to Sweden in 1946."[46]

Cassirer was a prolific writer with a wide range of interests and styles. However, he was consistent in raising before the eyes of all in Germany "that bright clear mirror fashioned by the Enlightenment"—its ideals of equality, human rights, and dignity.[47] *The Philosophy of the Enlightenment* (1932) was not only a philosophical study but also a direct response to the flight from reason and rationality in the last years of the Weimar Republic.

Enlightenment and Its Enemies

Cassirer never stood aloof from the rage of politics during World War I, the growing cancer of racism and anti-Semitism, the rise and fall of the Weimar Republic, the Nazi Revolution and World War II. He was well aware of the rising tide of popular opinion to exclude Jews from German culture and life. When Albert Einstein returned to Germany in 1914, he noted in horror: "worthy Jews [were] basely caricatured and the sight made my heart bleed. I saw how schools, comic papers, and innumerable other forces of the Gentile majority undermined the confidence of even the best of my fellow Jews."[48] Whatever the Weimar Republic's liberal pretensions, "anti-Semitism was even more precocious during the years of hyperinflation between 1919 and 1923 than in 1933, the year Hitler finally came to power."[49] Betty Scholem wrote in the 1920s to her son Gerhard in Jerusalem, "Anti-Semitism has so badly infiltrated and infected people that you hear them cursing the Jews wherever you go, completely openly and with less inhibition than ever before."[50] In this atmosphere, Cassirer did not retreat

---

46. Ibid., vii–viii.

47. Cassirer, *Philosophy of the Enlightenment*, xi.

48. Quoted in Paul Bookbinder, *The Weimar Republic: The Republic of the Reasonable* (Manchester: Manchester University Press 1996), 196.

49. Amos Elon, *The Pity of It All: A History of the Jews in Germany, 1743–1933* (New York: Metropolitan Books, 2002), 368.

50. Ibid., 374.

to an Ivory Tower but "showed a lively interest in all world-events."[51] He wrote "essays and delivered lectures in defense of constitutionalism and human rights." In August 1928, the Hamburg Senate invited him "to give the speech on Constitution Day," celebrating the Constitution of the German Reich (*Die Verfassung des Deutschen Reichs*), usually known as the Weimar Constitution. Cassirer delivered "an important statement in defense of the [Weimar] republic," declaring in plain words: "the idea of republican constitution as such is in no sense a stranger to . . . German intellectual history, let alone an alien intruder. . . . it has rather grown up on its own soil and been nourished by its very own forces, by the forces of idealist philosophy."[52]

The Nazis put an abrupt and violent end to such idiosyncratic constitutional and philosophical interpretations of German history. The conservative Austrian philosopher, sociologist, economist, and Catholic corporatist Othmar Spann felt free to make Cassirer his target in a February 1929 public lecture in Munich on "contemporary cultural crisis." According to the report in the *Frankfurter Zeitung*, the Austrian Spann lamented "that the German people should have to be reminded of their own Kantian philosophy by foreigners," among them "Hermann Cohen and Cassirer," both German. Spann warned his audience that Cassirer was "still teaching at Hamburg."[53]

Cassirer composed *The Philosophy of Enlightenment* with the goal, in his words, "simply to develop and to explain historically and systematically the content and point of view of the philosophy of the Enlightenment," arguing that "more than ever before, it seems to me, the time is again ripe for applying such self-criticism to the present age."[54] More specifically, he wrote it to refute "the verdict of the Romantic Movement" and the "slogan of the 'shallow Enlightenment'" that was "in vogue" in Weimar Germany.[55]

This political-philosophical goal determined the content and form of his study. In a 1953 review, Isaiah Berlin found it based on "efforts at reconciliation" that "can only be achieved at some sacrifice of the critical faculty. . . . for Professor Cassirer the history of human thought . . . is almost cloudlessly happy." He strove to build, Berlin argued, "the great cathedral of

---

51. Gawronsky, "Cassirer," in Schilpp, *Philosophy of Ernst Cassirer*, 27.
52. Skidelsky, *Ernst Cassirer*, 221, 4.
53. Ibid., 40–41.
54. Cassirer, *Philosophy of the Enlightenment*, xi.
55. Ibid.

human culture and knowledge."⁵⁶ Berlin was right. *The Philosophy of Enlightenment* fashioned a unified, unstained, and unsustainable humanist philosophy to convince Weimar Germany that the Enlightenment was a "clear mirror." To present it as a complex system of contradictory views would not have served Cassirer's fight against Nazism. The book was not a pure academic study of the philosophy of the Enlightenment but rather proposed a model for emulation by Germany in the last years of the Weimar Republic.

Berlin provides an important clue to Cassirer's opposition to Romanticism, which

> was the authenticity and sincerity of the pursuit of inner goals that mattered; this applied equally to individuals and groups—states, nations, movements. This is most evident in the aesthetics of romanticism, where the notion of eternal models, a Platonic vision of ideal beauty, which the artist seeks to convey, however imperfectly, on canvas or in sound, is replaced by a passionate belief in spiritual freedom, individual creativity. The painter, the poet, the composer do not hold up a mirror to nature, however ideal, but invent; they do not imitate (the doctrine of mimesis), but create not merely the means but the goals that they pursue; these goals represent the self-expression of the artist's own unique, inner vision, to set aside which in response to the demands of some 'external' voice—church, state, public opinion, family friends, arbiters of taste—is an act of betrayal of what alone justifies their existence for those who are in any sense creative.⁵⁷

In contrast to the Romantic's atavistic "pursuit of inner goals," the Enlightenment proposed universal, humanist concepts of reason, rationality, equality, and dignity. Cassirer sadly noted that much "that seems to us today the result of 'progress' will be sure to lose its luster when seen in this mirror; and much that we boast of will look strange and distorted in this perspective."⁵⁸

In a clear contrast to the myths, Aryanism, racism, and chauvinism that infected his age, Cassirer argued that the "eighteenth century is imbued

---

56. Isaiah Berlin, *English Historical Review* 68 (1953): 617–19.

57. Isaiah Berlin, *The Crooked Timber of Humanity: Chapters in the History of Ideas*, ed. Henry Hardy (London: John Murray, 1990), 57–58.

58. Cassirer, *Philosophy of the Enlightenment*, xi.

with a belief in the unity and immutability of reason. Reason is the same for all thinking subjects, all nations, all epoch, and all cultures."[59] Such a highly idiosyncratic reading of the Enlightenment mind reveals again how politics and philosophy were inseparable in Cassirer's thought. He emphasized that the "whole eighteenth century understands reason" more as

> an acquisition than as a heritage. It is not the treasury of the mind in which the truth like a minted coined lies stored; it is rather the original intellectual force which guides the discovery and determination of truth. This determination is the seed and the indispensable presupposition of all real certainty.[60]

The crisis of German politics, as Cassirer would later show in *The Myth of the State*, began with Romanticism's abandonment of these Enlightenment ideals, which he admired as a revival of Stoic ideas, emphasizing natural rights and the equality of all men. They were based on a "philosophical reorientation and self-criticism" sorely needed: "The age which venerates reason and science as man's highest faculty cannot and must not be lost even for us." He pleaded with readers: "We must find a way not only to see that age in its own shape but to release again those original forces which brought forth and molded this shape."[61] In *The Philosophy of the Enlightenment*, he still hoped to confront his country's distorted madness with a cool, still mirror. Despite this effort, Enlightenment ideas rapidly lost ground to old ideas and mythologies of race, blood, and soil. He had no success, and the German public and politics turned more and more away from reason and reality.

The Myth of the State will again posit a humanist Stoic culture of human rights and equality. However, its composition took place within a radically different historical context—in exile, in the United States, during the 1942–1943 Battle of Stalingrad. Cassirer knew by now that his earlier plea for return to reason had failed. With the German boot on humanity's throat, he could only explain the ideological, philosophical roots of the madness. *The Myth of the State* is his most political and polemical book, and its creation was in great part determined by his exile.

---

59. Ibid., 6.
60. Ibid., 13.
61. Ibid., xii.

Exile and Interpretation

The trauma of exilic displacement had tremendous impact on Cassirer and the content and form of his interpretations. The theme of crisis began to surface in his thought in 1935 when he spoke about "this disintegration . . . this crumbling down of our spiritual and ethical ideals of culture."[62]

In the same year, he gave an inaugural address at the University of Gothenburg, marking his departure from England to Sweden. He posited: "philosophy is the science of the relation of all knowledge to the essential end of human reason (*teleologias rationis humanae*)." That end "arises today more urgently and imperatively than ever before, not only for the philosopher, but for all of us who partake in the life of knowledge and the life of spiritual culture." In the face of Nazism, there should be no separation between philosophy and life, between modes of conviction and modes of conduct or modes of persuasion and modes of action. He quoted Albert Schweitzer (1875-1965), who, in his Olaus-Petri lectures in Uppsala,[63] argued that "in the hour of peril the watchman slept, who should have kept watch over us. So it happened that we did not struggle for our culture." Cassirer admitted that "all of us who have worked in the area of theoretical philosophy in the last decades deserve in a certain sense this reproach of Schweitzer." More specifically, he blamed himself, his peers, and colleagues:

> While endeavoring on behalf of the scholastic conception of philosophy, immersed in its difficulties as if caught in its subtle problems, we have all too frequently lost sight of the true connection of philosophy with the world. Theoretical, abstract philosophy should be replaced by philosophy which ought to explain and reveal the severe dangers to rationalism and humanism.

Today, Cassirer continued, "we can no longer keep our eyes closed to the menacing danger." Regarding his own vocation, he declared, "philosophy

---

62. Cassirer, "The Concept of Philosophy as a Philosophical Problem," in Verene, *Symbol, Myth, and Culture*, 60.
63. See Hansson and Nordin, *Ernst Cassirer*, 11.

cannot stand aside, mute and idle."[64] Philosophy and philosophers must be enlisted, and, gradually, he developed a more explicit denunciation of Nazism, as in his essay "The Tragedy of Culture" (1942).[65] He dedicated his last ten years in exile to salvaging European humanist culture.

While in Sweden, he wrote *Zur Logik der Kulturwissenschaften: Fünf Studien* (Göteborg: Göteborgs Högskolas Årsskrift 48, 1942), translated as *The Logic of the Humanities* (New Haven: Yale University Press, 1961), and "the fourth volume of *The Problem of Knowledge* (*Philosophy, Science, and History since Hegel*, 1950);" also published by Yale.[66] Both focused on overcoming the crisis in human knowledge and the growing fragmentation in philosophy and science since the death of Hegel. The first discussed human physical and cultural evolution and is considered "a genuine *tour de force* in treating the metaphysical problem as to 'mind and its place in nature.'"[67] In the second, Cassirer showed the interconnectedness of various ways of knowing from the work of physicists, mathematicians, biologists, and other natural scientists from Isaac Newton to the modern world. Cassirer's wife Toni described the historical context in which it was written: "unbelievable as it may seem the whole book was composed between July 9th and November 26th 1940." The reason for such great urgency? "Belgium, France, and Holland were overrun, Norway and Denmark were occupied, and we never knew whether Hitler would appear the next day in Sweden."[68]

These two works were very important to Cassirer, "as they represented his initial response to the madness that surrounded him." In particular, *The Logic of the Humanities* was "a political act of resistance for Cassirer."[69] In its "Introduction: Naturalistic and Humanistic Philosophies of Culture," he lamented the "continually erupting anxiety over the destiny and future of human civilization," advocating abandonment of "the Hegelian view of history" as determined by *Idee* and a return to the belief that "human action again has an open opportunity to determine itself by its own power and through its own answer, knowing full well that the direction and future

---

64. Cassirer, "The Concept of Philosophy," in Verene, *Symbol, Myth, and Culture*, 60–61.

65. Ernst Cassirer, "The Tragedy of Culture," in *Logic of the Humanities*, 182–217.

66. Lofts and Calcagno, "Translators' Introduction," xvi.

67. Clarence Smith Howe, "Translator's Foreword," in Cassirer, *Logic of the Humanities*, viii, x.

68. Toni Cassirer, as quoted in Hendel, "Preface," in Cassirer, *The Problem of Knowledge*, ix.

69. Lofts and Calcagno, "Translators' Introduction," xvi.

of civilization are dependent upon this kind of determination."[70] Like Popper, Cassirer raised his pen against Hegelian historical determinism and in favor of human freedom, human autonomy, and the self-direction of human actions in time and history.

Toni provides important glimpses into the gloomy and desperate context within which Cassirer wrote it—the outbreak of World War II in 1939 and the invasion of Norway in 1940. In "such an incomparable dreadful moment in world history," she wrote, "Ernst suddenly decided to undertake a *new work*." It aimed to combat "the horrible idea of the subjugation of the Western [European] countries" and was written at an "unusual pace . . . the first indication of the urgency that showed itself in his otherwise very quiet mode of working." He would keep it up "from the time of the invasion of Norway [1940] to his death [in 1945] . . . a completely new driving force. *The effort to 'finish' had become all determining*."[71]

The book signified a transformation in Cassirer's life of the mind, evidenced by the German title. He used the term *Kulturwissenschaften*, or cultural sciences, rather than *Geisteswissenschaften*, sciences of spirit, or the humanistic disciplines, to better describe his current project of "critique of culture" and to clearly associate himself "not with such neo-Kantians as Windelband and Rickert" but with "the Warburg Library for the Science of Culture (*Kulturwissenschaften*) and with the ideal of 'universal humanity,' a universal *humanitas*, which was the spirit of that institution."[72] Cassirer "finally returns to the project of establishing the logical foundations and

---

70. Cassirer, *Logic of the Humanities*, 37–38. According to George Wilhelm Friedrich Hegel's idealist philosophy, concepts determine the structure of reality; specifically, the concept of freedom in his philosophy of history. See Zakai, "Constructing and Representing Reality," 106–33.

71. Toni Cassirer is cited in S. G. Lofts, "Translator's Introduction," in Ernst Cassirer, *The Logic of the Cultural Sciences: Five Studies* (New Haven: Yale University Press, 2000), xiv–xv; emphasis original.

72. Ibid., xviii–xix. Compare Cassirer's humanist thought to that of Erich Auerbach, who believed that the study of philology should serve humanist aims and values, especially in the face of Nazi barbarism. Early in his life, Auerbach adopted a "Goethean humanism," closely following the views of Johann Wolfgang von Goethe (1749–1832), who believed that *Weltliteratur* meant "universal literature, or literature which expresses *Humanität*, humanity," and that "this expression is literature's ultimate purpose." *Weltliteratur*, Auerbach wrote, "considers humanity to be the product of fruitful intercourse between its members" (1950; "Philology and *Weltliteratur*," *Centennial Review* 13 [Winter 1969]: 2).

structure of the sciences of culture in contradistinction to the sciences of nature."[73]

After moving to the United States, Cassirer produced two books in English; the first, *An Essay on Man* (1944), serves as a concise introduction to his philosophy of symbolic forms and their application to different realms of human culture, thus providing a comprehensive view of his distinctive philosophical perspective. As he wrote: "the first impulse of writing this book came from my English and American friends who repeatedly and urgently asked me to publish an English translation of my *Philosophy of Symbolic Forms*."[74] The second book, *The Myth of the State* (1946), offered an explanation of the rise of Nazism and totalitarianism on the basis of Cassirer's conception of mythical thought. Both works were marked by great urgency, or the "crisis in man's knowledge of himself," as Cassirer put it in *An Essay on Man*, and by the realization that "human culture is by no means the firmly established thing that we once supposed it to be," as he stated in *The Myth of the State*.[75]

The crisis mode of historical and of philosophical thought pervaded Cassirer's work in exile and led to new interpretations as it had for Baron, Auerbach, Horkheimer and Adorno, Popper, Mann, and many other intellectual exiles. The strange claim that his two late works were "exceptions involving no new directions in Cassirer's thought. . . . seen as works of general interpretation writing for his English-speaking audience"[76] could not be farther from the truth, especially in regard to *The Myth of the State*, a direct attack on Nazi political thought and actions that inaugurated a new "political turn."

Considered "his main task," *The Myth of the State* explores and reveals "the driving forces of human history, especially those forces which made possible the appalling growth of totalitarianism" in the first half of the twentieth century.[77] Dramatic historical events demanded a dramatic analysis of the political thought that constructed them; his contemporary historian Hajo Holborn wrote, "the events cast a tragic shadow over the last years of his career."[78] The book opens with an analysis of the content and form of

---

73. S. G. Lofts, "Translator's Introduction," in Ernst Cassirer, *The Logic of the Cultural Sciences: Five Studies* (New Haven: Yale University Press, 2000), viii–xlii.

74. Cassirer as quoted by Hendel, "Preface," in Cassirer, *Language*, ix.

75. Lofts and Calcagno, "Translators' Introduction," xvii.

76. Verene, "Introduction," in Cassirer, *Symbol, Myth, and Culture*, 2.

77. Gawronsky, "Cassirer," in Schilpp, *Philosophy of Ernst Cassirer*, 32.

78. Holborn, "Ernst Cassirer," Schilpp, *Philosophy of Ernst Cassirer*, 45.

mythical thought, then delineates the development of political theory from early Greek philosophy to the twentieth century, exposing the technique of the modern, Nazi political myths that brought Western civilization to the brink of complete destruction. Cassirer wrote in the conclusion that as long as "intellectual, ethical, artistic forces" are "in full strength, myth is tamed and subdued. But once they begin to lose their strength," as was the case in Nazi Germany, "chaos arises again. Mythical thought then begins to rise anew and to pervade the whole of man's cultural and social life" (298).

"A Completely New Driving Force"

> Every great crisis in man's *thought* used to be accompanied by a deep crisis in his moral and social *conduct*.
>
> —Ernst Cassirer, "Philosophy and Politics," 1944

When the Nazi Revolution took place on January 30, 1933, and Hitler rose to power, Ernst wrote to Toni, "It was all in vain. I shall never write a word again."[79] This agonized vow did not materialize.[80] In fact, he continued his philosophical projects at full speed. Horrifying political crisis transformed the process, form, and content of his works in exile. What was implicit in earlier works, such *The Philosophy of the Enlightenment*, became more and more explicit—a scathing critique of Nazi mythology and antihumanism.

The desperate statement of 1933 and the decision to write *The Myth of the State* are linked directly and inseparably. The philosopher could not keep silent when the Nazis inaugurated their threatened "Thousand-Year Reich," or "Third Empire." By 1944, he said philosophy should provide "the 'spiritual' weapons" against the "new political systems" that had led to the "solemn enthronement of *myth*."[81] His answer to the political and cultural crisis of his time as well as the poverty of philosophy was clearcut: "If ever, now is the time for [philosophy] again to reflect . . . on its

---

79. Quoted by Skidelsky, *Ernst Cassirer*, 220.

80. In contrast, during his exile, Cassirer completed many works, among them *Determinismus und Indeterminismus in der modernen Physik* (1936; *Determinism and Indeterminism in Modern Physics* [1956]); *Axel Hägerström: Eine Studie zur Schwedischen Philosophie der Gegenwart* (1939; *Axil Hägerström: A Study of Contemporary Swedish Philosophy*); *Zur Logik der Kulturwissenschaften* (*The Logic of Cultural Sciences*); *An Essay on Man* (1944); and *The Myth of the State*.

81. Cassirer, "Judaism and the Modern Political Myth," 1944, in Verene, *Symbol, Myth, and Culture*, 234.

systematic, fundamental purpose, and on its spiritual-historical past." He blamed "the pessimism which believes that the hour of destiny for our culture has struck, that the 'decline of the West' is inescapable, that we can do nothing else than to observe this decline calmly and collectedly, *to this pessimism and fatalism we do not wish to resign ourselves.*"[82]

He was opposing the pessimistic and fatalistic views of Oswald Spengler (1880–1936), articulated in *The Decline of the West, or The Downfall of the Occident* (1918–1922). At the same time, Cassirer warned against adopting as an alternative Hegel's optimism as reflected in his famous words: "What is rational is real; what is real is rational."[83] In the rise and triumph of the culture of myths, legends, and heroes in Nazi Germany, the real was no longer rational, and the rational no longer real. Cassirer reiterated this view elsewhere, claiming, exactly as Auerbach did in the first chapter of *Mimesis*, "Odysseus' Scar,"[84] that "the Nazis based their power upon historical social myths," while "the Jews have always shown little inclination for mythical thought."[85]

These utterances reveal Cassirer's growing direct involvement in politics and his struggle to find an appropriate response to the Nazi menace. He indeed publicly addresses Judaism late in life, but he had always been quite actively devout. Although he lamented never learning Hebrew, he was religiously Jewish, but in a manner that was singular to Hermann Cohen's tradition. From Cohen he inherited very strong religious commitments, though these were underplayed publicly before the 1930s.[86] Finally, his was a version of liberal and cosmopolitan Judaism,

---

82. Cassirer, "The Concept of Philosophy as a Philosophical Problem," 1935, in Verene, *Symbol, Myth, and Culture*, 60–62, emphasis added.

83. Ibid., 60–62. Hegel's famous words—"*Was vernünftig ist, das ist wirklich, und was wirklich ist, das ist vernünftig*"—are found in *Outlines of the Philosophy of Right*, 14: "*What is rational is actual and what is actual is rational*" (emphasis original), meaning that "reason is an actual (*wirklich*) power in the world working to create the institutions of freedom" (*Outlines*, 326–27).

84. See Zakai, *Erich Auerbach and the Crisis of German Philology: The Humanist Tradition in Peril* (Dordrecht: Springer, 2017), and David Weinstein and Avihu Zakai, *Jewish Exiles and European Thought During the Third Reich: Auerbach, Baron, Popper, Strauss* (Forthcoming, Cambridge University Press, England, 2017).

85. Gawronsky, "Cassirer," in Schilpp, *Philosophy of Ernst Cassirer*, 33.

86. See Ned Curthoys, *The Legacy of Liberal Judaism: Ernst Cassirer and Hannah Arendt's Hidden Conversation* (New York: Berghahn Books, 2013), and Gregory B. Moynahan, *Ernst Cassirer and the Critical Science of Germany, 1899–1919* (London: Anthem, 2013).

and as such he was part of a distinct Jewish tradition that was not only cultural but also religious.

And now, in *An Essay on Man*, he publicly provided a strong defense of Jewish thought and belief and praised the Old Testament as one source of humanism, freedom, and the rise of the ethical standpoint of religious consciousness. He wrote in *An Essay on Man* about "our own European civilization," and he stressed that "the great prophets of Israel no longer spoke merely to their nations. Their God was a god of Justice and His message was not restricted to a special group." The ultimate message of this "prophetic religion" was "its ethical meaning."[87]

A clear example can be found in the question of taboo. The celebrated first chapter of Auerbach's *Mimesis*, "Odysseus' Scar," argued that Western civilization's representation of reality and its concepts of truth and history were based on the Old Testament.[88] Cassirer, too, claimed that with "the action of taboo," Judaism signified a "complete" and "decisive" change: "If we look at the development of Judaism we feel how complete and decisive this change of meaning was." In "the prophetic books of the Old Testament we find an entirely new direction of thought and feeling" with regard to a "taboo system" that clearly broke away "from all former mythical conceptions" of reality. Now,

> [t]o seek for purity or impurity in an object, in a material thing, has become impossible. Even human actions, as such, are no longer regarded as pure and impure. The only purity that has a religious significance and dignity is purity of the heart.[89]

Cassirer accordingly linked Judaism to other "higher ethical religions," which inaugurated "a new positive ideal of human freedom" in contrast to the "taboo system" based on "fear" and "passive obedience":

> All the higher ethical religions—the religions of the prophets of Israel, Zoroastrianism, Christianity—set themselves a common task. They relieve the intolerable burden of the taboo system, but they detect, on the other hand, a more profound sense of religious obligation that instead of being a restriction or compulsion is the expression of a new positive ideal of human freedom.[90]

---

87. Cassirer, *Essay on Man*, 103.
88. See Zakai, "Constructing and Representing Reality."
89. Cassirer, *Essay on Man*, 107.
90. Ibid., 108.

These words are not philosophical abstractions but important evidence of someone reclaiming his own ethnic and religious heritage. Such a strong defense of Judaism by such secular Jews as Cassirer and Auerbach cannot be understood without taking into account the racist, anti-Semitic Nazi culture of their times.

Like other German Jewish intellectual exiles, such as Hans Baron and Erich Auerbach, to name only two, Cassirer was very far from Jewish life and traditions. They were all what George L. Mosse calls "German Jews beyond Judaism," searching "for a personal identity beyond religion and nationality."[91] German nationalism, Nazism, and fascism "wrenched" their lives "out of their course," causing them "to marshal history, politics and literature in the fight against those who stood against the best of European civilization."[92] The horrors of National Socialism led Cassirer to acknowledge and embrace some features of Judaism, and two of Auerbach's most famous and celebrated works written in exile, "Figura" (1938) and *Mimesis* (1946), were not merely philological and literary studies but also polemical. They both rejected Aryan philology and Nazi historiography, which glorified a concept of *Kultur* based on racism, chauvinism, and communal mythologies of blood and soil and rejected the concept of European *civilization* based on a clear-eyed recognition of human equality. The first defended the Old Testament from depreciation and erasure by Aryan philology, and the second built a grand apology for Western humanist culture and civilization against Nazi tyranny and barbarism from the unique style and content of Old Testament.[93]

Cassirer's works do not evince such grand attempts to provide a comprehensive, systematic, and overarching defense of Jewish life, yet with the revelations of Nazi genocide, his essay "Judaism and the Modern Political Myth" (1944) addressed head-on Germany's unique anti-Semitism and its fatal consequences. It entangles a clear defense of Judaism with his longtime theory of myth, or the struggle between myth and reason. Like *The Myth of the State*, it is based on the crisis mode of historical, political, philosophical, and social thought. Cassirer sadly acknowledged the "disintegration and the sudden collapse of our social and political life in

---

91. Mosse, *German Jews beyond Judaism*, 2.
92. Ibid., 82.
93. See Zakai and Weinstein, *Exile and Interpretation*, and "Erich Auerbach and His 'Figura.'" See also Arthur Krystal, "The Book of Books: Erich Auerbach and the Making of *Mimesis*," *The New Yorker*, December 9, 2013, 83–88, http://pluto.mscc.huji.ac.il/~msavihu/AvihuZakai/AUERBACH-2.pdf.

the last decades" or "these last thirty years," which "have been a period of continuous war."⁹⁴ This war was fought not only by armies but by ideas; "philosophy began to play a new and unexpected role" in providing "the 'spiritual' weapons that were bound to complete and perfect the material weapons." The reason for this radical transformation, made most explicit in *The Myth of the State*, is that the "new political systems began with opposing to reason its oldest and most dangerous adversary. The open and solemn enthronement of *myth* is the distinctive and most characteristic feature in the political thought of the twentieth century."⁹⁵ Philosophy had to be enlisted when the triumph of myth threatened the whole rational structure of state and society.

Turning directly to the present misery, Cassirer argued that the "whole gamut of social passions, from the lowest to the highest notes, appeared and burst forth in the creation of the 'myth of the twentieth century.'" He is referring to Alfred Rosenberg's *The Myth of the Twentieth Century* (1930), "the Myth of the Blood, which, under the sign of the Swastika, released the World Revolution. It is the Awakening of the Soul of the Race, which, after a period of long slumber, victoriously put an End to Racial Chaos."⁹⁶ Now the whole spectrum of social passions was "personified and deified in the 'Leader,'" who became "the fulfilment of collective desires" and would inaugurate "the 'Millennium,'" or the Thousand-Year Reich, "promised to the German race by the modern political myths," in stark contrast to previous religious millennial visions of peace. Instead, "war was declared the true ideal and the only permanent thing in man's social and political life."⁹⁷ The reference shifts here to Ernst Jünger (1895–1998), who developed an aesthetics or ontology of industrial war in his *Storm of Steel* (1920).⁹⁸ According to Jünger:

---

94. Cassirer, "Judaism," in Verene, *Symbol, Myth, and Culture*, 240–41.

95. Ibid., 234.

96. Alfred Rosenberg, *Der Mythus des 20. Jahrhunderts. Eine Wertung der seelisch-geistigen Gestaltenkämpfe unserer Zeit* (München: Hoheneichen-Verlag, 1930); *Myth of the Twentieth Century: An Evaluation of the Spiritual-Intellectual Confrontations of Our Age* (Newport Beach: Noontide Press, 1982), http://www.gnosticliberationfront.com/myth_of_the_20th_century.htm.

97. Cassirer, "Judaism," in Verene, *Symbol, Myth, and Culture*, 238.

98. Ernst Jünger, *In Stahlgewittern, aus dem Tagebuch eines Stosstruppführers* (Berlin: E. S. Mittler & Sohn, 1920); *Storm of Steel; From the Diary of a German Storm-Troop Officer on the Western Front*, trans. Basil Creighton, intro. R. H. Mottram (Garden City: Doubleday, Doran & Company, 1929).

> Death for a conviction is the highest accomplishment. It is proclamation, deed, fulfillment, faith, love, hope and goal; it is, in this imperfect world, a perfect thing, absolute perfection. In this the cause is nothing and the conviction everything. One can die stubbornly for an indubitable error: that is the greatest thing there is.[99]

In the context of the political crisis that ushered in the Nazi Revolution's "devilization" of German state and society,[100] Cassirer referred directly in the essay's last paragraphs to the tragic fate of Jews in the Nazis' haunted, possessed imagination, which associated them with Satan:[101]

> In the mythical pandemonium we always find maleficent spirits that are opposed to the beneficent spirits. There is always a secret or open revolt of Satan against God. In the German pandemonium this role was assigned to the Jew. What we find here is much more than what is usually described by the name 'anti-Semitism.' . . . The German form of persecution was something that never had existed before. . . . What was proclaimed here was a mortal combat—a life and death struggle which could only end with the complete extermination of the Jews.[102]

---

99. See http://thedisorderofthings.com/2013/10/23/junger-meaning-on-the-industrial-battlefield/.

100. Cassirer, "Judaism," in Verene, *Symbol, Myth, and Culture*, 238. Thomas Mann also wrote in exile at exactly the same time about the Satanization, demonization, and barbarization of Nazi Germany. He began *Doctor Faustus* in 1943, and it was published in 1947. Mann argued that the "very definition of Germanness [is] a psychological state threatened by the poison of loneliness, by eccentricity, provincial standoffishness, neurotic involution, unspoken Satanism." The Nazis "entered the arena of history proclaiming themselves bearers of a barbarism that, while wallowing in ruthlessness, was to rejuvenate the world" (*Doctor Faustus*, 326, 184). No wonder that Mann believed in the "secret union of the German spirit with the Demonic" ("Germany and the Germans," 29 May 1945, in Tolzmann, *Thomas Mann's Addresses Delivered at the Library of Congress, 1942–1949*, 51).

101. This horrible association did not originate with Hitler and Nazism. Luther made the same association; see Barnes, *Prophecy and Gnosis*; Mark U. Edwards Jr., *Luther's Last Battles: Politics and Polemics, 1531–46* (Ithaca: Cornell University Press, 1983); Zakai, "Reformation, History and Eschatology in English Protestantism," *History and Theory* 26 (October 1987): 300–18, and "The Poetics of History and the Destiny of Israel."

102. Cassirer, "Judaism," in Verene, *Symbol, Myth, and Culture*, 239.

To explain "the campaign against Judaism launched by the leaders of the new Germany," Cassirer turned to "the National-Socialist propaganda" against the Jews. The Nazis understood that their "victory could not be gained by mere material weapons." Hence, the important role accorded *ideology* in Nazi Germany; "to deny or even to doubt this ideology was to them a mortal sin. It became a *crimen laesae majestatis*—a crime of high treason against the omnipotent and infallible totalitarian state. That the Jews were guilty of this crime was obvious." For Nazi leaders, the Jews "proved it by their whole history, by their tradition, by their cultural and religious life." Cassirer identified the demystification inherent in Judaism as the source. "In the history of mankind they had been the first to deny and to challenge those conceptions upon which the new [Nazi German] state was built; for it was Judaism which first made the decisive step that led from a *mythical* to *an ethical* religion."[103] Judaism inaugurated the antimythical turn in Western culture to reason. Later, in *The Myth of the State*, Cassirer will claim that Plato inaugurated the rational theory of the state.

In exile in Istanbul, Auerbach was also salvaging Judaism with a comparable argument. Against the Homeric culture of myths and heroes adored in Germany, he championed the Bible's rational conception of history based on the important Hegelian concept of "the historically becoming," or the "concept of universal history," which became "a general method of comprehending reality" in Western culture. The figural interpretation of history—the view that Old Testament events and persons are *figures*, or prefigurations, of events and persons in the New Testament—reached its culmination in Dante's *Divine Comedy* (1308-1321).[104]

In 1944, Hitler read his last address to the German people, marking the eleventh anniversary of his National-Socialist regime. Cassirer concluded his essay with an analysis of this speech, emphasizing the unique role the Jews occupied in Hitler's mind. As the Allied armies were storming German borders from all directions, Hitler did not speak of the desperate situation of the German people, the staggering losses of the German army and civilians, and the terrible destruction of German cities.

> Nothing of the kind. His whole attention is still fixed on one point. He is obsessed and hypnotized by *one* thing alone. He speaks of—the Jews. If I am defeated—he says—Jewry could celebrate a second triumphant Purim. Purim festival. What

---

103. Ibid., 239-40, emphasis original.
104. Auerbach, *Mimesis*, 16-17, 23.

> worries him is not the future destiny of Germany, but the 'triumph' of the Jews.[105]

Purim is a Jewish festival that commemorates the deliverance of the Jewish people from destruction in ancient Persia, as recorded in the book of Esther. Cassirer emphasized that by this utterance, Hitler proved once more "how little he knows of Jewish life and Jewish feeling." Not only did Cassirer expose Hitler's poor knowledge of Judaism, but he unmistakably reveals his own attachment to, and knowledge of, Jewish life and tradition. In contrast to Hitler, he wrote:

> In our life, in the life of a *modern Jew*, there is no room left for any sort of joy of complacency, let alone of exultation or triumph. All this has gone forever. No Jews whatsoever can and will ever overcome the terrible ordeal of these last years. The victims of this ordeal cannot be forgotten; the wounds inflicted upon us are incurable. Yet, amidst all these horrors and miseries there is, at least one relief. We may be firmly convinced that all these sacrifices have not been made in vain.

Cassirer's answer to Hitler's speech is very clear: the attempt to destroy European Jewry should bring a new evaluation of "Jewish ethical ideals" and their influence on the humanist culture of civilized nations. With "us" and "we," he also claims his own existential condition as a "modern Jew":

> What the *modern Jew* had to defend in this combat [against Nazism and Hitlerism] was not only his physical existence or the preservation of the Jewish race. Much more was at stake. *We had to represent all those ethical ideals that had been brought into being by Judaism and found their way into general human culture, into the life of all civilized nations.*[106]

The Jewish burden and destiny are to represent the ethical, humanist ideas of Judaism, which shaped "general human culture" on the one hand and the life of "civilized nations" on the other in the face of their destruction. This mission of Jewish life is the ground upon which modern Jews, like Cassirer, Baron, Auerbach, and many others, levied their battle against Nazism. In Cassirer's words:

---

105. Cassirer, "Judaism," 240–41, emphasis original.
106. Ibid., 241, emphasis added.

And here we stand on firm ground. These [ethical] ideals are not destroyed and cannot be destroyed. They have stood their ground in these critical days. If Judaism has contributed to break the power of the modern political myths, it has done its duty, having once more fulfilled its historical and religious mission.[107]

Exile and history had a tremendous impact on Cassirer, but their full meaning, his politicization of the history of political thought, reaches apotheosis in his last book, *The Myth of the State*.

The Myth of the State

The myth of the race worked like a strong corrosive and succeeded in dissolving and disintegrating all other values.

—Ernst Cassirer, *The Myth of the State*, 1946

In Hitler's world, the law of the jungle was the only law. People were to suppress any inclination to be merciful and were to be as rapacious as they could. Hitler thus broke with the traditions of political thought that presented human beings as distinct from nature in their capacity to imagine and create new forms of association. Beginning from that assumption, political thinkers tried to describe not only the possible but the most just forms of society. For Hitler, however, nature was the singular, brutal, and overwhelming truth, and the whole history of attempting to think otherwise was an illusion. Carl Schmitt, a leading Nazi legal theorist, explained that politics arose not from history or concepts but from our sense of enmity. Our racial enemies were chosen by nature, and our task was to struggle and kill and die.

—Timothy Snyder, "Hitler's World"

"The Whole Flight of Humanity"

The *Myth of the State* was the last book Cassirer wrote and, in many ways, can be read as a confession, the testament of a disillusioned humanist as the dark shadows of myth threatened to engulf history. Rooted in Cassirer's life and bitter time, it presents a very idiosyncratic, overarching interpretation of the history of political thought, or a philosophy of

---

107. Ibid., 241.

politics,[108] in light of the rise and triumph of Nazism. Cassirer was a philosopher, not a historian, and here he makes use and abuse of history in order to advance his thought and beliefs, an approach responsible for the book's many shortcomings.

Further, its form and content were greatly influenced by the Marburg School and its emphasis on *problemgeschichtliche Methode* (the problem-historical method), which Cassirer inherited from Hermann Cohen and ultimately Hegel and applied to the history of political thought. It traced the origins and transformation of philosophical problems in significant texts as opposed to assuming that they were perennial and passed intact between generations. In this ideological-methodological context, "Nazism dissolved . . . into a constellation of ideas. Its origins are sought not in the barracks and beer cellars of Munich and Vienna but in the works of Machiavelli, Hegel, Carlyle, and Arthur de Gobineau."[109]

Simply put, Cassirer's interpretation of the history of political thought is based on major, decisive turning points. A golden age of political thought beginning with the Pre-Socratic Greek philosophers, who first inaugurated the rational theory of the state, was followed by Plato's concept of the Legal State, or the state as the administrator of justice. Later, the Stoic philosophers added the principle of the fundamental equality of all human beings. These views prevailed throughout the Middle Ages until Machiavelli committed the "original sin," separating ethics from politics, which led to the concept of a totalitarian state. The Enlightenment's natural rights theory signified a return to Stoic principles with its credo of the equality and dignity of all human beings, which the German Romantic movement called into question by launching a radical shift to the concept of *Volk*: place and status in the political system were based exclusively on belonging to a tribe. Shortly thereafter, the German idealistic thinkers of the nineteenth century, Fichte and Hegel, became advocates and defenders of Machiavellianism. In fact, Hegel was the first eulogist of Machiavelli and his notion of an absolutist state.

---

108. Hans Morgenthau was right when he claimed that Cassirer "was not a historian of philosophy, but a philosopher who used history as a vehicle for philosophic thought" ("*The Myth of the State* by Ernst Cassirer," *Ethics* 57 [January 1947]:142). John M. Krois in *Cassirer: Symbolic Forms and History* (New Haven: Yale University Press, 1987) argued that *The Myth of the State* is the "most prominent" example in Cassirer's works of "philosophical questions concerning social and political history."

109. Skidelsky, *Ernst Cassirer*, 223.

Cassirer devotes the last part of his book, "The Myth of the Twentieth Century," to the nineteenth-century forerunners of the modern myth of the state. He identifies Thomas Carlyle's Hero Worship; Joseph Arthur Comte de Gobineau's Race Worship, or the Totalitarian Race, which prepared the ideology of the totalitarian state; and finally, Hegel's philosophy, which combined state worship with hero worship, leading to a New Type of Absolutism in the history of political thought. The book's theoretical arc can be summarized as follows: from Plato's legal state to the Nazi absolutist myth of the state based on the worship of heroes and blood or race.

Cassirer's interpretation hinges on certain crucial moments. For example, the Stoic philosophers, a school of Hellenistic philosophy founded by Zeno of Citium in the early third century BC, "introduced a principle that proved to be *a turning point* in the history of ethical, political and religious thought," namely, "the conception of the *fundamental equality of men*" (100, emphasis original). Other German Jewish intellectual exiles, such as Baron and Auerbach also defined the progress of history according to major turning points. In *The Crisis of the Early Italian Renaissance*, Baron argued that the "method of interpreting great turning-points in the history of thought against their social or political background has yet not rendered its full service in the study of the Italian Renaissance."[110] Of Auerbach, a critic remarked: "Turning a point of momentous cultural change upon a pivot of syntax (along with its meaning, of course) was an art he had fashioned for himself out of the welter of philological precisionism and Hegelian flight of visionary grandiosity."[111] The crisis of German ideology and politics led all these German Jewish exiles to read history in a very idiosyncratic way that reflected their own sudden historical uprooting. The same was true for Cassirer's idiosyncratic history of political thought. Hans Blumenberg (1920–1996), the German philosopher and intellectual historian, captured this idiosyncratic aspect of Cassirer's book:

> Against the background of his Neo-Kantianism, it is not without irony that Cassirer, the theorist of myth, completed as the last in the long sequence of his works *The Myth of the*

---

110. Hans Baron, *The Crisis of the Early Italian Renaissance: Civic Humanism and Republican Liberty in an Age of Classicism and Tyranny* (Princeton: Princeton University Press, 1966 [1955]), xxv.

111. Charles Breslin, "Philosophy or Philology: Auerbach and Aesthetic Historicism," *Journal of the History of Ideas* 22 (July–September 1961): 380.

> *State.* . . . Naturally this was a domain for which the philosophy of symbolic forms had least of all made provision, a domain in which it was at loss. *What Cassirer registers is fundamentally a unique Romantic regression, which it does not seem possible to fit into any philosophy of history.*[112]

In early 1943, when Cassirer turned to writing *The Myth of the State*, or to "the struggle against myth in the history of political theory" (51), he had already explored at large the relationship between myth and philosophy and witnessed firsthand the rise of fascism and Nazism. However, if in the past he had understood the struggle between rational and mythological thought mostly in philosophical, epistemological, abstract theoretical terms, now, in the terrible context of World War II, he transformed it into an existential battle for the humanist soul of Europe. Accordingly, his goal was to explain "the appearance of a new power: the power of mythical thought" in the political realm. Political philosophy was a new field for him. The historical, ideological, and philosophical reason for his "political turn" was the realization that in "the last thirty years, in the period between the first and second World Wars, we have not only passed through *a severe crisis of our political and social life* but have also been confronted with quite new theoretical problems. We experienced a radical change in the forms of political thought." The severe crisis he referred to was "the preponderance of mythical thought over rational thought in some of our modern political systems." As a result, he sadly noted, "after a short and violent struggle mythical thought seemed to win a clear and definitive victory" (3, emphasis added). Politics and philosophy were never so close in Cassirer's mind, and the crisis mode of political thought was never so apparent.

The Myth of the State is based on a great Manichean struggle between good and evil, rational thought and mythical thought. Crisis, or the crisis mode of historical, philosophical, and political thought, led to its composition. Cassirer's aim was to provide an account of the political crisis of his time, or "the new phenomenon that so suddenly appeared on our former political horizon and in a sense seemed to reverse all our former ideas of the character of our intellectual and social life" (3). His last book, so different in form and content from his previous, purely abstract philosophical studies, bears witness to his new consciousness of the change. Hajo Holborn (1902–1969), another German Jewish intellectual exiled

---

112. Hans Blumenberg, *Work on Myth*, trans. R. M. Wallace (Cambridge: MIT Press, 1985 [1979]), 51, emphasis added.

in the United States, who specialized in modern German history, wrote: "Cassirer confined his historical interest to the history of human thinking and avoided the discussion of the social and political forces."[113] *The Myth of the State* was the great exception to this contention.

Based on his experience of the failure of the Weimar Republic, the rise and eventual triumph of Nazism, exilic displacement, and World War II, Cassirer believed that "the defeat of rational thought seems to be complete and irrevocable," forcing "modern man" to "go back to the first rudimentary stage of human culture." In the scientific sphere, "we never aim to use anything but rational methods," but, he lamented, "in man's practical and social life," the defeat of rational thought was already a *fait accompli*. In view of this general regression and declension of European humanist culture, "rational and scientific thought openly confess their breakdown; they surrender to their most dangerous enemy" (3–4). His militaristic language is based on his explanation of a Manichean struggle between light and darkness, reason and myth. He had dedicated his life to revealing the struggle between philosophy and myth, and to see now the rise and triumph of myths as a feasible, concrete, and vital force in history was very painful.

How heart-breaking to see the elderly Cassirer engaged once again in this struggle, not only as an academic and philosopher, but now also as an eyewitness and a victim to the failure of rational thought. A deep frustration pervades the work; compared to his meticulous analysis of the glorious Enlightenment ideas of human equality, dignity, and liberty, with the rise of modern mythical thought, he sadly noted, "problems that had been unknown to the political thinkers of the eighteenth and nineteenth centuries came suddenly to the fore" (3). The mirror of Enlightenment thought he hoped to place before the Weimar Republic now showed it in retreat from Nazi Germany.

Plato's Legal State and the Administrator of Justice

Given the many storms and crises in Cassirer's life, no wonder he tended to read history in terms of a continuous struggle "between the forces of Light and Darkness."[114] *The Myth of the State* can be clearly seen as the history

---

113. Holborn, "Ernst Cassirer," in Schilpp, *Philosophy of Ernst Cassirer*, 43.
114. Eric Voegelin, "*The Myth of the State* by Ernest Cassirer," *Journal of Politics* 9 (August 1947): 446.

of Nazi Germany writ large, beginning with Plato's "Legal State" and "the administrator of justice" (68–69). He posits an immanent struggle between "Logos" and "Mythos, or between scientific and mythical thought" (53), and all history is depicted exclusively in these terms: as the battlefield where this inherent cosmological human dualism is decided. He uses militaristic terms: "victory," "conquest," "fortifications," "stronghold," concepts more befitting a military history than a philosophical treatise. In the chapter " 'Logos' and 'Mythos' in Early Greek Philosophy," the struggle is described in terms of strategy, plans, victory, leading readers to think they are reading about two mighty armies. The eventual triumph of the "rational theory of the state," wrote Cassirer, was based on "a preconceived strategic plan. One position after another was conquered; the firmest fortifications are laid low, till, at last, the stronghold of mythical thought is shaken to its foundations. All the great thinkers and different philosophical schools have their share in this common work" (53).

No aloof Ivory Tower philosopher is speaking but rather a scholar engaged in *Kulturkampf* against the evils of his times, especially the horrible battles of the last years of World War II. Remembering Cassirer's 1935 speech in Sweden about philosophy's failure to fight Nazi mythology and irrationalism—"philosophy cannot stand aside, mute and idle"[115]—his discussion of early Greek philosophers' war against myth appears in a new light. We can imagine Cassirer constantly looking at the globe to see the Allied Powers beating the Axis.

"Rational theory of state came to light in Greek philosophy," he wrote, and here, as in other fields, "the Greeks were the pioneers of rational thought" (53). He was referring to the Pre-Socratic philosophers, for example, the sixth-century BC Milesian school, people like Thales, Anaximander, and Anaximenes. According to Cassirer's studies on early modern science, in Greek history, "the elimination of the 'fabulous' " was also a main concern. Before studying politics, these Greek philosophers had studied nature and developed "a new [rational] method." Without this preliminary step, he argued, "it would not have been possible for them to challenge the power of mythical thought." In other words, a new conception of nature became the common ground for "a new conception of man's individual and social life." Scientific rationalism, the rational scientific method, paved the way for eliminating myth from politics because it totally rejects mythological thought:

---

115. Cassirer, "Concept of Philosophy," in Verene, *Symbol, Myth, and Culture,* 60–61.

We cannot hope to 'rationalize' myth by an arbitrary transformation and re-interpretation of the old legends of the deeds of gods or heroes.[116] . . . In order to overcome the power of myth we must find and develop a new positive power of 'self-knowledge.' We must see the whole of human nature in an ethical rather in a mythical light. Myth may teach man many things; but it has no answer to the only question which, according to Socrates, is really relevant: to the question of good and evil. (60)

In sum, "Only the Socratic 'Logos,' only the method of self-examination introduced by Socrates, can lead to a solution of this fundamental and essential problem" (60).

In his chapter on "Plato's *Republic*," Cassirer claimed that the Greek philosopher was "the founder and the first defender of the Idea of the Legal State," based on "a general principle of order, regularity, unity, and lawfulness" (69). This view stood in stark contrast to that of another German-speaking intellectual exile, the Austrian British philosopher Karl Popper (1902–1994), who argued that Plato's thought is rather marked by dangerous tendencies toward totalitarian ideology. Forced to flee Nazi Europe because of racism and anti-Semitism, each in his own place of exile, one in the United States and the other in New Zealand, Cassirer and Popper developed radically contrasting views of Plato's philosophy.

For Cassirer, Plato is an important figure in the struggle against myth in Western history because, since him, "all great thinkers have made the greatest efforts to find a rational theory of politics" (294). Cassirer also recognized that Plato was one of the greatest originators of myths, such as the "supercelestial place" of "the prisoners in the cave, of the soul's choice of its future destiny, of the judgment after death" (71–72), and, not least, the myth of Atlantis, the island of Atlas. However, in the last chapter of the book, Cassirer reiterated the claim that "Plato always makes a sharp distinction between mythical and philosophical thought" (291). Plato preserved "all the intellectual tendencies that formed Greek culture." In political terms, he believed that what "is written in 'small characters' in the individual soul, and is therefore almost illegible, becomes clear and understandable only if we read it in the larger letters of man's political and social life. This principle is the starting point of Plato's *Republic*" (61).

---

116. These words recall Auerbach's attack on Greek mythologies as unrealistic and, hence, unable to provide a true representation of reality in the first chapter of *Mimesis*, "Odysseus' Scar."

Following the Platonic moment in Greek political philosophy, "the whole problem of man was changed: politics was declared to be the clue to psychology." Thus, Plato constructed a new, rational foundation for the theory of the state:

> This was the last and decisive step necessary to the development of Greek thought which had begun with an attempt to conquer nature and continued by asking for rational norms and standards of ethical life. It culminated in a new postulate of *a rational theory of the state.* (61–62, emphasis added)

Self-knowledge became essential to rational politics once Plato realized that "the Socratic demand for self-knowledge could not be fulfilled so long as man was still blind with regard to the principle question and lacked a real insight into the character and the scope of political life" (62–63). The Platonic moment ushered in the rational theory of the state, as opposed to the mythological, confirming Cassirer's all-encompassing thesis that the main mark of the history of philosophy is "a single continuous struggle to effect a separation and liberation from myth."[117] In Plato, he found the first example, although by the end of his last book, he sadly concedes the triumph of myth.

However aware of Plato's use of myths, Cassirer designated him creator of the new postulate, "a rational theory of state" (62), and "first defender of the Idea of the Legal State" (69). Striving to organize and to bring rational rules into the empirical world, Plato found the ultimate principle of universal order "in geometry." He transferred the "geometrical equality of the right proportion between the elements which constituted a geometrical body" to politics in order "to discover the true constitution of the state." Believing that the political cosmos is only a symbol of "the universal cosmos," and given that the concept of cosmos as such denotes order, hence rationalism, Plato launched his "criticism of mythological thought." The philosopher or the ruler's first step should be "to replace the mythical gods by what is described by Plato as the highest knowledge: the 'Idea of the Good' " (69).

In contrast, Popper divorced Plato's ideas from those of Socrates in *The Open Society and Its Enemies* (1945), claiming that the former in his later years expressed none of the humanitarian and democratic tendencies of his teacher, and finally betraying Socrates in the *Republic* by portraying

---

117. Cassirer, *Mythical Thought*, xiii.

him as sympathetic to totalitarianism. Cassirer sees an integral continuity between the two.

Plato notoriously denounced poetry as "injurious to the minds which do not possess the antidote in a knowledge of its real nature." Seeing that the "art of representation" is "a long way from reality," Plato argued, "all poetry, from Homer onwards, consists in representing a semblance of its subject" with "no grasp of the reality." For him, "[d]ramatic poetry has a most formidable power of corrupting even men of high character"[118] and was unsuitable for educating the guardians of his ideal state. Justifying Plato on this point, Cassirer, again in clear contrast to Popper, argued that what "is combated and rejected by Plato is not poetry in itself, but the myth-making function. To him and every other Greek both things were inseparable." As Herodotus said, "Homer and Hesiod had made the generations of the gods," which was

> the real danger for the Platonic *Republic*. To admit poetry meant to admit myth, but myth could not be admitted without frustrating all philosophic efforts and undermining the very foundations of Plato's state. Only by expelling the poets from the ideal state could the philosopher's state be protected against the intrusion of subversive hostile forces. (67)

Note that in the first chapter of *Mimesis*, Auerbach claimed that the Homeric poems were based on myth, while the Old Testament strove to provide a more realistic representation of reality. Cassirer looked to Plato, whose "greatness depends on the new *postulate*"—a rational theory of the state—which was unforgettable: "It stamped the whole future development of political thought" (68, emphasis original).

Having broadly defined Plato's unique contribution to the history of political thought, Cassirer explains it in detail. Plato began his study of the social order by defining and analyzing "the concept of justice," claiming "the state has no other and no higher aim than to be the administrator of justice," which means establishing "a general principle of order, regularity, unity, and lawfulness." He thus "became the founder and the first defender of the Idea of the Legal State" (68–69). The only thing Plato absolutely rejected and condemned, argued Cassirer, was "the tyrannical soul and the tyrannical state" (71). Cassirer tended to emphasize an alternative

---

118. Plato, *The Republic of Plato*, trans. F. M. Cornford (New York: Oxford University Press, 1945), bk. 10, 595–608; 324, 328, 331, 337.

vision of the state based on the concept of justice—a legal state, whose sole function is the administration of justice—and he "found" in Plato's thought the most fruitful example: "the 'ideal' state" (71).

Plato was the first to introduce a rational "'theory' of the state, not as a knowledge of many and multifarious facts, but as *a coherent system of thought*" (69, emphasis added). To create it, "he had to lay the ax to the tree: he had to break the power of myth," although he was "one of the greatest myth makers in human history" (71). How to reconcile Plato the rationalist of the *Republic* with the myth-maker of the dialogue *Timaeus*, proposing a demiurge and twofold creation of the world? How could "the same thinker who admitted mythical concepts and mythical language so readily into his metaphysics and his natural philosophy [speak] in an entirely different vein when developing his political theories?" (72). Cassirer did not provide a serious answer to this arresting puzzle, simply saying that in the field of politics, "Plato became the professed enemy of myth." Instead, he put a warning into Plato's mouth that if "we tolerate myths in our political systems . . . all our hopes for a reconstruction and reformation of our political and social life are lost. There is only one alterative: we have to make our choice between ethical and mythical conceptions of the state. In the Legal State, the state of justice, there is no room left for the conception of mythology, for the gods of Homer and Hesiod" (72).

Behind Cassirer's history of political thought, or his political philosophy, lurks the devil of Nazism and the agonies of his life.

Cassirer emphasized that against Plato's Legal State and its role as the administrator of justice stood "the conception of the Power State" prevalent "in all the sophistical theories" and based on the view that "might is right." It appealed not only to the "wise men," or the "sophists," but also "to the practical men, the leaders of Athenian politics. To attack and destroy this dictum was the principal concern of Plato" (74). Note again the highly militaristic terms, befitting a military history perhaps, but hardly a serious work of philosophy. The Sophists' Power State is situated in direct opposition to "Plato's ethical and political philosophy." Justice is the cardinal virtue in Plato's thought: "Power can never be an end in itself" (75).

Cassirer transformed Plato's politics to make it an integral part of his struggle against Nazism and fascism. First, he claimed that Plato moved Socrates's ethic "to a new sphere, that of political life." Second, like the individual in Socratic thought, "the state too is under the same obligation," ethical obligation. Instead of accepting "its fate, it has to create it. To rule others it must first to learn to rule itself. But this is an ethical end which cannot be attained by a display of sheer physical force." In social life as well as individual life, "rational (*phronēsis*) thought must take the leading part." *The Myth of the State*'s strong plea for rationalism in a time when European humanity sank into fanaticism and madness applied not only within the boundaries of the state but also to its wars and annexation of other states:

> The welfare of a state is not its increase in physical power. The desire to have 'more and more' is just as disastrous in the life of a state as in individual life. If the state yields to this desire, that is the beginning of its end. The enlargement of its territory, the superiority over its neighbors, the advance in its military or economic power, all this cannot avert the ruin of the state but rather hasten it. (76)

These words apply more to Nazi Germany than to Plato and Athenian democracy.

Cassirer concluded that Plato excluded "myth from the *Republic*" because "of all things in the world myth is the most unbridled and immoderate. It exceeds and defies all limits; it is extravagant and exorbitant in its very nature and essence. To banish this dissolute power from the human and political world was one of the principal aims of the *Republic*" (77). These words represent a tremendous shift in Cassirer's thought. In the second volume of *The Philosophy of Symbolic Forms*, he included mythical thought as an integral part of human development. Now, in 1945, myth was accorded a unique, autonomous, eternally lurking evil force in the universe, and "to banish this dissolute power from the human and political world" was imperative. Culture could only arise when the "darkness of myth" was fought and overcome. When "intellectual, ethical and artistic" forces lose their strength, "chaos is come again," and myth pervades "man's cultural and social life" (298). Having experienced firsthand the great destructive power of myths in Nazi Germany and knowing the shocking magnitude of the Holocaust, no wonder Cassirer assigned to myth such a profound, concrete, and evil role in human history. The militaristic, aggressive terms pervading *The Myth of the State* show Cassirer himself making myth, or mythologizing its power as a living historical enemy.

Medieval Theory of the State

Plato's theory of the "Legal State became an everlasting possession of human culture," declared Cassirer. Moreover, "it was not bound to special historical conditions or to a particular cultural background." Based on reason, which knows no limitation, "Plato's ideal state was beyond space or time; it had no 'here' and 'now.' It was a *paradeigma*: a standard and pattern for human actions" (78). One of the many problems with this overly general interpretation, of course, is that the medieval scholastic philosophers did not have access to most of the works of Plato, which were essentially lost to Western civilization from circa 600 to 1100 CE and practically unknown until the fifteenth century. Cassirer did not—could not—substantiate his claim about the influence of Plato's *Republic* on medieval political thought.

Such an unhistorical, unphilosophical approach, leading to the glorification of the Platonic ideal state, stems from Cassirer's great urge to find a well-defined, solid, ideological, rationalist, and humanist starting point for his study. He wants to reconstruct the whole history of political thought in Manichean terms, as a fight between myth and reason that climaxes in the myth of the twentieth-century state. He knew firsthand the tragic end of the story, but he had to invent its beginning. Trying to establish Plato's influence on medieval thought, Cassirer eventually has to admit that even "by its great admirer Plato's *Republic* had always been described as a political utopia" and seems "to have little, if anything, to do with actual political life." Nevertheless, he continues, the Platonic thesis that "the first and principal task of the state is the maintenance of justice became the very focus of medieval political theory." Again, no clear proofs can be found for this bold assertion. Cassirer can only talk in general, superficial terms about "complete agreement between the medieval theory" of state "and that of classical antiquity" (97), while admitting that Plato "defined justice as 'geometrical equality,'" even though for Augustine and other medieval Christian thinkers, "all ethical laws are created things; they are the revelation" of the Deity's "personal will" (98). God, reason, and revelation ruled medieval history and thought, as in the title Étienne Gilson (1884–1978) gave his classic 1939 book.[119]

The role of Stoicism is also distorted in Cassirer's narrative. In the face of Aryanism, Nazi racism, and anti-Semitism, he elevated "the loftiest ideas of Stoic philosophy" about "the autonomy of the will and the independence of the wise man" (287). Stoic philosophers "introduced a principle that proved to be a turning point in the history of ethical, political and religious thought." To the Platonic ideal of justice, they "added an

---

119. Étienne Gilson, *Reason and Revelation in the Middle Ages* (New York: Charles Scribner's Sons, 1939).

entirely new conception: the conception of the *fundamental equality of men*" (100, emphasis original). The "principal ethical demand of the Stoics was 'to live in accordance with nature,'" or the moral, not the physical, "law of nature," rationalism. While many differences exist between human beings, "from an ethical point of view all these differences are declared to be of no account. They are of indifference because they do not affect the *form* of human life. What matters alone, what determines a man's personality, are not the things themselves but his *judgment* about things" (101, emphasis original).

Later Stoic philosophers like Cicero and Seneca believed in "the general virtue called 'humanity' (*humanitas*)," meaning that "all rational beings are members of the same commonwealth. Universus hic mundus," said Cicero, "una civitas communis deorum atque hominum existimanda est" (This whole world should be regarded as one commonwealth of gods and men). Their coalescence of political and philosophical thought was "a fact of paramount importance" since it changed "the whole conception of social life" (102). Cassirer will argue that the Enlightenment adopted the Stoic "conception of the *fundamental equality of men*" (100, emphasis original).

Virtue and rational judgment, ethics and reason, then, are the foundations of social and political life. They led to the Stoic maxim about "the fundamental equality of men" (103), or "the natural equality of men" (106), because all human beings are "endowed with the same reason." The consequences of these principles are far-reaching: not only are all human beings, but "no political power can ever be absolute" (104). Stoic thought radically transformed political life, grounding it in reason and rationalism and the equality of all people.

Machiavelli—the Modern Secular State Created and Maintained by Force

Cassirer's history of political thought is based on several decisive turning points: Plato first postulated a rational state and defended the idea of the legal state as administrator of justice; the Stoic philosophers introduced the concept of human equality based upon virtue and rationalism. Niccolò Machiavelli initiated a thorough and radical revolution in the history of political thought: he "decided to cut the Gordian knot" between politics and ethics, giving rise to the "modern secular state" (129, 133). This view stood in clear contrast to the Cambridge School of Political Thought, which included Quentin Skinner and J. G. A. Pocock, who saw Machiavelli as the source of the Atlantic Republican Tradition, which Pocock, following Hans Baron, traces back to Florentine civic humanism. The Cambridge School's historical methodology studied political philosophical texts in their own historical contexts.[120]

For Cassirer, Machiavelli created "*the structure of the new state,*" and he "foresaw its effects" and "anticipated the whole course of the future political life of Europe." Instead of clinging to the view that the state is based on tradition and the principle of legitimacy, the Florentine thinker held that a body politic is "created by force and was to be maintained by force" alone (134–35, emphasis original). This view was the essence of the Machiavellian revolution, or the Machiavellianism known to later generations. If Plato and the Stoics established a state based on reason and justice, Machiavelli destroyed its most cherished credo—the association between politics and ethics. The exclusion of ethical considerations from the realm of politics was Machiavelli's "original sin," according to Cassirer.

Cassirer devoted three chapters of over forty pages to Machiavelli's singular role, not least because it exercised enormous influence on German Romanticism and Idealism. He began his analysis with the saying "Pro captu lectoris habent sua fata libelli" (The fortune of a book depends upon the capacity of its reader, 116). These words apply most to Cassirer, who blamed Machiavelli for many evils of the twentieth-century totalitarian state, thus interpreting past thoughts and events in light of the political struggles of his own time. His politicized reading holds not only that Machiavelli's *The Prince* (1513; first printed version, 1532) "was immediately put into action" in "the hands of its first readers," but, most important, it "was used as a powerful and *dangerous weapon* in the great political struggle of our modern world" (116, emphasis added).

Cassirer sought confirmation of his thesis through time. In the seventeenth century, Machiavelli was "described as an incarnation of the devil" (123); Thomas Babington Macaulay (1800–1859), the British historian and Whig politician, wrote in his *Critical, Historical and Miscellaneous Essays* (1860): "Out of his surname" was "coined an epithet for a knave, and out of his Christian name a synonym for the Devil" (116–17). Cassirer moves from such excessive blame to excessive praise, saving special contempt for Germany: "Machiavelli, the counselor of tyrants, became a

---

120. J. G. A. Pocock, *The Machiavellian Moment: Florentine Political Thought and the Atlantic Republican Tradition* (Princeton: Princeton University Press, 1975; rpt. 2003).

martyr of freedom; the incarnate Devil became a hero and almost a saint" (117), drawing evidence from *Letters for the Advancement of Humanity* (1793-1797) by Johann Gottfried von Herder (1744-1803), who praised *The Prince* as "a political masterpiece written for the contemporaries of Machiavelli" (121). This view was shared by Hegel, who became "the first eulogist of Machiavelli." Hegel wrote:

> One has to read *The Prince* taking into consideration the history of centuries preceding Machiavelli and the contemporary history of Italy, and then this book is not only justified, but it will appear a highly magnificent and true conception of a genuine political genius of the greatest and noblest mind. (122)

Cassirer finds in these words a turning point in the history of political thought, citing the German liberal Friedrich Meinecke (1862-1954): "it was new and it was monstrous when Machiavelism was inserted into the idealistic system" of Hegel. "What happened was almost to be compared to the legitimization of a bastard" (122-23). Many other German idealists followed Hegel, such as Johann Gottlieb Fichte (1762-1814), who "praised Machiavelli's political realism and tried to exculpate him from all moral blame" (123). In sum, if "in the literature of the seventeenth century Machiavelli has been described as an incarnation of the devil; and then, in a curious hyperbole, the devil himself was sometimes styled a Machiavellian and tinged with Machiavelism," then, two hundred years later, "there was the complete reversal of this judgment. The devilization of Machiavelli was superseded by a sort of deification" (123-24), especially in Germany.

In his novel *Doctor Faustus* (1947), Thomas Mann, another exile from Nazi Germany, argued that "the very definition of Germanness" is "a psychological state threatened by the poison of loneliness, by eccentricity, provincial standoffishness, neurotic involution, unspoken Satanism."[121] In 1945, he denounced the "secret union of the German spirit with the Demonic."[122] Now, Cassirer argued that Machiavelli—Mephistopheles—brokered this special relationship between Germany and the devil.

Cassirer blamed "our [German] historicism" for misreading Machiavelli and Machiavellianism: "Since the time of Herder and Hegel we have been told that it was a mistake to regard Machiavelli's *Prince* as a systematic

---

121. Mann, *Doctor Faustus*, 326.
122. Mann, "Germany and the Germans," 29 May 1945, in Tolzmann, *Thomas Mann's Addresses*, 51.

book—as a theory of politics" (124). Historicism is based on skepticism about "the possibility of eternal truths and universal values," yet "this was not the attitude of Machiavelli nor was it that of the Renaissance. The artists, the scientists, the philosophers of the Renaissance did not know of our modern historical relativism; they still believed in an absolute beauty and absolute truth" (125). In contrast to German historicists, who claimed that *The Prince* was written "for a special purpose and for a small circle of readers," and should be considered solely "in its own surroundings" (124), Cassirer argued that its author strove "to build a new constructive theory, a real science of politics." Hence, "he certainly could not mean to restrict this science to special cases" or to Italy and Italy alone (126). In other words, "Machiavelli wrote not for Italy nor even for his own epoch, but for the world—and the world listened to him" (126), especially Germany. Note that both Karl Popper and Leo Strauss combined an idiosyncratic history of political thought with idiosyncratic hermeneutics to oppose historicism.[123] As we can see, Cassirer likewise believed that historicism helped the rise of fascism, Nazism, and totalitarianism with horrifying consequences.

Machiavelli sparked a "Copernican Revolution" in the history of political thought; he broke away from "the whole scholastic tradition" by destroying its "cornerstone . . . the hierarchic system" (135). Political power no longer resided in divine providence, the medieval concept of the Great Chain of Being, or a theological teleology of divine order inherent in the universe. Being "a political realist," Machiavelli had "to give up the whole basis of the medieval political system." For example, the theory of the "divine origin of the rights of kings seemed to him to be entirely fantastic." Instead, he "became the founder of a new type of science of a political static and a political dynamics" (136) because he had "eradicated root and branch" with his "theory all the previous theocratic ideas and ideals" (138). Similarly, "[r]eligion no longer bears any relation to a transcendental order of things and it has lost all its spiritual values." With Machiavelli the "process of secularization has come to its close; for the secular state exists not only de facto but also de jure; it has found its definitive theoretical legitimization" (139).

---

123. See Zakai and Weinstein, *Exile and Interpretation*; David Weinstein and Avihu Zakai, "Exile and Interpretation: Reinventing European Intellectual History in the Age of Nazi Tyranny and Barbarism," http://college.wfu.edu/politics/exileandinterpretation/; and David Weinstein and Avihu Zakai, *Jewish Exiles and European Thought in the Shadow of the Third Reich: Baron, Popper, Strauss, Auerbach* (Cambridge: Cambridge University Press, 2017).

The implications of such new political ideas were enormous and far-reaching: separating ethics and religion from politics provided the foundation for an absolute regime, a secular regime, bereft of any consideration above and beyond it. "With Machiavelli we stand at the gateway of the modern world. The desired end is attained; the state has won its full autonomy" (140, emphasis added). It had "cut off all the threads by which in former generations the state was fastened to the organic whole of human existence." In the new vision, the political world lost "its connection not only with religion or metaphysics but also with all other forms of man's ethical and cultural life" (140).

This is the marrow of Cassirer's conception of the Machiavellian moment in the history of political thought. It led eventually to "the most dangerous consequences," revealed in "our modern forms of dictatorship" (140). Machiavelli highly admired "the methods used by Cesare Borgia to liquidate his adversaries. Yet in comparison with the later much more developed technique of political crimes" used by Nazis and fascists, "these methods appear to be only child's play." Cassirer stressed that the consequences of "Machiavelli's theory were not brought to light until our own age. Now we can, as it were, *study Machiavellianism in a magnifying glass*" (140–41, emphasis added). Only by reading history backward, from the traumatic twentieth century to the sixteenth century, could Cassirer pass such grave, unjustified accusations against Machiavelli.

Cassirer's politicization of the history of political thought reaches its height when he claims that only with the totalitarian regimes of the twentieth century is Machiavellianism "coming to its full maturity." During the seventeenth and eighteenth centuries, "there were still great intellectual and ethical forces which counterbalanced" Machiavelli's influence. For example, with the single exception of Thomas Hobbes, the political thinkers of this period "were all partisans of the 'Natural Right of the state.'" Hugo Grotius, Samuel von Pufendorf, Jean-Jacques Rousseau, and John Locke all "looked on the state as a means, not as an end in itself"; the "concept of a 'totalitarian' state was unknown to these thinkers." For them, there was always "a certain sphere of individual life and individual freedom which remained inaccessible to the state." However, the nineteenth century called natural rights theory into question when German "Romanticism launched a violent attack against" it. With its collapse, Fichte and Hegel "removed" the last barrier to the triumph of Machiavellianism in the twentieth century. With the rise of fascism and Nazism, Machiavelli's "victory was complete and seemed to be beyond challenge" (141).

Cassirer knew that Machiavelli wrote not only *The Prince* but also *Discorsi sopra la prima deca di Tito Livio* (*Discourses on the First Decade of Titus Livy*, 1517). Still, he emphasized the first work, which "contains the most immoral things." More specifically, he claimed "that Machiavelli has no scruples about recommending to the ruler all sort of deception, of perfidy, and cruelty incontestable" (142). He was "dangerous—dangerous in his thought," and *The Prince* was the work of "a political thinker—and of a very radical thinker." For example, the "real politician, the great statesman" will not "shrink from such crimes as are stamped with an inherent greatness. He may perform many good actions, but when circumstances require a different course he will be 'splendidly wicked'" (144). Cassirer's Machiavelli became "the advocate of 'splendid wickedness'" (145), whose "fascination of Cesare Borgia is so strong that it seems completely to eclipse all republican ideals" expressed in *The Discourse*. Cassirer even claimed that the vicious, unscrupulous "methods of Cesare Borgia become the hidden center of Machiavelli's political reflections. His thought is irresistibly attracted to this center" (145–46).

The Machiavellian credo was "whoever will not keep to the fair path of virtue, must, to maintain himself, enter the path of evil." *Aut Caesar aut nihil*—either Caesar or nothing—"either to lead a private, harmless and innocuous life, or enter the political arena, struggle for power, and maintain it by the most ruthless and radical means" (148). He believed that human "depravity cannot be cured by laws; it must be cured by force" (149). Cassirer concluded that no "political writer before Machiavelli had ever spoken in this way." The ruler has "two ways of fighting: one with laws; the other, with force. The first way belongs to man, the second to beasts" (150). This saying reveals in "a sudden flash, the nature and purpose" of Machiavelli's "political theory." According to him, "political life" is "full of crimes, treacheries, and felonies," and no one before him "had undertaken to teach the *art* of these crimes." In the end, he "promised to become a teacher in the art of craft, perfidy, and cruelty" (151, emphasis original). His was "not only a new science" of politics "but a new *art* of politics. Accordingly he was the first modern author who spoke of the art of the state'"—*Arte dello Stato* (154–55, emphasis original). His theory of politics "was created by a clear, cool, and logical mind and by a man who could make use of both his rich personal experience in the affairs of the state and his deep knowledge of human nature" (162).

Both Plato and Machiavelli turned the tide of political thought, yet they could not have been more different; the first "tried to give a theory of the Legal State; Machiavelli was the first to introduce a theory that suppressed or minimized this specific feature" (155).

The Age of Reason and Enlightenment

After the modern secular state, "created by force" and "maintained by force" (135), the seventeenth century, the Age of Reason, introduced another profound transformation: "a rejuvenation of Stoic ideas," as the "best-known political books of this period show the clear and unmistakable imprint of the Stoic mind." The essence was rationalism and the natural rights of man, which had great impact on "the ethical and political conflicts of the modern world" (168). With the Renaissance, discovery of the Americas, the Protestant Reformation, and the Scientific Revolution, the "unity and the inner harmony of the Medieval culture had been dissolved." Now, if "there was to be a really universal system of ethics or religion, it had to be based upon such principles as could be admitted by every nation, every creed and every sect." To Cassirer, "Stoicism alone seemed to be equal to this task" and became "the foundation" of "a system of natural laws" (169). Further, it contained the more important "promise to restore man to his ethical dignity." This dignity "cannot be lost; for it does not depend on a dogmatic creed or any outward revelation. It rests exclusively on the moral will—on the worth that man attributes to himself" (169-70). The secularization of the European mind reached its height with the triumph of Stoicism in the Age of Reason, or, conversely, the theory of natural rights was indispensable to the modern world. "Without this theory there seemed to be no escape from a complete moral anarchy" (170). Needless to say, the great exaggeration in this statement is familiar to all who study early modern history.

The thinkers of the period, people like Galileo, Descartes, and Hugo Grotius, accepted "the Stoic principle of the 'autarky' of human reason. Reason is autonomous and self-dependent. It is not in need of any external help; it could not even accept the help if it were offered. It has to find its own way and to believe in its own strength." Bodin and Hobbes, the "defenders of popular rights and of the sovereignty of the people," assured that the "doctrine of the state-contract becomes in the seventeenth century a self-evident axiom of political thought" (172-73). Accepting this doctrine reduced the legal and social order "to free individual acts, to voluntary contractual submission of the governed." Hence, all mystery is gone from political thought and belief, for there is "nothing less mysterious than a contract" (173). This growing rationalization and secularization eventually led to disenchantment with the political realm. It should be noted again that in this highly idiosyncratic interpretation,

Cassirer tended to overlook the predominant absolutist trends, especially in England and France at the time.

The epitome of the Stoic revival is Thomas Jefferson's Declaration of Independence (1776), which stipulated: "We hold these truths to be self-evident; that all men are created equal; that they are endowed by their Creator with certain unalienable rights; that among these are life, liberty, and the pursuit of happiness." Only to secure these rights, Jefferson posits, "governments are instituted among men, deriving their just powers from the consent of the governed." Cassirer called these assertions "the language of the Stoic philosophy," expressing "the essence of men and the very character of human reason." The basis of the US Declaration of Independence and, later, the French Declaration of the Rights of Man and the Citizen (Déclaration des droits de l'homme et du citoyen, 1789), was "the intellectual Declaration of Independence that we find in the theoreticians of the seventeenth century." He expressed the view that concepts determine the structure of reality in Hegelian terms: in this century, "reason had first declared its power and its claim to rule the social life of man. It had emancipated itself from the guardianship of theological thought; it could stand on its own" (167). Cassirer argued that, with the revival of Stoic philosophy, "the theory of the natural right of man was no longer an abstract ethical doctrine but one of the mainsprings of political action" (168).

As can be clearly seen again and again, Cassirer "was not a historian of philosophy, but a philosopher who used history as a vehicle for philosophic thought."[124] His study is based on a teleological view of history, or a Whig interpretation of the annals of political thought.[125] He presents the past as an inevitable progression toward ever greater liberty and enlightenment, culminating in modern forms of liberal democracy.[126]

Cassirer had published a book on the Enlightenment in 1932, and in *The Myth of the State*, he begins, "In the development of political thought the eighteenth century, the period of the Enlightenment, proved to be one of the most fertile ages. Never before had the philosophy of politics played such an important and decisive role" (176). However, no thorough analysis of that role emerges. Most of the chapter is devoted to its German Romantic critics, as Cassirer strives to disassociate early German Romanticism and German nationalism.

---

124. Morgenthau, "*Myth of the State*," 142.

125. See Herbert Butterfield, *The Whig Interpretation of History*.

126. A typology of the Age of Enlightenment can be found in Avihu Zakai, "The Age of Enlightenment," in *The Cambridge Companion to Jonathan Edwards*, ed. Stephen Stein (New York: Cambridge University Press, 2006), 80–99.

Believing that the "the Enlightenment did not develop a new political philosophy," Cassirer argued that its thinkers expressed "much more concern about political *life* than political *doctrine.*" They drew on the new doctrines of Locke, Grotius, and Pufendorf "and never had the intention of being original" (176–77, emphasis original). The epitome of Enlightenment political thought was Jefferson's Declaration of Independence and the French Declaration of the Rights of Man and the Citizen. The bulk of the chapter addresses the Romantic movement's criticism of the Enlightenment's universal rationalist and humanist ideas.

Based on Stoic ideas, Enlightenment philosophy emphasizing natural rights and human equality was rejected at the beginning of the nineteenth century by "the critics of pure reason." Cassirer lamented, "How was it that all these achievements were suddenly called into question—that the nineteenth century began with attacking and openly defying all the philosophical and political ideals of the former generation?" (179). Among the most vehement adversaries were the "German romanticists who began the fighting and were the first heralds in the combat against the philosophy of the Enlightenment." The struggle was based, first, on "the new interest in history" and, second, on "the new conception and valuation of myth." On the one hand, all the Romantic writers held that "the period of the Enlightenment was an entirely unhistorical age" (180). Cassirer totally rejected this view, claiming that Enlightenment philosophers were "the first to introduce a new scientific method into the study of history" (180–81).[127] On the other hand, "the romantics love the past for the past's sake. To them the past is not only a fact but also one of the highest ideals." Such an "idealization and spiritualization of the past is one of the most distinctive characteristics of romantic thought." In other words, everything "becomes understandable, justifiable, legitimated as soon as we can trace it back to its origin" (181). In contrast to the Enlightenment belief that reason should "govern our thought, morality to conduct our feelings, and natural right," German Romanticism declared that "history," not reason, "was the source, the very origins of right. There is no authority above history." The philosophy of natural rights was replaced by "the Historic Right School" of German Romanticism (182).

Closely associated with this profound change from natural to historical rights was a transformation in the "metaphysical conception and value of myth" (182). For the Enlightenment, "myth had been a barbarous thing, a strange and uncouth mass of confused ideas and gross superstitions, a mere monstrosity." It believed that between "myth and philosophy there

---

127. On the Enlightenment science of history, see Zakai, "Age of Enlightenment."

could be no point of contact. Myth ends where philosophy begins—as darkness gives way to the rising sun" (182–83).[128] "[A]s soon as we pass to the romantic philosophers," however, "myth becomes not only a subject of the highest intellectual interest but also a subject of awe and veneration. It is regarded as the mainspring of human culture. Art, history, and poetry originated in myth" (183). At this historical juncture, Friedrich Wilhelm Joseph Schelling (1775–1854) gave "myth its right and legitimate place in human civilization." In his works, we find for the first time "a *philosophy of mythology* side by side with his philosophy of nature, history, and art." For Cassirer, Schelling's views signaled "a new step in the general history of ideas" because they "lead later to the rehabilitation and glorification of myth that we find in modern politics" (183, emphasis original). If Machiavelli paved the way to the modern secular state, German Romanticism legitimated the myths that based it on irrationalism and gave it power that allowed "no private sphere, independent of political life" (284).

German Romanticism signaled another decisive turning point in the history of political thought: it scorned Enlightenment universalism for *völkisch* particularism and nationalism, reason for myth. However, Cassirer made clear that to view "romanticism" as "the first and the most prolific source of the myth of the twentieth century" would be a mistake, nor did it invent "the concept of the 'totalitarian state'" (183–84).[129] We tend to forget, he argued, that the "'totalitarian' view of the romantic writers" was "*a cultural not a political view*." They "never meant to politicize but to 'poeticize' the world" (184, emphasis original). Likewise, early Romantic nationalism differed radically from that of Nazism: "To Herder every nation was only an individual voice in a universal, all-embracing harmony," and Goethe "was the first to use the term World Literature (Welt-Literatur)."[130]

---

128. Compare Jürgen Habermas, "The Entwinement of Myth and Enlightenment: Max Horkheimer and Theodor Adorno," 107, where he claimed that in "the tradition of the Enlightenment, enlightened thinking has been understood as an opposition and counterforce to myth."

129. See, for example, Peter Viereck, *Metapolitics: From Wagner and the German Romantics to Hitler*, and the important exchange between Arthur Lovejoy and Leo Spitzer: Arthur Lovejoy, "The Meaning of Romanticism for the Historian of Ideas," *Journal of the History of Ideas* 2 (June 1941): 257–78; Leo Spitzer, "*Geistesgeschichie* vs. History of Ideas as Applied to Hitlerism," *Journal of the History of Ideas* 5 (April 1944): 191–203; and Arthur Lovejoy, "Reply to Professor Spitzer," *Journal of the History of Ideas* 5 (April 1944): 204–19.

130. On Johann Wolfgang von Goethe's concept of *Weltliteratur*, see Auerbach, "Philology and *Weltliteratur*" (1952), *Centennial Review* 13 (Winter 1969): 1–17.

They all hoped not only for a unified Germany, "but also for a unified Europe." Hence, their nationalism was the "product of love" not "hatred" as in Nazism. The early German Romanticists, "even in their extreme nationalism," would "not disavow or renounce their universal ideals of human culture" (185–86).

Silent Echo

The book's third and last section, "The Myth of the Twentieth Century," clearly references Alfred Rosenberg's *Der Mythus des 20. Jahrhunderts* (*The Myth of the Twentieth Century*, 1930). Thomas Mann called Rosenberg "the preceptor of Hitler."[131] He was one of the principal ideologues of the Nazi Party and editor of its newspaper *Völkischer Beobachter* (*Populist Observer*), which for twenty-five years was its official public face. His racist interpretation of history was greatly influenced by Houston Stewart Chamberlain's bestselling and influential *Foundations of the Nineteenth Century* (*Die Grundlagen des neunzehnten Jahrhunderts*, 1899), in which the English son-in-law of the composer Richard Wagner and author of books on political philosophy and natural science advanced various racist and especially *völkisch* anti-Semitic theories; to wit, the Aryan race is superior to others; Teutonic peoples are the positive force in European civilization, and the Jews are a negative force.

Closely following Chamberlain, Rosenberg's *Myth of the Twentieth Century* develops a racial interpretation of history, concentrating on the Semitic influences that have corrupted modern culture, produced degenerate art, and degraded morality and society. In contrast, Aryan culture is defined by innate moral sensibility and an energetic will to power. He propounds that the higher race must rule the lower and never interbreed lest it destroy its divine physical and spiritual inheritance. This "organic" metaphor of race and state supports the claim that the Nazis must purify the race by cutting out non-Aryan elements in the same ruthless and uncompromising way a surgeon would cut a cancer from a diseased body. Rosenberg placed a quote from Meister Eckhart (ca. 1260–1328), the famous German theologian, philosopher, and mystic, on the first page: "The address is only for those who have already found its message in their own lives, or at least long for it in their hearts."[132]

---

131. *Thomas Mann's Addresses Delivered at the Library of Congress*, Don Heinrich Tolzmann, ed. (Peter Lang Publishing; 2nd ed. edition (January 1, 2003), 16–17.
132. Rosenberg, *Myth of the Twentieth Century*, 3.

The book attributes German defeat in World War I to the demonic powers of Norse mythology. Elsewhere, he argued more specifically that the victories of the Allied Powers were evidence of

> an age when the Fenris Wolf [fame-wolf] broke his chains, when Hel [the giant goddess who rules over the underworld where the dead dwell] moved over the earth and the Midgardschlange [a giant snake] stirred the oceans of the world. Millions upon millions were ready to sacrifice themselves to attain but one result embodied in the phrase: for the honour and freedom of the Volk. The world inferno continued to the end; nonetheless, sacrifices were demanded and made by all. All that was revealed, however, was that behind the armies daemonic powers had triumphed over divine ones. Unrestrained, they raged throughout the world, stirring up new unrest, new flames, new destruction.[133]

Strangely enough, Rosenberg is not mentioned in *The Myth of the State*, and Chamberlain only once. We know that Cassirer read Rosenberg, since in his lecture at Princeton on January 18, 1945, he compared this "notorious book of Alfred Rosenberg" to Oswald Spengler's *The Decline of the West* (1918).[134] Listen to Rosenberg:

> Today, a new belief is arising: the *Mythus* of the blood; the belief that the godly essence of man itself is to be defended through the blood; that belief which embodied the clearest knowledge that the Nordic race represents that *Mysterium* which has overthrown and replaced the old sacraments.[135]

The influence of this "Nazi manifesto" was deemed second only to Hitler's *Mein Kampf*. Rosenberg goes on: "History and the task of the future no longer signify the struggle of class against class . . . but the settlement between *blood and blood, race and race*, people and people. And that means

---

133. *Der Mythos des 20. Jahrhunderts* (Newport Beach, CA: Noontide Press, 1982). The quote is from *Race and Race History and Other Essays by Alfred Rosenberg*, ed. R. Pois (London: Jonathan Cape, 1970), 96–97.

134. See Cassirer's lecture at Princeton, January 18, 1945, "The Technique of Our Modern Political Myths," in Verene, *Symbol, Myth, and Culture*, 262.

135. See Pois, *Race and Race History*, 96–97.

the struggle of spiritual values against each other." He argued, therefore, "Humanity . . . divorced from the bond of blood" is "no longer absolute value for us."[136] Thomas Mann strongly denounced Rosenberg's use and abuse of the concept of myth, claiming: "the word 'myth' has a bad reputation nowadays—we have only to think of the title of the book, which the 'philosopher' of German fascism, Rosenberg, the preceptor of Hitler, has given to his vicious textbook: 'The Myth of the 20th Century.'"[137] Dripping with contempt, Mann and perhaps also Cassirer will not lower themselves to repeat words that far too many read and repeated.

Thomas Carlyle and "Hero Worship"

The first sections of part 3 are devoted to three writers who directly contributed to the myth of the twentieth-century state. Thomas Carlyle (1795–1881) and Joseph Arthur Comte de Gobineau (1816–1882) led the way "from hero worship to race worship" (224) and the "Totalitarian State" (231). Hegel wrought the most damage: "All our modern political ideologies show us the strength, the durability and permanence of the principles that were first introduced and defended in Hegel's philosophy of right and his philosophy of history" (248). The final section deals with the "Techniques of the Modern Political Myths."

Cassirer begins with a long discussion of the Scottish philosopher, satirist, essayist, and historian Thomas Carlyle and *On Heroes, Hero Worship and the Heroic in History* (1841), a collection of six lectures he delivered in May 1840. Cassirer argues that a hundred years later, Carlyle's ideas "had been turned into the most efficient weapons in the political struggle" marking the rise of fascism, Nazism, and totalitarianism (190). Readers will certainly recognize that this section is one of the best in the book, showing Cassirer's formidable erudition and establishing the close connection between Carlyle and Goethe with regard to nature and art, and Carlyle and Fichte, who provided Carlyle "with a whole *metaphysics* of hero worship" (213, emphasis original). Cassirer entitles this section

---

136. Rosenberg, *Myth*, xlv, 3, emphasis original. On Rosenberg, see Alfred Rosenberg, *Memoirs of Alfred Rosenberg*, trans. E. Posselt (Chicago: Ziff-Davis, 1949); Fritz Nova, *Alfred Rosenberg: Nazi Theorist of the Holocaust* (New York: Hippocrene Books, 1986); and Georg Lukács, *The Destruction of Reason* (Atlantic Highlands, NJ: Humanities Press, 1981 [1962]), 714–64.

137. Mann, "Theme of the Joseph Novels," 16–17.

"The Preparation: Carlyle," meaning that Carlyle's concept of hero worship prepared the ground for the twentieth-century myth of the state (189), yet he admits at the end of his book, not without irony, that Carlyle's was "a romantic conception of heroism—far different from that of all our modern political 'realists'" (281).

Carlyle's six lectures deal with the hero as divinity: Odin in Norse and Scandinavian mythology; the hero as prophet: Muhammad and Islam; the hero as poet: Dante and Shakespeare; the hero as priest: Luther and John Knox; the hero as writer: Samuel Johnson, Rousseau, and Robert Burns; and, finally, the hero as king: Oliver Cromwell, Napoleon, and modern revolutionaries. Faithful to his overall approach of reading political history as a series of decisive turning points that led to the problems and agonies of his own time, Cassirer argues that Carlyle preached "a new political evangelism," though "nobody could have foreseen" that these lectures were "pregnant with great political consequence," and the ideas expressed in them "contained a dangerous explosive" (189). Only fascism and Nazism fully revealed the frightening ramifications of Carlyle's views: "A hundred years later these ideas had been turned into the most efficient weapons in the political struggle" (190). At the same time, Carlyle's political theory was, at bottom, "nothing short of disguised and transformed Calvinism. True spontaneity is reserved to the few elect. As to the others, the mass of the reprobates, they have to submit under the will of these elect, the born rulers" (193).

Carlyle was a sworn enemy of "the political ideals of the eighteenth century: the ideals of liberty, equality and fraternity." Seeing no other "escape from the subversive influence of these ideals," the "Scotch Puritan" found it necessary to "return to hero worship" (243, 224), striving to locate "Hero-worship and the Heroic in human affairs."[138] As a consequence, he developed the nineteenth century's "Great Man theory," according to which history can be largely explained by the impact of "great men," or heroes, who, due to their personal charisma, intelligence, wisdom, or political skill, gained decisive power. He believed that "Universal History, the history of what man has accomplished in this world, is at the bottom the History of Great Men, Men who have worked here." They were "the leaders of men," the "modelers, patterns, and in a wide sense creators, of whatsoever the general mass of men contrived to do or attain." Consequently, "all things that we see standing accomplished in the world are properly the outer

---

138. Thomas Carlyle, *On Heroes, Hero-Worship and the Heroic in History* (London: Chapman and Hall, 1893), 1.

material result, the practical realization and embodiment, of Thought that dwelt in the Great Men sent into the world." For him, "the soul of the whole world's history, it may justly be considered, was the history of these" heroes.[139]

Great Men are "a profitable company" because we cannot look upon one

> without gaining something by him. He is the living light-fountain, which is good and pleasant to be near. The light which enlightens, which has enlightened the darkness of the world; and this not as kindled lamp only, but rather as a natural luminary shining by the gift of Heaven; a flowing light-fountain [of] native original insight, of manhood and heroic nobleness;—in whose radiance all souls feel that it is well with them.[140]

Looking at the six heroes whom Carlyle chose, "we should get some glimpses into the very marrow of the world's history." Their elevation is the epitome of the historical process: "the divine relation" that "in all times unites a Great Man to other men."[141] In times when the "confused wreck of crumbling and even crashing and tumbling all around us in these revolutionary ages, will get down so far," in these periods of trial and tribulation, he

> is an eternal corner-stone, from which they can begin to build themselves up again. That man, in some sense or other, worships Heroes; that we all of us reverence and must reverence Great Men: this is, to me, the living rock amid rushing-down whatsoever—the one fixed point in modern revolutionary history, otherwise as if bottomless and shoreless.[142]

Carlyle argued that "he to whose will our wills are to be subordinated, and loyally surrender themselves, and find their welfare in doing so, may be reckoned the most important of Great Men." He is the true "King, or Able-man, and he *has* a divine right over me." Further,

---

139. Ibid., 1–2.
140. Ibid., 2.
141. Ibid., 2.
142. Ibid., 14.

[t]hat we knew in some tolerable measure how to find him, and that all men were ready to acknowledge his divine right when found: this is precisely the healing which a sick world is everywhere, in these ages, seeking after![143]

Therefore, heroes and great men are sent to us by divine providence, and we cannot help but recognize and adore them: the "certainty of Heroes being sent to us: our faculty, our necessity, to reverence Heroes when sent: it shines like a polestar through smoke-clouds, and all manners down-rushing and conflagration." What is the great man's mission? "His mission is order; every man's is. He is here to make what was disorderly, chaotic, into a thing ruled, regular. He is the missionary of Order. Is not all work of man in this world *a making of Order?*"[144]

Nonetheless, the appearance of every new great man transforms the course of history to begin a new order. Cassirer paraphrases:

> . . . with every religious, philosophical, literary, political genius, there begins a new chapter in human history. The whole character of the religious world was completely changed, for example, by the appearance of Mahomet or Luther; the political worlds and the world of poetry were revolutionized by Cromwell or by Dante and Shakespeare. Every new hero is a new incarnation of one and the same great invisible power of the 'Divine Idea.' (230)

Perhaps "[i]n the Victorian era nobody could have divined the role that Carlyle's theory was to play in the twentieth century," and Cassirer admitted that blaming Carlyle for "the March of Fascism" (190) was unfair. His critique of "the Scotch Puritan" (224) may equally apply to him: "Carlyle's conception of history and politics always depends on his own personal history; it is much more biographical than systematic or methodical . . . he tried much more to persuade than to convince" (191, 197).

However, instead of the rationalist politics of Plato and the Stoics, based on ethics and justice; instead of the medieval view that stipulated *Rex nihil potest nisi quod jure potest*—the king can do nothing but what the law allows (104)—and not *Princeps legibus solutes* (the sovereign is not bound by the laws, nor is exempt from the laws; restrictions imposed

---

143. Ibid., 181, 184; emphasis original.
144. Ibid., 186–88, emphasis original.

by the laws don't apply to him), Carlyle's concept of hero worship opened the door to irrationality and mysticism in politics, especially with regard to political leaders. Hero worship led to blind obedience to the *Führer*, as in the Nazi's most famous slogan, *Ein Volk, ein Reich, ein Führer*—One People, One Empire, One Leader, which "left an indelible mark on the minds of most Germans who lived through the Nazi years. It appeared on countless posters and in publications; it was heard constantly in radio broadcasts and speeches."[145] Nazi Germany cultivated the *Führerprinzip* (leader principle), and Hitler was aggrandized as *der Führer*. Like much of the early symbolism of Nazi Germany, it was modeled after Italian fascism, where Benito Mussolini's chosen epithet was *il Duce*, or *Dux*, Latin for "the leader." On June 23, 1941, Hitler declared himself the Germanic Führer (*germanischer Führer*) to emphasize his professed leadership of what the Nazis described as the "Nordic-German master race," which included the Norwegians, Danes, Swedes, and Dutch, and was a transparent pretext to submerge their nations into the Third Reich in an "orderly" fashion.

Gobineau—"Race Worship" and the "Totalitarian Race"

Along with Carlyle's hero worship, another nineteenth-century political theory greatly contributed to the modern myth of the state: Joseph Arthur Count de Gobineau's theory of the "Totalitarian Race" (231) or "Race Worship," based on "the new god of race" and "race instinct" (224, 235, 237). In the political struggles of the early twentieth century, Cassirer argued, "hero worship and race worship have been in such a close alliance that, in all their interest and tendencies, they seemed to be almost one and the same thing"; by this alliance, "the political myths evolved into their present form and strength" (224). He called them "a new step, and a step of the greatest consequences, when hero worship lost its original meaning and was blended with a race worship and when both of them became integral parts of the same political program," or National Socialism. The modern myth of the state is a unique combination of a hero worship and a race worship "used for a common end" (224). Later, in the chapter on Hegel, Cassirer will add a third essential ingredient to the toxic brew—state worship.

Gobineau was a French aristocrat, novelist, and man of letters, who became famous for developing the theory of the Aryan master race in *An*

---

145. Joseph W. Bendersky, *A Concise History of Nazi Germany* (Lanham: Rowman & Littlefield Publishers, 2013 [2007]), 105–06.

Essay on the Inequality of the Human Races (1853–1855).[146] He is credited as the father of modern racial demography, producing very early examples of scientific racism. According to Cassirer, Gobineau "looked upon himself as a second Copernicus, the Copernicus of the historical world," and "the new god of race" as the "true center of this world" (225). Many cannot grasp "Hegel's *Phenomenology of the Spirit*, or his *Philosophy of History*," Cassirer wryly explained, but "anybody understands" Gobineau's language of "race and blood" (231).

Gobineau believed that race creates culture; he distinguished three races, black, white, and yellow, as natural barriers that race-mixing breaks, leading to chaos. "The negroid is the lowest, and stands at the foot of the ladder," he claimed.[147] "The yellow races" are indeed "superior to the black," but no "civilized society could be created by them."[148] Cassirer notes that Gobineau "could not even admit that the Negroes or the members of the yellow race belong to the same human family as the white races. What we find in those people is barbarism in its utter ugliness and egoism in its greatest ferocity" (233). Gobineau claimed that "according to an inexorable natural law, the inferior races are forever condemned 'to crawl before the feet of their masters'" (242); until the "mixture of blood," the "white race originally possessed the monopoly of beauty, intelligence, and strength."[149] It is an impenetrable argument since any flaw in any white person can be ascribed to race-mixing, and it is so stone-blind to non-Western history.

> Such is the lesson of history. It shows us that all civilizations derive from the white race, that none can exist without its help, and that a society is great and brilliant only so far as it preserves the blood of the noble group that created it, provided that this group itself belongs to the most illustrious branches of our species.[150]

---

146. Arthur de Gobineau, *The Inequality of the Human Races* (New York: Howard Fertig, 1967); Arthur de Gobineau, *The Moral and Intellectual Diversity of Races* (New York: Garland, 1984); and Michael D. Biddiss, ed., *Gobineau: Selected Political Writings* (London: Jonathan Cape, 1970). For an analysis of his theory of race, see Eric Voegelin, *Race and State*, trans. R. Hein (Baton Rouge: Louisiana State University Press, 1997 [1933]), esp. 160–76.

147. Gobineau, *Inequality*, 205.

148. Ibid., 206–07.

149. Ibid., 209–10.

150. Ibid., 210.

Gobineau accorded the white race superiority above all other races, yet "within this type," he gives "superiority" to "the Aryan family."[151] For him, Cassirer wrote, Aryans were "demigods" (234). He believed that they sprang from an ancient Indo-European culture and that, as Germans, were all that was positive. He attributed much of the economic turmoil in France to the pollution of the white race, but with the spread of British and American civilization and the growth of Germany, he began to believe that the white race could be saved.

Writing during the time of "great events—the bloody wars, the revolutions, and the breaking up of laws" in Europe during the first half of the nineteenth century, Gobineau attempted "to trace the more remote reasons for those social evils" and "the immediate causes of the plagues that are supposed to chasten" the "States of Europe," striving ultimately to find the clue to "obscure paths of philosophy and history."[152] Eventually, he stumbled upon an idea that would explain the whole course of human history and the historical process itself: "the racial question overshadows all other problems in history," he argued, and "it holds the key to them all." In other words, "the inequality of the races from whose fusion a people is formed is enough to explain the whole course" of history as well as "its destiny." This "colossal truth,"[153] which for Gobineau signaled nothing less than a great epistemological revolution comparable to the Copernican Revolution in astronomy, is the only clue to the progress of history. Recognizing that "both strong and weak races exist," he naturally preferred "to examine the former, to analyze their qualities, and especially to follow them back to their origins." Having discovered an Archimedean point ("*Punctum Archimedis*"), he pronounced that

> everything great, noble, and fruitful in the works of man on this earth, in science, art, and civilization, derives from a single starting-point, is the development of a single germ and the result of a single thought; it belongs to one family alone, the different branches of which have reigned in all the civilized countries of the universe.[154]

According to Cassirer's chronology of the rise and triumph of the modern political myth of the state, Gobineau forged the alliance between

---

151. Ibid., 205.
152. Ibid., xi.
153. Ibid., xiv.
154. Ibid., xiv–xv.

Carlyle's hero worship and race worship and between British and French intellectuals that proved fatal in the hands of fascists and Nazis: "It was by this alliance that the political myths evolved into their present form and strength" (224). Basically, Gobineau's racist view of history "was fatalistic. History follows a definite and inexorable law. We cannot hope to change the course of events; all we can do is to understand and accept it." In other words, the "destiny of the human race is predetermined from the very beginning." Race is "the principal point, the essential factor in human history"; without understanding it, "history remains a sealed book." With Gobineau, "the seal is broken and the mystery of human life and human civilization is revealed"; the self-styled "second Copernicus, the Copernicus of the historical world," had found "the true center" (225). Like Newton, who discovered "a fundamental fact of the physical world," the "law of gravitation," that enabled him to explain the "whole material universe," Gobineau had found race as "the common center toward which all" historical changes and transformations "gravitate" (231).

Based on the view that "race is the *only* master and ruler of the historical world," Gobineau framed his theory of the "Totalitarian Race." By doing so, he prepared "the ideology of the totalitarian state. It was the totalitarianism of race that marked the road to the later conceptions of the totalitarian state" in the first half of the twentieth century. Constantly viewing the history of political thought in the context "of our present problem" of Nazism and fascism, Cassirer argued that Gobineau's theory of race is "*an attempt to destroy all other values*," namely, human equality and dignity (231–32, emphasis original). In contrast to Stoic and Enlightenment thought, the Frenchman believed that to "seek universal ethical standards and values is absurd" (236). For him, the "god of race" was "a jealous god. He does not allow other gods to be adored beside himself. Race is everything; all other forces are nothing." They only acquire power from the "superior and sovereign" power of race: "the omnipotent race. This fact appears in all forms of cultural life, in religion, in morality, in philosophy and art, in the nation and in the state" (232).

Following "the new god of race," Gobineau emphasized "the instinct of the race," which is "highly superior to all our philosophical ideals and metaphysical systems." In his system, as reported by Cassirer, the ancient, glorious humanist concept of virtue is replaced by blood: "a man is not honorable by virtue of individual qualities but by the inheritance of his race"; he "is great, noble, virtuous not by his actions but by his blood. The only test that our personal work has to stand is the test of our ancestors. It is his birth certificate that gives to a man the certainty of his moral value. Virtue is not a thing to be acquired" (235–36).

Here is clear evidence of Gobineau's transformation of Carlyle's hero worship to race worship. Denying all "'humanitarian' ideals," Gobineau fashioned a "new religion" in which "the worship of the race, is firmly established." The discovery of "the excellence and the incomparable Aryan race" was for him a "cosmic moment—a spectacle not only for men, but for the gods and heavens." In Gobineau's exalted view, the "Aryan family" is "the noblest, the most intelligent and most energetic race" and "the real actor in the great historical drama." Race worship became "the highest form of worship, the worship of the highest god." As Cassirer notes, his "work begins with a sort of intoxication, an intoxication of race worship and self worship" (242, 244–45). Founded on "complete negativism and nihilism," it sacrificed all human values "to the new god, to the Moloch of the race" (246–47).

Hegel—"State Worship" as a "New Type of Absolutism"

Cassirer's politicization of the history of political thought as the road to Nazism reaches its height in his discussion of Hegel. Many other prominent German-speaking intellectual exiles saw Hegel the same way. Karl Popper, for example, viewed Plato, Hegel, and Marx as harbingers of modern fascism and claimed that he wrote *The Open Society and Its Enemies* (1945) and *The Poverty of Historicism* (1957) as his "war effort" and "as a defence of freedom against the totalitarianism and authoritarian ideas, and as a warning against the dangers of historicist superstitions," particularly Hegel's.[155] In *The Open Society*, he wrote that given the "responsibility of Hegel and the Hegelians for much of what happened in Germany," he felt obliged, "as a philosopher," to expose their politically perilous "pseudo-philosophy." According to Popper, Hegel's historicism "encouraged" and "contributed to" totalitarian philosophizing and political practice, and almost "all the more important ideas of modern totalitarianism are directly inherited from Hegel." He advocated "harsh words" for counterfeit liberals like Hegel as well as antiliberals like Plato and Marx if our "civilization is to survive."[156] These "harsh words" must be said in "memory of the countless" victims

---

155. Karl Popper, *Unended Quest* (London and New York: Routledge, 2002 [1992]), 131.

156. Popper, *Open Society*, 584–87; 315; xxxiii; and Weinstein and Zakai, *Jewish Exiles*.

of belief in the "Inexorable Laws of Historical Destiny."[157] Cassirer too blamed Hegel's glorification of the state and overt historicism for many of the problems of his time. In contrast, Auerbach was greatly influenced by Hegel's idealist philosophy and praised his aestheticism and historicism.

Although Cassirer blamed Machiavelli for separating politics from morality, Hegel's influence on political thought was much more radical and, hence, disastrous:

> No other philosophical system has exerted such a strong and enduring influence upon political life as the metaphysics of Hegel. All the great philosophers before him had propounded theories of the state which had determined the general course of political thought but played only a very modest role in political life. They belonged to the world of 'ideas' or 'ideals,' not to the 'actual' political world. (248)

For previous great philosophers, "the gulf between political thought and life remained insurmountable. Political theories were eagerly discussed; they were attacked and defended, proven and refuted; but all this had little, if any, effect upon the struggle of political life" (248). In contrast, Hegelian metaphysics took hold in the political arena and influenced formidable political powers.

> Hegelianism has had a rebirth not in the field of logical or metaphysical thought, but in the field of political thought. . . . All our modern political ideologies show us the strength, the durability and permanence of the principles that were first introduced and defended in Hegel's philosophy of right and his philosophy of history.

Eventually, this victory proved "Pyrrhic," and it "has had to pay the penalty for its triumph" (248).

> Bolshevism, Fascism and National Socialism have disintegrated and cut into pieces the Hegelian system. They are incessantly

---

157. Popper, *Poverty of Historicism*, dedication. See Zakai and Weinstein, *Exile and Interpretation*; Weinstein and Zakai, "Exile and Interpretation: Popper's Re-Invention of the History of European Political Thought," 185–209; and Weinstein and Zakai, "Exile and Interpretation," at http://college.wfu.edu/politics/exileandinterpretation/.

quarrelling with each other about the remnant of the booty. *And this is no longer a mere theoretical dispute. It has tremendous political effects.* (249, emphasis added)

Its use and abuse by various modern political forces had "become *a mortal combat*" (249, emphasis added).

With Hegel, the politicization of philosophy or, conversely, the philosophizing of politics, peaked. For example, Hajo Holborn argued that "the struggle of the Russians and the invading Germans in 1943" was "a conflict between the Left and Right wings of Hegel's school." The Battle of Stalingrad (1942–1943) and the Battle of Kursk (1943) called for a radical interpretation of Hegelian philosophy. Holborn's view, remarks Cassirer, was not exaggerated but "contains a nucleus of truth." It explained why, with Hegel, "we cannot proceed in the same way as in the case of other thinkers" (249).

In his *Philosophy of Right* (1821), Hegel famously argued, "*What is rational is actual and what is actual is rational*" (*Was vernünftig ist, das ist wirklich; und was wirklich ist, das is vernünftig*).[158] For many, wrote Cassirer, this saying signaled that "the Hegelian system" is "the firmest stronghold of political reaction"; hence, "*Hegel was the most dangerous enemy of all democratic ideals*" (250–51, emphasis added). Therefore, he argued, we must understand how and why Hegelian philosophy became "one of the greatest *revolutionary* forces in modern political thought"; the philosopher of "the Prussian State became the teacher of Marx and Lenin—the champion of 'dialectic Marxism'" (251, emphasis original); and the "Hegelian system" became "one of the explosive forces in the development of political thought during the nineteenth century" (253). To solve these puzzles, Cassirer emphasized the great and unbridgeable difference between Plato and Hegel; for the Greek thinker, "the principles of a true political life" are based, not upon "right opinion" (*doxa*), but rather upon "knowledge" (*epistēmē*), "a new form of rationality and moral consciousness." In contrast to this humanist ideal, Hegel wrote in his *Phenomenology of Spirit* (1807), "the realization of self-conscious reason . . . finds its actual fulfilment in the life of a nation" (251–52).

Hegel's political philosophy was inextricable from his philosophy of history: "The true life of the Idea, of the Divine, begins in history." In contrast to Spinoza's formula in his *Ethics* (1677), *Deus sive nature* (God

---

158. Hegel, *Outlines of the Philosophy of Right*, 14, emphasis original. See also Terry Pinkard, *Hegel: A Biography* (Cambridge: Cambridge University Press, 2001), 228.

or nature: "That eternal and infinite being we call God, or Nature, acts from the same necessity from which he exists"), Hegel's formula is "*Deus sive historia*." His radicalism is revealed in the fact that, for him, "history is no mere appearance of God, but his reality: God not only 'has' history, he *is* history" (262, emphasis original).

The Hegelian conception of the state follows directly: "*To Hegel the state is not only a part, a special province, but the essence, the very core of historical life. It is the alpha and omega*" (263, emphasis added). As Hegel wrote in his *Philosophy of History* (1831), "it is the State which first presents subject-matter that is not only *adapted* to the prose of history, but involves the production of such history in the very progress of its own being" (263, emphasis original). Reality can only be defined in terms of the history of the state. If "the state is the prerequisite of history, it follows that *we have to see in the state the supreme and most perfect reality*" (263, emphasis added). Here lay the unique radicalism in Hegel's political thought; no political theory before him, argued Cassirer, "ever proposed" that "the state is not only the representative but the very incarnation of the 'spirit of the world.'" In contrast to Saint Augustine, who regarded the *civitas terrena* as "a distortion and disfiguration of the *civitas divina*," Hegel sees in "the *civitas terrena* the 'Divine Idea as it exists on earth.'" Hegelian worship of the state, according to Cassirer, "is an entirely new type of absolutism" (263) with tremendous implications for the rise of the myth of the state and, concomitantly, the totalitarian regimes of the twentieth century.

Hegel's new type of absolutism was based on his denunciation of the "Natural Right theories of the state," according to which "the state originates in a contract" stipulating that it is "bound to certain conditions, to legal or moral obligations" (263). Instead, for Hegel, the "State is the self-certain absolute mind which acknowledges not abstract rules of good and bad, shameful and mean, craft and deception" (264). Duplicating Machiavelli's separation of ethics and politics, he radically abolished all previous ethical standards: "there is no longer any moral obligation for the state. Morality holds for the individual will, not for the universal will of the state." As Hegel wrote in *Philosophy of Right*, "The State is the spirit that dwells in the world and realizes itself in the world through *consciousness*. . . . It is the course of God through the world that constituted the State." The revolutionary implications of this theory are clear enough; the state is not the creation of free, autonomous people but a "Divine Idea" that "exists on earth" (265, emphasis original).

The absolutist dimension of the state is strengthened in Hegel's thought because for him, "the content of the particular will of the state is its welfare," and "this particularistic welfare is the highest law in the relation of one state to another." Humanitarian ideals have no place; he rejected the "universal love of mankind" as an "insipid invention" (266). Like Machiavelli, who argued that the political arena is based on a "struggle for power" and should be held "by the most ruthless and radical means" (148), Hegel sees only "the truth that lies in power." These words, wrote Cassirer, "*contain the clearest and most ruthless program of fascism that has ever been propounded by any political or philosophic writer*" (267, emphasis added).

The same exemption from all moral demands holds for political leaders, or "the real makers of history." Hence, in "Hegel's system *the worship of the state is combined with hero worship*." Since greatness means power, not virtue, in Hegel's thought, the "greatness of a hero has nothing to do with his so-called 'virtue'" (267, emphasis added). Napoleon is a clear example of this contention. After the Battle of Jena, in which he defeated the Prussian army, Napoleon visited the city, where Hegel saw him on Monday, October 13, 1806:

> I saw the Emperor—this world-soul—riding out of the city on reconnaissance. It is indeed a wonderful sensation to see such an individual, who, concentrated here at a single point, astride a horse, reaches out over the world and masters it . . . this extraordinary man, whom it is impossible not to admire.[159]

Facing Napoleon, the man who spread the ideas of the French Revolution throughout Europe, Hegel declared, "Gentlemen! We find ourselves in an important epoch, in a fermentation, in which Spirit has made a leap forward, has gone beyond its previous concrete form and acquired a new one."[160] A year later, 1807, he wrote in the same vein: "[I]t is not hard to see that ours is a birth-time and a period of transition to a new era. Spirit has broken with the world it has hitherto inhabited and imagined,

---

159. See G. W. F. Hegel, *Hegel: The Letters*, at https://www.marxists.org/reference/archive/hegel/works/letters/1806-10-13.htm.

160. Hegel, *Lectures at Jena* (1806), quoted by Alexander Kojève, *Introduction to the Reading of Hegel* (New York: Basic Books, 1969 [1947]), vi.

and is of a mind to submerge it in the past, and in the labour of its own transformation."[161]

Again, like Machiavelli, Hegel believed that " 'virtue' means strength; and there is no stronger and more powerful motive in human life than the great passions" (268). He was not afraid of egoism; in fact, "he was the first philosophic thinker who not only regarded it as unavoidable evil but elevated it to the rank of an 'ideal' principle," thus introducing "that concept of *sacro egoism* which after him has played such a decisive and disastrous role in modern political life." Hegel regarded individuals "as marionettes in the great puppet show of universal history"; according to him, "the author and the dramaturge of the historical drama is the 'Idea': the individuals are nothing but the 'agents of the world-spirit' " (269).

Seeing political history as defined by decisive turning points, Cassirer argued that "Hegel's political theory is a watershed between two great streams of thought. It marks the turning point between two ages, two cultures, two ideologies. It stands on the border line between the eighteenth and nineteenth centuries," or between "the spirit of the Enlightenment and the new spirit of the nineteenth century." While Enlightenment thinkers were "not afraid to think *against* their own time" and used philosophy to combat the *ancien régime*, Hegel "could no longer assign this role to philosophy. He had become the philosopher of *history*. History can be described and expressed but it cannot be created or transformed by philosophic thought" (269).

Here, Cassirer returns to the theme of the philosophers' betrayal in his inaugural speech at the University of Gothenburg (1935), where he quoted Schweitzer, "in the hour of peril the watchman slept, who should have kept watch over us. So it happened that we did not struggle for our culture."[162] He writes that the Hegelian system is "the firmest stronghold

---

161. G. W. F. Hegel, *Phenomenology of Spirit*, trans. A. V. Miller (Oxford: Clarendon Press, 1977), 6–7. See also "Preface to the first edition" of the *Science of Logic*, trans. and ed. George D. Giovanni (Cambridge: Cambridge University Press, 2010), 6, where he writes about "the youthful pleasure of the new epoch that has blossomed both in the realm of science [philosophy] and in the political realm. . . . [T]his pleasure greeted the dawn of the rejuvenated spirit giddily." Generally speaking, " '*Geist*' refers to some sort of *general consciousness, a single 'mind' common to all men*" (R. C. Solomon, "Hegel's Concept of 'Geist,' " *Review of Metaphysics*, 23 [June 1970]: 642, emphasis original).

162. Cassirer, "Concept of Philosophy," in Verene, *Symbol, Myth, and Culture*, 60–61.

of political reaction" and calls Hegel "*the most dangerous enemy of all democratic ideals*" (251, emphasis added). The philosophers' treachery is related, not only to their silence in the face of the destruction of Western humanist civilization, but also to their previous fierce opposition to the ideals of liberty and democracy, as in Hegel's case. Cassirer will return to this important point in the last chapter, when he denounces Spengler and Heidegger for supporting the German culture of pessimism and fatalism.

One of the main reasons for Cassirer's relentless attack on Hegel was that Hegel had once hailed the French Revolution, writing in his *Philosophy of History* that "the French Revolution resulted from philosophy," the philosophy of the Enlightenment, "and it is not without reason that Philosophy has been called 'Weltweisheit' (world wisdom)" because it is "truth in its living form as exhibited in the affairs of the world" (271). However, with the defeat of Napoleon, when Prussia became the predominant power in Germany, "the soul of the world" shifted to another part of the political body, and Hegel became "the philosopher of the Prussian State." When appointed to his professorship in Berlin in 1818, Hegel declared that the Prussian state is "based on intelligence" (272).

In *Philosophy of History*, Hegel wrote, "Reason is the Sovereign of the World"; hence, "the history of the world . . . presents us with a rational process."[163] However, looking at the great ordeals of the twentieth century, Hegel's philosophy, which "seemed to be the triumph of the rational," actually "unchained the most irrational powers that have ever appeared in man's social and political life." Indeed, no other "philosophical system has done so much for the preparation of fascism and imperialism as Hegel's doctrine of the state—'this divine Idea as it exists on earth'" (273).

Hegel's *Philosophy of History* first expressed the idea that in every epoch of history "there is *one* and only one nation that is the real representation of the world spirit and that this nation has the right to rule all the others" (273, emphasis original). In Hegel's own words:

---

163. G. W. F. Hegel, *Philosophy of History*, trans. J. Sibree (New York: Dover, 1956), 9, emphasis original. Hegel argues that "*nous* [reason], or its deeper determination, *spirit*, is the cause of the world" (*Science of Logic*, 36–37). On this point, he follows Aristotle, who believed that the world is governed by *nous*. The "ancients," wrote Hegel, thought that reason "governs the world" or "exists in the world and [they] mean by it that reason is the soul of the world, residing in it, immanent in it as its own most, innermost nature, its universal" (ibid., 58). Elsewhere: "Reason is Spirit when its certainty of being all reality has been raised to truth, and it is conscious of itself as its own world, and of the world as itself" (*Phenomenology of Spirit*, 263).

> Thus in universal history each nation in turn is for that epoch . . . dominant. Against this absolute right to be the bearer of the present stage of the development of the world-spirit, the spirits of the other nations are absolutely without right. (273–74)

Other nations have absolutely no rights against the chosen nation—self-chosen, in the case of Nazi Germany. Cassirer observes, "Never before had a philosopher of the rank of Hegel spoken in this way"; it was "a new event in the history of political thought, an event pregnant with far-reaching and fearful consequences, when a system of *Ethics* and a philosophy of *Right* defended such ruthless imperialistic nationalism" (274, emphasis original). Like Machiavelli, Hegel "exempted the state from all moral obligations" and "became a great admirer of 'the truth that lies in power'" (274–75). Readers can easily see the tragic implications of his support for an absolute, self-serving state, impermeable to criticism or attack, in the history of the twentieth century. Still, Cassirer stressed that Hegel "could extol and glorify the state, he could even apotheosize it," yet there was a great difference between "his idealization of the power of the state and that sort of idealization that is the characteristic of our modern totalitarian systems" (276).

"The Technique of the Modern Political Myths"

> *The ancient barbarism which has been held down for centuries . . . is waking again with a warlike delight in its own strength. This barbarism is what I call strong Race . . . the eternal warlike in the type of the beast of prey—Man. The only form-giving power is the warlike 'Prussian' spirit; not only in Germany the legions of Caesar march again.*
>
> —Oswald Spengler, *Jahre der Entscheidung*
> (*The Hour of Decision*), 1933

The last chapter is based on a 1945 lecture Cassirer gave in Princeton under the same title. Ultimately, both lecture and chapter reveal the sad lessons of an old, disillusioned man and his agonized history—the defeat of reason and the triumph of the political myths of hero worship, race worship, and state worship—in his time. Myth, once considered the subject of abstract philosophical inquiry or art, became, with Nazi power, real, vital, and threatening, responsible for the murder and immiserating of millions. James Joyce wrote in *Ulysses* (1922), "History . . . is a nightmare from which I am trying to awake." Cassirer could not entertain a metaphor that promised awakening.

Readers cannot avoid envisioning a discouraged, disappointed sage gazing down from his long experience at the terrible devastation of Western humanist civilization by National Socialism. Cassirer was seventy-one when he died in 1945, and his very pessimistic, even fatalistic, views of history are based on his witness to the worst period in all of human history. He had believed that since Plato, logos had overcome myth; his ultimate philosophical goal was to show the separation of myth from philosophy; but in the end, he was forced to recognize that myth had won. To fight it, we must understand it, but, first, it poisons the mind against understanding. The outcome is very bleak. This hard, agonizing lesson informed his life and time. Erich Auerbach felt the same way when he wrote in Istanbul at the end of *Mimesis* about "the decline of our world."[164] As René Wellek, Auerbach's colleague at Yale, noted, after World War II, Auerbach "wrote gloomily about the tomb of Western civilization," and this "gloom intensified in his last year."[165] Auerbach died in 1957.

In the last section, Cassirer reiterated his thesis that "our contemporary political myths" contained "no entirely new feature." All their elements were already well known in Carlyle's "hero worship and Gobineau's thesis of the fundamental moral and intellectual diversity of races." The great and essential difference was that, in the past, discussions on Gobineau and Carlyle's works "remained in a sense merely academic," while in the twentieth century, they were "accommodated to the understanding of a different audience." These ideas were no longer the possession of intellectuals alone but adopted by many. To achieve such popularity, "a fresh instrument was required—not only an instrument of thought but also of action," and a "new technique had to be developed." Referring obliquely to Rosenberg's treatise, he claimed that while "the soil for the Myth of the Twentieth Century had been prepared long before, it could not have borne its fruit without the skillful use of the new technical tool" (277), which removed the cuttings from the hands of intellectuals and put them into the hands of politicians.

---

164. Auerbach, *Mimesis*, 551.

165. René Wellek, *A History of Modern Criticism: 1750–1950*, Vol. 7, *German, Russian, and Eastern European Criticism:1900–1950*, 123.

Cassirer was well aware of the political and economic factors that led to the rise of the myth of the state: the First World War, inflation, and social unrest. In Germany, the problem was most acute: "In times of inflation and unemployment Germany's whole social and economic system was threatened with a complete collapse," forming "the natural soil upon which the political myths could grow up and in which they found ample nourishment" (277–78). Based on his previous overarching thesis about the decline of myth, he claimed that in the past "the mythical organization of society seems to be superseded by a rational organization." Now, he sadly admitted, rational organization of state and society could be maintained only in "quiet and peaceful times" and "relative stability and security." However, this peaceful social and political state should not mislead us because

> [i]n politics we are always living on a *volcanic soil and must be prepared for sudden convulsions and eruptions*. In all critical moments of man's social life, the rational forces that resist the rise of the old mythical conceptions are no longer sure of themselves. In this moment the time of myth has come again. *For myth has not been really vanquished and subjugated. It is always there, lurking in the dark and waiting for its hour of opportunity.* This hour comes as soon as the other binding forces of man's social life, for one reason or another, lose their strength and are no longer able to combat the demonic mythical powers. (280, emphasis added)

If, in the past, Cassirer studied myth as an integral part of the system of symbolic forms, now he regarded it as a real threatening political force capable of eradicating the rationalist and humanist foundation of Western society. An invention of the human mind was transformed into its great adversary.

A clear example of the flight from reason can be seen in the new status accorded to the political leader. In a time of crisis, "the intensity of the collective wish is embodied in the leader." When former social bonds, such as law, justice, and constitution, lose their power and validity, then what remains "is the mystical power of authority of the leader and the leader's will is supreme law" (280). Cassirer's idiosyncratic reading of the political history of his time can be seen in the fact the United States of America also passed through a severe economic and social crisis in the 1930s, but there, in England, and in other places, myth did not replace reason, and no leader was ever deemed above criticism.

Crisis, historical crisis, the crisis of German ideology, led to the rise of "present-day political myths." Surprisingly, Cassirer's explanation is most conventional; namely, that in "desperate situations man will always have recourse to desperate means—and our present-day means have been such desperate means. If reason has failed us, there remains always the *ultima ratio*, the power of the miraculous and mysterious" (279). In the old struggle between myth and reason, myth has gained the upper hand after many centuries of rationality. A unique place "has been reserved for the twentieth century, our own great technical age to develop a new technique of myth." More specifically, in modern times, "myths can be manufactured in the same sense and according to the same methods as any other modern weapon—as machine guns or airplanes." If in 1933, "the political world began to worry somewhat about Germany's rearmament," Cassirer is quick to point out, then "the real armament began with the origin and rise of the political myths" (282). Germany's military armament proceeded from, rather than preceded, the rise of political myths. Professor George H. Sabine argued that when "Professor Cassirer gives an explanation" for the rise of Nazism, it is very disappointing since "it is the one usually given—the disruption of Germany by the war, the destruction of the middle class by inflation," and so forth.[166]

The rise of Nazism and the consequent Nazi Revolution of 1933 signaled the return to "savage life." Of "all the sad experiences of these last twelve years [1933-1945] this is perhaps the most dreadful one," lamented Cassirer. At this point, he resorted to Greek mythology, as did Horkheimer and Adorno in their *Dialectic of Enlightenment*, comparing the Nazi role in Germany "to the experience of Odysseus on the island of Circe" in book 11 of Homer's *Odyssey*. The beautiful witch-goddess Circe drugs a band of Odysseus's men and turns them into pigs. In Germany, too, enchantment lured people away from reality and truth toward bestiality. In Nazi Germany, however, the situation is "even worse."

> Circe has transformed the friends and companions of Odysseus into various animal shapes. But here [in Nazi Germany] are men of education and intelligence, honest and upright men who suddenly give up the highest of human privileges. They have ceased to be free and personal agents. Performing the same

---

166. George H. Sabine, "*The Myth of the State* by Ernst Cassirer," *Philosophical Review* 56 (May 1947): 317.

> prescribed rites they begin to feel, to think, and to speak in the same way. Their gestures are lively and violent; yet this is but an artificial, a shame of life. In fact they are moved by external force. They act like marionettes in a puppet show—and they do not even know that the strings of this show and of man's whole individual and social life, are henceforward pulled by the political leaders.

The Nazi return to "savage life" was directly mediated by the type of myth that Homer recited. In his attempt to delegitimize myths, Cassirer vividly compared them to "a serpent that tries to paralyze its victims before attacking them. Men fell victim to them without any serious resistance. They were vanquished and subdued before they had realized what actually happened" (286). Note that Horkheimer and Adorno turned to the *Odyssey* but refer to the Sirens, dangerous and beautiful women who lure sailors to shipwreck with their enchanting voices. In both cases, these German Jewish intellectual exiles use myths about seductive women who lure men away from reality, sobriety, and sanity to condemn the awful experience of Nazism.

Nowhere in Cassirer's book can one find a more revealing passage than his description of his own personal agony, which drove him into exile. Here, his personal ordeal and the humanist, enlightened German ordeal converge: "Our modern political myths destroyed" humanist "ideas and ideals before they begin their work." More specifically, the "myth of the race worked like a strong corrosive and succeeded in dissolving and dismantling all other values" (287). For him, the political and historical lesson is clear:

> In times of a severe and dangerous social crisis [and] the breakdown of the whole public life . . . man tries to cast off this burden. Here the totalitarian state and the political myths step in. The new political parties promise . . . an escape from the dilemma. They suppress and destroy the very sense of freedom; but, at the same time, they relieve men from all personal responsibility. (288)

These views about the flight from reason bring to mind *Escape from Freedom* (1941) by Erich Fromm (1900–1980), in which the Frankfurt-born psychologist and social theorist emphasized the psychological conditions that facilitated the rise of Nazism.

The new political systems constituted a new social phenomenon: "in the totalitarian states the political leaders" took "all those functions that, in primitive societies, were performed by the magicians." Magicians in the past promised "to cure all social evils"; in modern totalitarian states, "political leaders" do so. The "soothsayer has his firm place and his indispensable role in primitive social life" (288), yet, Cassirer emphasized,

> our modern political life has abruptly returned to forms which seem to have been entirely forgotten. . . . We have developed a much more refined and elaborate method of divination. . . . Our modern politicians know very well that that great masses are much more easily moved by the force of imagination than by sheer physical force.

Referring to the threatened Thousand-Year Reich, Cassirer wrote: "The most improbable or even impossible promises are made; the millennium is predicted over and over again" (289).

Not only social, economic, and political crises contributed to the rise of modern political myths, and not only politicians, but also modern German intellectuals. They played the modern role of soothsayers by engaging in "the new art of divination," predicting the future, and thus greatly strengthening and enhancing "the force of imagination" in Germany. Sadly, Cassirer admitted, "the new art of divination first made its appearance not in German politics but in German philosophy" (289). Returning to the silence of the philosophers, he specifically denounces those who helped to create the culture of pessimism and fatalism in Germany that lofted modern political myths. First, he calls out Oswald Spengler's *Decline of the West* (1918–1923), which decidedly influenced the widespread sense of fatalism in Germany. "Perhaps never before had a philosophical book such a sensational success," with its translation "into almost every language and read by all sorts of readers—philosophers and scientists, historians and politicians, students and scholars, tradesman and the man on the street." The cause of this sensational success lay "rather in the title of this book than in its content," which was an "electric spark that set the imagination of Spengler's reader aflame" (289). Introduced by its author as a Copernican paradigm shift, it rejected the Eurocentric view of history. The meaningful units of history are not epochs but cultures, which evolve as organisms. Spengler argued that the Western world is ending; we are witnessing its last season.

Spengler's "philosophy of history" aimed to describe, "in the light of the decline of the Classical age, one world historical phase of several centuries upon which we ourselves are now entering," namely, "the Decline of the West," or "West Europe and America," since the eighteenth century. He considered this decline "a philosophical problem" that "includes within itself every great question of Being."[167] Like many Germans of his time, Spengler did not believe in the humanistic concept of Western civilization; culture, he believed, "has a soul, whereas Civilization is 'the most external and artificial state of which humanity is capable.'"[168] For him, "the 'Decline of the West' comprises nothing less than the problem of *Civilization*." Spengler lamented that "we are born as men of the early winter of full Civilization, instead of on the golden summit of a ripe Culture."[169] Indeed, the "keynote of Spengler's condemnation of his own time is in the word 'Civilization,' which, as used by him, connotes the death of a culture and a consequent transformation of values."[170] Spengler of course wasn't a Nazi and he distanced himself from that movement; yet the Nazis were attracted to him.

Claiming to find "a new method by which historical and cultural events could be predicted," Spengler stressed that his book "attempted for the first time the venture of determining history, of following the still unraveled stages in the destiny of a culture," or, more specifically, "the West European American." However, as Cassirer argued, Spengler's rise, decline, and fall of civilization is not based on laws of nature but on "a higher power, the power of destiny," or on sheer "Fatalism," which in turn signaled "the rebirth of one of the oldest mythical motives." Based on "a metaphysics of history that shows all the characteristic features of myth," Spengler's historical prognostics are exactly the same as "astrological prognostics" (290). In sum, his book is "an astrology of history—the work of a diviner who unfolded his somber apocalyptic visions." Spengler was not only "a prophet of evil"; his book "became one of the pioneer works of National Socialism" because his philosophy of history was "a philosophy of pessimism" (291). The Nazi "new men were convinced that they fulfilled Spengler's prophecy. They interpreted him in their own sense. If our culture—science, philosophy, poetry, and art—is dead, let us make a fresh start. Let us try our vast possibilities, let us create a new world and become the rulers of this world" (292).

---

167. Spengler, *Decline of the West* (1962 ed.), xv, 3, 16.
168. Ibid., 356, quoted by Mosse, *Crisis of German Ideology*, 6.
169. Spengler, *Decline of the West* (1934), 31, 44, emphasis original.
170. Arthur Helps, "Preface," in Spengler, *Decline of the West* (1962), xiv.

Spengler's influence on the Nazi movement may be imputed from *The Duties of German Youth* (1924): "Who cannot hate is no Man, and history is made by Men. That we Germans can at last hate is one of the few results of this period which holds no promise for the future." In his last publication, *Jahre der Entscheidung* (*The Hour of Decision*, 1933),[171] he wrote:

> *The ancient barbarism which has been held down for centuries . . . is waking again with a warlike delight in its own strength. This barbarism is what I call strong Race . . . the eternal warlike in the type of the beast of prey—Man. The only form-giving power is the warlike 'Prussian' spirit; not only in Germany the legions of Caesar march again.*[172]

The same trend of thought, the same new art of divination, fatalism, passivity, and pessimism, argued Cassirer, appeared in the work of another modern philosopher, Martin Heidegger,[173] who published in 1927 "the first volume of his book *Sein and Zeit* [*Being and Time*]" (292). In contrast to his teacher, Edmund Husserl (1859–1938), who strove "to make philosophy an 'exact science,'" Heidegger thought that in "vain we try to build up a logical philosophy." All we can do is to offer an *existenzialphilosophie* that "does not claim to give us an objective and universally valid truth." A philosopher can only supply the truth of his own existence, which "has a historical character" and is bound up with "the special conditions under which the individual lives." Most important to Cassirer's argument, to "change these conditions is impossible." The human condition is characterized by "the *Geworfenheit* of man," the state of being thrown into the stream of time and history:

> To be thrown into the stream of time is a fundamental and inalterable feature of our human situation. We cannot emerge from this stream and we cannot change its course. We have to accept the historical conditions of our existence. We can only try to understand and interpret them; but we cannot change them. (293)

---

171. Oswald Spengler, *Jahre der Entscheidung* (Munich: Beck, 1933).

172. Helps, "Preface," in Spengler, *Decline of the West* (1962), xix–xx; emphasis original.

173. On Cassirer and Heidegger's relationship, see Peter E. Gordon, *Continental Divide: Heidegger, Cassirer, Davos* (Cambridge: Harvard University Press, 2010).

Years of philosophical struggles between Cassirer and Heidegger, beginning in their famous Davos debate, 1929, in which Cassirer challenged Heidegger's relativism by invoking the universal validity of truths discovered by the exact and moral sciences, was transformed in the early 1940s, Peter E. Gordon wrote, "into a public dispute over the status of philosophy as ideology."[174]

The social, political, and philosophical ramifications of Spengler and Heidegger's "new philosophy" based on fatalism, passivity, and pessimism, were far-reaching in terms of the rise and triumph of political myths, or fascism and Nazism. Of course, neither was directly responsible for "the development of political ideas in Germany," but their new philosophical doctrines did

> enfeeble and slowly undermine the forces that could have resisted the modern political myths. A philosophy of history that consists in somber predictions of the decline and the inevitable destruction of our civilization and a theory that sees in the *Geworfenheit* of man one of his principal characteristics have given up all hopes of an active share in the reconstruction of man's cultural life. Such philosophy renounced its own fundamental theoretical and ethical ideals. It can be used, then, as a pliable instrument in the hands of political leaders.

The personal, existential, historical, and political situations were merged in Cassirer's mind; his exilic displacement, caused by the evil forces of Nazism and fascism, also contributed to his negative view of Spengler and Heidegger, who inaugurated "the return to fatalism in our modern world" (293).[175]

At the end of the book, Cassirer's gloomy tone intensifies. "The sudden rise of the political myth in the twentieth century" had a great impact on his soul. "Politics," he admitted, "is still far from being a positive science, let alone an exact science." He warns:

> ... we are always threatened with a sudden relapse into the old chaos. We are building high and proud edifices; but we forget

---

174. Ibid., 311.

175. On the relationship between Heidegger and Spengler, see Richard Wolin, "National Socialism, World Jewry, and the History of Being: Heidegger's Black Notebooks," *Jewish Review of Books*, Summer 2014, http://jewishreviewofbooks.com/articles/993/national-socialism-world-jewry-and-the-history-of-being-heideggers-black-notebooks/.

> to make their foundations secure. The belief that man by the skillful use of magic formulae and rites can change the course of nature has prevailed for hundreds and thousands of years in human history. In spite of all the inevitable frustrations and disappointments mankind still clung stubbornly, forcibly, and desperately to this belief. It is, therefore, not to be wondered at that in our political actions and our political thoughts magic still holds its ground. (295)

These words reveal desperation, a deep pessimism about the human condition. If "since the times of Plato all great thinkers have made the greatest efforts to find a rational theory of politics" (294), in the end, they did not dispel the power of myths and magic nor bring light to the dark abysses of the human soul and, hence, human history.

The crisis of German ideology and politics led many to reevaluate the whole history of political thought. The same remarkable, all-embracing endeavor was undertaken by Erich Auerbach in the field of philology and Popper in the field of political philosophy. Cassirer's vision of the return to myth and savage life appears in Max Horkheimer and Theodor Adorno's *Dialectic of Enlightenment*, where they argued that Nazism led to the "reversion of enlightened civilization to barbarism." They defined their goal in this work as "nothing less than to explain why humanity, instead of entering a truly human state, is sinking into a new kind of barbarism" and called on readers "to take up the cause of remnant freedom, of tendencies toward real humanity, even though they seem powerless in the face of the great historical trend" of the Nazi occupation of Europe.[176] Humanist civilization was besieged by Nazi barbarism and tyranny; Cassirer and his fellow intellectual expatriates in exile waged their grand *Kulturkampf* against it.

In his inaugural address at the University of Gothenburg, Cassirer declared that "philosophy cannot stand aside, mute and idle"[177] in the face of the Nazi menace. He reiterates this view at the end of his book, but now with the terrible knowledge and experience of World War II, he seems to have lost some faith in the power of his discipline. Rhetorically, he asks what "can philosophy do to help us in this struggle against the political myths?" The question is apt since "modern philosophers seem long ago to have given up all hope of influencing the course of political and social

---

176. Horkheimer and Adorno, *Dialectic of Enlightenment*, xix, xiv, xi.

177. Cassirer, "Concept of Philosophy," in Verene, *Symbol, Myth, and Culture*, 60–61.

events," as evidenced by Spengler and Heidegger's thought (295). It could be turned against Cassirer himself since he directly attacked political myths only in his last book. Nevertheless, his answer is a wake-up call to philosophers: leave the Ivory Tower and get involved in the hard political and social struggles of their times. They must follow "the classical example of Plato," he argues:

> The great thinkers of the past were not only 'their own times apprehended in thought.' Very often they had *to think beyond and against their times*. Without this intellectual and moral courage, philosophy could not fulfill its task in man's cultural and social life. (296, emphasis added)[178]

Such a desperate call to philosophers to save the humanist ideas and values of Western civilization may sound very naïve, yet Cassirer really believed that philosophers, such as Spengler and Heidegger, had betrayed humanity.[179] Of course, he was aware that "it is beyond the power of philosophy to destroy the political myths. A myth is in a sense invulnerable. It is impervious to rational argument; it cannot be refuted by syllogism." This statement is another clear example of the transformation of myth in Cassirer's thought from an abstract subject of theoretical, epistemological inquiry into an embodied historical force. In the crucial battle between mythological and rational forces, he urged philosophers at least to explain, if not to destroy, the menace of myth.

---

178. These words bring to mind Karl Marx's famous saying in his "Theses on Feuerbach," written in 1845, published in 1888: "The philosophers have only interpreted the world, in various ways; the point is to change it." What Marx means, wrote Louis Menand, was not that "philosophy is irrelevant; he was saying the philosophical problems arise out of real-life conditions, and they can be solved by changing these condition—by re-making the world." See Louis Menand, "He's Back: Karl Marx, Yesterday and Today," *The New Yorker*, October 10, 2016, 92.

179. Cassirer could not know but in 1941 Heidegger wrote in his famous "Black Notebooks" the following about Jews and "World Jewry," *Weltjudentum*: "World Jewry, spurred on by the emigrant that Germany let out, remains elusive everywhere. Despite its increased display of power, it never has to take part in the practice of war, whereas we are reduced to sacrificing the best blood of the best of our own people." See Adam Kirsch, "Heidegger Was Really a Real Nazi," *Tablet Magazine*, September 26, 2016. Adam Kirsch added: "This is a breathtaking example of how Nazi anti-Semitism precisely inverted reality: At just the moment when the Holocaust was killing millions of helpless Jews, Heidegger suggests that it was "elusive" World Jewry that was killing Germans."

Here, he returns to the militant voice of the chapter on "'Logos and 'Mythos' in Early Greek Philosophy," describing the formidable struggle between two armies, Logos and Mythos. He calls upon philosophers to "understand the adversary. In order to fight an enemy you must know him," admitting that in his discipline, all "of us have been liable to underrate this strength" of the political myths, including him:

> When we first heard of the political myths we found them so absurd and incongruous, so fantastic and ludicrous that we could hardly be prevailed upon to take them seriously. By now it has become clear to all of us that this was a great mistake. We should not commit the same error a second time. We should carefully study the origins, the structure, the methods, and the technique of the political myths. *We should see the adversary face to face in order to know how to combat it.* (296, emphasis added)

His words recall Pastor Martin Niemöller's powerful statement about the cowardice of German intellectuals when the Nazis rose to power and purged their targets, group after group:

> First they came for the Socialists, and I did not speak out—
> Because I was not a Socialist.
> Then they came for the Trade Unionists, and I did not speak out—
> Because I was not a Trade Unionist.
> Then they came for the Jews, and I did not speak out—
> Because I was not a Jew.
> Then they came for me—and there was no one left to speak for me.

Epilogue

Cassirer, a philosopher turned politician, transformed *The Myth of the State* into a grand *Kulturkampf* against the rise and triumph of fascism and Nazism. His transformation, caused by exilic displacement and ordeal, was not unique to him; Popper recounts that his decision to write *The Open Society and Its Enemies* "was made in March 1938, on the day I received the news of the invasion of Austria."[180] Auerbach, Baron, and, not least,

---

180. Popper, *Open Society*, xxxv.

Thomas Mann, who began writing *Doctor Faustus* about the "secret union of the German spirit with the Demonic"[181] in the early 1940s, adopted a new, direct, more activist tone. *The Myth of the State* was an integral part of German-speaking intellectuals' exilic *Kulturkampf* against the powers that drove them from their homes and endangered the foundation of humanist civilization of Europe.

Cassirer, Auerbach, Popper, Baron, and Walter Benjamin, to name only a few exiled German Jewish intellectuals were living in the "Age of Catastrophe," as Hobsbawm wrote.[182] Cassirer drew the sad lesson: "We must always be prepared for violent concussions that may shake our cultural world and our social order to its very foundations" (297). He and the others took upon themselves the mission of salvaging Western civilization's humanist tradition. Their goal was to explain why humanity was sinking "into a new kind of barbarism," attempting "to take up the cause of remnant freedom, of tendencies toward real humanity" in the face of the Nazi occupation of Europe.[183] Cassirer's *The Myth of the State* was an integral part of this mission and should be read and appreciated in this context.

The crisis mode of historical thought, or crisis history, is based on the view that history develops in a series of well-defined, decisive turning points. Walter Benjamin wrote "Theses on the Philosophy of History" shortly before his suicide, fleeing the Nazis, in 1940. In it, he depicts the "Angel of History": "His face is turned toward the past. Where we perceive a chain of events, he sees one single catastrophe which keeps piling wreckage upon wreckage and hurls it in front of his feet."[184] These words echo in Cassirer's sad recognition at the end of his study: "What we have learned in

---

181. Mann, "Germany and the Germans," May 29, 1945, in Tolzmann, *Thomas Mann's Addresses*, 51.

182. Hobsbawm, *Age of Extremes*, 6–7.

183. Horkheimer and Adorno, *Dialectic of Enlightenment*, xix, xiv, xi.

184. Benjamin, *Illuminations*, 257–58. On Benjamin's apocalyptic history, see Anson Rabinbach, *In the Shadow of Catastrophe: German Intellectuals between Apocalypse and Enlightenment* (Berkeley: University of California Press, 1997). Protestant Neo-Orthodoxy developed its crisis theology in the wake of the ravages of the First World War, more specifically in the theology of judgment of Karl Barth (1886–1968). That catastrophe also prompted the creation of a specifically Jewish philosophy of history in the writings of Ernst Bloch (1885–1977), Franz Rosenzweig (1886–1929), Walter Benjamin, Gershom Scholem (1897–1982), and others. Like crisis theology, Jewish philosophy following World War I severs the connection between divine goodness and human history, undermining the concept of historical progress. For example, in *The Star of Redemption*, Rosenzweig rejected Hegel's concept of "wisdom in history."

the hard school of our modern political life is the fact that human culture is by no means the firmly established thing that we once supposed it to be" (297). Crisis, not progress nor the glorious Enlightenment vision of human advance, is the marrow of the historical process.

A deep sense of crisis pervades *The Myth of the State* from beginning to end. On the first page, Cassirer writes about the "severe crisis" of Western civilization in his time (3). He concludes with these words: "the world of human culture could not arise until the darkness of myth was fought and overcome." Nazism and fascism clearly showed that the "mythical monsters were not entirely destroyed." To the contrary:

> In the past the powers of myth were checked and subdued by superior forces. As long as these forces, intellectual, ethical, and artistic, are in full strength, myth is tamed and subdued. But once they begin to lose their strength chaos is come again. Mythical thought then starts to rise again and to pervade the whole of man's cultural and social life. (297–98)

"Chaos is come again," Othello says (3.3.92), when Iago, whom Coleridge defined as "motiveless malignancy," infects the Moor's mind with falsehood and brings him to barbarous murder. Previously, Cassirer faulted Spengler and Heidegger's pessimism, but now he seems to succumb to it. In this broad historical and ideological context, *The Myth of the State* can be seen as a confession, a testament, a cry, uttered in the wilderness of exile as the dark clouds of myth threatened to engulf history and return us to barbarity.

Odysseus eventually returned to Ithaca after the Trojan War; Cassirer's "long Odyssey,"[185] was much different. No boat returned him to his beloved home. The Nazi Revolution of 1933 forced him into exile until his death. However, the hard existential experience of exilic displacement can forge new goals and missions. Dante and Machiavelli wrote their most significant works in exile, *The Divine Comedy* (1308–1321) and the *Discourses on the First Ten Books of Titus Livy* (*Discorsi*, 1517), respectively. Erich Auerbach composed his masterpiece *Mimesis*—"written in Istanbul between May 1942 and April 1945"[186]—in exile. Hans Baron wrote *The Crisis of the Early Italian Renaissance* and Thomas Mann, *Doctor Faustus*, in exile. Their hardship and misery were a source of heroic, lasting intellectual achievements.

---

185. Hendel, "Ernst Cassirer," 56. See also Verene, "Introduction," *Symbol, Myth, and Culture*, 7.

186. Auerbach, *Mimesis*, iv.

III

Erich Auerbach's Book of Books and the Rational Representation of Reality in Western Literature

with David Weinstein

> Philology itself, the branch of literary studies that most loudly cultivates distance from ideology and engagement with the most arcane details, might instead be an authentically—and repeatedly, in one strong voice after another—political activity.
>
> —María Rosa Menocal, *Shards of Love: Exile and the Origins of Lyric*, 1994

> There is no other work in contemporary literary criticism, known to me, that is comparable to it [*Mimesis*] in scope, in analytical and historical richness; it is actually a history of European history from the Odyssey to Ulysses and shows a quiet mastery of all the literature of the West.
>
> —Alfred Kazin, "Erich Auerbach," 1965

This chapter analyzes Erich Auerbach's writings in the wide ideological, philological, and historical context of his time. It deals specifically with his struggle against a twisted, fanatical Aryan philology that sought to eliminate the Old Testament from German *Kultur* and *Volksgeist* in particular and Western civilization in general and led him to develop a passionate *apologia* for Western Judeo-Christian humanist tradition at its gravest existential moment.

Auerbach began his struggle against Aryan philology in Germany in 1933 in his famous essay "Figura," which he published in exile in Istanbul in 1938.[1] "Figura" is traditionally regarded as a brilliant philological and literary study, but it should be seen, above all, as a defense of the Old Testament's validity and credibility.[2] Auerbach made clear that Western culture and civilization are based upon a figural interpretation of history—the traditional Christian doctrine that the New Testament is a "historical and typological fulfillment of the Old," establishing their intrinsic, inextricable connection.[3] Figural interpretation, he believed, "wished to preserve the full historicity of the Scriptures along with the deeper meaning." It "asserted both the historical reality of the Old and the New Testaments and also their providential connectedness," thus substantiating the Old Testament's authority.[4] "Figura" is a heroic mission. It seeks to define *figura* and its humanist ramifications as deployed by Saint Paul, Augustine, Aquinas, and Dante. Born "in the nexus of Judaism and Christianity," this approach embodies "one of the conditions of the literary project of the West."[5] Philology becomes an integral and formidable ideological tool and figural interpretation a powerful weapon against Aryan debasement and erasure.

Auerbach began writing *Mimesis: The Representation of Reality in Western Literature* (*Mimesis: Dargestellte Wirklichkeit in der abendländischen Literatur*, 1946)[6] in exile in Istanbul in 1942, as the crucial battles of Stalingrad, Midway, and El Alamein raged. Like "Figura," *Mimesis* was a groundbreaking philological study that inaugurated, among other things, the field of comparative literature. It was based on the idea that the Old Testament, not the classical Greek culture of myths, legends, and heroes

---

1. Erich Auerbach, "Figura," in *Scenes from the Drama of European Literature* (Gloucester: Peter Smith, 1973), 11–76. All references in the text to F are to this edition.

2. An analysis of "Figura" can be found in Zakai, *Erich Auerbach and the Crisis of German Philology*.

3. Lowry Nelson Jr., "Erich Auerbach: Memoir of a Scholar," *Yale Review* 69 (1979–1980), 314–15.

4. Lowry Nelson Jr., "Erich Auerbach (1892–1957)," in *Medieval Scholarship: Biographical Studies on the Formation of a Discipline*, 3 vols.; vol. 2, *Literature and Philology* (New York: Garland, 1998), 397, 316.

5. Galili Shahar, "Auerbach's Scars: Judaism and the Question of Literature," *Jewish Quarterly Review* 101 (Fall 2011): 611.

6. Erich Auerbach, *Mimesis: The Representation of Reality in Western Literature* (Princeton: Princeton University Press, 2003 [1946]). All references in the text to *M* are to this edition.

recently revived by Nazi culture, is the source of history and, hence, the way Western culture conceives reality.[7] Auerbach sets the history of European literature, not from Homer, but "from Genesis all the way to Virginia Woolf" (*M*, 563). His main aim is to confront Aryan philology with concrete evidence that Scripture leads "from distant legend and its figural interpretation into everyday contemporary reality" (*M*, 159), while Aryan premises lead from legend to flight from reality—*Schwärmerei*.[8] Thomas Mann described the Nazis "enter[ing] the arena of history proclaiming themselves bearers of a barbarism that, while wallowing in ruthlessness, was to rejuvenate the world."[9] In contrast to their recidivist revisionism, *Mimesis* stresses the rationalist, realist view of history as a teleological progression toward democracy. It was written to "those whose love for our western history has serenely persevered" (*M*, 557) through the horrors of World War II yet finds in early twentieth-century works by Virginia Woolf, Marcel Proust, and James Joyce a confused subjectivity supporting Oswald Spengler's claims in *The Decline of the West*. Rejecting his previous adherence to Vico and Hegel's belief in historical progress, Auerbach sees dissolution in modern literature.

His growing pessimism is more than understandable; many tense years at home followed by a hard life in exile left their indelible marks. While Auerbach made constant struggle against Nazism his chosen field, he could not ignore the terrible impact of two bestial World Wars on Western history and culture.

Knowing the Enemy

> [The Nazi's] furious onslaught aimed at eliminating any trace of 'Jewishness,' any sign of 'Jewish spirit,' any remnant of Jewish presence (real or imaginary) from politics, society, culture, and history.
>
> —Saul Friedländer, *The Years of Extermination: Nazi Germany and the Jews, 1939–1945*, 2007

---

7. An analysis of the content and form of *Mimesis*, as well as of its whole twenty chapters, can be found in Zakai, *Erich Auerbach and the Crisis of German Philology*.

8. In his last book, *The New Leviathan: Or Man, Society, Civilization, and Barbarism*, R. G. Collingwood, the English philosopher, historian, and archaeologist, devoted a long chapter to modern German barbarism, claiming, among other things, that "the Nazis advocate 'thinking with your blood'" (377).

9. Mann, *Doctor Faustus*, 184.

> Auerbach's writing is, first and foremost, that of an historian and critic of culture in the tradition of Jakob Burckhardt and German *Kulturgeschichte*; beneath the surface of scholarly detachment and aristocratic urbanity there is a pathos, an urgency of involvement born of a passionate commitment to the variety of attitudes and the shared values and assumptions of Western civilization.
>
> —Arthur R. Evans Jr., "Erich Auerbach as European Critic," 1971
>
> The idea that Auerbach is simply a neutral observer, purely committed to his extreme historical relativism, is not correct.
>
> —René Wellek, *A History of Modern Criticism: 1750-1950*, 1991

In the introduction to his *Literary Language and Its Public in Late Latin Antiquity and in the Middle Ages* (1958),[10] Auerbach described the close connection in his thought between philology and ideology, the intrinsic relationship of literary expression to the contemporary "inward and outward crises of Europe" (*LLP*, 6). His works entitled him to an important place among "European philologists," and he noted three scholars whose "breadth of vision" made them "without equal in any other field of philology or in any other country": Karl Vossler, Ernst Robert Curtius, and Leo Spitzer. Vossler (1872-1949) was a German linguist and scholar, a leading Romanist known for his interest in Italian thought, and a follower of the Italian critic and idealist philosopher Benedetto Croce. Curtius (1886-1956) was a German literary scholar, philologist, and critic of Romance-language literature. Spitzer (1887-1960) was an Austrian Romanist and Hispanist, an influential and prolific literary critic known for his emphasis on stylistics (*Stilistik*), linking linguistics and literature.[11] Auerbach positions his own work as springing "from the same presuppositions as theirs," namely,

---

10. Erich Auerbach, *Literary Language and Its Public in Late Latin Antiquity and in the Middle Ages* (1993), trans. Ralph Manheim (Princeton: Princeton University Press, 1993), 6. All references in the text to *LLP* are to this edition.

11. According to René Wellek, the famous Czech American literary critic, these "four prominent German specialists in Romance literature" were influenced by Wilhelm Dilthey (1833-1911), the German historian, psychologist, sociologist, and hermeneutic philosopher, and Benedetto Croce (1866-1952), the Italian idealist philosopher and historian. See *A History of Modern Criticism: 1750-1950*; Vol. 7, *German, Russian, and Eastern European Criticism, 1900-1950*, 92. Among them, Wellek argues, Auerbach "seems to be the most widely read" (92).

"embracing *Europe as a whole.*" However, he claimed a "much clearer awareness of the European crisis" (*LLP*, 6, emphasis added).

Many studies have dealt with Auerbach's response to the crisis in Germany, but few if any explain against what and whom he fought. One argues that Auerbach's goal was "salvaging . . . some vestiges of Western tradition or precious survival of the past."[12] Another claims that in writing *Mimesis*, he "was not only merely practicing his profession despite adversity: he was performing an act of cultural, even civilizational, survival of the highest importance" or offering "a massive reaffirmation of the Western cultural tradition."[13] The same author declares that *Mimesis* is "an alternative history for Europe."[14]

Auerbach's philological, historical, and philosophical enterprise in "Figura" and *Mimesis* was directed against a well-defined crisis in Germany and the Europe of his time.[15] He addressed not only the general political and social crises[16] but the specific crisis in his own discipline: the development of Aryan philology, based on racism, anti-Semitism, narrow nationalism, and chauvinism, which strove to eliminate the Old Testament from the Christian canon and, hence, the very fabric of European culture and civilization.[17] My goal is to analyze the extent to which Aryan philology,

---

12. Nelson, "Erich Auerbach: Memoir of a Scholar," 319.

13. Edward W. Said, "Introduction: Secular Criticism," in *The Word, the Text, and the Critic* (Cambridge: Harvard University Press, 1983), 6, 8.

14. Edward W. Said, "Introduction to the Fiftieth Anniversary Edition," in Auerbach, *Mimesis* (2003), xxxi.

15. See Zakai and Weinstein, "Erich Auerbach and His 'Figura,'" 320–38.

16. During the first half of the twentieth century, Germany witnessed many crises in ideology, politics, theology, historicism, culture, philology, and more. See Mosse, *The Crisis of German Ideology*; Fritz Stern, *The Politics of Cultural Despair: A Study in the Rise of the Germanic Ideology* (Berkeley and Los Angeles: University of California Press, 1961); and Lukács, *The Destruction of Reason*, 1981.

17. The German humanistic and philological crisis of the early twentieth century was inextricably connected to the crisis of historicism. According to Michael Holquist, "the crisis of historicism was in effect a crisis in belief. The long three stage descent from A. belief in an absolute god, through, B. a succeeding belief in the absolute of reason, to C. the 19th century loss of faith in *any* absolute after the Romantic appropriation of Kantian epistemology led to a re-formulation of subjectivity" (letter to the author, July 29, 2011). See also Michael Holquist, "The Place of Philology in an Age of World Literature," *Neohelicon* 38 (2011): 267–87.

"*völkisch* mysticism,"[18] and Nazi historiography influenced "Figura," and, later, how the spread of Nazi barbarism throughout Europe contributed to *Mimesis*, Auerbach's *magnum opus* and *opus famosum*. In both works, he followed Augustine's famous saying: "*nonnulla enim pars inventionis est nosse quid quaeras*" (a considerable part of discovery is to know what you are looking for).[19] In the same spirit, one may identify these works as a fierce, systematic rejection of the premises of Aryan philology. This uniquely German belief system strove to fashion new origins for the German people, to shape a new Germanic or Nordic Christianity, and to cut the Old Testament from the Christian canon.[20] Alfred Rosenberg, the Nazi party's chief ideologue, described Germany's defeat in World War I in terms of the dark, demonic powers of Norse mythology; the victories of the Allied Powers were evidence of

> an age when the Fenris Wolf [fame-wolf] broke his chains, when Hel [the giant goddess who rules over the underworld where the dead dwell] moved over the earth and the Midgardschlange [a giant snake] stirred the oceans of the world. Millions upon millions were ready to sacrifice themselves to attain but one result embodied in the phrase: for the honour and freedom of the *Volk*. The world inferno continued to the end; nonetheless, sacrifices were demanded and made by all. All that was revealed, however, was that behind the armies daemonic powers had triumphed over divine ones. Unrestrained, they raged throughout the world, stirring up new unrest, new flames, new destruction.[21]

---

18. Max Horkheimer, *Between Philosophy and Social Sciences: Selected Early Writings*, trans. G. F. Hunter and M. S. Kramer (Cambridge: MIT Press, 1993), 300.

19. Auerbach, *Literary Language*, 24.

20. In his last work *The Myth of the State* (1946), the German Jewish philosopher Ernst Cassirer, who fled Germany when the Nazis came to power, attempted to understand the intellectual origins of Nazi Germany. He saw Nazi Germany as a society in which the dangerous power of myth is not checked or subdued by superior forces and claimed that in twentieth-century politics there was a return back to the irrationality of myth, and in particular to a belief that there is such a thing as destiny. Hence, in the Nazi and fascist mythologies of Blood, *Volk*, and Soil, Cassirer argued, "the myth of the race worked like a strong corrosive and succeeded in dissolving and disintegrating all other values." See *The Myth of the State* (New Haven: Yale University Press, 1975 [1946]), 287.

21. *Der Mythos des 20. Jahrhunderts*. The quote is from Pois, *Race and Race History and Other Essays by Alfred Rosenberg*, 96–97.

"Figura" and *Mimesis* countered such absurd premises while also addressing, according to William Calin, Auerbach's research assistant at Yale during the 1950s, the "wish-fulfillment passion for everything Greek" among German intellectuals since "Johann Gottfried von Herder," reaching "culmination in Heidegger's notion that there are only two truly philosophical languages: Greek and German. Hitler took the trouble to have his picture taken next to (or in front of) the Acropolis," and one can recall the Greek trappings of Leni Riefenstal's *Olympia*. "[T]his German model was directed not only against the Jewish Old Testament; it also pushed aside the Latin/Roman and, consequently, repudiated the French and Italian traditions," which may explain "why Auerbach centered on French and, to a lesser extent, Italian."[22]

During the Weimar Republic, "Philology had become a metaphor for numbing drudgery, authoritarian discipline."[23] In contrast, Auerbach's "historicist humanism"[24] (PW, 4) sought to locate a broad narrative of Western civilization, not of a specific "race" or ethnic group. Auerbach was an avid student of the Italian political philosopher, historian, and jurist Giovanni Battista (Giambattista) Vico, who presented the third age of history, the age of fully developed reason, "only as potentiality . . . only a stage, doomed to degenerate and relapse into barbarism" (*LLP*, 16). Auerbach's first paper on Vico, dating from 1922, explains his attraction; he finds "no *Volksgeist* in Vico, no interest in the particular conditions of nations, no patriotism, no egotism, no romantic folklore, no domestic feeling of closeness, no idyllic joy in the beautiful and noble in man."[25]

The Nazi reversion was widely acknowledged. Thomas Mann had no illusions about the new Germany; in 1940, he wrote: "Where there is Nazism, there is to be found the denial of every decent human attribute and a reversion to the pagan and barbaric state of life in which murder, corruption, and intrigue are not merely condoned but advocated. Truth, justice, dignity have been ideals cherished by free men through the ages, but under Hitlerism they are simply empty words."[26] He complained that these beliefs "involve the abandonment of cultural achievements for the sake

---

22. Letter to the author, July 11, 2011.

23. Suzanne L. Marchand, *German Orientalism in the Age of Empire: Religion, Race, and Scholarship* (New York: Cambridge University Press, 2009), 316.

24. Erich Auerbach, "Philology and *Weltliteratur*" (1952), *Centennial Review* 13 (Winter 1969), 4. All references in the text to (PW) are to this edition.

25. Wellek, *German, Russian, and Eastern European Criticism*, 130.

26. Mann to Edward Edwards, June 23, 1940, in *Letters of Thomas Mann, 1889–1955*, 340.

of simplification or 're-barbarization'" based on "total rejection of truth," which he sums up as "the German Will to Legend in full flower after 1933."[27] D. H. Lawrence, the English novelist, poet, playwright, essayist, literary critic, and painter, likewise observed in his remarkable *Letter from Germany* (1924) that during the Weimar Republic, time was "whirling to the ghost of the old Middle Ages of Germany, then to the Roman days, then to the days of the silent forest and the dangerous, lurking barbarians."[28] In the same vein, Georg Lukács saw the "danger of a barbaric underworld latent in German civilization as its necessary complementary product."[29] Max Horkheimer and Theodor Adorno declared in the *Dialectic of Enlightenment* that Nazism led to the "reversion of enlightened civilization to barbarism" and defined their goal in this work as "nothing less than to explain why humanity, instead of entering a truly human state, is sinking into a new kind of barbarism." They "take up the cause of remnant freedom, of tendencies toward real humanity, even though they seem powerless in the face of the great historical trend" of the Nazi occupation of Europe.[30]

Within this broad historical, philological, and humanist context, Auerbach's "Figura" can be described as an apologia for the Old Testament and *Mimesis* as an apologia for the Western Judeo-Christian humanist tradition, not in terms of regret or remorse, but rather as a strong defense or justification. Augustine wrote *City of God* as a defense of the Christian faith in the early fifth century, when Christians and Christianity were blamed for the Fall of Rome. Pascal wrote *Pensées*, originally entitled *Apologie de la religion Chrétienne*, during the seventeenth century as a defense of Christianity against the rise of the modern mechanical philosophy of nature, especially as articulated by René Descartes.[31] These authors claimed to know the truth and strove to show its full range of

---

27. Reed, *Thomas Mann: The Uses of Tradition*, 375, 377–78.
28. Quoted in ibid., 399n88.
29. Quoted in ibid., 385.
30. Horkheimer and Adorno, *Dialectic of Enlightenment*, xix, xiv, xi.
31. On Augustine's apologia, see Avihu Zakai and Anya Mali, "Time, History and Eschatology: Ecclesiastical History from Eusebius to Augustine," *Journal of Religious History* 17 (December 1993): 393–417. On Pascal's apologia, see Zakai, *Jonathan Edwards's Philosophy of Nature*, chap. 4, "'God of Abraham' and 'Not of Philosophers': Pascal against the Philosophers' Disenchantment of the World," 125–62.

colors to a world that denied or denounced it. As Wellek wrote, *Mimesis* "was oriented toward truth"[32] or, in Auerbach's own words, "an absolute claim to historical truth" (*M*, 14).

Auerbach was more than familiar with the thought and lives of Augustine and Pascal; they are discussed throughout his works. He is clearly closer to Augustine because they both drew similar conclusions from their own and their civilizations' ordeals. Augustine termed his world *Terra aliena*; exile led to alienation. Auerbach believed that "the spirit (*Geist*) is not national" and after two terrible world wars, described the world as "*Paupertas* [poverty] and *terra aliena*" (PW, 17),[33] an indigent, devastated, strange land, echoing Augustine's remarks to his fellow Christians in Carthage: "Citizens of Jerusalem . . . you do not belong here [earth], you belong somewhere else."[34] Their existential state in the world is that of "resident stranger" or "resident aliens."[35]

Auerbach's apologetic moment, his turn to reveal, explore, and defend the Judeo-Christian humanist tradition and, ipso facto, the Jewish foundation of Western culture and literature, coincided with the 1933 Nazi Revolution, as his list of publications makes clear.[36] Before he published "Figura," most of his works concentrated on Italian and French literature. In exile during the 1930s and 1940s, he made a major turn, exploring and justifying the credibility and authority of the biblical foundations of Western civilization. This *Ansatzpunkt*,[37] or point of great epistemological departure, drilled into the question of realism as "an investigation into

---

32. René Wellek, "Erich Auerbach (1892–1957)," *Comparative Literature* 10 (1958): 94; René Wellek, "Review: Auerbach's Special Realism," *Kenyon Review* 16 (Spring 1954): 299–307.

33. Generally speaking, "'*Geist*' refers to some sort of *general consciousness, a single 'mind' common to all men.*" See R. C. Solomon, "Hegel's Concept of 'Geist,'" *Review of Metaphysics* 23 (June 1970): 642.

34. Peter Brown, "Saint Augustine," in *Trends in Medieval Political Thought*, ed. B. Smalley (Oxford: Oxford University Press, 1965), 11.

35. Peter Brown, *Augustine of Hippo: A Biography* (Berkeley: University of California Press, 1969), 313–14.

36. See "Bibliography of the Writings of Erich Auerbach," in *Literary Language*, 395–405.

37. Auerbach borrowed the crucial concept of *Ansatzpunkt* from Wilhelm Dilthey, *Das Erlebnis und die Dichtung: Lessing, Goethe, Novalis, Hölderlin* (Göttingen: Vandenhoeck & Ruprecht, 1968 [1914]).

the literary representation of reality in European culture" (*M*, 23). Until "Figura" and *Mimesis*, Auerbach had not dealt with Jewish thought and life. Evidently, with the triumph of Nazism and Aryan philology in 1933, he had something to prove that was so important, he changed the course, themes, and goals of his life's work.

In what follows, my goal is not to provide an exhaustive analysis of the ideological sources of Auerbach's philological philosophy, which has been accomplished elsewhere.[38] Likewise, I am not concerned with the impact of Jewishness on Auerbach's works, an important subject receiving more attention in recent years.[39] My aim is more modest: to reveal the formation, content, and form of "Figura" and *Mimesis* in light of his life and times; in other words, to illuminate the space of experience and horizon of expectation behind their composition. As David Damrosch wrote about *Mimesis*, but it applies to "Figura" as well, Auerbach "knew too much about his own time, and that knowledge, so often repressed, continually returned to shift the course of his argument away from the free play of the material in itself."[40] These works had an ideological-philological mission: to achieve a grand, overarching teleology of literary history, or literary historiography,

---

38. See, for example, Michael Holquist, who, in his important essay, "The Last European: Erich Auerbach as Precursor in the History of Cultural Criticism," *Modern Language Quarterly* 54 (September 1993): 371–91, brilliantly analyzes the ideological origins of Auerbach's philological method in the context of the Marburg and Southwest German schools of Neo-Kantianism. See also Paul A. Bové, *Intellectuals in Power: A Genealogy of Critical Humanism* (New York: Columbia University Press, 1986); Stephen G. Nichols, "Philology in Auerbach's Drama of Literary History," in *Literary History and the Challenge of Philology: The Legacy of Erich Auerbach*, ed. Seth Lerer (Stanford: Stanford University Press, 1996), 63–77; and Luiz Costa-Lima, "Erich Auerbach: History and Metahistory," *New Literary History* 19 (Spring 1988): 467–99.

39. See Stephen G. Nichols, "Erich Auerbach: History, Literature and Jewish Philosophy" *Romanistisches Jahrbuch* 58 (2008): 166–85; Geoffrey H. Hartman, "The Struggle for the Text" in *Midrash and Literature*, ed. G. H. Hartman and S. Budick (New Haven: Yale University Press, 1986), 3–18; Malachi H. Hacohen, "Typology and the Holocaust: Erich Auerbach and Judeo-Christian Europe" *Religions* 3 (2012): www.mdpi.com/journal/religions/special_issues/jewish-emigres/; and Matthias Bormuth, "Meaning and Progress in History: Karl Löwith and Erich Auerbach," *Religions* 3 (2012): www.mdpi.com/journal/religions/special_issues/jewish-emigres.

40. David Damrosch, "Auerbach in Exile," *Comparative Literature* 47 (Spring 1995): 116.

based on an "ethical dimension in which humanistic values and a sense of the tragic coexist."[41]

Auerbach wrote about Dante that "his unfortunate situation was one of his main reasons for framing his work," and that with the writing of the *Comedy*, "he overcame the crisis and it vastly enriched his personal experience."[42] The same may be said about Auerbach. Exile led to a mission: "*Mimesis* was intended to be something more than a contribution to literary criticism,"[43] and "*Mimesis* is quite consciously a book that a particular person, in a particular situation, wrote at the beginning of the 1940s" (*M*, 574). Both its form and content declare a singular historical moment; hence, it demands historicization and contextualization, for as Auerbach argued, "[w]e are constantly endeavoring to give meaning and order to our lives in the past, the present, and the future, to our surroundings, the world in which we live" (*M*, 549). This task was urgent, given the major historical upheavals through which Auerbach lived. *Mimesis* can be seen as not only a literary odyssey, but his private, long, eventful odyssey. As he wrote, crisis demands interpretation: "The need to constitute authentic texts manifests itself typically when a society becomes conscious of having achieved a high level of civilization, and desires to preserve from the ravages of time the works that constituted its spiritual patrimony."[44]

I argue that "Figura" should not be regarded as a simple "technical essay," nor *Mimesis* understood as a mere "calm affirmation of the unity and dignity of European literature in all its multiplicity and dynamism," as one scholar suggested.[45] Rather, both works are unambiguous signs of Auerbach's *Kulturkampf* against Aryan philology and the spread of fascism

---

41. Kevin Brownlee, "The Ideology of Periodization: *Mimesis* 10 and the Late Medieval Aesthetic," in *Literary History and the Challenge of Philology: The Legacy of Erich Auerbach*, ed. Seth Lerer (Stanford: Stanford University Press, 1996), 158, emphasis added.

42. Auerbach, *Dante: Poet of the Secular World*, trans. Ralph Manheim (New York: New York Review of Books, 2007 [1929]), 75, 83. All references in the text to *D* are to this edition.

43. Brian Stock, "The Middle Ages as Subject and Object: Romantic Attitudes and Academic Medievalism," *New Literary History* 5 (Spring 1974): 531–32.

44. Auerbach, Introduction aux études de philology romane, quoted in Lerer, "Introduction," Literary History and the Challenge of Philology, 1, emphasis added.

45. Said, "Introduction to the Fiftieth Anniversary Edition," xx, xvi. See also "Erich Auerbach, Critic of the Earthly World," *Boundary 2* 31, 2 (2004): 550.

in Europe.⁴⁶ Each is an apologia written for a specific crisis Auerbach faced in his life. As he wrote in his typical reserved tone, "My own experience, and by that I mean not merely my scientific experience, is responsible for the choice of problems, the starting points, the reasoning and the intention expressed in my writing" (*LLP*, 30, emphasis added).

In what follows, I wish to explain "the reasoning and the intention" behind Auerbach's "choice of problems" and "starting points" in "Figura" and *Mimesis* in light of his experiences in Weimar, Nazi Germany, and exile. In 1942, R. G. Collingwood fretted about "the incessant tempests through which we have precariously lived for close to thirty years."⁴⁷ English poet, novelist, and essayist Stephen Spender wrote in 1945 that these years and especially World War II "brought nearly all those things which we hold firm and sacred into danger and collapse: truth and humanity, reason and right. We lived in a possessed world. For many of us the result was not unexpected when the insanity of a day broke out into delirium in which this poor European humanity sank back, fanatical, stupefied and mad."⁴⁸ "Figura" and *Mimesis* were constructed to preserve European Judeo-Christian humanist tradition during an "Age of Catastrophe" or "the age of absolute sinfulness."⁴⁹ Auerbach's was an acutely urgent mission in a time of tyranny, barbarism, and genocide.

Philology and History

[T]he romantics introduced the conception of natural and organic evolution into history itself; they developed an evolutionary conservatism, based on the traditions of the folk genius, directed as much against rationalistic forms of absolutism as against rationalistic tendencies toward revolutionary progress. Their organic conservatism resulted from their prevailing interest in the individual roots and forms of the folk genius, in folklore, national traditions, and the national individual-

---

46. For the rise of the concept of *Kulturkampf* in Germany during the second half of the nineteenth century, see Uriel Tal, "The *Kulturkampf* and the Status of the Jews in Germany," in *Christians and Jews in Germany: Religion, Politics, and Ideology in the Second Reich, 1870–1914* (Ithaca: Cornell University Press, 1975), 18–20.

47. Collingwood, *New Leviathan*, lx.

48. *European Witness*, 231.

49. Lukács, *Theory of the Novel*, 18. The "Preface" from which these words are taken is from 1962.

ity in general. Although this interest was extended to foreign national forms in the literary and scientific activities of the romantics, it led many of them, especially in Germany, to an extremely nationalistic attitude toward their own fatherland, which they considered as the synthesis and supreme realization of folk genius.

—Erich Auerbach, "Vico and Aesthetic Historicism," 1949

The ancient barbarism which has been held down for centuries . . . is waking again with a warlike delight in its own strength. This barbarism is what I call strong Race . . . the eternal warlike in the type of the beast of prey—Man. The only form-giving power is the warlike 'Prussian' spirit; not only in Germany the legions of Caesar march again.

—Oswald Spengler, *Jahre der Entscheidung*
(*The Hour of Decision*), 1933

[Auerbach's] historicism seeks to generate by purely scholarly means testimony to oppose the forces of uniformity and intolerance.

—Geoffrey Hartman, *A Scholar's Tale: Intellectual Journey of a Displaced Child of Europe*, 2007

Like Hans Baron, Karl Popper, Leo Strauss,[50] and other German-speaking Jewish intellectual exiles, crisis led Auerbach toward innovative, confrontational interpretations. He admitted: "At an early date, and from then on with increasing urgency, I ceased to look upon the European possibilities of Romance philology as mere possibilities and came to regard them as a task specific to our time—*a task which could not have been envisaged yesterday and will no longer be conceivable tomorrow*" (*LLP*, 6, emphasis added). He believed that in the wake of two world wars, "European civilization is approaching the terms of its existence," and "its history as a distinct entity" seemed "to be at an end" (*LLP*, 5-6). This sense of impending doom drove him, in *Mimesis*, to provide an apologia for Western culture, or "a coherent picture of European civilization as it is mirrored in its exemplary literary masterpieces."[51]

---

50. For these exiles from Nazism and fascism, see: David Weinstein and Avihu Zakai, *Jewish Exiles and European Thought in the Shadow of the Third Reich: Baron, Popper, Strauss, Auerbach* (Cambridge: Cambridge University Press, 2017).

51. Arthur R. Evans, "Erich Auerbach as European Critic," *Romance Philology* 25 (1971): 200.

"Figura" and *Mimesis* cannot be properly analyzed without exploring Auerbach's exile. "Modern Western culture is in large part the work of exiles, émigrés, refugees," Said wrote,[52] and Adorno thought "the only home truly available" to exiles, "though fragile and vulnerable, is in writing."[53] In exile, writing against the premises of Aryan philology and Nazi barbarism, Auerbach found his true home.[54] The experience of exile determined not only the form of *Mimesis* but also its unique content. Auerbach "found himself perforce in the position of writing a more original kind of book than he might otherwise have attempted, if he had remained within easy access to the stock of professional facilities."[55] He wrote: "it is quite possible that" *Mimesis* "owes its existence" to "the lack of a rich and specialized library. If it had been possible for me to acquaint myself with all the work that has been done on so many subjects, it might never have reached the point of writing" (*M*, 557).

Auerbach proposed that "[t]he science which seeks, by interpreting documents, to determine what they held to be true is called philology. Thus philology is enlarged to mean what in Germany is called *Geistesgeschichte*, to include all historical disciplines, including the history of law and economic history" (*LLP*, 15). His "philological philosophy or philosophical philology" is "concerned with only one thing—mankind" (*LLP*, 16). He "exercised" it for the "sake of humanism." Its "strong humanist avowal that literature has an ethical potential to modify the reader"[56] contrasts with Leo Spitzer's view. For Spitzer, "philology" is "the love of the word";[57] his literary and cultural analysis was based "mainly upon the word or cluster of related

---

52. Said, *Reflections on Exile*, 173.

53. Quoted in ibid., 184.

54. I criticize Said's interpretation of Auerbach's works in "Exile and Criticism: Edward Said's Interpretation of Erich Auerbach," *Society* 57 (2015): 275–82, and "Professor of Exile: Edward Said's Misreading of Erich Auerbach," *Moment Magazine*, August 14, 2014, www.momentmag.com/edward-said-erich-auerbach.

55. Harry Levin, "Two *Romanisten* in America: Spitzer and Auerbach," in *The Intellectual Migration: Europe and America*, ed. Donald Fleming and Bernard Bailyn (Cambridge: Harvard University Press, 1969), 466.

56. Jan M. Ziolkowski, "Foreword," *LLP*, xxiii, xxvii.

57. René Wellek, "Leo Spitzer (1887–1960)," *Comparative Literature* 12 (Autumn 1960): 312.

words," or *explication de texte*.[58] He situates his work in "the enchanted garden of literary history,"[59] although he "never published a book of literary history but, instead, collections of discrete critical and linguistic essays."[60] He was "interested primarily in the use of language by an individual writer, seeking the clue to the writer's personality in his deviation from the norm."[61] Even when he wrote *Anti-Chamberlain* (1918) as an antidote to "the toxins of race hatred" in H. Stewart Chamberlain's racist works, he called it "the purely scholarly protest of an academic specialist."[62] As late as 1949, he described *Mimesis* as "written by a German in exile without any resentment against current German movements."[63] He could not have been more wrong. Auerbach was very sensitive to the political and social transformations in Weimar and Nazi Germany and an acute observer of the horrors of his contemporary history. Evidently, Spitzer's assessment is based on his own inclination to avoid political questions to deal only with the "philological circle"[64] by which he meant "the continuous movement of the interpreter's mind from the text at hand to the context of widening awareness and back again."[65]

---

58. Nelson, "Erich Auerbach: Memoir of a Scholar," 314. On Auerbach and Spitzer, see Thomas R. Hart, "Literature as Language: Auerbach, Spitzer and Jakobson"; Seth Lerer, *Error and the Academic Self: The Scholarly Imagination, Medieval to Modern*, 267–71; and Hartman, *A Scholar's Tale*, 165–80.

59. Leo Spitzer, *Linguistic and Literary History: Essays in Stylistics* (Princeton: Princeton University Press, 1948), 1. See also Wellek, "Leo Spitzer."

60. William Calin, *The Twentieth-Century Humanist Critics: From Spitzer to Frye* (Toronto: University of Toronto Press, 2007). 52. See also Wellek, "Leo Spitzer": Spitzer "did not write a single unified book" (312). On the complex relationship between Auerbach and Spitzer, see Hans Ullrich Gumbrecht, "'Pathos of the Earthly Progress': Erich Auerbach's Everydays," in Lerer, *Literary History and the Challenge of Philology*, esp. 23–25. According to Calin, Auerbach "never mentioned Spitzer" (letter to the author, July 10, 2011).

61. Calin, *Twentieth-Century Humanist Critics*, 52.

62. Hartman, *Scholar's Tale*, 182.

63. Leo Spitzer, review of Curtius, *Europäische Literatur und lateinisches Mittlelalter*, *American Journal of Philology* 70 (1949): 430.

64. Spitzer, "Introduction," in *Linguistic and Literary History: Essays in Stylistics*, 1, 24. On the definition of Spitzer's philological circle as moving "from the detail to the whole and then back to the details," see Wellek, "Leo Spitzer," 315.

65. Levin, "Two *Romanisten*," 476.

Auerbach's "'philosophical circle' transcends Spitzer's *Stilforschung* [research of styles]." He embraced the "historical sociology of literature," namely, "historical process and change."[66] While Spitzer "starts with the analysis of a detail, assuming that the whole of the work is still unknown to him," Auerbach "starts with an unrivaled knowledge" of the work.[67] During the 1930s, while both Auerbach and Curtius increasingly moved toward historicist philology in their struggle against Aryan philology; Spitzer focused on "the ultimate unity of linguistic and literary history."[68] Auerbach and Curtius emphasized European literary history over narrow nationalism, racism, and Nazism; Spitzer believed that "the best document of the soul of a nation is its literature."[69] Auerbach saw "language as a key to the character of a particular society,"[70] texts "almost always have a general significance, which goes beyond the text itself and reveals something about the writer, the period in which he wrote, the development of his mode of thought, an artistic form, or a way of life."[71] He was engaged "in a process too multidimensional to be called a philological or interpretive circle." If Spitzer's philological system was based on "passing from observed detail to hypothesis and back to details,"[72] Auerbach's treated individual texts, not in isolation, but as "part of a narrative history of one aspect of western literature."[73]

Expressing the inextricable relationship between philology and history was Auerbach's ultimate goal: "Turning a point of momentous cultural change upon a pivot of syntax (along with its meaning, of course) was an art he had fashioned for himself out of the welter of philological precisionism and Hegelian flight of visionary grandiosity." In "Figura," he developed "the great insight of his life," namely, figural interpretation.[74] It was the source of his famous statement: "My purpose is always to write history," meaning: "I never approach a text as an isolated phenomenon. I address a question to

---

66. Calin, *Twentieth-Century Humanist Critics*, 44–45.

67. Wellek, "Leo Spitzer," 315.

68. Spitzer, "Introduction," 1.

69. Ibid., 10, emphasis added.

70. Hart, "Literature as Language," 228.

71. Auerbach, *Introduction aux etudes de philologie romane* (1949), 36, quoted in Hart, "Literature as Language," 228.

72. Wellek, "Leo Spitzer," 315.

73. Hart, "Literature as Language," 238.

74. Nelson, "Erich Auerbach: Memoir of a Scholar," 314–15.

it, and my question, not the text, is my primary point of departure" (*LLP*, 20).[75] For Auerbach, then, "the language of both literary and nonliterary text is a key to the conception of everyday reality in a particular time and place."[76] In contrast to Spitzer, but in clear parallel with the works of the other exiles addressed in this study, philology in "Figura" and *Mimesis* is an endless *Kulturkampf* and contributes to idiosyncratic interpretations and canonical reconstructions.[77]

Early in his life, Auerbach adopted a "Goethean humanism" (PW, 2), closely following Johann Wolfgang von Goethe's belief in *Weltliteratur*, "universal literature, or literature which expresses *Humanität*, humanity," and that "this expression is literature's ultimate purpose."[78] *Weltliteratur*, Auerbach wrote, "considers humanity to be the product of fruitful intercourse between its members" (PW, 2). Goethe also "contributed decisively to the development of historicism and to the philological research that was generated by it."[79] Auerbach conceives *Weltliteratur* as impelled by "historicist humanism," or the search for the "inner history of mankind" (PW, 2–4). Since publication of the works of Vico and von Herder, Auerbach continues, this search "*has been the true purpose of philology*" (emphasis added). Auerbach became an avid follower of historicism, which sees "man not only immersed in history but always relative to his historical position."[80] He believed that "because of this purpose philology became the dominant branch of the humanities" (PW, 2–4). Overall, according to Wellek, historicism was for Auerbach a "secular religion."[81]

---

75. According to W. W. Holdheim in "Auerbach's Mimesis: Aesthetic as Historical Understanding," the right translation should be: "again and again I have the purpose of writing history" (143).

76. Hart, "Literature as Language," 232.

77. According to Wellek, "Review: Auerbach's Special Realism": "Mr. Auerbach's extreme reluctance to define his terms," such as realism, "and to make his supposition clear from the outset . . . certainly would open the door to unlimited idiosyncrasies" (304–05).

78. Maire Said and Edward Said, "Introduction," in Auerbach, "Philology and Weltliteratur," 1.

79. On the impact of historicism on Auerbach's thought and philology, see Breslin, "Philosophy or Philology." Frank R. Ankersmit argues that Auerbach's historicism was influenced by the "historicist historical writing" of Friedrich Meinecke and "classical historicism as developed by Ranke, Humboldt, or Dilthey" ("Why Realism? Auerbach on the Representation of Reality," 54).

80. Wellek, *German, Russian, and Eastern European Criticism*, 120.

81. Ibid., 131.

Auerbach was also influenced by Immanuel Kant, who, in 1784, coined the famous dictum: "Enlightenment is mankind's exit from its self-incurred immaturity. Immaturity is the inability to make use of one's own understanding without the guidance of another. . . . *Sapere Aude*! [dare to know] Have courage to use your own understanding! That is the motto of enlightenment."[82] Similarly, Auerbach argued, "The inner history of the last thousand years is the history of mankind achieving self-expression: *this is what philology, a historicist discipline, treats*. This history contains the records of man's mighty adventurous advance to a consciousness of his human condition and to the realization of his given potential" (PW, 4–5, emphasis added). Like Kant, who claimed that his idealist philosophy constituted a Copernican revolution,[83] Auerbach declared that "historicism" is "the Copernican discovery in the cultural sciences" (*LLP*, 10).[84]

Philology, history, and humanism were inseparable in Auerbach's mind. Following Vico, he argued that through "the manifold expressions of linguistic activity the historical dimension of human existence makes itself known to men."[85] During the rise and triumph of Nazism in Germany, he

---

82. Immanuel Kant, "What Is Enlightenment?," in *What Is Enlightenment? Eighteenth-Century Answers and Twentieth-Century Questions*, ed. James Schmidt (Berkeley: University of California Press, 1996), 58.

83. In the preface to the second edition of the *Critique of Pure Reason* (1787), Kant states: "Hitherto it has been assumed that all our knowledge must conform to objects. But all attempts to extend our knowledge of objects by establishing something in regard to them a priori, by means of concepts, have, on this assumption, ended in failure. We must therefore make trial whether we may not have more success in the tasks of metaphysics, if we suppose that objects must conform to our knowledge. This would agree better with what is desired, namely, that it should be possible to have knowledge of objects a priori, determining something in regard to them prior to their being given. We should then be proceeding precisely on the lines of *Copernicus' primary hypothesis*. Failing of satisfactory progress in explaining the movements of the heavenly bodies on the supposition that they all revolved round the spectator, he tried whether he might not have better success if he made the spectator to revolve and the stars to remain at rest. A similar experiment can be tried in metaphysics, as regards the intuition of objects." See *Critique of Pure Reason*, 110.

84. However, Hartman writes that Auerbach went "so far as to call historicism's enrichment of the human adventure, its revelation of diversity, an inspiring scholarly myth: only a myth, that is, but one valid to his time" (*Scholar's Tale*, 179).

85. Breslin, "Philosophy or Philology," 372.

declared, "our philological home is the earth: it can no longer be the nation," and pleaded, as did Curtius, "We must return . . . to the knowledge that prenational medieval culture already possessed: the knowledge that that the spirit is not national" (PW, 17).[86] Auerbach and Curtius, as Geoffrey Hartman wrote, were "restorative scholars"[87]—philologists who strove to rescue European humanist tradition by reconstructing its literary history.

Philology and Ideology

[Auerbach] does not leave the present behind. The study of history comprises not just what lies in the past but what remains actual.

—Geoffrey Hartman, *A Scholar's Tale*, 2007

The Old Testament as a book of religious instruction must be abolished once and for all. With it will end the unsuccessful attempts of the last one-and-a-half millennia to make us all spiritual Jews.

—Alfred Rosenberg, *Myth of the Twentieth Century*, 1930

Auerbach was no ivory tower scholar. As Arthur Evans writes, "Auerbach's writing is, first and foremost, that of an historian and critic of culture in the tradition of Jakob Burckhardt and German *Kulturgeschichte*; beneath the surface of scholarly detachment and aristocratic urbanity there is a pathos, an urgency of involvement born of a passionate commitment to

---

86. These words about the Spirit clearly exemplify the great transformation of German thought from the time of Hegel to that of Auerbach. For according to Hegel, too, the Spirit is not national. See Yirmiyahu Yovel, *Hegel's Preface to the Phenomenology of Spirit*, trans. and commentary by Y. Yovel (Princeton: Princeton University Press, 2005 [1807]), 82–84: "It is . . . not hard to see that our time is a time of birth and transition into a new era. Spirit has broken away from its former world existence and imagining; it is about to sink all that into the past, and is busy shaping itself anew . . . self-shaping spirit matured slowly and silently toward a new shape, while shedding the edifice of its former world piece by piece. . . . This gradual crumbling . . . is broken by the rising day which, in a flash, outlines the features of the new world."

87. Hartman, *Scholar's Tale*, 167.

the variety of attitudes and the shared values and assumptions of Western civilization."[88] Auerbach believed his task was related not only to the past but also to the present: "we must today attempt to form *a lucid and coherent picture of this civilization and its unity*. I have always tried, more and more resolutely as time went on, to work in this direction, at least in my approach to the subject matter of philology, namely literary expression" (*LLP*, 6, emphasis added).

Upholding the unity of European humanist civilization became Auerbach's ultimate goal amid the crisis of German philology.[89] Note that in his first book, *Dante: Poet of the Secular World* (1929), he adhered to traditional German literary historiography, claiming that "European literature" began "in Greece" (*D*, 1). By 1942, when he began writing *Mimesis*, the picture had changed radically; he claimed that Greek pagan culture produced the Homeric, unrealistic, legendary, and irrational style, which stood in contrast to the historic, realist, and rational style of the Hebrew Bible.

Although *Mimesis* begins with Homer's *Odysseus* and ends with Joyce's *Ulysses*, Auerbach argued that its conception was based on the history of European literature "from Genesis" (*M*, 563). This decision represents a crucial, ideological, epistemological stand. His aim in "Figura" and *Mimesis* was not "only a literary inimitable masterpiece of individual, and in some other ways peculiar, interpretation of one great tradition of Western culture, but also an affirmation, while in exile in Turkey, of a complex" and "passionate attitude toward that culture."[90]

Against Aryan philology's attempt to eliminate the Old Testament from the Christian Western canon in general and German cultural and religious life in particular as an antiquated Book of Laws or the history of a despised people, Auerbach upheld it as a prophetic book that prefigures Christ's life and message, the central theme in the Christian drama of salvation, situating both in the sacred dimension of time in which a promise in the Old Testament is realized in the New. Through figural, typological

---

88. Evans, "Erich Auerbach as European Critic," 200–01.

89. According to Hartman, *Scholar's Tale*, *Mimesis* provides "a generous conception of the unity of European literature, shaped by its capacity to absorb the *imaginaries* of two very different civilizations" (166).

90. Nelson, "Erich Auerbach: Memoir of a Scholar," 312.

interpretation, the Old and New Testaments are inextricable from each other and from the history of Christian Europe as a whole.

Changing historical circumstances prompted this humanist ideology, emphasizing the power and influence of the Old Testament. *Dante: Poet of the Secular World* (1929) presents no serious analysis of Old Testament events and heroes but discusses the influence of the classical world, Christianity, and Thomas Aquinas's theology and philosophy on Dante and Western culture. In "Figura" and *Mimesis*, the Old Testament plays a crucial, momentous role in the development of European culture and literature; moreover, Auerbach claims its superiority to classical culture because it provides the content and form for European identity and its unique sense of time and vision of history. Confronting the premises of Aryan philology first led Auerbach to interpretation, and interpretation led him to construct a magisterial new vision of European literary history based on universalism, or humanism, founded in the Judeo-Christian tradition. The clear, coherent ideological agenda of *Mimesis* informs its unique teleological analysis of realism in the West as well as its structure and texture. Like his beloved Dante, and Popper and Baron in his own time, Auerbach found his great mission in exile.

To understand the transformation of Auerbach's mind, we must first understand his life in Germany and the rise of Aryan philology. Next, I will explore the crisis of his existential displacement, which led him to conceive a comparative approach to *Weltliteratur* and to attack Aryan philology head-on.

Erich Auerbach: Life, Time, and Works

[In] Auerbach's experience, individuality as fate emerges out of the inevitably tragic sphere of everyday life.

—Hans Ulrich Gumbrecht, "'Pathos of the
Earthly Progress': Erich Auerbach's Everydays," 1996

From this sketch of his life it should appear that [Stendhal] first reached the point of accounting for himself, and the point of realistic writing, when he was seeking a haven in his 'storm-tossed boat,' and discovered that, for his boat, there was no fit and safe haven . . .

—Erich Auerbach, "In the Hôtel De La Mole," *Mimesis*, 1946

Erich Auerbach was born in Berlin on November 9, 1892,[91] the only son of a prosperous and distinguished merchant family: "I am Prussian and of Jewish faith," he noted on the curriculum vitae appended to his 1921 inaugural dissertation.[92] He was "a member of the humanly liberal, financially comfortable, Prussian Jewish *haute bourgeoisie*. His father bore the honorary title of *Kommerzienrat* [roughly, Councilor of Commerce], conferred by Wilhelmina Germany upon her distinguished financiers, industrialists, and business executives."[93] Young Auerbach received his preliminary education in the capital's prestigious French Lycée (*Französisches Gymnasium*), where he benefited from its "strong program of classical studies, and learned to speak French fluently and to write forcefully."[94] From 1910 to 1913, after completing his secondary studies, he studied law in Berlin, Freiburg, Munich, and Heidelberg and had the time and leisure to travel elsewhere in Europe as well. In 1913, at the age of twenty-one, he received the Doctor of Law degree, *doctor juris*, from the University of Heidelberg, with a thesis "devoted to a program of reform in German penal law."[95] He then "undertook further journeys abroad and began in early 1914 to study Romance philology in Berlin."[96] Before the outbreak of World War I, he had completed most of the requirements toward his doctorate: perhaps already "Auerbach saw Roman philology as holding an unparalleled promise" because of its "potential to demonstrate a basic unity in European culture."[97]

From 1914 to 1918, he volunteered as an infantryman, fought in northern France, and in April 1918 severely injured his foot and was

---

91. On Auerbach's life and works, see Jan M. Ziolkowski, "Foreword," *LLP*, ix–xxxix; Geoffrey Green, *Literary Criticism and the Structure of History: Erich Auerbach and Leo Spitzer* (Lincoln: University of Nebraska Press, 1982); Levin, "Two *Romanisten*," 463–84; Gumbrecht, " 'Pathos,' " 13–35; Lewis Coser, *Refugee Scholars in America: Their Impact and Their Experiences* (New Haven: Yale University Press, 1984), 262–64; Nelson, "Erich Auerbach: Memoir of a Scholar," 312–20; and Evans, "Erich Auerbach as European Critic," 193–215. See also, more recently, Krystal's excellent "The Book of Books: Erich Auerbach and the Making of 'Mimesis.' "

92. See Nelson, "Erich Auerbach: Memoir of a Scholar," 313.

93. Evans, "Erich Auerbach as European Critic," 212.

94. Ibid., 212–13.

95. Shahar, "Auerbach's Scars," 606.

96. Auerbach, *curriculum vitae*, in Nelson, "Erich Auerbach: Memoir of a Scholar," 313.

97. Ziolkowski, "Foreword," *LLP*, xvi, emphasis added.

awarded a second-grade military medal.⁹⁸ After the war, he continued Romance Studies in Berlin. When his adviser, Erhard Lommatzsch, transferred to the University of Greifswald, Auerbach defended his dissertation, *The Technique of the Early Renaissance Novelle in Italy and France* (*Zur Technik der Frührenaissancenovelle in Italien und Frankreich*) "to that university faculty." He received his PhD in 1921.⁹⁹

During the Weimar Republic (1919–1933), Jewish origin was considered an obstacle to obtaining an academic appointment,¹⁰⁰ which may explain why, from 1923 to 1929, Auerbach served as a librarian, or *Bibliotheksrat*—a senior civil service rank—at the Prussian State Library in Berlin.¹⁰¹ There, he met other Jewish scholars, including Walter Benjamin.¹⁰² At thirty-one, he married Marie Mankiewitz; their only son, Clemens, was born later that year. These seven years proved most productive. He published an abridged translation of Vico's *The New Science* (1924) as well as a collaborative translation of Benedetto Croce's introductory study, *The Philosophy of Giambattista Vico* (1927). The Italian political philosopher, rhetorician, historian, and jurist exercised enormous influence on Auerbach, not least, Auerbach wrote, because Vico argued that the "entire

---

98. Kader Konuk, *East West Mimesis: Auerbach in Turkey* (Stanford: Stanford University Press, 2010), 25. See also Jan N. Bremmer, "Erich Auerbach and His Mimesis," *Poetics Today* 20 (Spring 1999): 4.

99. Auerbach, *curriculum vitae*, in Nelson, "Erich Auerbach: Memoir of a Scholar," 313.

100. For a description of life in Germany between 1914 and 1933, written by a German who opposed Nazism and Hitlerism, see Sebastian Haffner, *Geschichte eines Deutschen* [*The Story of a German*] (Stuttgart/München: Deutsche Verlags-Anstalt, 2000). Good descriptions of Weimar and Nazi Germany can be found in Eric D. Weits, *Weimar Germany: Promise and Tragedy* (Princeton: Princeton University Press, 2007); Elon, *The Pity of It All*; Saul Friedländer, *Nazi Germany and the Jews: The Years of Destruction, 1933–1939* (New York: HarperCollins, 1997), and *The Years of Extermination: Nazi Germany and the Jews, 1939–1945* (New York: HarperCollins, 2007); and Mosse, *Crisis of German Ideology* and *Confronting History—A Memoir*.

101. Later in life, Auerbach joked that "his parents—of the high bourgeoisie—secured for him a sinecure in the National Library in Berlin." "With that wonderful smile," Calin reports in a July 10, 2011, letter to the author, he said, "'So, having nothing to do, I wrote a book on Dante and translated Vico. Then they asked me to be Professor of Romance Philology in Marburg. Me! What did I know about that? So, I read up on it over the summer.'"

102. See Shahar, "Auerbach's Scars," 607.

development of human history, as made by men, is potentially contained in the human mind, and may therefore, by a process of research and re-evocation, be understood by men."[103] This observation is clearly the source for the essential and unique link in Auerbach's thought between philology, humanism, literature, and history.

During this period, he also completed his *Habilitationsschrift*, which he published as *Dante: Poet of the Secular World* (1929). He "spent 7 years at the Staatsbibliothek, and was almost 38 when I brought out the [study on] Dante and arrived at the university" of Marburg.[104] He took the motto for the study from Heraclitus of Ephesus: "A man's character is his fate," because he deemed Dante "the first European poet who had painted characters in their individuality."[105] However, this motto, did not apply to Auerbach. His life was soon engulfed and eventually shattered, not by any fault of character, but by the great social and political transformation taking place in Germany and Europe. His life and career were forcefully and radically determined by anti-Semitism; in Auerbach's experience, "individuality as fate emerges out of the inevitably tragic sphere of everyday life."[106]

With the success and wide recognition of his book on Dante, Auerbach was appointed professor (*ordinarius*—a professor with a chair representing the area in question) and chair of Romance philology at the University of Marburg, succeeding Leo Spitzer, who went to the University of Cologne.[107] He was thirty-seven years old and would spend only six years in this position. After Hitler was elected chancellor in 1933, a law was passed that barred Jews from holding official positions. The Law for the Re-Establishment of Professional Civil Service was part of "a compre-

---

103. Auerbach, "Vico and Aesthetic Historicism," 197. On Vico's crucial influence on Auerbach, see Timothy Bahti, "Vico, Auerbach and Literary History," in *Vico: Past and Present*, ed. Giorgio Tagliacozzo (Atlantic Highlands: Humanities Press, 1981), 99–114; and Wellek, "Auerbach and Vico," in *Vico: Past and Present*.

104. Auerbach to Dr. Martin Hellweg, May 22, 1939, in Elsky, Vialon, and Stein, "Scholarship in Times of Extremes," 755.

105. Gumbrecht, "'Pathos,'" 20. Compare Goethe's letter to Lavater, 1780, "Have I not already written to you, 'Individuum est ineffabile,' from which I drive a whole world," quoted in Friedrich Meinecke, *Historicism: The Rise of a New Historical Outlook*, trans. J. E. Anderson (London: Routledge & Kegan Paul, 1972 [1936]), 1.

106. Gumbrecht, "'Pathos,'" 32.

107. According to Bremmer ("Erich Auerbach and His Mimesis"), during 1929, Auerbach "was transferred to the University Library at Marburg, then recommended for *Habilitation* on the basis" of his book on Dante, and only later, in 1930, "was appointed chairman of the Department of Romance Philology" (4).

hensive legal policy aimed at diminishing the presence of the Jews in the German public, especially 'in professions that shape and express the essence of Germandom, the Aryan character,' such as schools and institutions of higher learning, and also in the areas of law, medicine and art."[108] Auerbach was dismissed in 1935 and went into exile in Turkey in 1936 to teach at Istanbul State University. There, he launched his systematic repudiation of Aryan philology, first in the essay "Figura" (1938) and culminating in the majestic *Mimesis* of 1946.

Turkey was the only place that offered him an academic job that would allow him to escape Nazi Germany with his wife and young son. He arrived at Istanbul State University in the fall, once again replacing Spitzer, who went to Johns Hopkins University in Baltimore. Auerbach spent the next eleven years as chair of Turkey's "leading faculty for Western language and literature."[109] In a 1938 letter to the Romanist Karl Vossler, he quoted Dante: "the bread of exile . . . tastes salty."[110] He must have felt "the deep loneliness of exile."[111] Indeed, according to Edward Said, who knew firsthand, exile is above all "life led outside habitual order"; it "is like death but without death's ultimate mercy, it has torn millions of people from the nourishment of tradition, family, and geography."[112] Thomas Mann, who lived in California during the war, wrote that for exiles "homeland . . . has become foreign," and "here in the foreign land that has become home we cannot help feeling we are in the wrong place, something which robs our own existence of a certain moral authority."[113] Hence, "exile's predicament" is "as close as we come in the modern era to tragedy."[114] At Yale University during the 1950s, Auerbach told Hartman a sad "anecdote of a concert violinist, a refugee like himself, who complained that in America his violin emitted a different tone."[115]

---

108. Uriel Tal, *Religion, Politics and Ideology in the Third Reich: Selected Essays* (London: Routledge, 2004), 130.

109. Konuk, *East West Mimesis*, 3–4.

110. Quoted in Hacohen, "Typology and the Holocaust," 23.

111. María Rosa Menocal, *Shards of Love: Exile and the Origins of Lyric* (Durham: Duke University Press, 1994), 92.

112. Said, *Reflections on Exile*, 186.

113. Mann to Adorno, September 1, 1950, in Adorno and Mann, *Correspondence, 1943–1955*, 41.

114. Said, *Reflections on Exile*, 174, 183.

115. Hartman, *Scholar's Tale*, 169.

However, the hard existential experience could forge new goals. Dante and Machiavelli wrote their most significant works in exile, the *Divine Comedy* and the *Discourses on the First Ten Books of Titus Livy* (*Discorsi*, 1517), respectively. In 1938, Auerbach wrote that his challenge in exile was "to find a point of departure (*Ausgangspunkt*) for those historical forces that can be set against it."[116] "Figura," which he published in 1938, should be seen as a point of departure, namely, the discovery of the Christian figural interpretation of history, and later, *Mimesis* was structured so that "each part of the investigation" or chapter "raises problems of its own and demands its points of departure" (*LLP*, 20).

In early 1937, Auerbach complained about the "whole monstrous mass of difficulties" he encountered in Turkey as well as the "troubles, cross-purposes, and misarrangements on the part of local authorities that drive some colleagues to despair."[117] He grumbled that "as far as research goes, my work is entirely primitive," and that although "wonderfully situated," the city was "also unpleasant and . . . rough."[118] Like so many other exiles, he lived "a life in translation." Exiles crossed "from one meaning of *Übersetzung* [translation] to the other, from one *Übersetzung* to another *Übersetzung*."[119] In the words of George Steiner, it "seems proper that those who create art in a civilization of quasi-barbarism, which has made so many homeless, should themselves be poets unhoused and wanderers across language."[120]

After two years in Istanbul, Auerbach began an agonizing, soul-searching quest for a mission that would mitigate his hardships and, above all, provide his life some meaning. In an October 1938 letter to Traugott Fuchs (1906–1997), Spitzer's doctoral assistant, who also lived in Istanbul, he claimed: "The challenge is not to grasp and digest all the evil that's happening—that's not difficult—but much more to find a point of departure (*Ausgangspunkt*) for those historical forces that can be set against it." The philologist was more than willing to enlist his skills and scholarship, but,

---

116. Auerbach to Traugott Fuchs, October 22, 1938, in Elsky, Vialon, and Stein, "Scholarship," 752.

117. Auerbach to Herr Benjamin, January 3, 1937, in Elsky, Vialon, and Stein, "Scholarship," 751.

118. Ibid., 750.

119. Azade Seyhan, "German Academic Exiles in Istanbul: Translation as the *Bildung* of the Other," 286.

120. Quoted in Said, *Reflections on Exile*, 174.

he continued, all "those who today want to serve the right and the true are united only in negative—in matters active and positive they are weak and splintered."[121]

The historical reasons for wielding his pen as a weapon are not hard to find. In a speech to the 1937 annual Nazi Party rally in Nuremberg, Reich Minister of Propaganda Joseph Goebbels spelled out the official view of Jews: "Look, this is the enemy of the world, the destroyer of cultures, the parasite among the nations, the son of chaos, the incarnation of evil, the ferment of decomposition, the visible demon of the decay of humanity."[122] In March 1938, Austria was occupied and annexed to Germany. In Vienna, "[u]niversity professors were obliged to scrub the streets with their naked hands, pious white-bearded Jews were dragged into the synagogue by hooting youth and forced to do knee-exercises and to shout 'Heil Hitler.'"[123] On October 1, the German army invaded Czechoslovakia and occupied the Sudetenland. Nazi malice was no longer confined to Germany but expanded by military might and aggression into other countries in Europe. On November 9–10, *Kristallnacht*, or the Night of Broken Glass, or *Reichskristallnacht, Pogromnacht, Novemberpogrome*, fully revealed Nazi sadism. In a series of coordinated attacks throughout Germany and parts of Austria, at least ninety-one Jews were killed, and thirty thousand arrested and incarcerated in concentration camps. The Hebrew Bible, the Old Testament, was burned,[124] as were over one thousand synagogues, ninety-five in Vienna alone. Over seven thousand Jewish businesses were damaged or destroyed; Jewish homes, hospitals, and schools were ransacked; attackers demolished buildings with sledgehammers. The Twelve Theses manifesto of the students who organized the 1938 book burnings stated: "The Jews can only think in a Jewish way. When he writes in German, he lies. We want to eradicate the lie. Jewish works should be published only in Hebrew. If

---

121. Auerbach to Traugott Fuchs, October 22, 1938, in Elsky, Vialon, and Stein, "Scholarship," 752.

122. Peter Fritzsche, *Life and Death in the Third Reich* (Cambridge: Harvard University Press, 2008), 131.

123. Stefan Zweig, *The World of Yesterday: An Autobiography* (London: Cassell, 1943 [1942]), 305.

124. For example, in the small town of Fürth, "the Hebrew Bible, one of the most sacred symbols of European-Christian civilization" was "publicly burned." The same took place in many German cities. See Alon Confino, *A World without Jews: The Nazi Imagination from Persecution to Genocide* (New Haven: Yale University Press, 2014), 3.

they appear in German, they should be identified as translation. German writing should be available for use only to Germans." Therefore, "*not one copy but thousands, not in one place but in hundreds of communities across the Reich . . . [b]y fire and other means, the destruction of the Book of Books was at the center of Kristallnacht, when fourteen hundred synagogues were set on fire.*"[125] No other event in the history of German Jewry between 1933 and 1945 was so widely reported as it was happening, and the accounts of foreign journalists sent shock waves around the world.

In this gloom and desperation, Auerbach looked for "historical forces" that could fight the savagery spreading before his eyes: "To seek for them in myself, to trace them down in the world[,] completely absorbs me," he confessed, yet the "old forces of resistance," such as "churches, democracies, education, economic laws—are useful and effective only if they are renewed and activated through a *new force not yet visible to me*" (emphasis added). Traditional institutional modes of resistance no longer fit. Europe desperately needed a humanist renewal. He knew "well what the most general rules and direction of the expected renewal must be," but he did not know what to do "concretely." It was "now hidden not only from me but from everyone who cares for the dignity and freedom of man." He could not turn "away from world events" as did so many people he knew; he was "too deeply convinced of the historical order," yet he had learned "too much (from life and from books) to allow myself to be deceived by illusory hopes."[126]

In June 1939, two months before Germany invaded Poland and World War II began, Auerbach wrote that despite "no lack of uncertainty and restlessness even now . . . life is for the time being is enchanting here—Only books, that is, a usable U[niversity] L[ibrary] is lacking, and travel is impossible."[127] In a few weeks, the whole of Europe was engulfed

---

125. Ibid., 56, 115.

126. Auerbach to Fuchs, October 22, 1938, in Elsky, Vialon, and Stein, "Scholarship," 752-55.

127. Auerbach to Dr. Martin Hellweg, May 22, 1939, in Elsky, Vialon, and Stein, "Scholarship," 756. Later in life, Auerbach said that in Turkey, "I needed texts even if I could do without scholarship. There was a Greek monastery on a hill; in the library was the entire Patrologia Latina. So I climbed the hill every morning and came down every evening" (Calin, letter to the author, July 10, 2011). Compare Niccolò Machiavelli's description of exile: "When evening comes, I return home and go to my study. On the threshold, I strip naked, taking off my muddy, sweaty work day clothes, and put on the robes of court and palace, and, in this graver

in brutality. On August 22, as final preparations were made for the invasion of Poland, Hitler told his generals how he envisaged what was to come:

> Our strength lies in our speed and brutality. Genghis Khan hunted millions of women and children to their deaths, consciously and with a joyous heart . . . I have put my Death's Head formations at the ready with the command to send man, woman and child of Polish descent and language to their deaths, pitilessly and remorselessly. Poland will be depopulated and settled with Germans.[128]

In these years, the Third Reich "demonstrate[d] with terrible clarity the ultimate potential consequences of racism, militarism and authoritarianism."[129]

Fascism had gained the upper hand. As Lukács wrote, "Fascist ideology and its pseudo-revolutionary rejection of the past" was "in reality a rejection of culture and humanism."[130] Likewise, the German Jewish philosopher Ernst Cassirer observed in *The Myth of the State* (1946) that "the myth of the race worked like a strong corrosive and succeeded in dissolving and disintegrating all other values."[131] Thomas Mann, who moved with his family to Switzerland in 1933 after Hitler's rise to power, had no doubt about the outcome. Writing "Bruder [Brother] Hitler" in summer 1939, he describes how the Führer, with

> masterly adroitness . . . exploits the weariness of the continent, its agony of fear, its dread of war. He knows how to stir up the

---

dress, I enter the courts of the ancients, and am welcomed by them, and there I taste the food that alone is mine, and for which I was born. And there I make bold to speak to them and ask the motives of their actions, and they, in their humanity, reply to me. And for the space of four hours I forget the world, remember no vexation, fear poverty no more, tremble no more at death; I pass indeed into their world" (Machiavelli to Francesco Vettori, December 10, 1513, in James B. Atkinson and David Sices, eds., *Machiavelli and His Friends: Their Personal Correspondence* (DeKalb: Northern Illinois University Press, 1996), 262–65.

128. Quoted in Evans, *Third Reich at War*, 11.

129. Ibid., 764.

130. Georg Lukács, *Studies in European Realism* (New York: Grosset & Dunlap, 1964), 4. Lukács wrote these words in 1948.

131. Cassirer, *Myth of the State*, 3, 287.

people over the heads of their rulers and win large sections of opinion to himself. Fortune is his slave, all walls fall before him. The one-time melancholic ne'er-do-well, simply because he has learned—for aught he knows, out of patriotism—to be a political animal now bids fair to subjugate Europe, or, God knows, maybe the whole world.[132]

In this dark moment, Auerbach assumed a "combative stance." By 1942, he found his unique voice, based on his epiphany in Istanbul, and, in *Mimesis*, would deliver an overarching humanist apologia for Western humanist civilization through a sophisticated, evidentiary, and luminous analysis of Western literary realism.

After the war, in 1947, Auerbach immigrated to the United States, teaching first at Pennsylvania State University and then at the Institute for Advanced Study in Princeton. He held the position of Professor of Romance Philology at Yale University from 1950 until his death in 1957.

Auerbach had time and cause to reflect on the relationship of exile to revelation, creation, confrontation, and interpretation. The example dearest to him, Dante, wrote the *Divine Comedy* in exile, and like "Figura" and *Mimesis*, it bears the signs of its author's devastating experience even while it announces his new revelation and mission in life; exile fueled creation and focused confrontation. While Dante used the *Comedy* to condemn his enemies to eternal damnation, "Figura" and *Mimesis* confronted the vicious, specious premises of an Aryan philology that led to the murder of millions and world war with a learned journey through the human struggle to render truth.

Aryan Philology and the Elimination of the Old Testament

> We expect our national Churches to shake themselves free of all that is un-German, in particular the Old Testament and its Jewish morality and rewards.
>
> —"Resolution of the German Christians,"
> rally at Berlin Sportpalast, November 13, 1933

---

132. "Bruder Hitler," March 25, 1939; it appears as "A Brother," in *Death in Venice, Tonio Kröger and Other Writings*, ed. F. A. Lubich (New York: Continuum, 1999), 298.

> Did Christianity arise out of Judaism being thus its continuation and completion, or does it stand in opposition to Judaism? To this question we respond: Christian faith is the unbridgeable religious contradiction to Judaism.
>
> —"The Godesberg Declaration," Evangelical Lutheran Church, April 4, 1939

> Elimination of Jewish influence on German life is the urgent and fundamental question of the present German religious situation . . . the de-Judaization of Christianity would continue the work of the Lutheran Reformation.
>
> —Walter Grundmann, 1939

Philology studies the grammar, rhetoric, history, and critical traditions associated with a given language to establish the authenticity, original form, intent, and meaning of literary texts and written records. During the nineteenth and the first half of the twentieth century, it became enmeshed in ideological and historical transformations related to the rise of Aryanism, racism, anti-Semitism, and Nazism in Europe: it became "war by other means."[133]

During the nineteenth century, European philologists and historians searched for an alternative to the traditional Judeo-Christian origins of Western civilization. Their quest actually began at the end of the eighteenth century, when the Anglo-Welsh philologist William Jones (1746–1794) "discovered the similarities between the European languages" and the "Sanskrit and Persian" languages, laying "the foundation for the hypothesis of an Indo-European language [*Indo-Germanische*] affinity and an Indo-European primal population."[134] Like the sixteenth-century Copernican Revolution, which replaced the geocentric conception of the universe with the heliocentric view, the discovery of Sanskrit literature displaced classical antiquity. "Henceforward the Greco-Roman world could only be regarded as a single province, a small sector of the universe of human culture."[135]

---

133. Lerer, "Philology and Criticism at Yale," 18.
134. Stefan Arvidsson, *Aryan Idols: Indo-European Mythology as Ideology and Science*, 10.
135. Cassirer, *Myth of the State*, 17.

The historical-linguistic construction of Indo-Europeans also had tremendous implications for the Judeo-Christian tradition. The bible's authority was called into question by a "comparative linguistics that supported the new people."[136] The interest stemmed—and still stems—"from a will to create alternatives to those identities that have been provided by tradition," or the Judeo-Christian tradition.[137] European research on the "Indo-Europeans and their culture and religion [was] used . . . in the service of various ideological interests."[138] Aryan philology "became the primitive homeland of Western man in search of legitimation." It sought to provide "answers to a series of questions that first became urgent in the nineteenth century, questions pertaining to the origins and vocation of a Western world in search of a national, political, and religious identity."[139] Particularly in Germany, it strove to develop a new ancestral lineage and to eliminate the Old Testament stories from history as well as the Christian canon. Philology was inextricable from, not only ideology and history, but anthropology. Germany witnessed the "transformation of nineteenth century scholarly studies of philology into racist and even genocidal rant in the twentieth century."[140] By the end of the nineteenth century, "*culturist* philology was unable to prevent the word 'race' from being usurped by *naturalist* forces, and human beings came to be seen more and more as part of the necessary realm of nature, rather than the contingent realm of culture."[141]

The full depravity of Aryan racial anthropology was evident in Nazi Germany. "From about 1940 to 1944," historian Léon Poliakov wrote, "the most important differentiation between the inhabitants of Europe was that between Aryans and Semites: the former were permitted to live, the latter

---

136. Arvidsson, *Aryan Idols*, 60.

137. Suzanne L. Marchand shows the close connection between Aryanism and Orientalism in nineteenth-century Germany in her important study, *German Orientalism in the Age of Empire: Religion, Race, and Scholarship* (New York: Cambridge University Press, 2009). See also Marchand, "Nazism, Orientalism and Humanism," 267–305.

138. Arvidsson, *Aryan Idols*, xi, 4.

139. Maurice Olender, *The Language of Paradise: Race, Religion, and Philology in the Nineteenth Century*, trans. A. Goldhammer (Cambridge: Harvard University Press, 2008 [1989]), 139.

140. Susannah Heschel, *The Aryan Jesus: Christian Theologians and the Bible in Nazi Germany*, (Princeton: Princeton University Press, 2008), 32.

141. Arvidsson, *Aryan Idols*, 61.

were condemned to die."¹⁴² Thanks to the work of philologists and linguists, this absolute dividing line "was accepted as a dogma by the majority of researchers," and by "about 1860 this conviction was already a part of the intellectual baggage of all cultivated Europeans." Linguistics imposed its "tyrannical influence" on "anthropology" and the other sciences[143] and, in turn, crucially influenced the course of history. Language was used to support spurious "blood relationships" that justified murder, torture, and slavery in Nazi Germany and Europe generally during World War II.

As "scholars established the disciplines of Semitic and Indo-European" studies, they invented "the mythical figures of the Hebrew and the Aryan," a "providential pair" that revealed "to the people of Christianized West the secret of their identity" and "bestowed upon them the patent of nobility that justified their spiritual, religious, and political domination of the world."[144] Although the "Aryan" concept is very problematic since it refers to a language, not a people—in Sanskrit, it means noble or pure—it affected all the human sciences from history to mythology "and soon to include 'racial science.'" Scholars believed they were now "in a position to make an accurate portrayal of prehistoric society."[145] Throughout Europe, "the terms Aryan and Semite embarked on new ideological and political careers outside philology and physical anthropology."[146]

The first to spread "the doctrine of Indomania in Germany" was the Lutheran priest and pre-romantic Johann Gottfried Herder (1744–1803).[147] Later, the polymath German biblical scholar and orientalist Paul de Lagarde (1827–1891) promoted the idea of a new Germanic Christianity, which could be cleansed or purged of its Jewish dross. He claimed, "Every Jew is a proof of the weakness of our national life and of the small worth of what we call the Christian religion."[148] Therefore, Jesus would be elevated as the discoverer

---

142. Léon Poliakov, *The Aryan Myth: A History of Racist and Nationalist Ideas in Europe*, (New York: Barnes & Noble, 1974), 1.

143. Ibid., 255–56.

144. Jean-Pierre Vernant, "Foreword," in Olender, *Language of Paradise*, x.

145. Olender, *Language of Paradise*, 7–8.

146. Ibid., 12–13.

147. Arvidsson, *Aryan Idols*, 24.

148. Poliakov, *Aryan Myth*, 309. For an important study about the search for the historical Jesus in Germany during the nineteenth and early twentieth centuries, see Albert Schweitzer, *The Quest for the Historical Jesus* (London: SCM Press, 2000 [1906]).

of eternal truth, a pure human genius and proclaimer of the Kingdom of God, but not as a Jew or the Jewish Messiah. These misconceptions arose from his disciples and were exacerbated by Paul's Jewish Pharisaic corruption of Jesus's original message.[149] In theology, Lagarde was radically anti-Pauline.

The search for a non-Jewish or Aryan Jesus as founder of a Germanic or Nordic Christianity[150] started in the same decades when "a special word is coined and 'anti-Semitism' begins to be used for racial animosity against Jews."[151] The term first appeared in 1879 in a pamphlet called "The Way to Victory of Germanicism over Judaism" by the German journalist Wilhelm Marr (1819–1904) and was used overwhelmingly in reference to Jews, not other Semitic peoples. As part of "the revival of a mythical *Deutschtum* and the creation of political institutions that would embody and preserve this peculiar character of the Germans,"[152] Aryan philology contributed major efforts to decanonize and exclude the Old Testament from Christian history and German culture and life. "The Aryan Jesus was the confession of those who sought a Teutonic brand of Christianity, rejecting the Old Testament and anything else that smacked of Jewish influence in the church."[153]

In 1899, Houston Stewart Chamberlain's *Die Grundlagen des neunzehnten Jahrhunderts* (*The Foundations of the Nineteenth Century*) became

---

149. Peter M. Head, "The Nazi Quest for an Aryan Jesus," *Journal for the Study of the Historical Jesus* 2 (2004): 63. On Lagarde, see Eugene Sheppard, "Foreword," *Germany's Prophet: Paul de Lagarde and the Origins of Modern Antisemitism* (Waltham/Boston: Brandeis University Press/University Press of New England, 2013), an English translation of Ulrich Sieg, *Paul de Lagarde und die Ursprünge des modernen Antisemitismus* (Munich: Carl Hanser Verlag, 2007). See also Stern, *Politics of Cultural Despair*.

150. On attempts to build a new Germanic or Nordic church in Nazi Germany, see Cardinal Michael von Faulhaber, *Judaism, Christianity and Germany* (New York: Macmillan, 1934), 92; and Heschel, *Aryan Jesus: Christian Theologians and the Bible in Nazi Germany* (Princeton: Princeton University Press, 2010); Heschel, "When Jesus was an Aryan," in *Betrayal: German Churches and the Holocaust* (Minneapolis: Fortress, 1999), 68–89; Heschel, "Nazifying Christian Theology: Walter Grundmann and the Institute for the Study and Eradication of Jewish Influence on German Church Life," *Church History* 63 (December 1994): 587–605; and Heschel, "Reading Jesus as a Nazi," in *A Shadow of Glory: Reading the New Testament after the Holocaust*, ed. Tod Linafelt (New York: Routledge, 2002), 27–41.

151. Head, "Nazi Quest," 62. The term *anti-Semitic*, or *anti-Semite*, overwhelmingly refers to Jews only. It was coined in 1879 by the German journalist Wilhelm Marr (1819–1904) in a pamphlet called "The Way to Victory of Germanism over Judaism."

152. Stern, *Politics of Cultural Despair*, xiii.

153. Heschel, "Reading Jesus as a Nazi," 27.

one of the main references for the early twentieth-century pan-Germanic movement and, later, Nazi racial policy. Its fifteen hundred pages were "the new Bible of hundreds of thousands of Germans."[154] Constructing Western history since the time of the Greeks in terms of a race struggle, "the chief prophet of Aryanism"[155] argued that "only Aryans were . . . capable of creative culture," and "the intermingling of Aryans with other races leads inevitably to decline." As "the best representative of the western Aryan people," the German was "best placed to establish a new European order." Chamberlain "spends around eighty pages in an attempt to prove the 'Aryanism' of Jesus."[156] In contrast, the Jews' "existence is sin, their existence is a crime against the holy laws of life."[157] Scholars regard Chamberlain's work as pivotal: "perhaps no book has contributed so much to the spreading of the anti-Jewish theory of race as this book, with its innocent-sounding title drawn from the philosophy of culture."[158] Another historian termed it "this lofty bible of anti-Semitism."[159]

Alfred Rosenberg was a leading proponent of racial theory, persecution of the Jews, and German *Lebensraum*. In *The Myth of the Twentieth Century* (1930), he declared: "Today, a new belief is arising: the *Mythos* of the blood; the belief that the godly essence of man itself is to be defended through the blood; that belief which embodied the clearest knowledge that the Nordic race represents that *Mysterium* which has overthrown and replaced the old sacraments."[160] Inspired by Chamberlain, where "the eternal Aryan values were contrasted to *Judaeo-Christian depravity*," Rosenberg

---

154. Poliakov, *Aryan Myth*, 318.

155. Ibid., 313.

156. Head, "Nazi Quest," 64–65.

157. Poliakov, *Aryan Myth*, 317.

158. A. Bein, "Modern Anti-Semitism and Its Place in the History of the Jewish Question," in *Between East and West: Essays Dedicated to the Memory of Béla Horovitz*, ed. A. Altman (London: East West Library, 1958), 181.

159. Poliakov, quoted in Head, "Nazi Quest," 64.

160. On Rosenberg, see *Memoirs of Alfred Rosenberg*; Nova, *Alfred Rosenberg: Nazi Theorist of the Holocaust*; Rosenberg, *Race and Race History and Other Essays by Alfred Rosenberg*; and Lukács, *Destruction of Reason*, 714–64. In "The Theme of the Joseph Novels" (1942) in *Thomas Mann's Addresses Delivered at the Library of Congress, 1942–1949*, 16–17, Mann strongly denounced Rosenberg's use and abuse of the concept of myth: "the word 'myth' has a bad reputation nowadays—we have only to think of the title of the book, which the 'philosopher' of German fascism, Rosenberg, the preceptor of Hitler, has given to his vicious textbook: 'The Myth of the 20th Century.'"

declared: "The Old Testament as a book of religious instruction must be abolished once and for all. With it will end the unsuccessful attempts of the last one-and-a-half millennia to make us all spiritual Jews." As for Jesus, Rosenberg followed Chamberlain and others in claiming "there is not the slightest reason to believe" that "Jesus was of Jewish ancestry."[161] And he contemplated the creation of a National Reich Church based not on the Bible but on *Mein Kampf*.[162] Chamberlain and Rosenberg figured in Hans Baron's struggle to rescue the Renaissance from the purported humanism "north of the Alps."[163]

Attempts to eradicate the Jewish Bible and all Jewish influence reached their nadir after 1933. A mass rally organized Nazi Party–style by the German Christians (*Deutsche Christen*) on November 13, 1933, at the Berlin Sportpalast shows the omnipresent anti-Semitism fueled by Aryan philology.[164] The group formed "in 1921 for the racial survival and de-judaizing of the Christian faith and had been represented in sundry Church parliaments."[165] In 1931, it was officially organized as the Nazi wing of the Evangelical Church, and in June 1932 its leaders published a letter in *Christliche Welt* expressing their goals: "rejection of the liberal spirit of the

---

161. Rosenberg, quoted in Head, "Nazi Quest," 69.

162. Rosenberg, quoted in Marvin Olasky, "If we lose the battle [Dietrich Bonhoeffer on living in totalitarian times]," July 3, 2010; www.freerepublic.com/focus/f-news/2549521/posts.

163. Hans Baron wrote that he "came upon the prevailing [nationalist and *völkisch*] theories of those years, according to which Humanism north of the Alps, and in particular in Germany, developed from a native, late medieval background essentially independent of any—at least and salutary—influence from the south," namely, Italy. See Hans Baron, "The Course of My Studies in Florentine Humanism," in Baron, *In Search of Florentine Civic Humanism: Essays on the Transition from Medieval to Modern Thought*, 2 vols. (Princeton: Princeton University Press, 1988), 1: 183. On Hans Baron, see Weinstein and Zakai, *Jewish Exiles and European Thought in the Shadow of the Third Reich*.

164. Heschel, "Nazifying Christian Theology," 588. On the German Christian movement, see Doris L. Bergen, *Twisted Cross: The German Christian Movement in the Third Reich* (Chapel Hill: University of North Carolina Press, 1996); Jack Forstman, *Christian Faith in Dark Times: Theological Conflicts in the Shadow of Hitler* (Louisville: Westminster, 1992); and Richard Steigmann-Gall's important critical reevaluation of Nazi ideology in *The Holy Reich: Nazi Conceptions of Christianity, 1919–1945* (New York: Cambridge University Press, 2003).

165. Waldmar Gurin, *Hitler and the Christians* (New York: Sheed & Ward, 1936), 68.

Judaic-Marxist 'enlightenment,'" the "overthrow of humanitarianism born of the Judaic-Marxist spirit, with its resultant pacifism, internationalism, Christian world-citizenship, etc.," and the "purification and preservation of the race."[166] The movement emphasized "Christ in the Community of Blood and Fate" in its 1933 guidelines, claiming: "Through God's creation we have been put directly into the community of blood and fate of the German people and as the bearers of this fate we are responsible for its future. Germany is our task, Christ our strength."[167] Horkheimer and Adorno wrote: "Among the 'German Christians,' all that remained of the religion of love was anti-Semitism."[168]

At the rally, before a hall packed by twenty thousand supporters, banners proclaiming the unity of National Socialism and Christianity were interspersed with swastikas. Speakers proposed such popular ideas as the removal of all pastors unsympathetic to National Socialism and expulsion of members of Jewish descent. Not least among these demands was "the removal of the Old Testament from the Bible" or the Christian canon and the adoption of a more "heroic" and "positive" Jesus, who should be portrayed battling mightily against corrupt Jewish influences.[169] A resolution was passed: "We expect our national Churches to shake themselves free of all that is un-German, *in particular the Old Testament and its Jewish morality and rewards*"[170] (emphasis added).

According to *Time* magazine, the "great gathering of the 'German Christians'" demanded "the super-Nazification of the Church." The reporter describes "[t]heir presiding officer" as "brisk, sleek, pomaded young Rev. Joachim Hossenfelder, Bishop of Berlin and Brandenburg," yet the "prime hot-head" was Dr. Reinhold Krause, a pastor associated with the extreme wing of the Nazi movement. "Meeting a few days after the 450th birthday of their Church's founder, Martin Luther," the Berlin rally "proceeded to juggle ecclesiastical dynamite." Krause claimed German Protestantism needed a "'second Reformation.'" He submitted three reforms, among them

---

166. Ibid., 68–69.

167. "Christ in the Community of Blood and Fate," in *Nazi Culture: Intellectual, Cultural and Social Life in the Third Reich*, ed. George L. Mosse (Madison: University of Wisconsin Press, 1966), 241–42.

168. Horkheimer and Adorno, *Dialectic of Enlightenment*, 145.

169. Victoria Barnett, *For the Soul of the People: Protestant Protest against Hitler* (New York: Oxford University Press, 1992), 34–35.

170. The November 13, 1933, resolution appears in Faulhaber, *Judaism, Christianity and Germany*, 35.

the "*Elimination of the Old Testament and of 'palpably misrepresenting or superstitious passages in the New Testament.'*"[171] He claimed that the Old Testament presented Jewish "commercial morality" and "unedifying stories of 'cattle-dealers and pimps,'" and he rejected the theology of "Rabbi Paul."[172] The "meeting enthusiastically adopted a resolution supporting Dr. Krause's reforms."[173] Indeed, many "*Deutsche Christen* theologians who were loyal to Nazi ideology rejected the OT precisely because they thought of it as a Jewish book."[174] For example, Ludwig Müller (1883–1945), leader of the German Christians and Reich's Bishop (1933) of the German Evangelical Church, declared in 1934: "*We must emphasize with all decisiveness that Christianity did not grow out of Judaism but developed in opposition to Judaism.*"[175] Likewise, the Synod of the Evangelical Church of the Church Province of Saxony (Evangelische Kirche der Kirchenprovinz Sachsen; KPS), the most important Protestant denomination in the German state of Saxony-Anhalt, stated in 1933: "[W]e recognize . . . in the Old Testament the apostasy of the Jews from God, and therein their sin. This sin is made manifest throughout the world in the Crucifixion of Jesus. From henceforth until the present day, the curse of God rests upon this people."[176]

Hitler, of course, went further, insisting that the "Christian religion is nothing but a Jewish sect. It always has been and it will always remain just that, as long as it will exist." He added:

---

171. See www.time.com/time/magazine/article/0,9171,746354,00.html, emphasis added.

172. Mordecai Paldiel, *Churches and the Holocaust: Unholy Teaching, Good Samaritans, and Reconciliation* (Jersey City: Ktav, 2006), 33.

173. See www.time.com/time/magazine/article/0,9171,746354,00.html.

174. Pamela Eisenbaum, "The Christian Canon and the Problem of Antisemitism," in *Shadow of Glory*, 11. See also E. C. Helmreich, *The German Churches under Hitler* (Detroit: Wayne State University Press, 1979).

175. Bergen, *Twisted Cross*, 21, emphasis original. For an analysis of three distinguished, scholarly, and influential theologians who greeted the rise of Hitler with great enthusiasm and support, see Robert P. Ericksen, *Theologians under Hitler: Gerhard Kittel, Paul Althaus and Emanuel Hirsch*. On the relationship between Christian theology and the rise of Nazism in Germany, see the important study of Paul R. Hinlicky, *Before Auschwitz: What Christian Theology Must Learn from the Rise of Nazism* (Eugene: Cascade Books, 2013).

176. Confino, *A World without Jews*, 130.

After the destruction of Judaism, the extinction of Christian slave morals must follow logically. I shall know the moment when to confront, for the sake of the German people and the world, their Asiatic slave morals with our picture of the free man, the god-like man. . . . We are fighting against the most ancient curse that humanity has brought upon itself. We are fighting against the perversion of our soundest instinct. Ah, the God of the deserts, that crazed, stupid, vengeful Asiatic despot with his powers to make laws! The slave keeper's whip. . . . It's got to get out of our blood, that curse from Mount Sinai.[177]

These accusations against Judaism, the Old Testament, and the belief that Jesus was of Jewish origin stood in clear contrast to the teachings of the Apostles. The first gospel—Matthew—opens with a genealogy showing that Jesus descended from Abraham, the first Jew, through forty-two generations of Jews. Luke's gospel also contains a genealogy (3: 23–38) that proves Jesus came from a long line of Jews going back to Abraham and then all the way back to Adam. Jesus was inseparable from the history of Israel. Likewise, in Romans, Paul said that the gospel is all about "the blessing of Abraham . . . coming to the Gentiles" (3: 14), and in Galatians, that from the "Israelites . . . Christ *came*" (3: 4–5). In the same vein, Paul continues, "If you belong to Christ, then you are Abraham's offspring, heirs according to the promise" (3: 29).

On Advent Sunday in December 1933, Cardinal Michael von Faulhaber addressed the faithful congregated in a Munich cathedral and fiercely defended the Old Testament as an integral part of Christian tradition. His greatest fears were the attacks on the validity and credibility of the Old Testament, the assertion that Jesus was not a Jew but an Aryan, and the grave and pressing threat to establish a "national church," free of Semitic taint, Teutonic, and endowed with special favor from Hitler. He feared that in "the German nation a movement is afoot to establish a Nordic or

---

177. Quoted in Michael Wood, "Afterword," in Mann, *The Tables of the Law*, 114. Wood took these words from Herman Rauschning, "Preface" to *The Ten Commandments*, ed. Armin L Robinson (New York: Simon & Schuster, 1943), xi–xii. According to Wood in a letter to the author, December 29, 2013, "Rauschning's preface to the Robinson book reports the conversation verbatim. As I say, there is some skepticism about its authenticity."

Germanic religion, which is to take its place side by side with the two Christian [Catholic and Protestant] creeds."[178]

Cardinal Faulhaber began his first sermon by reminding the congregation that already in "the year 1899 on the occasion of an anti-Semitic demonstration in Hamburg, and simultaneously in Chamberlain's book, *The Foundation of the Nineteenth Century*, a demand was raised for the total separation of Judaism from Christianity, and for the complete elimination from Christianity of all Jewish elements."[179] Two decades later, he argued, these views had become widespread and were propounded in many other books; for example, *The Sin against the Blood* (*Die Sünde wider das Blut*, 1917) a bestseller by Artur Dinter (1876–1948). The cardinal also mentioned *The Great Deception* (*Die große Täuschung*), published in two volumes in the early 1920s by Friedrich Delitzsch, a German Assyriologist and specialist in ancient Middle Eastern languages, remembered today for his scholarly critique of the Old Testament's historical accuracy. He also called for the removal of the Old Testament from the Christian canon and assumed that Jesus was Aryan. In other works, he claimed the absolute superiority of "Babylonia" over "Israel" and that the Bible is devoid of religious and moral value. The cardinal also mentioned *The False God* (*Der falsche Gott*, 1911) by Theodor Fritsch, a notorious and influential German political scientist, who wrote that "the Jahve [sic] cult of the Old Testament is the deification of Jewish greed, egotism in the form of religion, which is bound to destroy the Germans."[180] Fritsch's Hammer Verlag in Leipzig published anti-Semitic propaganda hammering on the moral inferiority of Judaism.

Faulhaber warned his audience, "these single voices have swelled together into a chorus": "*Away with the Old Testament! A Christianity which still clings to the Old Testament is a Jewish Religion, irreconcilable with the spirit of the German people*" (emphasis added). Some "have indeed tried to save Him [Jesus] with a forged birth-certificate, and have said that He

---

178. Faulhaber, *Judaism, Christianity and Germany*, 92. It should be noted that after Kristallnacht, Cardinal Faulhaber "sent a van to the chief Rabbi of Munich when he heard that the temple was in flames in order to help salvage the sacred relics." See Dumbach and Newborn, *Sophie Scholl and the White Rose*, 63.

179. Faulhaber, *Judaism, Christianity and Germany*, 1.

180. Quoted in American Jewish Committee, *The Jews in Nazi Germany: A Handbook of Facts regarding Their Present Situation* (New York: American Jewish Committee, 1935), 65. On Fritsch and Delitzsch, see Tal, *Christians and Jews in Germany*, and *Religion, Politics and Ideology*.

was not a Jew at all but an Aryan, because there were Aryans among the inhabitants of Galilee."[181] These attacks on the Jews, Judaism, and the Old Testament were inextricable from attacks on Christianity: "antagonism to the Jews of the present days is extended" not only "to the sacred books of the Old Testament," but "Christianity" too is "condemned because it has relations of origin with pre-Christian Judaism." In contrast, the cardinal stressed time and again the crucial importance of "the Old Testament and its fulfillment in Christianity." Against the view that "Christianity has corrupted the German race because it is burdened with Old Testament ideas," he repeated, "Let us venerate the Scriptures of the Old Testament!"[182]

Clearly, voices like Cardinal Faulhaber's were rare in Nazi Germany. In contrast, the Godesberg Declaration of the Evangelical Lutheran Church on April 4, 1939, reiterated the same harsh, negative attitudes toward the Jews and the Old Testament, particularly the relationship between Christianity and Judaism: "Did Christianity arise out of Judaism being thus its continuation and completion, or does it stand in opposition to Judaism? To this question we respond: *Christian faith is the unbridgeable religious contradiction to Judaism.*"[183] The Godesberg Declaration was "intended to establish a common basis for German Christians" and "greeted with widespread support by most of the regional churches in the Reich." Point three out of five stated:

> The National Socialist worldview is against the political and spiritual influence of the Jewish race, on our national life. In full obedience to the divine rules of creation, the evangelical Church affirms its responsibility for the purity of our people. Over and above that, *in the domain of faith there is no sharper opposition than the one existing between the message of Jesus*

---

181. Faulhaber, *Judaism, Christianity and Germany*, 1–2.

182. Ibid., 3, 5, 108, 13.

183. Head, "Nazi Quest," 76, emphasis added. On the 1930s crisis and the Church in Germany, see Klaus Scholder, *A Requiem for Hitler and Other New Perspectives on the German Church Struggle* (London: SCM Press, 1988). Another translation of this infamous Declaration is: "What is the relation between Judaism and Christianity? Is Christianity derived from Judaism and has therefore become its continuation and completion, or does Christianity stand in opposition to Judaism? We answer: Christianity is in irreconcilable opposition to Judaism." See Confino, *World without Jews*, 135.

Christ and that of the Jewish religion of laws and political messianic expectation.[184]

The declaration stated further that "National Socialism carried forward the work of Martin Luther and would lead the German people to a true understanding of Christian faith."[185] In the same vein, the Confessing Church (or Confessional Church, *Bekennende Kirche*), which arose in opposition to government-sponsored efforts to Nazify the German Protestant church, responded in May 1939 to the Godesberg Declaration: "In the realm of faith, there is a sharp opposition between the message of Jesus Christ and the Jewish religion's legalism and political messianic hope, already criticized in the Old Testament. In the realm of life, the preservation of the purity of our people demands an earnest and responsible racial policy."[186]

The Godesberg Declaration was followed in May with the creation of the Institute for the Study and Eradication of the Jewish Influence on German Church Life in Eisenach, Thuringia, by professors of Christian theology, Protestant bishops, and pastors.[187] One of five anti-Jewish research institutes organized between 1933 and 1939,[188] it was located in the castle of Wartburg, where Martin Luther translated the New Testament into German in 1521 and founded "several days after Kristallnacht." At its opening ceremony on May 6, its "scientific" director and Professor of New Testament Walter Grundmann spoke on "The Dejudaisation of the Religious Life as the Task of German Theology and Church."[189] He claimed that the "elimination of Jewish influence on German life is the urgent and fundamental question of the present German religious situation" and "would continue

---

184. See Friedländer, *Years of Extermination*, 56, emphasis added.

185. Heschel, "When Jesus was an Aryan," 82. Luther's anti-Semitism is discussed in Zakai, "The Poetics of History and the Destiny of Israel," 313–50.

186. Friedländer, *Years of Extermination*, 56.

187. Heschel, *Aryan Jesus*, esp. 67–105.

188. Head, "Nazi Quest," 70. See also Alan E. Steinweis, *Studying the Jew: Scholarly Antisemitism in Nazi Germany*.

189. Head, "Nazi Quest," 76–77. See also Heschel, "Nazifying Christian Theology," 587–605; and "For 'Volk, Blood, and God': The Theological Faculty at the University of Jena during the Third Reich," in *Nazi Germany and the Humanities*, ed. W. Bialas and A. Rabinbach, 365–98.

the work of the Lutheran Reformation."[190] The significance of his institute lay in "its efforts to identify Christianity with National Socialist antisemitism by arguing that Jesus was an Aryan who sought the destruction of Judaism"[191] and to frame "Nazism as the very fulfillment of Christianity" and Christ as "a pre-figuration of Nazi Germany's fight against the Jews." It began working to create "a dejudiazed New Testament, hymnal, and catechism that made it possible to begin worshiping Christianity without Judaism." This new testament was entitled *God's Message*. All references to Jewish names and places and all quotations from the Old Testament were erased along with Jesus's descent from the House of David and his fulfillment of any Old Testament prophecy about the Messiah.[192] In 1943, Grundmann wrote: "In the fateful battle of the Greater Germany, which is a fateful battle against World Jewry and against all destructive and nihilistic forces, the work of the Institute gives the tools for the overthrow of all religious foreigners . . . and serves the belief of the Reich."[193]

Volk means more than people; to German thinkers since the birth of romanticism in the eighteenth century, it has "signified the union of a group of people with transcendental 'essence.' This 'essence' infused man's innermost nature, and represented the source of his creativity, his depth of feeling, his individuality, and his unity with other members of the *Volk*."[194] Ethnic ideology captured the German imagination well before the nation's defeat in World War I and greatly contributed to the rise of German fascism. It sharply distinguishes culture and civilization.[195] According to Spengler, culture "has a soul, whereas civilization is 'the most external and artificial state of which humanity is capable.' "[196] Hence, "we are born as men of the early winter of full Civilization, instead of the golden summit

---

190. Heschel, "Nazifying Christian Theology," 591, and "Reading Jesus as a Nazi," 31–32.

191. Heschel, "When Jesus was an Aryan," 80.

192. Confino, *World without Jews*, 148, 178.

193. Head, "Nazi Quest," 81.

194. Mosse, *Crisis of German Ideology*, 4.

195. On the question of culture versus civilization in modern German history, see Viereck, *Metapolitics*.

196. Spengler, *Decline of the West* (1931), 1: 356, quoted in Mosse, *Crisis of German Ideology*, 6.

of a ripe Culture."[197] Such thinking adored culture but denounced the view of a unified European civilization based on common humanist values and shared history. Mann's *Doctor Faustus* mocks it in the figure of literary historian Georg Vogler, who holds that "the history of German literature" should be viewed "from the perspective of tribal membership, whereby each writer" should be "treated and valued not as a writer per se, not as a universally trained mind, but as the genuine, blood-and-soil product of a real, concrete, specific corner of the world, out of which he was born and to which he bore witness."[198]

European civilization "as a distinct entity" was always on Auerbach's mind. His mission, probably conceived during the Weimar Republic, was "to form a lucid and coherent picture" of it (*LLP*, 6). In "Vico and Aesthetic Historicism" (1949), he continuously attacks "'Nordic' admiration for primitive and early forms of civilization" or "folk genius" as opposed to rationalism. Germans developed "an extremely nationalistic attitude toward their fatherland," which "the romantics" considered "the synthesis and supreme realization of folk genius." They developed an evolutionary conservatism based on their interest in the roots and forms of folklore, national traditions, and national identity in general, directed as much against rationalistic forms of absolutism as rationalistic views of revolutionary progress.[199]

Not only in Germany but all over Europe, fascism "exhibited a flight from reality into the realm of emotional and mystical ideology." Fascist movements "were all part of the 'displaced revolution' which moved from a rejection of reality to glorification of ideology,"[200] or as Mann observed in 1943, "[i]ntellectual-spiritual fascism, throwing off of human principle, recourse to violence, blood-lust, irrationalism, cruelty, Dionysiac denial of truth and justice."[201] Especially in Germany, with defeat in World War I, rabid nationalism led to the flight from reason and reality, or reading historical situations in apocalyptic terms. Many Germans believed "themselves involved in a permanent crisis of nationhood and ideology . . . as knights riding bravely between death and the devil."[202] According to Adam

---

197. Helps, "Preface" to Spengler, *Decline of the West*, xiv.
198. Mann, *Doctor Faustus*, 383.
199. Auerbach, "Vico and Aesthetic Historicism," 186–87, emphasis added.
200. Mosse, *Crisis of German Ideology*, 203.
201. Mann, quoted in Reed, *Thomas Mann*, 365.
202. Mosse, *Crisis of German Ideology*, 203.

Kirsch, "Nazism taught the Germans to see themselves as a beleaguered nation, constantly set upon by enemies external and internal. Metaphors of infection and disease, of betrayal and stabs in the back, were central to Nazi discourse. The concentration camp became the place where those metaphorical evils could be rendered concrete and visible. Here, behind the barbed wire, were the traitors, Bolsheviks, parasites, and Jews who were intent on destroying the Fatherland."[203]

Auerbach's reaction was to focus on *realism* in his many studies, especially rejecting legendary, mythological discourse. The struggle against the Old Testament was only part of Aryan philology; Ludwig Woltmann (1871–1907), the father of political anthropology in Germany, claimed in *The Teutons and the Renaissance in Italy* (1905) that Dante and Michelangelo were descendants of Germanic tribes. Chamberlain argued that the Italian Renaissance and Dante signaled "the new Teutonic epoch" in history.[204] Once in exile, the fight against these distortions became Auerbach's central concern. If in *Dante: Poet of the Secular World* he adhered to the traditional German philological literary historiography that placed the cradle of European literature in Greece, by 1942, when he began writing *Mimesis*, he moved it to the Near East, securing the power of the biblical worldview and style in European life, imagination, and civilization.

It's Personal

In September 1933, at the Nuremberg party rally called the Congress of Victory (*Reichsparteitag des Sieges*) because the Nazis had seized power over the Weimar Republic, Adolf Hitler expressed his views about the racial foundations of art and culture: "It is a sign of the horrible spiritual decadence of the past epoch that one spoke of styles without recognizing their racial determination. . . . Each clearly formed race has its own handwriting in the book of art, insofar as it is not, like Jewry, devoid of any creative artistic ability."[205] Auerbach no doubt heard these views, and he surely contemplated their barbaric and inhuman implications for his own existential condition. At the end of January 1933, he had written to

---

203. Kirsch, "The System," 80–81.

204. Mosse, *Crisis of German Ideology*, 100; Sheila Faith Weiss, *Race, Hygiene and National Efficiency: The Eugenics of Wilhelm Schallmayer* (Berkeley: University of California Press, 1987), 96; Chamberlain, *Foundations*, vol. 1, lxxiii.

205. Quoted in Friedländer, *Nazi Germany and the Jews*, 71.

Dr. Erich Rothacker (1888–1965), professor of philosophy, sociology, and psychology at the University of Bonn, complaining that Rothacker's racial views denied him "the right to be a German."[206] Things went from bad to worse for German Jews in general and Erich Auerbach and his family in particular. In May 1933, Auerbach began recording his fear of "suspension" from his post at the University of Marburg.[207]

Two years later, on October 16, 1935, following enactment of the Nuremberg Laws in September, "the administrators at Marburg University had summoned" Auerbach to a meeting.[208] Naturally, he and his wife had no good expectations. The Nuremberg Laws excluded Jews from any participation in German political life and culture, deprived Jews of German citizenship, and prohibited marriage between Jews and other Germans. Since they defined Auerbach as a "full Jew," hence, "non-Aryan," the university had to terminate his employment.

The Nuremberg Laws were a watershed in European Jewish history. For Jean Améry, they were "the death threat—better, the death sentence" for German-speaking Jews. "Had I not already heard a hundred times the appeal to fate—coupled with the call for Germany's awakening—that the Jew should perish?" (Deutschland erwache! Juda verrecke). Since then, he continued, or after 1935, to "be a Jew" meant "to be a dead man on leave. Someone to be murdered, who only by chance was not yet where he properly belonged." No wonder that young Améry felt that the "degradation proceedings directed against us Jews, which began with the proclamation of the Nuremberg Laws" led "all the way to Treblinka."[209] As the Jewish "international music agent and concert producer" Saul Fitelberg tells the composer Adrian Leverkühn in Mann's *Doctor Faustus*: "We Jews have everything to fear from the German character, *qui est essentiellement anti-sémitique.*"[210]

---

206. Auerbach to Dr. Erich Rothacker, January 29, 1933, in Elsky, Vialon, and Stein, "Scholarship," 745.

207. Auerbach to Dr. Karl Vossler, May 22, 1933, in Elsky, Vialon, and Stein, "Scholarship," 745.

208. Konuk, *East West Mimesis*, 3.

209. Jean Améry, "On the Necessity and Impossibility of Being a Jew," in Améry, *At the Mind's Limits: Contemplations by a Survivor on Auschwitz and Its Realities*, trans. S. Rosenfeld and S. P. Rosenfeld (Bloomington: Indiana University Press, 1980 [1966]), 85–89.

210. Mann, *Doctor Faustus*, 427.

Auerbach's last paper before he went into exile was "Giambattista Vico and the Idea of Philology," in which he defined philology, following Vico, as "the study of the principles of humanity" and argued that Vico's *New Science* was the first work "understanding philology" as a science of man "as far as he is a historical being." However, in contrast to the progressive Enlightenment view of history, he claimed that philology "presupposes a common world of man" in "the whole great and terrible reality of history"—in other words, in his own historical situation.[211]

In September 1935, a month before his dismissal from the University of Marburg, Auerbach and his family vacationed in Italy. He wrote from Siena, "Only this voyage liberated me from my error. . . . I believe that my family and I (I have a wife and a child of 12) cannot endure it much longer in Germany."[212] In another letter from Siena at the same time, he acknowledged that because of the political situation and its effect on his university "my own work on realism," probably "Figura," will "have to wait a while; there may still be more to get out of it."[213]

The gloomy prospect of exile looms in a September 23rd letter to Benjamin from Rome. After reading Benjamin's memoir *Berlin Childhood around 1900*, Auerbach wrote movingly about the "memories of a home that vanished so long ago!"[214] He hoped despairingly, "if only there are still people who read documents" like his friend's book, and in the last paragraph of *Mimesis* he wonders whether, with the end of World War II, his book will find an audience: "Nothing now remains but to find him—to find the reader, that is. I hope that my study will reach its readers—both

---

211. Wellek, *German, Russian, and Eastern European Criticism*, 130, emphasis added.

212. Auerbach to Herr Saxl, September 12, 1935, in Elsky, Vialon, and Stein, "Scholarship," 746.

213. Auerbach to Dr. Karl Vossler, September 15, 1935, in Elsky, Vialon, and Stein, "Scholarship," 747.

214. Begun in Poveromo, Italy, in 1932 and extensively revised in 1938, *Berlin Childhood around 1900* was not published during Benjamin's lifetime. Auerbach apparently read the short version of 1932. On Benjamin, see Michael P. Steinberg, *Walter Benjamin and the Demands of History* (Ithaca: Cornell University Press, 1996). Auerbach to Herr Benjamin, September 23, 1935, in Elsky, Vialon, and Stein, "Scholarship," 747. Benjamin's letters to Auerbach can also be found in Walter Benjamin, "Walter Benjamin and Erich Auerbach: Fragments of Correspondence," *Diacritics*, 22 (Autumn-Winter 1992).

my friends of former years, if they are still alive, as well as all the others for whom it was intended" (*M*, 557). Many, like Benjamin, were not still alive. This pessimism, or "quiet tone," grew throughout 1935. It is "impossible to give you a picture of the oddity of my situation" in Germany, he wrote to Benjamin. "[I]t becomes more senseless day by day."[215]

Auerbach's letters to Benjamin are more open than his other letters, which usually avoided "any dramatic expressions and complaints."[216] Auerbach's typical style "is unruffled, at times even lofty and supremely calm,"[217] but in September 1935, he wrote with rare enthusiasm after receiving a letter from Benjamin: "What a joy! That you are still there [Paris], that you are writing—and with a tone that evokes memories of a home."[218] In October 1935, Auerbach wrote from Florence of Marburg: "I lived there among honorable people who are not of our stock, who have completely different presuppositions," yet it was foolish to think that individuals, however good, could stand up to the evil forces of Nazism and fascism: "the opinions of individuals, even if there are many of them, don't matter at all."[219] The impersonal forces of history were withering the meaning and value of all personal opinions and relationships, like his friendship with a fellow Jew who had already fled Germany because of them.

In September 1935, a German newspaper recorded Auerbach's predicament: "Anti-Semitism also is causing troubles for several Marburg professors whose names were inscribed on the pillory of the university as punishment for defending Jewish business."[220] We have no additional details, but the economist Fritz Neumark (1900–1991), who also fled to Istanbul after his dismissal from the Goethe-University in Frankfurt am Main, wrote that the "Nazi student union" demanded that "all publications of the Jewish professors . . . be considered 'translation from the Hebrew.'" This absurd defamation "of people who had never considered anything other than German as their mother tongue" finally convinced Neumark "that it

---

215. Auerbach to Herr Benjamin, September 23, 1935, in Elsky, Vialon, and Stein, "Scholarship," 747.

216. Gumbrecht, "'Pathos,'" 14.

217. Said, "Introduction to the Fiftieth Anniversary Edition," x.

218. Auerbach to Herr Benjamin, September 23, 1935, in Elsky, Vialon, and Stein, "Scholarship," 747.

219. Auerbach to Herr Benjamin, October 6, 1935, in Elsky, Vialon, and Stein, "Scholarship," 748.

220. Ibid., 759n35.

was no longer possible for me to work at an institution which continued to call itself 'The Johann Wolfgang von Goethe University' for appearances sake."[221] Two universities, Berlin and Munich, offered the following courses: Geography in the Service of the National Socialist State; The Life of the Soul in Its Racial, National, and Historical Form; *Volk* and Race (including legislation on racial improvement and eugenics, with slides and field trip); Birth, Marriage, and Death: The Role of Race in the *Völkisch* Character (with slides); and The Sociology of War (open to the public).[222]

In exile, Auerbach's pessimism about the political situation in Germany only worsened. As he wrote to Benjamin in 1937, "the contemporary world situation is nothing other than the cunning of providence to lead us along a bloody and circuitous route," which, he thought, was evident "already in Germany and Italy, especially in the horrifying inauthenticity of 'Bluebopropaganda,'" eliding *Blut und Boden*, blood and soil, the Nazi criteria for defining "Germanness." This cunning was revealed to him "for the first time" in Turkey, in exile,[223] and this utterance is one of the very rare occasions when Auerbach disclosed the abyss of his heart and mind. The experience of exile allowed him to express important new revelations about Nazi Germany and the true course of history. Auerbach would soon experience many more desperate moments, such as the outbreak of World War II and the great success of the German army in 1942, which posed a serious, existential threat, not only to his new life in Turkey but to his beloved Western European humanist tradition as a whole.

Epiphany in Istanbul

The writing of *Mimesis* was based on a decisive spiritual, intellectual epiphany in Istanbul. Evidence can be found in the "Epilegomena to *Mimesis*" (1953), where he admits that it deals "with *a version of thought*, which was formed by me around 1940"; the idea of "realism, which is present in *Mimesis*, was dealt with previously only rarely—and even then in another context" (*M*, 562–63, emphasis added). In chapter 2, his words about Peter's denial of Jesus capture his own exilic condition; it "prepared him for the visions which contributed decisively" (*M*, 42) to its composition. Spurned by the Nazis as

---

221. Quoted in Seyhan, "German Academic Exiles in Istanbul," 286.

222. Dumbach and Newborn, *Sophie Scholl*, 83.

223. Auerbach to Benjamin, January 3, 1937, in Elsky, Vialon, and Stein, "Scholarship," 751.

a worthless human being of inferior race, he exacted perfect revenge: rescuing the Western humanist tradition, based on its Judeo-Christian heritage and Scriptures, in a text that has captured the imagination of readers for far longer than the blither of the "Thousand-Year Reich."

The Istanbul epiphany gave Auerbach his epistemological, methodological point of departure, which enabled him to construct his response to Aryan philology in a grand survey of European humanist literary civilization. This *a primo capite libri ad ultimum caput* (from the first chapter of the book to the last one) clearly reflects the book's overt ideological, philological, and literary goal, in a way that the cover illustration to the fiftieth-anniversary edition, depicting the central panel of Max Beckmann's 1932–1933 triptych *Departure*, does not. Its Greek figures sitting on a boat contradict both the criticism of classical, pagan culture and the stated theme, the representation of reality.[224] Auerbach's choice for the cover illustration was the image of Christ in the Amiens Cathedral, 1220–1288, and he "insisted that Christ's hands should appear in the picture."[225]

Both "Figura" and *Mimesis* are heated with ideological aims and missionary zeal. As in "Figura," the book of Genesis is the *Ansatzpunkt* for Auerbach's reconstruction of the history of Western literature, but the literal *Ansatzpunkt*—"Written in Istanbul between May 1942 and April 1945" (*M*, iv)—was charged with apocalyptic and eschatological dimensions. As Benjamin wrote: "History is the subject of a structure whose site is not homogeneous, empty time, but *time filled by the presence of the now*."[226] Auerbach was witnessing a time when the Nazi *"propaganda device"* led

---

224. Beckmann (1884–1950), the famous German painter who fled Nazi Germany in 1937, explains the meaning of the central panel: "The King and Queen, Man and Woman, are taken to another shore by a boats-man whom they do not know, he wears a mask, it is the mysterious figure taking us to a mysterious land. . . . The King and Queen have freed themselves of the tortures of life—they have overcome them. The Queen carries the greatest treasure—Freedom—as her child in her lap. Freedom is the one thing that matters—it is the departure, the new start." See www.artchive.com/artchive/b/beckmann/departure.jpg.

225. Calin to the author, August 2, 2013: "The paperback edition of *Mimesis* came out while I was Auerbach's research assistant. I remember his speaking on the telephone with the publisher. He wanted the Christ of Amiens as the cover illustration, and insisted that Christ's hands should appear in the picture. Which was done."

226. Benjamin, "Theses on the Philosophy of History," 261, emphasis added.

to "*an ocean of filth and blood*" all over Europe (*M*, 404, emphasis added). On the verso of the first page, he placed the dates of composition to show his space of experience and horizon of expectation; they mark the urgency of the immediate threat and point to eventual redemption from Nazi barbarism.[227]

He also chose the prophetic, apocalyptic, and eschatological motto, "Had we but world enough, and time . . . ," that Marvell wrote in 1651–1652 during the Puritan Revolution (1640–1660); King Charles I had been executed, and many believed Christ's Second Coming was at hand to establish the Kingdom of God on Earth. Auerbach chose the rhetorical question to which Marvell responds in the next lines:

> But at my back I always hear
> Time's winged chariot hurrying near;
> And yonder all before us lie
> Deserts of vast eternity.

This highly charged scenario signaling the end of time and history was a very common motive in Puritan apocalyptic tradition, especially during the revolution, and can be seen in the thought and writings of Marvell's friends Oliver Cromwell and John Milton, among others.[228]

Marvell wrote the poem while serving as tutor to twelve-year-old Mary Fairfax, the daughter of Sir Thomas Fairfax, commander of the Parliamentary army during the English Civil Wars (1642–1651). Between 1653 and 1657, he tutored a ward of Oliver Cromwell, Lord Protector of England, Ireland, and Scotland during the Commonwealth period (1653–1658), and in a 1650 poem, "An Horatian Ode upon Cromwell's Return from Ireland," praised Cromwell:

---

227. In contrast, Bremmer argues that Auerbach recorded the dates because he wanted readers to know that it was written in Istanbul, which "lacked most European books and journals" ("Erich Auerbach and His Mimesis," 5).

228. For an analysis of English Puritan millennial, eschatological, and apocalyptic visions and thought, see Zakai, "Reformation, History, and Eschatology in English Protestantism," *History and Theory* 16 (October 1987): 300–18, *Exile and Kingdom: History and Apocalypse in the Puritan Migration to America* (Cambridge: Cambridge University Press, 1992), and *Jonathan Edwards's Philosophy of History: The Re-Enchantment of the World in the Age of Enlightenment* (Princeton: Princeton University Press, 2003).

218 / The Pen Confronts the Sword

> Then burning through the air he went,
> And palaces and temples rent;
> And Cæsar's head at last
> Did through his laurels blast. (ll. 21–24)[229]

In 1657, Marvell served in the Foreign Office under the great scholar and poet John Milton, and in 1659 he was elected to Parliament.[230]

"To His Coy Mistress" continues:

> I would
> Love you ten years before the Flood;
> And you should, if you please, refuse
> Till the conversion of the Jews.

Hence, the young lovers have little time, with apocalypse impending and the whole mystery of sacred, providential history soon to be unveiled and resolved. In this moment, the conversion of the Jews signaled the approach of Christ's Second Coming and the transformation of the world into the Kingdom of God. In other words, the essence of the poem is time or its lack; the lovers squabble between two apocalyptic, eschatological moments—ten years before the great flood that Noah outlasted in his ark (Gen. 5: 28–10: 32) and the end of the world, when all Jews become Christians.[231]

In light of the German army's frighteningly successful advances on the European and North African fronts, Auerbach must have felt, like Marvel, bereft of world and time. The real meaning of Marvell's poem is not *carpe diem* (seize the day), hedonistic advice from the ancient Roman poet Horace, but the urgent need to take action before the world ends. Marvel's view was also not *foied venom pipafo carefo* (today I will drink wine, tomorrow I will do without). Time and eternity, not love and present joy, are the essence of the poem—time running according to God's plan

---

229. See Andrew Marvell, "An Horatian Ode upon Cromwell's Return from Ireland," ll. 21–24.

230. On Marvell's life and work, see J. M. Wallace, *Destiny His Choice: The Loyalism of Andrew Marvell* (Cambridge: Cambridge University Press, 1981).

231. Oliver Cromwell's decision to readmit the Jews to England in 1655 after their expulsion in 1290 should be understood in this millennial and eschatological context. On the important role of the Jews in English apocalyptic tradition, see Zakai, "Reformation, History, and Eschatology in English Protestantism" and "The Poetics of History and the Destiny of Israel."

like a speeding chariot. Since we know that Auerbach believed in divine providence—"I am more and more convinced," he wrote in 1937, "that the contemporary world situation is nothing other than the cunning of providence"[232]—he adopted Marvell's apocalyptic and eschatological scenario as the motto to *Mimesis*.

In the eyes of contemporaries as well as historians, 1942 was the most crucial year of World War II because of three decisive battles on three different fronts. The Battle of Midway in the Pacific took place between June 4 and 7, the First Battle of El Alamein in Egypt from July 1 to 27, and the Battle of Stalingrad, Russia, between August 1942 and February 1943. These battles eventually turned the tide of the war in favor of the Allies, but in Istanbul, Auerbach could not know what the outcome would be, let alone whether the German army would reach Turkey from the south via Egypt or the north after conquering Russia. On May 8, 1942, for instance, the German army withstood a Soviet counteroffensive near Kharkov and inflicted heavy losses. The *Wehrmacht* was on the move and winning in Russia: it reached the Donets, recaptured the Crimea, and took Sevastopol by mid-June. Voronezh was taken while the bulk of the German forces moved toward the oil fields and the Caucasus. At the same time, Friedrich Paulus's Sixth Army advanced along the Don in the direction of Stalingrad. The German army clearly had the upper hand.[233]

It also seemed invincible in North Africa. Panzer Army Africa (Panzerarmee Afrika) under Field Marshal Erwin Rommel (1891–1944) started the second phase of its advance toward Egypt, and from February to May 1942, the front line settled down near Tobruk. Rommel thought his army would soon "secure the oilfields of the Middle East, Persia, and even Baku on the Caspian Sea."[234] He attacked in June, defeating the Allies and reaching the El Alamein line just one hundred kilometers from Alexandria and the vital Suez Canal. The British army prepared to make its last stand.[235]

---

232. Auerbach to Benjamin, January 3, 1937, in Elsky, Vialon, and Stein, "Scholarship," 751.

233. See Friedländer, *Years of Extermination*, 331. For a description of the atrocities the German army inflicted on Russia, see Evans, *Third Reich at War*; and Littell, *The Kindly Ones* (*Les Bienveillantes*). For terrible eyewitness accounts, see Ehrenburg and Grossman, *The Black Book*; and Snyder, *Bloodlands*. On the atrocities in Poland, see Göran Rosenberg, *A Short Stop on the Road from Auschwitz*.

234. Evans, *Third Reich at War*, 467.

235. See Roberts, *Storm of War*, chaps. 4 and 9; and Atkinson, *An Army at Dawn*.

The extent to which Auerbach was aware of these critical military threats can be seen in a letter written in summer 1946, where he describes in his aloof, reserved way some of the anxieties of 1942: "Things have gone well for us *against all odds. The new order did not reach these straits; that really says it all.* We have lived in our apartment and *suffered* nothing but small discomfort and fear: *until the end of [19]42 it looked very bad,* but then the clouds gradually withdrew."[236] He had more than enough reasons to begin writing his apologia for Western humanism in May 1942, and he was not alone in his sense of urgency. In the same year, Hans Baron started *The Crisis of the Italian Renaissance*; Adorno and Horkheimer, *Dialectic of Enlightenment*; Cassirer, *The Myth of the State*; Mann began to conceive *Doctor Faustus*; Franz Neumann published *Behemoth: The Structure and Practice of National Socialism*; R. G. Collingwood published *The New Leviathan: Or Man, Society, Civilization, and Barbarism*; and Stefan Zweig committed suicide in Brazil when he felt that "the world of my own language sank and was lost to me and my spiritual homeland, Europe, destroyed itself." He concluded, "I salute all of my friends! May it be granted them yet to see the dawn after this long night! I, all too impatient, go before them."[237] In 1942, "the apparently steady dissolution of moral and political order, and the rise of a barbaric 'new order' justify the sense of urgency and fear that surface throughout *Mimesis*."[238]

Philology, Teleology, and Historicist Humanism

Mimesis is ultimately an elegy for the difference and otherness that he [Auerbach] named the West.

—Michael Holquist, "The Last European: Erich Auerbach as Precursor in the History of Cultural Criticism," 1993

---

236. Auerbach to Dr. Martin Hellweg, June 22, 1946, in Elsky, Vialon, and Stein, "Scholarship," 757, emphasis added.

237. From his suicide letter, February 22, 1942. See Friedman, "70 years later, a handwritten note recalls the end of a literary life"; Leo Carey, "The Escape Artist: The Death and Life of Stefan Zweig," *The New Yorker*, August 27, 2012, 70; and Oliver Matuschek, *Three Lives: A Biography of Stefan Zweig* (London: Pushkin Press, 2011).

238. Thomas DePietro, "Literary Criticism as History: The Example of Auerbach's *Mimesis*," *Clio* 8 (1979): 377–78.

> In many learned writings one finds a kind of objectivity in which, entirely unbeknownst to the composer, modern judgments and prejudices ... cry out from every word, every rhetorical flourish, every phrase. *Mimesis* is quite consciously a book that a particular person, in a particular situation, wrote at the beginning of the 1940s.
>
> —Erich Auerbach, "Epilegomena to *Mimesis*," 1953

Mimesis presents "western literary history as a story of 'fulfillment' of the 'figure,'" or figural interpretation. Hence, "every 'representation' is also presentation," and the concept of fulfillment (*Erfüllung*) "is crucial for understanding the peculiar nature of Auerbach's conception of historical redemption,"[239] or his teleological conception of literary history, based on a unique combination of Vico and Hegel.[240] Within the context of "figurality" and "fulfillment," one can understand Auerbach's claim: "History is the science of reality" (PW, 4). Against the Nazi flight from reason and reality, *Mimesis* sets out the realist, rationalist representation of reality as the guiding principle and standard of judgment by which all historic-literary theories are measured.

What is the promise and its fulfillment? What is represented in *Mimesis*?[241] It aims to describe "the rise of more extensive and socially inferior human groups to the position of subject matter for problematic-existential representation" (*M*, 491). His humanist ideology led, in the first place, to the selection of literary works and passages that "must not be sought exclusively in the upper strata of society and in major political events but also in art, economy, material and intellectual culture, in the depths of the workaday world and its men and women, because it is only there that one can grasp what is unique, what is animated by the inner forces, and what, in both a more concrete and a more profound sense, is universally valid" (*M*, 444). As philology was inseparable from ideology, *Mimesis* takes on the politics of presentation and representation against

---

239. Hayden White, "Auerbach's Literary History: Figural Causation and Modernist Historicism," in *Figural Realism: Studies in the Mimesis Effect* (Baltimore: Johns Hopkins University Press, 1999), 124–25.

240. See Zakai, "Constructing and Representing Reality."

241. For the complexities of "representation," see Thomas Docherty, "Anti-Mimesis: The Historicity of Representation," *Forum for Modern Language Studies* 26 (1990): 272–81.

the "Nazi world view," where the "flight from reason became a search for myths and heroes."[242]

The politics of the 1930s and 1940s determined the subject matter; as Wellek wrote, "Auerbach never rests content with analysis of style but moves from that to reflection on the attitude of a writer toward reality and his technique of reproducing it, and these topics, in turn, lead to reflection about periods and cultures, social conditions and assumptions." He works toward "the breakdown of the limits" of "ancient doctrines of the three levels of style"[243]—"the sublime, the intermediate, and the low, or lowly" (*LLP*, 33)—and "the breakdown of the hierarchy of genres and stylistic levels which came with the dissolution of French classicism and the rise of modern realism."[244] In classical culture theory, the low style (*sermo remisus or humilis*) was associated with comedy and the popular classes; the elevated style (*sermo gravis or sublimis*) with the tragic, the historic, the heroic, and the sublime. In other words, "the realistic depiction of daily life was incompatible with the sublime and had a place only in comedy" (*M*, 22).

These epistemological transformations—breaking down the three styles as well as the overall hierarchy of genres and styles—were inseparable from the progress of the Western egalitarian, humanist, and realist tradition. The first transformation took place in early Christianity with the figural interpretation of history, when "the deep subsurface layers, which were static for the observers of classical antiquity, began to move" (*M*, 45, emphasis added). The second came with historicism in which "the thing we call separation of styles, the exclusion of realism from high tragedy, was overcome, and this is a basic prerequisite both for a historical and contemporary realism" (*M*, 444). *Mimesis* does not deal with the history of the representation of reality in Western literature per se but only Auerbach's presentation of the "evolution of realism" in Western literature, namely, his idiosyncratic interpretation based on his humanist ideology and struggle against Aryanism and Nazism. His recovery of texts searches for the "inner history" of Western culture in which "mankind achiev[es] self-expression" (*PW*, 5). Consequently, *Mimesis* is not "about the triumph of realism over nonrealist literature, or an attempt to account for this triumph; it is rather an account of the struggle between the different proposals made over three thousand years as to how reality should be represented. Auerbach approaches

---

242. Mosse, *Nazi Culture*, 93–96.
243. Wellek, "Review: Auerbach's Special Realism," 300–01.
244. Ibid.

realism and its history from the inside, as it were, rather than the outside." This "history of how writers from Homer to Virginia Woolf have attempted to represent reality" implies that "realism can only be defined by means of a history of realism," or that realism and history are the same.[245]

However, the question remains: why write the book at all? The answer lies in the importance he attached to philology, or "historicist humanism." Auerbach maintains "that humanism was not only the overt discovery of materials and the development of methods of research, but beyond that their penetration and evaluation so that the inner history of mankind . . . could be written" (PW, 4, emphasis added). *Mimesis* is driven by this understanding:

> *Imitation of reality is imitation of the sensory experience of life on earth*—among the most essential characteristics of which would seem to be its possessing a history, its changing and developing. Whatever degree of freedom the imitating artist may be granted in his work, he cannot be allowed to deprive reality of this characteristic, which is its very essence. (*M*, 191, emphasis added)

At the same time, in many cases, Auerbach's ideological, teleological approach in *Mimesis* stands in clear contrast to his overt historicist approach, which stipulated that "epochs and societies are not to be judged in terms of a pattern concept of what is desirable absolutely speaking but rather in every case in terms of their own premises" (*M*, 443). The discrepancy suggests that *Mimesis* is based on a serious self-contradiction. Auerbach's analysis is pervaded by many value judgments, which stand in clear contrast to his professed historicist approach. For example, he talks about "God's incarnation in a human being of the humblest social station, through his existence on earth amid humble everyday people and conditions" (*M*, 41). Saint Peter was called from "the humdrum existence of his daily life," and Christianity is "the birth of a spiritual movement in the depths of the common people, from within the everyday occurrences of contemporary life" (*M*, 42-43). He denounces Ammianus Marcellinus's *Res Gestae* of the second half of the fourth century as "magical and sensory" at "the expense of the human and the objectively rational," thus leading to "the stage of

---

245. Ankersmit, "Why Realism?," 59, 53, 73. See also Frank R. Ankersmit, *History and Tropology: The Rise and the Fall of Metaphor* (Berkeley: University of California Press, 1994).

a magical and sensory dehumanization" (*M*, 53), the "dominance of the mob," "irrational and immoderate lust," and the "spell of magical powers," while Christianity is the "fight against magical intoxication" (*M*, 68–69).

Based on his negative views of nobility, Auerbach stresses time and again that Christ came "as a human being of the lower social station," and his first disciples were simple men and women. The critic stresses the "new *sermo humilis*," low style or ordinary speech, born with Christianity (*M*, 72). Likewise, although of humble origins, "nothing human is foreign" to the sixth-century Gregory of Tours, whose "soul faces living reality." His Latin style may be very simple and different from that of other late antiquity authors, but "it exists as a language which is spoken, which is used to deal with everyday reality" (*M*, 92–94). He criticizes Marcellinus, the Roman historian, "of a half silly, half spectral distortion of ordinary average occurrences in human life" (*M*, 62–63), and characterizes the realism of the late Middle Ages as "poor in ideas; it lacked constructive principles and even the will to attain them" (*M*, 259). Finally, he claims that Molière "constantly avoids any realistic concretizing, or even any penetrating criticism, of the political and economic aspects of the milieu in which his characters move" (*M*, 370).

Auerbach's preference for ordinary, simple people, and the widespread value judgments, especially his negative assessment of the ruling classes, stand in clear contrast to his historicist humanist credo. Historicism aims to eschew judging past centuries and people in favor of understanding them in their own historical contexts. Aesthetic, historicist humanism, Auerbach explained, "is based on historicism, i.e., on the conviction that every civilization and every period has its own possibilities of aesthetic perfection; that the works of arts of the different peoples and periods, as well as their general forms of life, must be understood as products of variable individual conditions, and have to be judged each by its own development, not by absolute rules of beauty and ugliness."[246] Still, especially in *Mimesis*, he judges past events, people, and classes constantly in the name of rationalism, realism, and history. For example, he argues that Tacitus's historiography lacks "methodological research into the historical growth of social as well as intellectual movements" (*M*, 40). Clearly, this claim is anachronistic. In his analysis of the French classicists, such as Corneille,

---

246. Auerbach, "Vico and Aesthetic Historicism," 183–84, emphasis added; cf. *LLP*, 6. On Vico's humanism, see Sandra R. Luft, *Vico's Uncanny Humanism: Reading the New Science between Modern and Postmodern* (Ithaca: Cornell University Press, 2003).

Molière, and, above all, Racine, "Auerbach's relativist tolerance begins to strain." Here, as in other places in *Mimesis*, "the historicist fails to meet the standard of his own historicist relativism," and, "despite his historicism," he saw fit "to condemn the French classicists so harshly."[247]

Why was Auerbach more than willing to betray his own self-professed credo of historicism, or, more specifically, why did French classicism arouse his "unhistoricist wrath"?[248] The cause is his ideological struggle against Nazi barbarism. In the moment of grave crisis, his zeal led him to abandon some of the basic principles of historicist humanism in support of his own commitments. This contradiction is the main source of his idiosyncratic approach, but we find idiosyncratic interpretations arising in the work of other intellectual exiles of the time—Popper, Strauss, and Baron, for example. In a time of terrible danger, they all made ideological concessions. Auerbach used philology to advance his humanist ideology at the expense of his historicism.

Mimesis: Form and Content

> Only in the entirety of history is there truth, and only by the understanding of its whole course may one obtain it.
>
> —Erich Auerbach, "Vico's Contribution to Literary Criticism," 1958

Mimesis is driven by an essential antagonism between two radically different interpretations of reality and, hence, history—rationalistic realism, originating in the Judeo-Christian tradition, and pagan, Homeric, irrational, mythological, legendary antirealism. Historicist humanist philology aims to find the real in history, which is equal to the truth. It is no exaggeration to say that "history and existence" for Auerbach "coalesced into one."[249] He wrote, "Whatever we are, we became in history, and only in history can we remain the way we are and develop therefrom; it is the task of philologists, whose province is the world of human history, to demonstrate this so that it penetrates our lives unforgettably" (PW, 6).

---

247. Ankersmit, "Why Realism?," 55, 57. On 55, he argues that Auerbach "had a profound dislike" of Schiller.
248. Ibid., 55.
249. Claus Uhlig, "Auerbach's 'Hidden'? Theory of History," in Lerer, *Literary History and the Challenge of Philology*, 49.

In Plato's allegory of the cave in *The Republic*, the prisoners mistake appearance for reality, thinking the shadows they see on the wall are substance; they know nothing of real causes or reality. This view was radically transformed by the Judeo-Christian tradition in which history and reality, not abstract, Platonic eternal ideas, are the source of the truth. Literary text is intrinsically connected to its historical context "not to some Platonic archetype of literature or art or beauty, nor to any changeless canon of classics."[250] Auerbach's philology, based on an *Ansatzpunkt*, a major "point of departure of a literary-historical analysis,"[251] can provide insight into very large literary or cultural movements like the epistemological, semantic departure from the pagan to the biblical view of reality. According to "Figura," the rise of the figural interpretation of reality or history in early Christianity provided the *Ansatzpunkt* from the classical, pagan world. "A solution which struck me as on the whole satisfactory," Auerbach wrote, "resulted from an investigation of the semantic history of the word *figura*" (*M*, 555). *Mimesis* depicts the progress of Western literature as a series of major literary, semantic, cultural, and historical turning points described in each chapter. "The procedure I have employed—that of citing for every epoch a number of texts and *using these as test cases for my ideas*—takes the reader directly into the subject and makes him sense what is at issue long before he is expected to cope with anything theoretical" (*M*, 556, emphasis added).

Each text or translation at the beginning of the sections in *Mimesis* is "a theme of a chapter devoted to its stylistic interpretation. But the sequence of twenty chapters also comprises an anthology—or, better, an imaginary museum—of European civilization extending across three millennia and eight languages."[252] In this sense, *Mimesis* is "Figura" writ large, but for Auerbach, unlike Spitzer, no text is an isolated, autonomous phenomenon: "Auerbach led the reader immediately into the concrete. He then was able to work outwards from the text as a totality of stylistic relations to the 'other forms of life' in the period."[253] For example, the analysis of the three levels of style ("the sublime, the intermediate, and the low, or lowly"[254]) was only a way to explain "the dialectical relationship between

---

250. White, "Auerbach's Literary History," 136.

251. W. Wolfgang Holdheim, "The Hermeneutic Significance of Auerbach's *Ansatz*," *New Literary History* 16 (Spring 1985): 627.

252. Levin, "Two *Romanisten*," 466.

253. Stock, "Middle Ages as Subject and Object," 531–32.

254. Auerbach, "Sermo Humilis," 33.

representation and reality" or "between experience and expression" in history.²⁵⁵ For Auerbach, style is a sufficient but never a necessary condition for explaining a given text.

Auerbach restructured "Figura" to serve as the framework for *Mimesis* by making philological, semantic, epistemological turning points, or "semantic development," the core.²⁵⁶ In *Mimesis*, "chapter after chapter analyzes different techniques of representation, each of which captures a particular culture's most basic forms for organizing experience."²⁵⁷ For example, the universe of the Old Testament is "a different world of forms" than Homer's (*M*, 7) because "it organizes representation according to quite different categories." With respect to style and text, "Homer's syntax and tropes are less important in themselves as a style than they are as a formal index of the ancient Greek worldview," and "Hebrew theology is less significant as such than the organizational principles it presupposes."²⁵⁸ In other words, *Mimesis* is structured on "disconnected fragments: each of the book's chapters is marked not only by a new author who bears little overt relationship to earlier ones but also by a new beginning, in terms of the author's perspective and stylistic outlook." This structure determines the content: the representation of reality is described as "an active dramatic presentation of how each author actually realizes, brings characters to life, and clarifies his or her world."²⁵⁹ Auerbach argues elsewhere that "each part of the investigation" or chapter "raises problems of its own and demands its points of departure" (*LLP*, 20). As a historical survey, the book is "organized in autonomous, self-contained units, and deals with a tradition of glorious achievement from its origins through its continuous evolution to the present."²⁶⁰ Overall, however, the teleological historicist and humanist view of Western literature stands in contrast to pagan, mythological, and legendary delusion.

Auerbach's philological enterprise relies on a singular and coherent structure: "Turning a point of momentous cultural change upon a pivot of syntax (along with its meaning of course) was an art he had fashioned for

---

255. Stock, "Middle Ages as Subject and Object," 531–32.

256. Auerbach, "Figura," 76.

257. Holquist, "Last European," 378.

258. Ibid.

259. Said, "Introduction to the Fiftieth Anniversary Edition," xx.

260. Vassilis Lambropoulos, *The Rise of Eurocentrism: Anatomy of Interpretation* (Princeton: Princeton University Press, 1993), 6.

himself."[261] He looked for radical epistemological semantic literary changes in the presentation and representation of reality in each period discussed, "[b]ut the task that my theme *imposed* on me was a different one: *I had to show* not the transition but rather the complete change" (*M*, 562, emphasis added). He believed that "every text must provide a partial view on the basis of which a synthesis is possible" (*LLP*, 19). Thus, he moves "from specific phenomena—specific passages in specific texts—to general principles or observations and from the general back to the specific."[262]

In "Figura," Auerbach wrote that his goal was to move from words to history, or "to show *how on the basis of its semantic development a word may grow into a historical situation and give rise to structures that will be effective for many centuries*" (F, 76, emphasis added). He describes the structure of *Mimesis* as follows:

> I started with the ancient conception of the three levels of style and *asked all the selected texts* in what way they were related to it. This was tantamount to asking what their authors regarded as sublime and significant and what means they employed to represent them. *In this way I was able . . . to disclose something of the influence of Christianity on the development of literary expression, and even to throw light on an aspect of the development of European culture since antiquity.* (*LLP*, 20, emphasis added)

History and historical development, rather than merely philology, semantics, or stylistic analysis, were his ultimate concern. For example, "Christianity posited a new vision of existence" in its "fusion of styles" and "the equalization of lives propagated by Christian doctrine."[263] This method clearly explains the unique structure of the chapters in *Mimesis*: almost each is based on a different *Ansatzpunkt*: "Of course *a single starting point* cannot suffice for such enormous subjects; at most it can perform a function of guidance and integration; *each part of the investigation raises problems of its own and demands its points of departure*" (*LLP*, 20, emphasis added).[264] Here again, following Vico, "through the manifold expressions of linguistic

---

261. Nelson, "Erich Auerbach," 314–15.

262. Ziolkowski, "Foreword," xi.

263. Costa-Lima, "Erich Auerbach: History and Metahistory," 488.

264. See also James I. Porter, "Erich Auerbach and the Judaizing of Philology," *Critical Inquiry* 35 (Autumn 2008): 141.

activity the historical dimension of human existence makes itself known to men."[265] In *Mimesis*, his "immediate and explicit historical concern is to capture and record the whole of European civilization through an examination of select literary fragments."[266]

Faithful to the premises of aesthetic historicism acquired from Vico, the "underlying premises of *Mimesis*" are "that literary style and language" portray "the view of reality in a given text"; that "the chronological organization of these views explains the 'movement' or change of literary styles in European literature"; and, finally, that "through an understanding of an individual's style," we can "understand the view of reality, or, more broadly, the general milieu of a given historical period."[267] In other words, figural interpretation "accounted for western culture's unique achievement of identifying 'reality' as 'history'" because "historical things are related to one another as elements of structures of figuration."[268]

The project was driven by fury, ideological zeal, and enthusiasm. Apart from the first chapter of his book on Dante, Auerbach explicitly addresses method only in his introduction to *Literary Language and Its Public in Late Latin Antiquity and in the Middle Ages* (1958). In *Mimesis*, we are "plunked into particularity without an introduction. Auerbach shies away from generalization, though a brief epilogue draws together the guiding threads of his approach."[269] His passionate defense of Western Judeo-Christian civilization in an age of peril rendered methodological questions secondary.

Nevertheless, a coherent, well-defined humanist ideology pervades *Mimesis*. Auerbach divides and structures the chapters in time and space according to an "ideology of periodization," a grand teleological framework, "an overarching forward movement toward the *goal of fully actualized, universal realism*, in which the limitations of style separation and 'class boundaries' are overcome, *and a profound and informing awareness of 'creatural' sensoriness is maintained in tandem with a full consciousness of historical process*."[270] He is "looking for representation of everyday life in which that life is treated seriously, in terms of its human and social problems or even of its tragic complications" (*M*, 342–43). History is seen

---

265. Breslin, "Philosophy or Philology," 372.

266. DePietro, "Literary Criticism as History," 377–78.

267. Ibid., 378.

268. White, "Auerbach's Literary History," 134, 137.

269. Ibid., 467.

270. Brownlee, "Ideology of Periodization," 157–58, emphasis added.

as the representation of reality, reaching apotheosis in the French realist novels of the nineteenth century. In this teleological view, the "history of the last thousand years is the history of mankind achieving self-expression" (PW, 5), and it also has an "ethical dimension in which *humanistic values and a sense of the tragic coexist.*"[271] In Auerbach's words: "what we are tracing is the combination of the everyday with tragic seriousness" (*M*, 282). *Mimesis*, then, is a "teleological literary history" based on "the two opposing mimetic modes adumbrated in chapter 1," namely, the Homeric and biblical styles. More specifically, *Mimesis* "privileges moments in the history of western realism in which *the common and everyday came to be the subject of truly serious literature*," emphasizing "*the everyday reality of the lower social strata of European society.*"[272]

This framework is based on Hegelian dialectic, according to which history progresses toward a better and more egalitarian condition in three stages: a thesis; an antithesis, which contradicts or negates the thesis; and the tension between the two, which is resolved in a synthesis. In *Mimesis*, we have "a modified Hegelian model in which literary discourses play the role of historic-political forces. A humanist ideology of progress is built into this model, with the nineteenth-century 'realistic' French novel serving as a provisional end-point."[273] In this view, the Homeric style serves as the thesis; biblical Judeo-Christian style as antithesis; and French realism as synthesis. Hence, "*Mimesis* is not only a history of a specific kind of literary representation, that is 'figuralism,' but also a history conceived as a sequence of figural-fulfillment relationship"[274] or "a figural fulfillment in the beyond" (*M*, 116). For example, Auerbach explains that the all-inclusive subject of Dante's *Comedy* is *status animarum post mortem* ("the condition of souls after death"), which reflects "God's definitive judgment," or God's providential "design in active fulfillment" (*M*, 189–90).

Auerbach's aim is "recreating, still in German, the *Weltliteratur* of a fallen *Welt*."[275] Given that "*mímesis* is realistic by definition, and *figura* is symbolic mode, one of the contributions of Auerbach's book is to demon-

---

271. Ibid., emphasis added.

272. Carl Landauer, "Auerbach's Performance and the American Academy, or How New Haven Stole the Idea of *Mimesis*," in Lerer, *Literary History and the Challenge of Philology*, 181, 186, emphasis added.

273. Ibid., 158.

274. White, "Auerbach's Literary History," 128.

275. Lerer, *Error and the Academic Self*, 274.

strate precisely how they conjoin and enmesh"[276] in the dialectic of Western history. However, as Auerbach explains, a "systematic and complete history of realism would not only have been impossible, it would not have served my purpose" (*M*, 556). *Mimesis* does not trace the history of European realism per se but rather its evolution in Western literature,[277] or Auerbach's idiosyncratic humanist interpretation of it in opposition to Aryanism and Nazism. His realism "is the representation of the historical, concrete aspects of human being"[278] in contrast to simplistic, irrational tales of heroes.

Auerbach writes that he belongs to "a certain group of modern philologists who hold that the interpretation of a few passages from *Hamlet*, *Phèdre*, or *Faust* can be made to yield more, and more decisive, information about Shakespeare, Racine, or Goethe and their times than would a systematic and chronological treatment of their lives and works" (*M*, 548).[279] Accordingly, he "could never have written anything in the nature of a history of European realism." His "method . . . consists in letting *myself be guided* by a few motifs which I have worked out gradually and *without a specific purpose*, and in trying them out on a series of texts which have become familiar and vital to me in the course of my philological activity" (*M*, 548, emphasis added). In contrast, I argue that his method has a specific, clear, coherent ideological aim; his claim that his book was written without "a specific purpose" is far from the truth. The whole thrust of "Figura" and *Mimesis* is based on an overarching mission to demonstrate the poverty of Aryan philology. In a blatant contradiction, he claims, "*He who represents the course of a human life*, or a sequence of events extending over a prolonged period of time, *and represents it from beginning to end, must prune and isolate arbitrarily*" (*M*, 548–49, emphasis added); surely, to "prune and isolate arbitrarily" is a specific purpose.

Like "Figura," *Mimesis* has a definite agenda, aim, and goal—probing and proving the centrality of the Judeo-Christian tradition to Western

---

276. Levin, "Two *Romanisten*," 467.

277. Ziolkowski, "Foreword," xi. According to Wellek, *Mimesis* "concerns not realism but man's attitudes toward the world in general." See Levin, "Two *Romanisten*," 466.

278. Shahar, "Auerbach's Scars," 608.

279. Compare these words to Georg Lukács's views about the school of "intellectual sciences," people like "Dilthey, Simmel and Max Weber," for whom it "became the fashion to form general synthetic concepts on the basis of only a few characteristics—in most cases only intuitively grasped—of a school, a period, etc." (*Theory of the Novel*, 12–13).

literary tradition. In *Mimesis*, the biblical interpretation "is treated as the most important one, and is used systematically throughout the book as the basic approach to Western literature," with chapters 18 and 19 "form[ing] the apogee of *Mimesis*, a celebration of the Biblical understanding of history which entered its modern maturity with the nineteenth-century realist novel." The last chapter examines, among other works, Virginia Woolf's *To the Lighthouse* (1927), comparing it "extensively to the *Odyssey*," to reveal how "the pagan element reappears" in Western culture.[280] In this context, *Mimesis* moves from Odysseus ("child of wrath")[281] to James Joyce's *Ulysses* (Odysseus in Latin) to reflect Auerbach's pessimism after the two World Wars that wrecked European life and culture. Figural dominance, or the triumph of the Hebrew Bible in early Christianity, has ended, and now "the Homeric, the pagan element, threatens to take over again."[282] In "Auerbach's survey of the canon" of Western literature, "the central dialectic evolves between the Homeric and the Biblical, the pagan and the religious, the mythical and the historical, the Hellenic and the Hebraic."[283] In 1942, the crisis was not solely a specific German crisis of philology and ideology but a general Western humanist crisis that could arbitrarily and murderously deny humanity to anyone and everyone.

Mimesis: Method and Approach

> [A] solution which struck me as on the whole satisfactory resulted from an investigation of the semantic history of the word *figura*. For this reason, I use the term figural to identify the conception of reality in late antiquity and the Christian Middle Ages.
>
> —Erich Auerbach, *Mimesis*, 1946

Scholars have argued that Auerbach did not provide an adequately systematic introduction or coherent methodology in *Mimesis*, but its epilogue clearly and fully develops both. Why didn't he make it the introduction?

---

280. Lambropoulos, *Rise of Eurocentrism*, 13–14.
281. Lerer, *Error and the Academic Self*, 225.
282. Lambropoulos, *Rise of Eurocentrism*, 14.
283. Ibid., 15.

We know that he started this ambitious book with great urgency in 1942. Hence, the first chapter, "Odysseus' Scar," provides the general introduction. Clear proof can be found in Auerbach's 1957 letter to Martin Buber, the Austrian-born Israeli philosopher, best known for his philosophy of dialogue. In 1956, Buber wrote to Auerbach asking if he could write an introduction to the Hebrew translation of *Mimesis* that would appear in 1957. Auerbach replied, "But *Mimesis* is a book without an Introduction; *the chapter on Genesis and Homer is conceived as an introduction*; a theoretical polemic at the beginning of the book would have contradicted the intention of the book."[284] Apparently, only after he finished *Mimesis* in 1945 did he have the time and will to explain its unique philological form and content. He begins the epilogue: "The subject of this book, the representation of reality through literary representation or 'imitation,' has occupied me for a long time," probably since the 1929 book on Dante.[285] With regard to the concept of realism, his "original starting point was Plato's discussion in book 10 of the *Republic*—mimesis ranking third after truth—in conjunction with Dante's assertion that in the *Commedia* he presented true reality" (*M*, 554). Plato thought that poetic *mimêsis*, like that in a painting, is the mere imitation of appearance and ranked its products far below truth. Further, he found that it corrupts the soul, weakening the control of reason over other drives and desires (*Republic* 10, 596e–608b).[286] As Auerbach "studied the various *methods of interpreting human events in the literature of Europe*," his "interest" became "more precise and focused." At this moment, "*guiding ideas* began to crystallize," and he "sought to pursue" them in *Mimesis* (*M*, 554, emphasis added).

He first considered "*the doctrine of the ancients regarding the several levels of literary representation . . . which was taken up again by every later classicist movement.*" However, in teaching, he had found that "*modern realism in the form it reached in France in the early nineteenth century is, as aesthetic phenomenon, characterized by complete emancipation from that doctrine*" (*M*, 554, emphasis added). It broke with the view "that the

---

284. Auerbach to Buber, January 12, 1957, National Library of Israel, Martin Buber Archive, ARH Ms. 350, emphasis added.

285. Hacohen, personal letter to the author, January 10, 2012, "The rudiments of 'everyday tragic realism' are already in *Dante*."

286. On Plato's views on mimesis, see Zakai, "Constructing and Representing Reality," 110–12.

realistic depiction of daily life was incompatible with the sublime and had a place only in comedy" (*M*, 22):

> When *Stendhal and Balzac took random individuals from daily life in their dependence upon current historical circumstances and made them the subjects of serious, problematic, and even tragic representation, they broke with the classical rule of distinct levels of style,* for according to this rule, everyday practical reality could find a place in literature only within the frame of *a low or intermediate kind of style,* that is to say, as either grotesquely comic or pleasant, light, colorful, and elegant entertainment. (*M*, 554, emphasis added)

In exercising the intermediate style between tragedy and comedy, "in which the realistic mixes with the serious" (*M*, 401), the French realists "*opened the way for modern realism,* which has ever since developed in increasingly rich forms, in keeping with the constantly changing and expanding reality of modern life" (*M*, 554, emphasis added).

This "*revolution early in the nineteenth century against the classical doctrine of levels of style*" was the first turning point, in Auerbach's search for the evolution of realistic representation in Western literature. It dawns on him that the French realist revolution "could not possibly have been the first of its kind." In fact, he finds that "[t]he barriers which the romanticists and the contemporary realists tore down had been erected only toward the end of the sixteenth century and during the seventeenth by the advocates of rigorous imitation of antique literature" (*M*, 554). He makes an important discovery: "both during the Middle Ages and on through the Renaissance, a serious realism had existed." In these periods, "it had been possible in literature as well as in the visual arts to represent the most everyday phenomena of reality in a serious and significant context." Thus, the classic "doctrine of the levels of style" did not have "absolute validity." Despite their many differences, "medieval and modern realism" agreed on this point (*M*, 554–55).

Now, Auerbach confesses that "it had long been clear" to him "how this medieval conception of art had evolved, and when and how the first break with the classical theory had come about. It was the story of Christ, with its ruthless mixture of everyday reality and the highest and most sublime tragedy, which had conquered the classical rule of styles" (*M*, 555). This last discovery delivers a new chronology, or literary history, in which the Christian representation of reality, based on the figural interpretation of history, is consummated in Dante during the Middle Ages and the secular representation of reality, based on historicism, culminates in the nineteenth-century French realists. With historicism, "the thing we call separation of styles, the exclusion of realism from high tragedy, was overcome, and this is a basic prerequisite both for a historical and for a contemporary realism of tragic dimensions" (*M*, 444). In every instance of realistic representation, "Auerbach uncovers the same underlying pattern: the mixture of styles, that is, the breakdown of hierarchical divisions of style and subject matter (elevated style for heroes, kings, and nobles; comic style for low-born characters). The principal turning points in the history of realistic representation—sublime realism (the Gospels), figural realism (the literature of late Antiquity and the Middle Ages), contingent realism (the nineteenth-century French novel)—all share a common structure."[287]

The third theme of *Mimesis* thus becomes the figural interpretation of history, or representation of reality, first formulated in "Figura." Auerbach explains that "the two breaks with the doctrine of stylistic levels" (*M*, 555)—"the medieval and figural or the modern and practical type of realism" (*M*, 440)—took place under "completely different conditions and yielded completely different results" (*M*, 555). Their perceptions of reality are also completely different, and the early view "is very difficult to formulate." He solves the problem based on his previous "investigation of the semantic history of the word *figura*," using "the term figural to identify the conception of reality in late antiquity and the Christian Middle Ages" (*M*, 555). He defines his meaning in many places in *Mimesis*, especially in chapter 3, "The Arrest of Peter Valvomeres" (73–77). In sum, the "three closely related ideas, *which gave the original problem form*" are "*the base upon which the entire study is built*" (*M*, 555, emphasis added).

Had the epilogue introduced *Mimesis*, many readers might have better understood this otherwise complex and difficult study. It enunciates the central problem: "to what degree and in what manner realistic subjects were treated seriously, problematically, or tragically." Therefore, he decides to exclude "comic works, works which indubitably remained within the realm of the low style" (*M*, 556), ideologically restricting the field. Even regarding his own category, "realistic works of serious style and character," he claims that he has "not seen fit to analyze it theoretically and to describe it systematically." Since "even the term 'realistic' is

---

287. Robert Doran, "Literary History and the Sublime in Erich Auerbach's *Mimesis*," *New Literary History* 38 (2007): 354.

unambiguous," he concedes that his "interpretations are no doubt guided by a specific purpose," yet he then claims to have been "guided only by the texts themselves," selecting them "*at random, on the basis of accidental acquaintance and personal preference rather than in view of a definite purpose.*" We are right to be suspicious. We have seen that he was not guided by the texts themselves and did not choose them at random. He had a very definite view of history and literary history, and his subtitle denotes a specific humanist worldview, opposing realism to irrational myths, legends, and heroes. Above all, his study aims at "bringing together again," after the horrors of World War II, "*those whose love for our western history has serenely persevered*" (*M*, 556–57, emphasis added). The book's historical context—Armageddon—determined its form and content.

Whether *Mimesis* was written with a "definite purpose" may be judged from its moving final paragraph: "Nothing now remains but to find him—to find the reader, that is. I hope that my study will reach its readers—both my friends of former years, if they are still alive, as well as the others for whom it was intended" (*M*, 557). From first to last, it was written against a time of utter callousness for those, living and dead, who held fast to humanist culture and values. Hartman writes, Auerbach's "historicism seeks to generate by purely scholarly means testimony to oppose the forces of uniformity and intolerance."[288]

Epilogue: Exile, Interpretation, and Alienation

> [F]leeing Nazi Europe, fueled by adversity, many wrote criticism as a kind of message in a bottle dispatched to former interlocutors whose whereabouts were unknown, whose lives were uncertain.
>
> —Emily Apter, *The Translation Zone: A New Comparative Literature*, 2006

> [Auerbach] was not alone either in his desire to create a new world for himself or in his desire to make a terrain of that world somehow familiar. Many other German refugees were involved in similar experiments with their past, redefining themselves by creating a new world to inhibit. That world was often not as new as they may have suggested. The new structure often bore a remarkable resemblance to the old.
>
> —Carl Landauer, " 'Mimesis' and Erich Auerbach's Self-Mythologizing," 1988

---

288. Hartman, *Scholar's Tale*, 179.

In America from 1947 until his death in 1957, Auerbach belonged to a distinguished group of German-speaking intellectual exiles, who were, in Walt Whitman's words, "Language-shapers on other shores."[289] They included Leo Strauss, Hans Baron, Max Horkheimer, Theodor W. Adorno, Ernst Cassirer, and Hannah Arendt. Their language and concepts were formed during a specific, wretched moment in German history, and in opposition they all developed idiosyncratic interpretations in their own disciplines, directed by their common humanist ideology. In exile, each strove to save Western society from the menace of Nazism.

The idiosyncrasy of *Mimesis* can be seen in its reception. Auerbach wrote to Harry Levin that "his European reviewers, though they were friendly, looked upon *Mimesis* as no more than 'an amusing series of analyses of style.'"[290] How insulting to an author whose goal was not merely "to show, by stylistic study, the forms of literary realism shifting from Homer and Petronius through the age of Zola,"[291] but to emphasize how "literary discourses play the role of historic-political forces."[292] One of these European critics, whom Auerbach names in the letter to Levin, was Curtius. In fall 1949, at a Princeton seminar in literary criticism where Auerbach presented his work on realism, Curtius strongly criticized its philological-philosophical system and continued his argument in a 1952 review of *Mimesis*.[293] According to one participant at the Princeton seminar, every "blow" Curtius "struck at Auerbach was meant to break down" his concept of "realism." For example, Curtius objected to "the whole category of 'realism' as applied to Flaubert." Auerbach replied in these revealing words, which capture much of his tendency to impose his rigid categories on the course and progress of Western literary history: "No matter if Flaubert did not want to be called realist; he worked the same way *whether he liked it or not*"[294] (emphasis added). Eventually, one participant reported, "Auerbach

---

289. Walt Whitman, *Leaves of Grass*, ed. W. Blodgett and S. Bradley (New York: New York University Press, 1965), 18.

290. Levin, "Two *Romanisten*," 467–68.

291. Robert Fitzgerald, *Enlarging the Change: The Princeton Seminars in Literary Criticism 1949–1951* (Boston: Northeastern University Press, 1985), 32–33.

292. Brownlee, "Ideology of Periodization," 158.

293. Ernst Robert Curtius, "Die Lehre von den drei Stilen in Altertum und Mittelalter (zu Auerbachs *Mimesis*)" (The Teaching of the Three Styles in Antiquity and the Middle Ages [on Auerbach's *Memesis*]), *Romanische Forschungen* 64 (1952): 57–70.

294. Fitzgerald, *Enlarging the Change*, 39, 36.

concede[d] that only part of Flaubert was realist. 'But,' Auerbach added and no doubt putting his finger on what was, in a sense, the heart of the matter, 'I was writing a book on the treatment of everyday life.'"[295]

Auerbach responded more completely to Curtius's criticism later in "Epilegomena to Mimesis" (1953). He explained that Curtius "sees in the book a theoretical construct, from which he seeks to extract theses in order to refute it." Curtius apparently struck a chord here. "But the book is no *theoretical construct*," Auerbach complains, because "*it aims to offer a view*, and the very elastic thoughts or ideas that hold it together cannot be grasped and proven wrong in single isolated phrases" (*M*, 562, emphasis added). First, he asserts his particular circumstances: *Mimesis* deals "with a version of thought, which was formed by me around 1940," when "the idea of realism . . . present in *Mimesis*, was dealt with previously only rarely—and even then in another context" (*M*, 562–63, emphasis added). Exile led to interpretation, or Auerbach's unique presentation and representation of the Western humanist "version of thought" in light of the crisis of European civilization during World War II.

He then focuses on two points in Curtius's criticism, the doctrine of the three styles and typology that support his concept of realism. He argues that he began to work on the motif of typology "seventeen years ago," in 1936, when he was writing "Figura," and he dealt with it "from Paul up to the seventeenth century," or the Enlightenment. Curtius tended to minimize the influence of typology, which supported Auerbach's whole mission, and Auerbach responded angrily and personally: "The effect of typology is most certainly just as important and permanent a phenomenon for the medieval structure of expression as is the survival of ancient rhetorical topoi of form and content," which Curtius had developed in *European Literature and the Latin Middle Ages* (1948). He answered Curtius's imputation that he was exaggerating the role and power of figural interpretation, claiming "that typology is the real vital element of Bible poetry and hymns, or, even more, of almost the whole Christian literature of late antiquity and the Middle Ages" (*M*, 568–69). This post–World War II controversy between two German humanist philologists is most revealing. Both struggled against the menace of Aryan philology, yet Curtius's attack shows how idiosyncratic Auerbach's interpretation of reality is. Naturally, Curtius's criticisms were very hard for Auerbach to accept since figural interpretation was inextricable from his existential exiled predicament in Turkey and his *Kulturkampf* against Aryan philology and Nazism.

---

295. Ibid., 36.

However, countering criticism of *Mimesis* was not Auerbach's primary subject after the war. In 1952, he published the essay "Philology and *Weltliteratur*," which elucidates his concepts of humanism and the human condition in general. In expressing his deep pessimism about the fate of Western civilization, it continues the last chapter of *Mimesis*, and we may regard it as an extended epilogue.

Goethe conceived the notion of *Weltliteratur* around 1827. Here, Auerbach deploys it to discuss the relationship between historicism, philology, and humanism, noting that "approximately five hundred" years ago, "the national European literatures won their self-consciousness from and superiority over Latin civilization." A mere two hundred years had "passed since the awakening of our sense of historicism, a sense that permitted the formation of the concept of *Weltliteratur*" by which Goethe "contributed decisively to the development of historicism and to the philological research that was generated out of it." Philology became queen of the humanities because it "drew the history of the other arts, the history of religion, law, and politics after itself, and wove itself variously with them into certain fixed aims and commonly achieved concepts of order" (PW, 4).

For Auerbach, humanism was not based on the glorious cultural past of the classical world and the early Italian Renaissance, as Burckhardt and Baron, for example, believed, but a new phenomenon related crucially to the rise of historicism in early eighteenth-century Germany. Likewise, his humanism was not Baron's civic humanism of the fourteenth- and fifteenth-century Italian Renaissance but "historicist humanism"; hence, the singular and prominent role he attaches to the realm of history:

> History is the science of reality that affects us most immediately, stirs us most deeply and compels us most forcibly to a consciousness of ourselves. It is the only science in which human beings step before us in their totality. Under the rubric of history one is to understand not only the past, but the progression of events in general; history therefore includes the present. (PW, 4–5)

Auerbach closely follows Kant's famous 1784 dictum about the Enlightenment[296] as well as Vico's epistemology to define the specific task of the philologist: "Whatever we are, we became in history, and only in history can we remain the way we are and develop therefrom: it is the

---

296. Kant, *What Is Enlightenment?*, 58.

task of the philologist, whose province is the world of human history, to demonstrate this so that it penetrates our lives unforgettably" (PW, 5–6). He never forgot the great historical lesson of his time, the horror of Nazism and fascism: "our philological home is the earth: it can no longer be the nation" (PW, 17).

Clearly, like "Figura" and *Mimesis*, "Philology and *Weltliteratur*" is not simply a philological study but an important statement about the human condition. It is very pessimistic. In the last paragraph, Auerbach writes, "*Paupertas and terra aliena*" (PW, 17); *Geist* now finds itself in an indigent, devastated, and strange land. In other words, "the whole world is a foreign land"—*mundus totus exilium est*—for Spirit, a view in clear contrast to Hegel's teleological philosophy of history, which Auerbach had embraced in the past. After two terrible world wars, alienation from, not reconciliation with, the world is the mark of the human existential condition: exile. The important theme of exile and alienation was the main subject of a series of sermons that the Bishop of Hippo Regius preached following the sack of Rome: "Citizens of Jerusalem . . . O God's own people, O Body of Christ, O high-born race of foreigners on earth . . . you do not belong here, you belong somewhere else."[297] Christian life is figured as a permanent pilgrimage upon earth as "resident aliens."[298]

Exile and alienation dominated the respective crises of both the Doctor of Grace and the German philologist. For Augustine, it meant that Christianity's fate on earth was once again exile, as it had been before the Conversion of Constantine the Great in 312, when the Christian Church was transformed from a persecuted sect into the established faith of the Roman Empire. Auerbach felt that Western humanism was once again exiled after World War II. In the modern, "standardized" world of culture, the concept of *Weltliteratur* comes to an end: "There is no more talk now—as there had been—of a spiritual exchange between peoples, of the refinement of customs and of reconciliation of races" (PW, 1, 4, 6–7, 17). *Weltliteratur*, as a unique and important ideal of historicist humanism, reached its end, and Auerbach and his method are excluded from modern Western culture. His sense of exile in Istanbul and his deep, atavist sense of alienation never left him.

Two world wars, one in which he was seriously wounded; the upheavals of the Weimar Republic; the rise of Nazism; and the triumph

---

297. Brown, "Saint Augustine," 11. See also Zakai, *Exile and Kingdom*, especially 12–55.

298. Brown, *Augustine of Hippo*, 313–14.

of Aryan philology had a great impact not only on the composition of *Mimesis* and "Philology and *Weltliteratur*" but also on their fate. Auerbach became convinced that the story of Western civilization did not end in success.[299] He defended it with all his might, but he was not blind to its faults and shortcomings.

However, immediately following his claim about historicist humanism's exile and alienation from the world, he quotes a moving passage from the medieval philosopher, theologian, and mystic Hugh of St. Victor (ca. 1096–1141), a monk from Saxony:

> It is, therefore, a source of great virtue for the practiced mind to learn, bit by bit, first to change about invisible and transitory things, so that afterwards it may be able to leave them behind altogether. *The man who finds his homeland sweet is still a tender beginner; he to whom every soil is as his native one is already strong; but he is perfect to whom the entire world is as a foreign land.* The tender soul has fixed his love on one spot in the world; the strong man has extended his love to all places; the perfect man has extinguished his. (PW, 17, emphasis added)[300]

Auerbach wrote that "Hugo intended these lines for one whose aim is to free himself from a love of the world. But it is a good way also for one who wishes to earn a proper love for the world" (PW, 17). He seems to identify with "the perfect man," whose love of the world has been "extinguished" and to "whom the entire world is as a foreign land."[301] Now in America, Auerbach quotes these beautiful, haunting words, which provide

---

299. Auerbach's deep pessimism was not unique. Three years after the end of World War II, on March 8, 1948, the American weekly newsmagazine *Time* featured on the cover of its twenty-fifth-anniversary edition a picture of Reinhold Niebuhr (1892–1971) captioned "Man's Story is Not a Success Story." See Zakai, "The Irony of American History: Reinhold Niebuhr and the American Experience," *La Revue LISA/LISA e-journal*, World War II Thematic dossier, 2008, 1–21, www.unicaen.fr/mrsh/lisa/publicationsGb.php?p=2&numId=1&it=inTheWar.

300. See also Said, *Reflections on Exile*, 185, and Aamir R. Mufti, "Auerbach in Istanbul: Edward Said, Secular Criticism, and the Question of Minority Culture," *Critical Inquiry* 25 (Autumn 1998): 97.

301. Compare the General Epistle of James, 4: 4: "the friendship of the world is enmity with God" and "whosoever therefore will be a friend of the world is the enemy of God."

a good summary of his entire philological enterprise or, in fact, his entire life and works.

In the end, the man who was excluded from German culture and life—his *Heimat*—forced into exile in Istanbul, where he discovered his mission to save the European humanist world, changed radically after the war with the rise of industrial capitalist society—standardized, uniform, and dehumanized. Wellek, Auerbach's colleague at Yale, noted that after World War II he "wrote gloomily about the tomb of Western civilization," and this "gloom intensified in his last year."[302] Ironically, the historical reality that Auerbach strove so hard to portray in *Mimesis* seemed blunted and stunted by standardization and uniformity.

However, out of his agonizing exilic experience, he gave us a majestic, magisterial work of humanist literary history. In its broad cross-cultural analyses and sense of a world historical humanist ideological debate beginning with the Old Testament and Homeric epic, it enlarged the scope and significance of literary criticism and sparked the future field toward comparative rather than national perspectives that, in fact, enact *Weltliteratur*. If only he had lived a little longer, "had [he] but world enough, and time," to see authors in India, Africa, the Caribbean, Latin America, and excluded Western communities adopt the techniques of Western realistic representation to assert their political, economic, and social relevance and to demand readers' attention. Even at his most tendentious, pushing his idea of progress through such recalcitrant authors as Rabelais, his pure love of the texts and brilliant illumination of their insights shine through.

---

302. Wellek, *German, Russian, and Eastern European Criticism*, 123.

IV

Enlightenment and Its Enemies

Max Horkheimer, Theodor Adorno, and the Dialectic of *Dialectic of Enlightenment*

> [The year 1942] will most probably be a decisive one for all our existence.
>
> —Theodor Adorno, *Letters to His Parents*," 1942
>
> In their blackest book, *Dialectic of Enlightenment*, Horkheimer and Adorno [conceptualize] the Enlightenment's process of self-destruction. On their analysis, it is no longer possible to place hope in the liberating force of Enlightenment.
>
> —Jürgen Habermas, *The Philosophical Discourse of Modernity*, 1985

Among the books begun in the crucial year 1942, the year of Stalingrad, which signified a great epistemological watershed in modern Western history, *Dialectic of Enlightenment* is the saddest, gloomiest, most desperate. Jürgen Habermas called it Horkheimer and Adorno's "blackest book."[1] All the books under discussion—*Doctor Faustus, Mimesis, Dialectic of Enlightenment,* and *The Myth of the State*—were written in a time of horrors and atrocities and marked by deep pessimism and a strong sense of world decline, yet only *Dialectic of Enlightenment* is devoid of hope and conceives society as a jungle stripped of humanist values. The end of *Doctor Faustus* provides a moment of grace when the hero finally escapes the grip of the Devil; while acknowledging decline, *Mimesis* defends a well-defined, coherent, and unified humanist vision of European civilization against Nazi barbarism, and *The Myth of the*

---

1. Habermas, *Philosophical Discourse of Modernity*, 106.

State reveals the permanent struggle between myth and reason. *Dialectic of Enlightenment* differs radically: it revives Thomas Hobbes's *Leviathan or The Matter, Forme and Power of a Common-Wealth Ecclesiastical and Civil* (1651),² which describes "the natural condition of mankind" as "the war of all against all" or "each against all"—*Bellum omnium contra omnes*.³

Dialectic of Enlightenment constructs the Hobbesian view that might is right in Hegelian and Marxist terms. The primary concepts are power, force, naked force, domination, subjugation, violence, terror, horror, and deception. Bereft of the conceit of human progress, might is right ruled the day. As in Hobbes, self-preservation is the source and final drive of all human action; "Spinoza's proposition: 'the endeavor of preserving oneself is the first and only basis of virtue,' contains the true maxim of all Western civilization" the authors agreed.⁴ More specifically, with capitalism, inextricably connected to the Age of Reason and the Enlightenment, "the process of self-preservation is based on the bourgeois division of labor" (23). In the authors' hands, class struggle replaces Hobbes's war of all against all or the law of the jungle.⁵ In this inhumane and unjust society,

---

2. Another important attempt to read history after the outbreak of World War II in Hobbesian terms is Collingwood, *New Leviathan*.

3. Thomas Hobbes, *De Cive (On the Citizen)*, 1642: ". . . *ostendo primo conditionem hominum extra societatem civilem (quam conditionem appellare liceat statum naturae) aliam non esse quam bellum omnium contra omnes; atque in eo bello jus esse omnibus in omnia.*" (I demonstrate, in the first place, that the state of men without civil society [which state we may properly call the state of nature] is nothing else but a mere war of all against all; and in that war all men have equal right unto all things.") See: https://en.wikipedia.org/wiki/Bellum_omnium_contra_omnes.

4. Max Horkheimer and Theodor W. Adorno, *Dialectic of Enlightenment: Philosophical Fragments*, ed. Gunzelin Schmid Noerr, trans. Edmund Jephcott (Stanford: Stanford University Press, 2002 [1944]), 22. All references in the text are to this edition.

5. Hitler's views give clear proof of this contention: "the law of the jungle was the only law. People were to suppress any inclination to be merciful and were to be as rapacious as they could. Hitler thus broke with the traditions of political thought that presented human beings as distinct from nature in their capacity to imagine and create new forms of association. Beginning from that assumption, political thinkers tried to describe not only the possible but the most just forms of society. For Hitler, however, nature was the singular, brutal, and overwhelming truth, and the whole history of attempting to think otherwise was an illusion. Carl Schmitt, a leading Nazi legal theorist, explained that politics arose not from history or

they wrote, clearly reflecting on their own exilic condition, "No one who seeks shelter shall find it; those who express what everyone craves—peace, homeland, freedom—will be denied it, just as nomads and traveling players have always been refused rights of domicile. Whatever someone fears, that is done to him" (150).[6] This vision of human society as a cruel wilderness appears in the last chapter, "Elements of Anti-Semitism: Limits of Enlightenment," which reveals how much the authors' personal experience of exilic displacement, racism, and anti-Semitism determined the content and form of Dialectic of Enlightenment.

In Hegelian and Marxist dialectic, a thesis provokes its antithesis, which contradicts or negates it; a synthesis that resolves the tension between the two advances social progress. In stark contrast, the Dialectic of Enlightenment posits human regression and decline. Its overt dismissal of a "philosophy of history, which had been, in the Marxist tradition, basically progressive," clearly contradicted the views of the Institute for Social Research (Institut für Sozialforschung) with which Horkheimer and Adorno were affiliated.[7] This philosophical turn, based on "undialectical pessimism,"[8] had a tremendous impact on the human condition. As Horkheimer wrote:

> Dialectic of Enlightenment—Men no longer experience themselves as individuals, in need of a goal that transcends their

---

concepts but from our sense of enmity. Our racial enemies were chosen by nature, and our task was to struggle and kill and die." See Snyder, "Hitler's World," New York Review of Books, 24 September 2015.

6. Compare Rainer Maria Rilke (1875–1926), "Autumn Day" (Herbsttag), trans. Guntram Deichsel.

> Who's homeless now, will for long stay alone.
> No home will build his weary hands,
> He'll wake, read, write letters long to friends
> And will the alleys up and down
> Walk restlessly, when falling leaves dance.

7. Richard Wolin, The Terms of Cultural Criticism: The Frankfurt School, Existentialism, Poststructuralism (New York: Columbia University Press, 1992), 41.

8. Anson Rabinbach, "The Cunning of Unreason: Mimesis and the Construction of Anti-Semitism in Horkheimer and Adorno's Dialectic of Enlightenment," in In the Shadow of Catastrophe: German Intellectuals between Apocalypse and Enlightenment (Berkeley: University of California Press, 1997), 170. See also, Rabinbach, "Why Were the Jews Sacrificed? The Place of Anti-Semitism in Dialectic of Enlightenment," New German Critique 81 (Autumn 2000): 49–64.

existence. Le Grand Etre and Hegel's objective spirit have become unnecessary. And man no longer thinks of himself as finite, as being unable to live without an infinite, or at least, meaning. Instead, he is unreflectedly [sic] 'positive,' an element of social reality. Dialectic of Enlightenment.[9]

The writing of *Dialectic of Enlightenment* originated in the struggle against Nazism and fascism, but as Horkheimer made clear in 1957, its origins should be traced to the beginning of modern history and the rise of bourgeois society: "The tendency to subordinate the truth to power did not first emerge with fascism; irrationalism, just as deeply rooted in the economic situation of the bourgeoisie as the liberal traits, pervades the entire history and limits its concept of reason."[10] The origins of fascism and Nazism, symbolized by the flight from reason, should be located in the Enlightenment and capitalist, bourgeois society.

Horkheimer and Adorno's ultimate goal was to reveal why humanity is sinking into "a new kind of barbarism" and to demonstrate a cultural progress turned "into its opposite" (xiv, xiii).

Written during the early 1940s, the authors cannot find any progress or even hope in history, like their friend and colleague Walter Benjamin, whose "Theses of the Philosophy of History" greatly influenced them. It depicted the Angel of History: "His face is turned toward the past. Where we perceive a chain of events, he sees one single catastrophe which keeps piling wreckage upon wreckage and hurls it in front of his feet."[11] Hegel and Marx's philosophy of history is based on constant progress, as the

---

9. Max Horkheimer, *Dawn and Decline: Notes 1926-1931 and 1950-1969*, trans. Michael Shaw (New York: Seabury Press, 1978), 144-45, emphasis original. *Le Grand Etre* [Great Being] references the work of Auguste Comte (1798-1857), who founded the discipline of sociology and the doctrine of positivism—the belief that positive knowledge is based on natural phenomena and their properties and relations; information derived from sensory experience, interpreted through reason and logic, is the exclusive source of all authoritative knowledge. Comte's secular and positive religion was a complete system of belief and ritual, with liturgy and sacraments, priesthood and pontiff, all organized around the public veneration of Humanity, referred to as the *Nouveau Grand-Être Suprême* (New Supreme Great Being).

10. Max Horkheimer, *Between Philosophy and Social Sciences: Selected Early Writings*, trans. G. F. Hunter and M. S. Kramer (Cambridge: MIT Press, 1993), 278.

11. Benjamin, *Illuminations*, 257-58.

representative of the *Spirit*,[12] in Hegel's case, or, for Marx, toward a communist society in which class-based human conflict would be overcome. *Dialectic of Enlightenment* sees steady decline and regress.

Given the predominance of Aryan philology based on *völkisch* mysticism in Nazi culture and historiography, *Dialectic of Enlightenment* had to reflect on the power of myth in history. *Doctor Faustus, Mimesis, The Myth of the State*, and many other works struggled to provide a new historiography of German history (Mann), literature (Auerbach), politics (Cassirer), and sociology (Horkheimer and Adorno). As Hannah Arendt wrote: "All historiography is necessarily salvation and frequently justification."[13] Horkheimer and Adorno strove to understand how enlightened thought gave way to the myth of power. Politics in Nazi Germany determined to a large extent the content and form as well as the politics of representation in all these works, sparking *Kulturkampf* against fascism and Nazism.

Biographical Sketches

Horkheimer

> Only one thing is certain, the irrationality of society has reached a point where only the gloomiest predications have any plausibility.
>
> —Max Horkheimer, 1932

> The hope that earthly horror will not have the last word, is without a doubt, nonscientific desire.
>
> —Max Horkheimer to Martin Jay, 1971

Max Horkheimer (1895–1973) was the director of the Institut für Sozialforschung (Institute of Social Research, now known as the Frankfurt School of Critical Thinking) and Professor of Social Philosophy at the University of Frankfurt from 1930 to 1933 and 1949 to 1958; between those periods, he led the institute in exile, primarily in America. As a philosopher, he is best known, especially in the Anglophone world, for his 1940s works,

---

12. On Hegel's philosophy of history, see Zakai, "Constructing and Representing Reality."
13. Hannah Arendt, "A Reply to Eric Voegelin" (1953), *The Portable Hannah Arendt* (New York: Penguin, 2000), 158.

including *Dialectic of Enlightenment* (1944), coauthored with Theodor Adorno, and *The Eclipse of Reason* (1947).[14]

Horkheimer was the only son of Moritz and Babetta Horkheimer, born into a conservative, wealthy, orthodox Jewish family. His father was a successful businessman who owned several textile factories in the Zuffenhausen district of Stuttgart, where Max was born. In 1911, at sixteen, he graduated from prep school and went to work in his father's factory. He was drafted into the army during World War I in 1916, but by the spring of 1919, he was enrolled at Munich University. Shortly thereafter, he moved to Frankfurt am Main, where he studied philosophy and psychology and met his most important intellectual collaborators, especially Adorno, with whom he developed a lasting friendship. In 1926, the year he married Rose Riekher, he was appointed *Privatdozent*, meaning that he had permission to teach and to supervise PhD students at the conferring university without holding a professorial chair and that he was qualified to be appointed full professor. He was promoted to professor of philosophy at Frankfurt University in 1930.

In the same year, director Carl Grünberg left the Institute for Social Research he had founded in 1923 as a freestanding center for Marxist scholarship. He had been a Marxist professor of law and politics at the University of Vienna and an adjunct at the University of Frankfurt. The institute was the first Marxist-oriented research center affiliated with a major German university. When Horkheimer was elected director, he changed it to a more heterodox center for critical social research. He proposed a program of collective research on specific social groups, especially the working class, that would highlight the problematic relationship of history and reason. Under his leadership, the institute focused on systematically integrating the views of Marx and Freud, attempting to bring together the different conceptual structures of historical materialism and psychoanalysis. His goal was to make the institute a purely academic enterprise. In 1971, he explained the institute's credo under his directorship in a letter

---

14. The following intellectual biography of Horkheimer is based in part on the editors' "Introduction: Max Horkheimer: Between Philosophy and Social Science," in *On Max Horkheimer: New Perspectives*, ed. Seyla Benhabib, Wolfgang Bonss, and John McCole (Cambridge: MIT Press, 1993), 1–25; John Abromeit, *Max Horkheimer and the Foundations of the Frankfurt School* (New York: Cambridge University Press, 2011); Martin Jay, *The Dialectical Imagination: A History of the Frankfurt School and the Institute of Social Research, 1923–1950* (Berkeley: University of California Press, 1996); and Rolf Wiggershaus, *The Frankfurt School: Its History, Theories, and Political Significance* (Cambridge: MIT Press, 1995).

to Martin Jay: "the Marxist interpretation of social events without a doubt continued to be definitive for us," as well as "the conviction that in the epoch of transition it was more important to articulate the negative than to pursue an individual academic career." He summed up his life in the Age of Catastrophe: "The hope that earthly horror will not have the last word is, without a doubt, a nonscientific desire."[15]

When Horkheimer became Professor of Social Philosophy and director of the institute in 1930, tremendous social and political transformations were wrenching Weimar Germany. The Nazis became the second largest party in the Reichstag. Horkheimer's observation in 1932 proved chillingly prophetic: "Only one thing is certain," he wrote, "the irrationality of society has reached a point where only the gloomiest predictions have any plausibility."[16] From the rise and triumph of Nazism, the theme of irrationalism informed his work. In 1933, Hitler became chancellor. The new Nazi government revoked Horkheimer's *venia legendi* (permission to lecture) because of the institute's Marxian ideas and prominent Jewish associations. It was forced to move, first to Geneva in 1933, and in the following year, to New York, where the president of Columbia University agreed to host it in exile and offered Horkheimer a building. The Nazis drove into exile not only individuals but also academic institutions.[17]

The breakout of World War II in 1939 and especially the Nazi invasion of France in 1940 led to the important collaboration of Horkheimer and Adorno and a thorough reconstruction of the content and form of their works. In America, they began planning a joint work on "dialectical logic," which would later become *Dialectic of Enlightenment*.[18] Alarmed by reports from Europe, where Adorno's parents suffered increasing discrimination and their friend Walter Benjamin was arrested by the French government and incarcerated for three months in a prison camp near Nevers, in central Burgundy, following the Nazi invasion of France. Horkheimer and Adorno had no delusions about the fate of Europe: "In view of what is now threatening to engulf Europe," Horkheimer wrote in 1939,

---

15. Max Horkheimer, *A Life in Letters: Selected Correspondence*, ed. and trans. M. R. Jacobson and E. M. Jacobson (Lincoln: University of Nebraska Press, 2007), 379–80.

16. Müller-Doohm, *Adorno*, 175.

17. See Thomas Wheatland, *The Frankfurt School in Exile* (Minneapolis: University of Minnesota Press, 2009).

18. For an important analysis of the making of *Dialectic of Enlightenment*, see Rabinbach, "Cunning of Unreason," 166–98.

"our present work is essentially destined to pass things down through the night that is approaching: a kind of message in a bottle."[19] They aimed to write a message that would salvage European humanist civilization from the menace of Nazi barbarism, although the approaching night brought despair and deep pessimism, a burden they all shared. Adorno used the same metaphor, describing their work as the "surviving message of despair from the shipwrecked."[20]

Dialectic of Enlightenment was a message they could write only as shipwrecks in America; they did not aim to solve their own existential crisis but rather to salvage European humanist tradition, like Cassirer and Auerbach in the books they began in 1942. But who in Nazi Europe would receive the message? In the context of despair and agony, the crisis mode of historical thought became the dominant and overarching theme of *Dialectic of Enlightenment* as well as many other works written by exiles from Nazi Germany, such as Mann's *Doctor Faustus*, Cassirer's *The Myth of the State*, Auerbach's *Mimesis*, and many more. Despair was the portion of those who cared about the humanist soul of Western culture. In the face of the seemingly invincible Wehrmacht, what was left but to send a "surviving message of despair" from exile?

The crisis mode of historical thought, or crisis history, is based on the view that history proceeds in a series of crises, or well-defined, decisive turning points. Walter Benjamin's "Theses on the Philosophy of History"[21] takes this view,[22] as does Cassirer's sad recognition in the "Conclusions" to

---

19. Müller-Doohm, *Adorno*, 262.

20. Ibid., 549n107. Müller-Doohm argues that in *The Philosophy of Modern Music* (1949), Adorno translated Horkheimer's "message in a bottle" to "surviving message of despair from the shipwrecked" of Europe. Walter Benjamin too used this metaphor. See Benjamin's letter to Gerhard Scholem, April 17, 1931: "Like one who keeps afloat on a shipwreck by climbing to the top of a mast that is already crumbling. But from there he has a chance to give a signal leading to his rescue." Quoted in Arendt, *Men in Dark Times* (New York: Harcourt, Brace & World, 1955), 172. Needless to say, Benjamin committed suicide in 1940, relinquishing all hope of rescue and help.

21. Benjamin, *Illuminations*, 245–55. On Benjamin's philosophy in general and philosophy of history in particular, see Eli Friedlander, *Walter Benjamin: A Philosophical Portrait* (Cambridge: Harvard University Press, 2012).

22. On Benjamin's apocalyptic view of history, see Anson Rabinbach, "Between Apocalypse and Enlightenment: Benjamin, Bloch, and Modern German Messianism," *In the Shadow of Catastrophe*, 27–65.

The Myth of the State: "What we have learned in the hard school of our modern political life is the fact that human culture is by no means the firmly established thing that we once supposed it to be."[23] Auerbach wrote in *Mimesis* that the dissolution of the representation of reality prefigured "the decline of our world."[24] In the same vein of pessimism and despair, Horkheimer and Adorno wrote, "The present time is without turning points. A turn of events is always for the better. But when, as today, calamity is at its height, the heavens open and hurl their fire on those who are lost in any case" (182). Crisis, not progress, or the glorious Enlightenment vision of human advance, is the marrow of the historical process.

The same sense of impending existential and historical crisis developed from the ravages of the First World War in the crisis theology of Protestant Neo-Orthodoxy, more specifically, Karl Barth's theology of judgment, and a new Jewish philosophy of history, evidenced in the writings of Benjamin, Ernst Bloch (1885–1977), Franz Rosenzweig (1886–1929), Gershom Scholem (1897–1982), and others.[25] In both strains, the connection between divine goodness and human history was severed, undermining the concept of historical progress. For example, in *The Star of Redemption*, Rosenzweig rejected Hegel's concept of "wisdom in history."

Saint Augustine was the first to develop the view that divine providence and the course and progress of history are not connected.[26] In fact, the Bishop of Hippo and his celebrated *City of God* provided a model for modern shipwrecks. Living on the outskirts of the Roman empire, the Doctor of Grace (*Doctor gratiae*) wrote his ecclesiastical history to explain that the Christian faith did not cause the fall of Rome, as many claimed. His apology defended and justified the Christian faith at its gravest existential moment. Likewise, Horkheimer and Adorno's *Dialectic of Enlightenment* aimed to explain the causes of the fall of European humanist civilization at its gravest existential moment. The Janus-faced dialectic of enlightenment, a dramatic epistemological turning point in modern history, entwines knowledge and power. If Augustine's *City of God* provided an alternative explanation of the fall of Rome, then Horkheimer and Adorno provided an alternative explanation of the fall of Western civilization under Nazi barbarism.

---

23. Cassirer, *Myth of the State*, 297.

24. Auerbach, *Mimesis*, 551.

25. See Rabinbach, "Introduction: Apocalypse and Its Shadow," *In the Shadow of Catastrophe*, 1–23, and "Between Apocalypse and the Enlightenment: Benjamin, Bloch, and Modern Jewish Messianism," *In the Shadow of Catastrophe*, 27–65.

26. See Zakai and Mali, "Time, History and Eschatology."

Trauma caused by the triumph of Nazi irrationalism and, consequently, forced exile, led to the two important studies Horkheimer wrote in America during the 1940s, *Dialectic of Enlightenment* (1944) and *Eclipse of Reason* (1947). In 1940, he received American citizenship and moved to the Pacific Palisades district of Los Angeles, where, in 1942, he and Adorno began writing *Dialectic of Enlightenment: Philosophical Fragment* in light of "the National Socialist terror" and "National Socialist rule" (xiii). Its goal was "to take up the cause of the remnants of freedom, of tendencies toward humanity, even though they seem powerless in face of the great historical trend" of the rise and triumph of totalitarianism (xi). Originally, the authors argued, "Enlightenment, understood in the widest sense as the advance of thought, has always aimed at liberating human beings from fear and installing them as masters." Its "program was the disenchantment of the world," to "dispel myths, to overthrow fantasy with knowledge" (1). However, with the rise of fascism and National Socialism, reason seemed to collapse; discourse regressed into superstition and myth.

The struggle against myth, as in Cassirer's *The Myth of the State*, Auerbach's *Mimesis*, and Mann's *Doctor Faustus*, was central to *Dialectic of Enlightenment*. Alfred Rosenberg, the chief ideologist of the Nazi Party, proclaimed in *The Myth of the Twentieth Century* (1930) that "a new belief is arising: the Myth of the blood, the belief that the godly essence of man itself is to be defended through *the blood*."[27] The rise of fascism and the demise of the liberal state and the market constituted the theoretical and historical frame for Horkheimer and Adorno's overall argument: "What we had set out to do was nothing less than to explain why humanity, instead of entering a truly human state, is sinking into a new kind of barbarism" (xiv) or the "reversion of enlightened civilization to barbarism in reality" (xix). Devoted "predominantly to philosophical questions," the book provides "a critique of philosophy" (xii) in response to the crisis of German philosophy. Paradoxically, the authors noted, reason itself had become irrational.

The second study Horkheimer wrote in exile was *Eclipse of Reason*, a continuation of *Dialectic of Enlightenment*, that sprang from the same crisis of Western civilization or, more specifically, the horrors of Nazi barbarism, which shattered conventional and traditional concepts of reason and rationality. It reflected the "universal feeling of fear and disillusionment" that the advance in "technical facilities for enlightenment is accompanied

---

27. Pois, *Race and Race History and Other Essays by Alfred Rosenberg*, 82.

by a process of dehumanization," which led to "a victorious re-emergence of the new-barbarism recently defeated on the battlefields."[28] The book is based on a series of lectures he delivered at Columbia University in spring 1944, before the end of World War II. He discusses how the Nazis were able to project their agenda, based on myths, legends, and heroes and hence a flight from reason, as "reasonable": "If by enlightenment and intellectual progress we mean the freeing of man from superstitious belief in evil forces, in demons and fairies, in blind fate—in short, the emancipation from fear—then denunciation of what is currently called reason is the greatest service we can render."[29]

Eclipse of Reason should also be seen in the wider context of the political and philosophical crisis of the first half of the twentieth century. Erich Fromm was another member of the Frankfurt Institute of Social Research. He joined in 1930 and in 1934, after the Nazi Revolution, also moved to Columbia University. In his *Escape from Freedom* (or *Fear of Freedom*, 1941), he emphasizes the psychological conditions that facilitated the rise of Nazism—the dark side of the human soul. Other works intrinsically connected to this crisis are R. G. Collingwood's *The New Leviathan: Or Man, Society, Civilization, and Barbarism* (1942), a reaction to the Second World War and Nazism and fascism's threat to civilization, and *Behemoth: The Structure and Practice of National Socialism, 1933-1944* (1942) by Franz Leopold Neumann, another member of the Frankfurt Institute of Social Research who wrote this work in New York. A wide range of works sought to unveil the cultural, political, and philosophical origins of these antihumanist movements. The Nazi horrors revealed the black hole of the human soul, fleeing freedom and reason in fear, and allowing the triumph of irrational myths and murderous prejudices.

After World War II ended, Horkheimer did not publish much but continued to edit *Studies in Philosophy and Social Science*, the official journal of the Institute for Social Research. In 1949, he returned to Frankfurt for its reopening in 1950, and in 1951, he became rector of the University of Frankfurt. He stepped down from that position in 1953 and took on a smaller role at the institute, while Adorno became its director. The two were seen as the institute's fathers.

---

28. Max Horkheimer, *Eclipse of Reason* (New York: Oxford University Press, 1947), v–vi.

29. Ibid., 187.

Adorno

> I find death in exile, even though it was a blessing compared to an existence over there [in Nazi Germany], particularly dreadful—that the continuity of a person's life is senselessly broken in two, that he cannot live his own life to its natural conclusion, as it were, but instead ultimately has the entirely external identity of the 'emigrant' forced upon him, a representative of a category rather than an individual.
>
> —Theodor Adorno, July 19, 1946, in *Letters to His Parents*

Theodor W. Adorno (1903–1969) was a sociologist, philosopher, and musicologist.[30] Along with Horkheimer, he was a leading member of the Frankfurt School of Critical Theory, which held that social inquiry ought to combine, rather than separate, the poles of philosophy and social science, the better to explain structure and agency, regularity and normativity.[31] His work has come to be associated with such thinkers as Walter Benjamin, the Marxist philosopher Ernst Bloch (1885–1977), and Herbert Marcuse (1898–1979), the German American philosopher, sociologist, and politic theorist for whom the works of Hegel, Marx, and Freud were essential to a critique of modern society. Adorno is widely regarded as one of the twentieth century's foremost thinkers on aesthetics and philosophy and one of its preeminent essayists. Like many other intellectual exiles from Nazi Germany, he wrote several books for which he later became famous in exile, including *Dialectic of Enlightenment*, *Philosophy of New Music* (1946), *The Authoritarian Personality* (1950), in collaboration with Else Frenkel-Brunswik, Daniel Levinson, and Nevitt Sanford at the University of California, Berkeley, and *Minima Moralia: Reflections from Damaged Life* (1951).

Born Theodor Ludwig Wiesengrund, Adorno was the only child of Oscar Alexander Wiesengrund and Maria Calvelli-Adorno della Piana. His mother, a devout Catholic from Corsica, was once a professional singer, and his father, an assimilated Jew who had converted to Protestantism, ran a successful wine export business.[32] He changed his name to Theodor

---

30. The following intellectual biography of Adorno is based, in part, on Müller-Doohm, *Adorno*; Jäger, *Adorno*; and Brian O'Connor, "Introduction," in *The Adorno Reader*, ed. O'Connor (Oxford: Blackwell, 2000), 1–19.

31. See Seyla Benhabib, *Critique, Norm, and Utopia: A Study of the Foundations of Critical Theory* (New York: Columbia University Press, 1986).

32. Adorno wrote: "I was born in Frankfurt in 1903. My father was a German Jew, while my mother, herself a singer, was born to a French officer of Corsican,

W. Adorno when he applied for US citizenship. He attended Deutschherren middle school in Frankfurt before transferring to the Kaiser-Wilhelm Gymnasium, where he studied from 1913 to 1921. Then he went on to study philosophy, psychology, and sociology at Johann Wolfgang Goethe University in Frankfurt. In 1924, before reaching his twenty-first birthday, he received his doctorate; his dissertation addressed *The Transcendence of the Real and the Noematic in Husserl's Phenomenology*. At the same time, he met his most important intellectual collaborators, Max Horkheimer and Walter Benjamin. In 1925, he moved to Vienna to study with the composer Alban Berg, whom Adorno called "my master and teacher." In 1929, he accepted the Christian existentialist philosopher and theologian Paul Tillich's offer to present a Habilitation on *Kierkegaard: The Construction of the Aesthetic*. Receiving favorable reports from Professors Tillich and Horkheimer as well as Walter Benjamin,[33] the university conferred the *venia legendi* (permission to lecture) on Adorno in February 1931.

Several months later, he secured an academic position at the University of Frankfurt and delivered an inaugural lecture at the Institute for Social Research, which had recently appointed Horkheimer director. With the arrival of the literary scholar Leo Löwenthal, social psychologist Erich Fromm, and philosopher Herbert Marcuse, it sought to exploit recent theoretical and methodological advances in the social sciences. Adorno spent two years as a university instructor (*Privatdozent*) before he and other professors of Jewish heritage or on the political left were expelled by the Nazis.

In 1933, Adorno's right to teach was revoked; in March, as the swastika was run up the town hall flagpole, the Frankfurt criminal police searched the institute. Adorno's house was searched in July, and his application for membership in the Reich Chamber of Literature was denied on the grounds that membership was limited to "persons who belong to the German nation by profound ties of character and blood." As "a non-Aryan," he was informed, "you are unable to feel and appreciate such an obligation."[34]

Adorno was forced into fifteen years of exile. In 1934, he went to Oxford and registered as an advanced student at Merton College. While in England, he received a letter from Benjamin in Paris, claiming that as

---

originally Genoese, origin and a German singer." See Adorno to Thomas Mann, July 5, 1948, in Adorno and Mann, *Theodor Adorno and Thomas Mann: Correspondence*, 24.

33. See Adorno and Benjamin, *The Complete Correspondence, 1928–1940*, ed. H. Lonitz, trans. N. Walker (Cambridge: Harvard University Press, 1999), 3–4.

34. Müller-Doohm, *Adorno*, 178.

far as "Germany is concerned," it "seems highly probable that the crisis" of ideology and politics "is imminent—but the outcome is uncertain."[35] In the same year, Horkheimer began sending "urgent invitations" to Adorno to join him in New York, where the Institute for Social Research had relocated.[36] Adorno sailed for New York in 1938, and Horkheimer soon found him a permanent post at the institute. Only during the American phase did Adorno officially become a member.

Unlike some other members, in 1941, Adorno followed Horkheimer to a Pacific Palisades neighborhood of German émigrés, which included playwright Berthold Brecht and composer Arnold Schoenberg. After the United States entered the war in 1941, the émigrés were classed as "enemy aliens." They were forbidden to go more than five miles from their homes or to leave them between 8 p.m. and 6 a.m. Émigrés like Adorno, who would not be naturalized until November 1943, were severely restricted in their movements.

In California, Horkheimer and Adorno worked to complete their joint project, no longer on dialectical logic, but a rewriting of the history of rationality and the Enlightenment. First published privately in a small mimeographed edition in May 1944 as *Philosophical Fragments*, the text would wait until 1947 before it was published under the definitive title *Dialectic of Enlightenment: Philosophical Fragments*. It was a "reflection on the destructive aspect of progress," aiming to show "tendencies which turn cultural progress into its opposite" (xiii). It proceeded in chapters that treated rationality as both the liberation from, and further domination of, nature; interpreted Homer's *Odyssey* and works of the Marquis de Sade; and analyzed the culture industry and anti-Semitism. The study's goal was "to investigate" the "self-destruction of enlightenment" (xvi), striving to show that in clear contrast to the traditional glorious vision, "the cause of enlightenment's relapse into mythology is to be sought not so much in the nationalist, pagan, or other modern mythologies concocted specifically to cause such a relapse as in *the fear of truth* which petrified enlightenment itself" (xvi, emphasis added).[37]

---

35. Benjamin to Adorno, May 25, 1934, in Adorno and Benjamin, *Complete Correspondence*, 51.

36. Ibid., 60, 63.

37. This phrase recalls the work of Erich Fromm (1900–1980), *Escape from Freedom* (1941), known outside North America as *The Fear of Freedom*. It explores humanity's shifting relationship with freedom, particularly the personal consequences of its absence. Fromm was also associated with the Frankfurt School of Critical Theory and focused on the psychological conditions that facilitated the rise of Nazism.

This thesis is revolutionary and original; enlightenment's relapse into the myth of power caused modern barbarism and the flight from reason, not fascism and Nazism. *Dialectic of Enlightenment* is both revelation and critique: "Myth becomes enlightenment and nature mere objectivity" (6).

In addition to *Dialectic of Enlightenment*, Adorno put together a collection of aphorisms in honor of Horkheimer's fiftieth birthday that would later be published as *Minima Moralia: Reflections from Damaged Life* (1951). In California, he became an acquaintance of Charlie Chaplin and friends with Fritz Lang, the Austrian German filmmaker and screenwriter, and Hans Eisler, the Austrian composer, with whom he completed a study of film music in 1944 that pushed for greater use of avant-garde music to supplement, not simply accompany, the visual aspect of films. Adorno also assisted Thomas Mann on his novel *Doctor Faustus* after the latter asked for his help[38] and wrote "Research Project on Anti-Semitism: Idea of the Project" and "Anti-Semitism and Fascist Propaganda."[39]

At the end of October 1949, following Horkheimer, Adorno returned to Frankfurt to take a position in the philosophy department, quickly establishing himself as a leading German intellectual and a central figure in the Institute for Social Research. He became its director in 1958. He wrote *In Search of Wagner*, critiquing the ideology of the Nazis' favorite composer; *Prisms*, a collection of social and cultural studies; *Against Epistemology*, an antifoundationalist critique of Husserlian phenomenology; and the first volume of *Notes to Literature*, a collection of essays in literary criticism.

Dialectic of Enlightenment—Historical Context

> In view of what is now threatening to engulf Europe, our present work [*Dialectic of Enlightenment*] is essentially destined to pass things down through the night that is approaching: a kind of message in a bottle.
>
> —Max Horkheimer, 1939

---

38. See Gretel Adorno (née Karplus), January 7, 1946: "Thomas Mann is here at the moment, and Teddie [Adorno] is giving him musical advice for his new novel (about a musician)" (Adorno, *Letters to His Parents*, 243). According to Lorenz Jäger, "Adorno provided sketches for Leverkühn's chamber music and his cantata *The Lamentation of Dr. Faustus*, which interprets Faust's final meeting with his pupil as a 'negative communion'" (*Adorno*, 129).

39. Both essays appeared in Theodor Adorno, *The Stars Down to Earth*, ed. Stephen Crook (London: Routledge, 1994), 135–61 and 162–71.

> My work [like *Dialectic of Enlightenment*] is so deeply connected to the war effort.
>
> —Theodor Adorno, 1943

> The present time is without turning points. A turn of events is always for the better. But when, as today, calamity is at its height, the heavens open and hurl their fire on those who are lost in any case.
>
> —Horkheimer and Adorno, *Dialectic of Enlightenment*, 1944

Reunited in California in 1941, Horkheimer and Adorno started in earnest on their joint project to elucidate the origins of the dark clouds gathered over the humanist civilization of Europe.[40] Other German-speaking intellectual exiles began studies in 1942 with the same goal: Cassirer's *The Myth of the State*, Mann's *Doctor Faustus*, Auerbach's *Mimesis*, Baron's *The Crisis of the Early Italian Renaissance*, and more. Nazi victories all over Europe in the early 1940s threatened the total collapse of Western civilization and a reign of darkness; those who had witnessed firsthand the menace of the new barbarian hordes sought to awaken the human conscience.

Five hundred years earlier, Augustine had the same goal in writing his celebrated book *City of God* to defend Christianity after the Visigoths under Alaric I sacked Rome in 410. The Visigoths were a branch of the nomadic Germanic tribes referred to collectively as the Goths. No wonder Adorno compared his age to the Migration Age, or the Barbarian Invasions (*Völkerwanderung*: wandering of the peoples), a period of human migration from 300 to 700 CE in Europe marking the transition from Late Antiquity to the Early Middle Ages. He wrote, "I do not like to use such grand words, but *what is going on here is not simply a world war, but rather the collapse of that form of culture which has lived in the world since the Migration Age*."[41] Now, in the early 1940s, he observed, "Hitler is the most dreadful thing there ever was . . . the Germans have pulled the whole of civilization down with them."[42] Horkheimer concurred: the Nazi "regime secret" is a "horror worse than death."[43]

---

40. Müller-Doohm, *Adorno*, 262.

41. Adorno to his parents, May 20, 1940, in Adorno, *Letters to His Parents*, 50, emphasis added.

42. Adorno to his parents, May 1, 1945, in Adorno, *Letters to His Parents*, 217.

43. Horkheimer, *Life in Letters*, 242.

Theirs was the "Age of Catastrophe," or *historia calamitatum*, in the words of Eric Hobsbawm: the "decades from the outbreak of the First World War to the aftermath of the Second," when European civilization "stumble[d] from one calamity to another. And there were even times when even intelligent conservatives would not take bets on its survival."[44] In Hannah Arendt's summation, "two world wars" took place "in one generation, separated by an uninterrupted chain of local wars and revolutions"; hence, the "subterranean stream of Western history has finally come to the surface and usurped the dignity of that tradition."[45] According to Ernst Cassirer, "In the last thirty years, in the period between the first and second World Wars, we have . . . passed through a severe crisis of our political and social life." His generation experienced "a radical change in the form of political thought . . . the appearance of a new power: the power of mythical thought."[46] Georg Lukács called it "the age of absolute sinfulness."[47] By the same token, the English philosopher and historian R. G. Collingwood wrote in 1942 about "the incessant tempests through which we have precariously lived for close to thirty years."[48] English poet, novelist, and essayist Stephen Spender wrote in 1945 that these years, especially World War II, "brought nearly all those things which we hold firm and sacred into danger and collapse: truth and humanity, reason and right. We lived in a possessed world. For many of us the result was not unexpected when the insanity of a day broke out into delirium in which this poor European humanity sank back, fanatical, stupefied and mad."[49]

Horkheimer and Adorno's lives were broken by exile, but their personal tragedy was only part of a larger, more pressing one. In a June 5, 1935, letter to Benjamin, Adorno revealed his deeply pessimistic view of the course of German and European history and his growing adherence to the crisis mode of historical thought: "What has recently happened always presents itself as if it were something destroyed by a series of catastrophes."[50]

---

44. Hobsbawm, *Age of Extremes*, 6–7.

45. Arendt, "Preface to the First Edition" (1950), in *Origins of Totalitarianism*, vii, ix.

46. Cassirer, *Myth of the State*, 3.

47. Lukács, "Preface" (1962) to *Theory of the Novel*, 18. See also Lukács, *Destruction of Reason*, 714–64.

48. Collingwood, *New Leviathan*, lx.

49. Spender, *European Witness*, 231.

50. Adorno and Benjamin, *Complete Correspondence*, 94.

Later the same year, he wrote, "Hell wanders through mankind," repeating "the recent past always presents itself as though it had been destroyed by catastrophes" or "earthquakes and catastrophes."[51] Benjamin wrote in 1938 about "the collision of historical events"—the Italian invasion of Ethiopia in 1935, the Spanish Civil War, which lasted from 1936 to 1939, the Japanese invasion of China in 1937, and the German annexation of Austria and the Sudetenland in 1938—that made him wonder "how long it will still physically be possible to breathe this European air."[52] Adorno was more than sure "another European crisis is now approaching" and would "end in war"[53] just before World War II began and engulfed the whole of Europe. Facing such horrifying historical events, he resorted, however ironically, to a Hegelian interpretation of history: "the world spirit [*Geist*] has had an occupational accident, and the world of appearances has gained control over the intrinsic order—or rather disorder—of the present historical phase in a truly demonic fashion."[54]

A year later, Benjamin was trapped in France after the German invasion: "The complete uncertainty about what the next day, even the next hour, may bring has dominated my life for weeks now," and he sadly acknowledged, "we have much less time at our disposal than we imagined."[55] A month later, in September, after failing to cross the border into Spain, Benjamin committed suicide. In his last letter, he wrote: "In a situation with no escape, I have no other choice but to finish it all. It is in a tiny village in the Pyrenees, where no one knows me, that my life must come to its end."[56] Far from the war zone, on the other side of the ocean, Adorno had seen doom a few months earlier: "the world has to

---

51. Adorno to Benjamin, August 2, 1935, in Adorno and Benjamin, *Complete Correspondence*, 106–7.

52. Benjamin to Adorno, October 4, 1938, in Adorno and Benjamin, *Complete Correspondence*, 277.

53. Adorno to Benjamin, February 1, 1939, in Adorno and Benjamin, *Complete Correspondence*, 299.

54. Adorno to his parents, September 8, 1939, in Adorno, *Letters to His Parents*, 16–17. Generally speaking, "'*Geist*' refers to some sort of *general consciousness, a single 'mind' common to all men.*" See Solomon, "Hegel's Concept of 'Geist,'" 642, emphasis added.

55. Benjamin to Adorno, August 2, 1940, in Adorno and Benjamin, *Complete Correspondence*, 339–40.

56. "Benjamin to Henry Gurland [and Adorno?]," September 25, 1940, in Adorno and Benjamin, *Complete Correspondence*, 342.

go through this hell completely and utterly before it finds the chance to come to its senses."[57]

German success in the year 1940 was astonishing: in April, the Wehrmacht invaded Denmark and Norway; in May, France, Belgium, the Netherlands, and Luxembourg. Immediately afterward, on May 20, Adorno wrote a most revealing letter about the whole crisis of Western civilization to his parents:

> in these immeasurably horrific times, and I am not exaggerating when I say that the present time is worse for me than everything previous . . . I am now unable to regain my balance even to a moderate degree, which has never happened to me before, am barely sleeping at all, and stare as if paralyzed into the black abyss sucking everything into its eddies and destroying it. I am quite certain that the madness of fascism, once it has taken hold of the earth, will act in such opposition to the incredibly progressive elements also present in fascism that it cannot last forever, and that humanity will ultimately come to its senses. But I believe neither that we will have the chance to see that, nor that much will be salvaged of these things on which all possibility of meaningful existence for us once depended.[58]

This desperate moment, followed, in 1942, by the all-or-nothing Battle of Stalingrad, should be considered the ideological, philosophical, and political context of the writing of *Dialectic of Enlightenment*. In June 1940, Adorno wrote: "We are trying at least to keep a cool head and not be numbed by horror. But this horror has meanwhile taken on such proportions that even that is no easy matter, one falls into a sort of frozen state, like the bird staring at the snake."[59] The image of the snake would reappear in *Dialectic of Enlightenment*.

In April 1941, Horkheimer planned to write down "the layout of the book," which would deal, not surprisingly, with "the collapse of 'culture.'" Given the dissolution of Western humanist civilization, it would propound, first, that "culture was itself untruthful, contradictory, friable (Sade's and Nietzsche's criticism)" and, second, that "the disintegration of existent forms of society is related to their opposition to the truth

---

57. Adorno to his parents, May 8, 1940, in Adorno, *Letters to His Parents*, 48.
58. Adorno to his parents, May 20, 1940, in Adorno, *Letters to His Parents*, 50.
59. Adorno to his parents, June 11, 1940, in Adorno, *Letters to His Parents*, 56.

(Hegel's and Marx's dialectic)." Third, "truth is the principle that caused the disintegration of what is bad—it is critical, negative." Consequently, "the European idea of culture" should be "investigated." If truth and culture are intrinsically connected, then "the notion that one 'can make use of' the truth [Hitler] instead of fulfilling it [Jesus] is the secret conflict of modern history." Following Hegel, Horkheimer argued that "art [and philosophy] is, therefore, so central because only it at least intends the fulfilment of truth." Finally, believing "[s]cience is inextricably connected to the control of nature," presenting "the dialectic of the control of nature will be one of our primary tasks."[60]

The thesis developed to trace how reason and enlightenment's quest for power and for control of nature were transformed into modern totalitarian society's quest to control human beings. In June 1941, Horkheimer wrote to Adorno, expressing his great aim "to begin working on the dialectic project sometime soon," and informing him that Benjamin's "theses on history" had reached the Institute for Social Research in New York. He mentioned meeting with Benjamin in Paris and how Benjamin had influenced their ideas about "the identity of barbarism and culture" that would acquire such a prominent role in *Dialectic of Enlightenment*.[61]

Adorno first mentioned beginning the writing of *Dialectic of Enlightenment* in a letter dated April 19, 1942, revealing the singular place of the year 1942 to this project: "Max and I are well into the schemata for our book (definitely: *not* about the Jews!)" and predicted a long war: "as far as the war is concerned, I *do* actually think that Hitler will be beaten! If only

---

60. Horkheimer, *Life in Letters*, 175. In this broad context of negative thought, note that in 1966, Adorno published *Negative Dialectics* (*Negative Dialektik*) in which he rejected the idea of a positive synthesis. He sought in this work to update the philosophical process known as the dialectic, freeing it from traits previously attributed to it that he believed to be fictive. In short, for Hegel, the dialectic was a process of realization that things contain their own negation and through this realization the parts are *sublated* into something greater. Based on the gloomy experience of his times, Adorno's dialectics rejected this positive element wherein the result was something greater than the parts that preceded and argued for a dialectics that produced something essentially negative. Adorno's book begins: "*Negative Dialectic* is a phrase that flouts tradition. As early as Plato, dialectics meant to achieve something positive by means of negation; the thought figure of the 'negation of the negation' later became the succinct term. *This book seeks to free dialectics from such affirmative traits without reducing its determinacy.*" *Negative Dialectics* (New York: Seabury Press, 1973), xix, emphasis added.

61. Horkheimer, *Life in Letters*, 179, 181.

we might live to witness it."[62] The book would expose the true causes of Western humanist civilization's destruction, not by defending its glorious past, as Auerbach and Cassirer did, but rather by tracing its fateful ambitions from the control of nature to control of human beings, following the concept of negative dialectic. Mann's *Doctor Faustus* had the same goal, using a core German legend to track the agonizing course of German history from the Protestant Reformation to Nazi barbarism.

Adorno saw, as many did, that the year 1942 would *"most probably be a decisive one for all our existence."*[63] Awareness of the Holocaust was growing. From the end of 1941 to summer 1942, the terrible news of the massacre of European Jews reached England and the United States.[64] Jan Karski (1914–2000), a Polish resistance fighter, reported in 1942 and 1943 to the Polish government in exile and the Western Allies on the destruction of the Warsaw Ghetto and the secretive German Nazi extermination camps.[65] From July 1942 to February 2, 1943, the Battle of Stalingrad on the eastern boundary of Europe struck many as the most crucial struggle of the war for the humanist soul of European civilization against Nazi barbarism. Often regarded as the largest and bloodiest battle in the history of warfare, the heavy losses inflicted on the Wehrmacht make it arguably the most strategically decisive battle of World War II. It was a turning point in the European theater; German forces never regained a foothold in the East and withdrew a vast military force from the West to replace their losses.

---

62. Adorno, *Letters to His Parents*, 92, emphasis original.

63. Ibid., 111, emphasis added.

64. The ways in which early news about the Holocaust reached Britain and the United States are discussed in Rafael Medoff, "How America First Learned of the Holocaust," *Jewish News Service*, June 11, 2012, http://www.jns.org/latest-articles/2012/6/11/how-america-first-learned-of-the-holocaust.html#.VTiUXPAauZE; Hillary Kelly, "The Article That Told the World about the Holocaust: Varian Fry's Landmark Report, 'The Massacre of the Jews,'" *New Republic*, July 22, 2014, http://www.newrepublic.com/article/118800/first-american-report-holocaust; and Raziye Akkoc and Andrew Marszal, "Holocaust Commemorations Mark 70th Anniversary of Auschwitz Liberation—As It Happened," *Telegraph*, January 27, 2015, http://www.telegraph.co.uk/history/world-war-two/11371241/Holocaust-Memorial-Day-commemorations-across-Europe-mark-70th-anniversary-of-Auschwitz-liberation-latest.html.

65. E. Thomas Wood and Stanisław M. Jankowski, *Karski: How One Man Tried to Stop the Holocaust* (Hoboken: John Wiley & Sons, 1994).

Adorno was more than sure that his work with Horkheimer against "fascist propaganda" constituted "genuinely a contribution, however small, to the fight against this evil, which even a victorious end to the war will naturally not eliminate." He boldly declared in 1943: "my work"—he was writing *Dialectic of Enlightenment* and on anti-Semitism—"*is so deeply connected to the war effort.*"[66] He and Horkheimer viewed the book in these missionary, humanist terms as a "sacred text."[67] In March 1943, Adorno wrote that he had finished "some of the most difficult sections of my historic-philosophical excursus on Homer," referring to "Excursus 1: Odysseus or Myth and Enlightenment." For this digression, he explained, not without great irony, that he had to read "countless works of classical philology" as well as "various anthropological and ethnological material, with the reward that a 'theoretical' thinker always has when devouring . . . something that is as neutral as possible, and has not already been pre-digested by clever Jews."[68]

The first edition of *Dialectic of Enlightenment* appeared in April 1944, only two years after it was begun, clearly showing the great urgency of the times, which also contributed to its unique content and form. Horkheimer well summarized its content and form in these pessimistic words: "The dialectic of Enlightenment consists largely in the change from light to darkness,"[69] more specifically, as he articulated elsewhere, when "[m]en no longer experience themselves as individuals, in need of a goal that transcends their existence."[70]

Dialectic of Enlightenment—Content and Form

> If by enlightenment and intellectual progress we mean the freeing of man from superstitious belief in evil forces, in demons and fairies, in blind fate—in short, the emancipation from fear—then denunciation of what is currently called reason is the greatest service reason can render.
>
> —Max Horkheimer, *Eclipse of Reason*, 1947

---

66. Adorno to his parents, November 11, 1943, and May 14, 1943, in *Letters to His Parents*, 156, 134, emphasis added.

67. Adorno to his parents, October 30, 1942, in *Letters to His Parents*, 114.

68. Adorno to his parents, March 29, 1943, and March 8, 1943, in *Letters to His Parents*, 131, 129.

69. Horkheimer, *Dawn and Decline*, 180.

70. Ibid., 144–45.

> The 'dark' writers of the bourgeoisie, such as Machiavelli, Hobbes, and Mandeville, always had an appeal for Max Horkheimer. . . . These writers still thought in a constructive way; and there were lines in their works leading from their disharmonies to Marx's social theory. The 'black' writers of the bourgeoisie, foremost among them the Marquis de Sade and Nietzsche, broke these ties. In their blackest book, *Dialectic of Enlightenment*, Horkheimer and Theodor Adorno joined with these writers to conceptualize the Enlightenment's process of self-destruction. On their analysis, it is no longer possible to place hope in the liberating force of Enlightenment.
>
> —Jürgen Habermas, *The Philosophical Discourse of Modernity*

Jürgen Habermas, who studied philosophy and sociology under Horkheimer and Adorno at the Institute for Social Research at the Johann Wolfgang Goethe University in Frankfurt am Main, wrote that the " 'dark' writers of the bourgeoisie, such as Machiavelli, Hobbes, and Mandeville, always had an appeal for Max Horkheimer." These writers "still thought in a constructive way" and lines in their works led "to Marx's social theory." In contrast, the " 'black' writers of the bourgeoisie, such as Donatien Alphonse François, Marquis de Sade (1740–1814), and Friedrich Wilhelm Nietzsche (1844–1900), broke these ties." Accordingly, in their "blackest book" Horkheimer and Adorno "joined with these [black] writers to conceptualize the Enlightenment's process of self-destruction" because they believed "it is no longer possible to place hope in the liberating force of enlightenment."[71] Instead, they followed Walter Benjamin's now ironic "hope for the hopeless."[72] In contrast to Auerbach's *Mimesis*, which dealt with the most illustrious humanist writers of Western literature, or Baron's *The Crisis of the Early Italian Renaissance*, which focused on the proponents of the humanist republican tradition, Cassirer's *The Myth of the*

---

71. Habermas, *Philosophical Discourse of Modernity*, 106. See also Jeffrey Herf, "*Dialectic of Enlightenment* Reconsidered," *New German Critique* 117 (Fall 2012): 81–89.

72. "Only for the sake of the hopeless ones have we been given hope," in Walter Benjamin, *Selected Writings*, I, *1913–1926* (Cambridge: Belknap Press, 1996), 356. It is the concluding sentence of his essay on "Goethe's Elective Affinities," in the translation by Stanley Corngold. Herbert Marcuse translated it as "It is only for the sake of those without hope that hope is given to us" in *One-Dimensional Man* (Boston: Beacon Press, 1964), 257. The original reads: "Nur um der Hoffnungslosen willen ist uns die Hoffnung gegeben."

State and Mann's *Doctor Faustus* also dealt with the dark side of Western civilization and German history. To this dark literature, Horkheimer and Adorno piled on their book.

Habermas wrote that *Dialectic of Enlightenment* is "an odd book," not only because it was written at various times, but also its "unperspicuous form of presentation renders the clear structure of its train of thought almost indiscernible at first glance."[73] He notes that in the "tradition of the Enlightenment, enlightened thinking has been understood as an opposition and counterforce to myth," and given that "Enlightenment contradicts myth, [it] thereby escapes its violence." In contrast, Horkheimer and Adorno emphasize that "it is no longer possible to place hope in the liberating force of Enlightenment."[74] Their devastating criticism of the Enlightenment and reason is based on their dark reading of contemporary history. Based in part on the deep historical pessimism Spengler expressed in *The Decline of the West* (1918) and Hobbes's dark vision of human society as "a war of all against all," *Dialectic of Enlightenment* asserts that everything in modern Western civilization is based on the inhumane, unrestricted play of terror and naked struggle for self-preservation, domination, control, and subjugation. It posits history as the span of time in which human lives are destroyed or deformed by irresistible political and social forces.

In *Eclipse of Reason* (1947), Horkheimer summed up the crushing disappointment that led to the writing of *Dialectic of Enlightenment*: "If by enlightenment and intellectual progress we mean the freeing of man from superstitious belief in evil forces, in demons and fairies, in blind fate—in short, the emancipation from fear—then denunciation of what is currently called reason is the greatest service reason can render."[75] Enlightenment brought not light, but darkness and misery. Horkheimer therefore summarized *Dialectic of Enlightenment* in these pessimistic words: "The dialectic of Enlightenment consists largely in the change from light to darkness."[76] This cynicism must be understood as inextricable from the unique historical moment of the first half of the twentieth century.

Since reason failed to liberate humanity from myth, Horkheimer and Adorno turned to Homer and found in the character of Odysseus the beginning of human striving to overcome myths. They saw "a description

---

73. Habermas, *Philosophical Discourse of Modernity*, 107.

74. Ibid., 107, 106.

75. Horkheimer, *Eclipse of Reason*, 187.

76. Horkheimer, *Dawn and Decline*, 180.

of the retreat of the individual from the mythic powers" in his struggle against the Sirens, the six-headed monster Scylla, and the whirlpool Charybdis; for him, the "mythic world is not the homeland, but the labyrinth from which one has to escape for the sake of one's own identity."[77] In Horkheimer and Adorno's moving words, which clearly reflect their agonizing exilic displacement, "[i]t is a yearning for the homeland which sets in motion the adventures by which subjectivity, the prehistory of which is narrated in the *Odyssey*, escapes the primeval world. The fact that—despite the fascist lies to the contrary—the concept of homeland is opposed to myth constitutes the innermost paradox of epic" (60). In their own odyssey, Horkheimer and Adorno sought "retreat from the mythic powers" of enlightenment; for them, as for Odysseus, the "mythic world" was "not the homeland, but the labyrinth from which" they had "to escape" to preserve their "own identity."

In the 1944 preface to the first edition, the authors stressed the inherent difficulty of their project: "we still placed too much trust in contemporary consciousness," but based on their explorations in "sociology, psychology, and epistemology," the "fragments we have collected here show" that "we have had to abandon this trust" (xiv). Faithful to their Marxist beliefs, Horkheimer and Adorno saw "the present collapse of bourgeois civilization" as evidence that "not only the operations but the purpose of science have become dubious." Modern science, born in the Enlightenment during the early modern period, betrayed any trust in consciousness. In political terms, "the tireless self-destruction of enlightenment hypocritically celebrated by implacable fascists and implemented by pliable experts in humanity compels thought to forbid itself its last remaining innocence regarding the habits and tendencies of the *Zeitgeist* [spirit of the time]." In a world in which "thought is being turned inescapably into a commodity and language into celebration of the commodity, the attempt to trace the sources of this degradation must refuse obedience to the current linguistic and intellectual demands before it is rendered entirely futile by the consequence of those demands for world history" (xiv–xv). They were in a race to conceive and to articulate their analysis before time rendered its thought and language futile.

Their pessimistic views sparked action: "The aporia which faced us in our work thus proved to be the first matter we had to investigate: *the self-destruction of enlightenment*." They admitted that in the beginning their "*petitio principia*" was that "freedom in society is inseparable from

---

77. Habermas, *Philosophical Discourse of Modernity*, 108.

enlightenment thinking," but later they found that "the very concept of that thinking, no less than the concrete historical forms, the institutions of society with which it is intertwined, already contains the germs of the regression which is taking place everywhere today." The gravest existential moment in the history of Western civilization, marked by the triumphs of the Nazi army, prompted both their mission and a formidable warning: "If enlightenment does not assimilate reflection on this regressive moment, it seals its own fate" (xvi, emphasis added). Away from the bloody battlefields, on the Pacific shore in California, the authors sought the cause of the present disaster of Western humanist civilization as well as their own exile.

They found it in progress, which is traditionally inextricably associated with reason and enlightenment: "By leaving consideration of the destructive side of progress to its enemies, thought in its headlong rush into pragmatism is forfeiting its sublating character, and therefore its relation to truth" (xvi). The Hegelian concepts—reason, enlightenment, and progress—were used to define and to construe reality.[78] The flight from truth and reason were thought to be most evident in the cultures of industry and nationalism; however, "[i]n the mysterious willingness of the technologically educated masses to fall under the spell of any despotism, in its self-destructive affinity to nationalist paranoia, in all this uncomprehended senselessness the weakness of contemporary theoretical understanding is evident" (xvi). A radical rethinking of "truth," no less than victory in the battlefield, was requisite to any possibility of overcoming the present crisis of Western civilization.

Horkheimer and Adorno show some affinity with Ernst Cassirer's views about the role of myth in modern history, yet Cassirer praised the Enlightenment as the revival of Stoic ideas about natural rights and human equality and dignity.[79] In contrast, Horkheimer and Adorno argued that Enlightenment thought and modes of reasoning degenerated into mythology. They believed that "the cause of enlightenment's relapse into mythology is to be sought not so much in the nationalist, pagan, or other mythologies," such as the myth of the state, "concocted specifically to cause such a relapse," but rather "in the fear of truth which petrifies enlightenment itself" (xvi). In the word *fear*, we may feel the influence of their associate at the Frankfurt School, German social psychologist, psychoanalyst, sociologist, humanistic philosopher, and democratic socialist Erich Fromm, whose *Escape from Freedom* (1941) analyzes the psychological conditions that facilitated the rise of Nazism. Trauma, especially political trauma,

---

78. See Zakai, "Constructing and Representing Reality," 106–33.

79. See Cassirer, *Myth of the State*, 167–68.

leaves its signature in the works written in its wake, despite our efforts to hide it behind the veil of careful, objective scholarship. Fromm, Auerbach, Cassirer, Mann, Horkheimer, and Adorno were all marked.

The authors of *Dialectic of Enlightenment* argued that "[b]oth these terms, enlightenment and truth, are to be understood as pertaining not merely to intellectual history" as such "but also to current reality." If "enlightenment expresses the real movement of bourgeois society as a whole from the perspective of the idea embodied in its personalities and institutions," then "truth refers not merely to rational consciousness but equally to the form it takes in reality" (xvi). In light of "the calamitous situation today," they wrote, "even the most honorable reformer who recommends renewal in threadbare language reinforces the existing order he seeks to break by taking over its worn-out categorical apparatus and the pernicious power-philosophy lying behind it. *False clarity is only another name for myth. Myth was always obscure and luminous at once. It has always been distinguished by its familiarity and its exemption from the work of concepts*" (xvii, emphasis added).

Following Francis Bacon's famous dictum "Nature to be commanded must be obeyed,"[80] Horkheimer and Adorno argued that the "enslavement to nature of people today cannot be separated from social progress." Based on their Marxist belief, they claimed that "the increase in economic productivity which creates the conditions for a more just world also affords the technical apparatus and the social groups controlling it a disproportionate advantage over the rest of the population." In the brave new world of capitalist economy, the "individual is entirely nullified in face of the economic powers" that "are taking society's domination over nature to unimagined heights." Individuals "are vanishing before the apparatus they served." Thus, the Enlightenment gospel about "a more just world" delivers "the unjust state of society." In contrast to the views of Aldous Huxley (1894–1963), the English writer, philosopher, and author of *Brave New World* (1931); Karl Theodor Jaspers (1883–1969), the German Swiss psychiatrist and philosopher; and Ortega y Gasset (1883–1955), the Spanish liberal philosopher and essayist, Horkheimer and Adorno argued that "what is at issue here is not culture as a value," as these "critics of civilization" understood it, "but the necessity for enlightenment to reflect on itself if humanity is not to be totally betrayed." They do not advocate "conservation of the past but the fulfilment of past hopes" and boldly claim: "Today" the "past is being continued as destruction of the past." For example, "[i]f up to the nineteenth century, respectable education was a privilege

---

80. Aphorism 3, book 1, *Novum Organum* (1620).

paid for by the increased sufferings of the uneducated, in the twentieth the hygienic factory is bought with the melting down of all cultural entities in the gigantic crucible" (xvii).

In Marxist terms, the destruction of the past is caused in part by economic considerations: "If . . . the volume of goods took the form of so-called overproduction in domestic economic crises in the preceding period, today, thanks to the enthronement of powerful groups . . . it is producing the international threat of fascism: progress is reverting to regression." Capitalist economy profoundly transforms human society: "That the hygienic factory and everything pertaining to it, Volkswagen and the sports palace, are obtusely liquidating metaphysics does not matter in itself, but that these things are themselves becoming metaphysics, an ideological curtain, within the social whole *behind which the real doom is gathering*, does matter. *That is the basic premise of our fragments.*" Faithful to their critical theory, the authors stressed that ideology, or "the international threat of fascism," is the principal obstacle to human liberation (xviii, emphasis added).[81]

The first chapter, "The Concept of Enlightenment," examines "the intertwinement of rationality and social reality as well as of the intertwinement, inseparable from the former, of nature and the mastery of nature." The authors' goal is to provide "a positive concept of enlightenment" that will free it "from its entanglement in *blind domination*" (xviii, emphasis added). Their critique rests on two premises about the connection between myth and enlightenment: "Myth is already enlightenment, and enlightenment reverts to mythology" (xviii). Both myth and enlightenment thought are founded in and pursue an irrational quest for power. To elaborate on these ideas, first, "Odysseus or Myth and Enlightenment," the second chapter, looks at Homer's *Odyssey*, "one of the earliest representative documents of bourgeois Western civilization," in which "the concepts of sacrifice and renunciation" expose "the difference between and the unity of mythical nature and enlightenment mastery." Second, "Juliette or Enlightenment and Morality," the third chapter, addresses Kant, Sade, and Nietzsche, the dark writers of the Enlightenment, "whose works represent the implacable consummation of enlightenment" (xviii). "Culture Industry," the fourth chapter, shows "the regression of enlightenment to ideology which is graphically expressed in film and radio. . . . the specific content of the ideology

---

81. See Brian J. Shaw, "Reason, Nostalgia, and Eschatology in the Critical Theory of Max Horkheimer," *Journal of Politics* 47 (February 1985): 160–81.

is exhausted in the idolization of the existing order and of the power by which the technology is controlled" (xviii–xix). Finally, the fifth chapter, "Elements of Anti-Semitism," finds "the reversion of enlightenment civilization to barbarism in reality." Their argument is not an academic exercise; the "tendency toward self-destruction . . . inherent in rationality from the first . . . is emerging nakedly" (xix) in the mass murder of a people based on rationally supported, yet irrational myths. Myth is the core of *Dialectic of Enlightenment* and the target of other works by German-speaking intellectual exiles from Nazi Germany, such as Cassirer's *The Myth of the State*, Mann's *Doctor Faustus*, and Auerbach's *Mimesis*.

The preface to the Italian edition, written in 1966, provides more insights into the concrete historical, ideological, and political context within which *Dialectic of Enlightenment* was composed, illuminating its unique content and form. "Begun as early as 1942," the authors wrote, "during the Second World War, it was supposed to form the introduction to the theory of society and history we had sketched during the period of National Socialist rule." This statement shows that the work was conceived as *Kulturkampf*. Indeed, the authors stress: "It is self-evident that, with regard to terminology and the scope of the questions investigated, *the book is shaped by the social conditions in which it was written*." The study was not merely philosophical or sociological scholarship but aimed to reveal concrete historical "*tendencies which turn cultural progress into its opposite*" (xiii, emphasis added). Over time, the influence of historical context became more apparent.

In the preface of 1969, the final one, the authors explain that they agreed to the new edition because "not a few ideas in it are timely now and have largely determined our later theoretical writings." However, they "do not stand by everything we said in the book in its original form." Their theory imputes "a temporal core to truth" as opposed to "something invariable to the movement of history" and was necessarily influenced by a unique historical, social, and political context "*when the end of the National Socialist terror was in sight.*" Nonetheless, while, "[i]n not a few places" the "formulation is no longer adequate to the reality of today," the book connects with the Cold War: "The conflicts in the third world and the renewed growth of totalitarianism are not mere historical interludes any more than, according to the *Dialectic*, fascism was at that time." Their great humanitarian starting point applied to the 1940s as well as the 1960s: "Critical thought, which does not call a halt before progress itself, *requires us to take up the cause of the remnants of freedom, of tendencies toward real humanity, even though they seem powerless in face of the great historical trend*" (xi, emphasis added).

The 1969 preface also explains that their "prognosis regarding the associated lapse from enlightenment into positivism, into the myth of that which is the case, and finally of the identity of intelligence and hostility to mind, has been overwhelmingly confirmed."[82] Twenty-five years after the first edition was mimeographed for publication, *Dialectic of Enlightenment* still held true. Upon returning to Germany, the authors entertained "the idea of taking further the concepts formulated in *Dialectic*" and continued "to develop our theory." They did not want to rewrite it: "what matters today is to preserve and disseminate freedom, rather than to accelerate, however indirectly, the advance toward the administered world" (xii).

The Concept of Enlightenment

> What human beings seek to learn from nature is how to use it to dominate wholly both it and human beings. Nothing else count. Ruthless toward itself, the Enlightenment has eradicated the last remnant of its own self-awareness.
>
> —Horkheimer and Adorno, *Dialectic of Enlightenment*, 1944

> Human beings have always had to choose between their subjugation to nature and its subjugation to the self. With the spread of bourgeois commodity economy the dark horizon of myth is illuminated by the sun of calculating reason, beneath whose icy rays the seeds of the new barbarism are germinating. Under the compulsion of power, human labor has always led away from myth and, under power, has always fallen back under its spell.
>
> —Horkheimer and Adorno, *Dialectic of Enlightenment*, 1944

In the first chapter, "The Concept of Enlightenment," Horkheimer and Adorno begin from the common view of the Enlightenment and then refute it according to their own dialectic reasoning. Traditionally, "Enlightenment, understood in the widest sense as the advance of thought, has always aimed at liberating human beings from fear and installing them as masters." However, the agonizing *historia calamitatum* of the twentieth

---

82. Positivism is a philosophical system that holds that every rationally justifiable assertion can be scientifically verified or is capable of logical or mathematical proof and therefore rejects metaphysics and theism.

century had taught them a lesson, "the wholly enlightened earth is radiant with triumphant calamity." Francis Bacon (1561–1626), as "'the father of experimental philosophy,'" according to Horkheimer and Adorno, "despised the exponents of tradition, who substituted belief for knowledge and were as unwilling to doubt as they were reckless in supplying answers." He aimed to design a systematic methodology for studying natural phenomena. "Knowledge obtained through such enquiry would not only be exempt from the influence of wealth and power but would establish man as a master of nature." They quote Bacon's *In Praise of Knowledge*: "now we *govern* nature in opinions, but we are thrall unto her in necessity; but if we would be led by her in invention, we should *command* her in action" (1, emphasis added). The will to dominate nature is the crux of the problem for Horkheimer and Adorno. It signals a crucial turning point in history, when knowledge and power became intertwined, and the Enlightenment absorbed the myth of domination. "Myth becomes enlightenment and nature mere objectivity" (6), they argue, because Bacon "envisaged" the "'happy match' between human understanding and the nature of things," or the natural world, as "a *patriarchal one*; the mind, conquering superstition, is to rule over disenchanted nature. Knowledge, which is power, knows no limits, either in its *enslavement* of creation or in its deference to worldly masters" (2, emphasis added). In its irrational, irresistible quest for power and domination, enlightenment moved humanity far from the truth and true knowledge of its ambiguous place in the natural order and disorder. Reason surrendered to myth in modern history and politics with fascism and Nazism, as Ernst Cassirer showed in *The Myth of the State*. *Dialectic of Enlightenment* saw Bacon's gospel of scientific inquiry in particular and enlightenment as a whole as Janus-faced.

The conversion of knowledge to power, Horkheimer and Adorno argued, began with the Enlightenment and had a crucial impact on modern history with the rise and triumph of capitalism: "Just as it serves all the purposes of the bourgeois economy both in factories and on the battlefield, it is at the disposal of entrepreneurs regardless of their origins." In modern history, "[t]echnology is the essence of this knowledge" because it aims "to produce neither concepts nor images, nor the joy of understanding, but method, exploitation of the labor of others, capital." The domination and enslavement of nature led to the unrestrained drive to control human beings: "What human beings seek to learn from nature is how to use it to dominate wholly both it and human beings. Nothing else counts. Ruthless toward itself, the Enlightenment has eradicated the last remnant of its own self-awareness" (2).

Becoming blind to rational thought, Enlightenment thought believed a myth: that with knowledge, some human beings could dominate and enslave both nature and other human beings. The authors claim that, dialectically, "[o]nly thought which does violence to itself is hard enough to shatter myths." Rational critique is prerequisite to rejecting myths, yet Enlightenment thought became monolithic and unimpeachable and degenerated into a defense of naked power and nothing else: "Power and knowledge are synonymous" (2). Hence, "[j]ust as myths already entail enlightenment, with every step enlightenment entangles itself more deeply in mythology" (8). In dialectic terms, enlightenment is evidence of the process by which "progress is reverting to regression" (xviii), or the tendency of rational progress to become irrational regress, which means, *ipso facto*, totalitarianism. In the political context, the authors are explicit: "Enlightenment is totalitarian" (4). Instead of a rational, humanist program for social, political, and philosophical progress, Enlightenment is the forerunner of oppressive fascism, Nazism, and capitalism. *Dialectic of Enlightenment* reveals its inherent antihumanism and antirationalism.

In propounding the view that ideology is the principal obstacle to human liberation, these two famous representatives of the Institute for Social Research and its philosophical system of Critical Theory left nothing standing of the traditional, cherished, and glorious humanist vision of the Enlightenment as the Age of Reason. They viewed it as a Pandora's box from which all the evils of the modern world escaped. The enslavement of nature led to the enslavement and, worse, murder of human beings in the Holocaust and Nazi concentration camps. Human society is the stage on which the quest for power and domination rages constantly, controlling every sphere. Everything is based on "naked force" (37): "Enlightenment stands in the same relationship to things as the dictator to human beings. He knows them to the extent that he can manipulate them" (6). The authors note that "patriarchal myth was itself an enlightenment, fully comparable . . . to the philosophical one. . . . Mythology itself set in motion the endless process of enlightenment by which, with ineluctable necessity, every definite theoretical view is subjected to the annihilating criticism that it is only a belief, until even the concepts of mind, truth, and, indeed, enlightenment itself have been reduced to animistic magic" (7).

The tendency of rational progress toward irrational regress is evident, not only in the realm of thought, but also in psychology and social life. Given that the "self never quite fitted the mold, enlightenment throughout the liberalistic period has always sympathized with social correction." As a result, the "unity of the manipulated collective consists in the negation

Enlightenment and Its Enemies / 275

of each individual and in the scorn poured on the type of society which could make people into individuals." Horkheimer and Adorno found ample evidence in the Nazi Party of psychological and social transformations in which the "horde, a term which doubtless is to be found in the Hitler Youth organization, is not the relapse into the old barbarism but the triumph of repressive *égalité*, the degeneration of the equality of rights into the wrong inflicted by equals" (9).[83]

Nazi Germany was only one example of "the trajectory of European civilization" as a whole. In their very eclectic mode of reasoning, the authors argue that "[a]bstraction, the instrument of enlightenment, stands in the same relationship to its objects as fate, whose concept it eradicates: as liquidation. Under the leveling rule of abstraction, which makes everything in nature repeatable, and of industry, for which abstraction prepared the way, the liberated finally themselves become the 'herd' (*Trupp*)" (9). If "*Myth is already enlightenment, and enlightenment reverts to mythology,*" and "progress is reverting to regression" (xviii), then "[t]he step from chaos to civilization" reverts to chaos in modern history (12, emphasis added).

The forms and variety of enlightenment mythology are revealed in a series of important historical concepts that reject human capacity to shape and order the social and political world rationally: "mythology had reflected in its forms the essence of the existing order—cyclical motion, fate, domination of the world as truth—and had renounced hope" (20). Cassirer expresses the same criticism of myth in *The Myth of the State* when he attacks Oswald Spengler's *The Decline of the West, or The Downfall of the Occident* (1918–1922), claiming it is based on "a metaphysics of history that shows all the characteristic features of myth." Spengler's historical prognostics are exactly the same as "astrological prognostics."[84] He argued further that Spengler's book is "an astrology of history—the work of a diviner who unfolded his somber apocalyptic visions." Spengler

---

83. On the barbaric turn in early twentieth-century German history, see the views of two contemporaries, D. H. Lawrence, the English novelist, poet, playwright, essayist, literary critic, and painter, who, in his remarkable *Letter from Germany* (1924), describes the Weimar Republic "whirling to the ghost of the old Middle Ages of Germany, then to the Roman days, then to the days of the silent forest and the dangerous, lurking barbarians." In the same vein, Georg Lukács saw the "danger of a barbaric underworld latent in German civilization as its necessary complementary product." See Reed, *Thomas Mann*, 399n88 and 385.

84. Cassirer, *Myth of the State*, 290.

was not only "a prophet of evil"; his book "became one of the pioneer works of National Socialism" because his philosophy of history was "a philosophy of pessimism." The Nazi "new men were convinced that they fulfilled Spengler's prophecy. They interpreted him in their own sense. If our culture—science, philosophy, poetry, and art—is dead, let us make a fresh start. Let us try our vast possibilities, let us create a new world and become the rulers of this world."[85]

The power of mythical thought was an integral part of modern German thought, according to Horkheimer, Adorno, Cassirer, and Thomas Mann, whose *Doctor Faustus* revives a the sixteenth-century German myth.

Dialectic of Enlightenment also raises fears about standardization.[86] The authors saw "countless agencies of mass production and its culture impress standardized behavior on the individual as the only natural, decent, and rational one. Individuals define themselves now only as things, statistical elements, success or failure." In such a brave new world, the ultimate "criterion is self-preservation, successful or unsuccessful adaptation to the objectivity of their function and the schemata assigned to it. Everything which is different, from the idea to criminality, is exposed to the force of the collective, which keeps watch from the classroom to the trade union." Behind this enforced uniformity lurked "the powers which manipulated the collective as an agent of violence" (21–22). No sphere of human society can be free of, or divorced from, power and violence. These views obviously mirror fascism and Nazism, but they are applied to capitalist society and economy as a whole, for the collective "brutality, which keeps the individual up to the mark, no more represents the true quality of people than value represents that of commodities." In the history of their time, the authors found a "demonically distorted form which things and human beings have taken." It is "Enlightenment's mythic terror," which "springs from a horror of myth" (22).

Myth, terror, and horror are inseparable since the foundation of modern society is based on "self-preservation." As a proof, the authors cite "Spinoza's proposition: 'the endeavor of preserving oneself is the first

---

85. Ibid., 291–92.

86. In 1937, Erich Auerbach wrote that "the cunning of providence" was transforming European civilization into "an International of triviality and a culture of Esperanto," or a nightmarish, uniform, standard world that would eventually leave no room for humanist philology. See Auerbach to Walter Benjamin, January 3, 1937, in Elsky, Vialon, and Stein, "Scholarship," 750–51. See also Auerbach, *Mimesis*, chap. 18 and "Epilogue"; Auerbach, "Philology and *Weltliteratur*," 17; and Zakai, *Erich Auerbach and the Crisis of German Philology*.

and only basis of virtue,'" which "contains the true maxim of all Western civilization" (22), although in modern political and economic history, the "more heavily the process of self-preservation is based on the bourgeois division of labor, the more it enforces the self-alienation of individuals, who must mold themselves to the technical apparatus body and soul" (23). From the individual sphere to political and social life, everything is based on the law of the jungle, or self-preservation.

Evidently, the price for mingling the principal of self-preservation, bourgeois economy, and technology is very high; it not only led to the "intertwinement of myth, power, and labor" (25) but replaced true knowledge with the "automatic mechanisms of order." More specifically, the "transcendental subject of knowledge, as the last reminder of subjectivity, is itself seemingly abolished and replaced by the operations of automatic mechanisms of order, which therefore run all the more smoothly." The resulting "expulsion of thought from logic ratifies in the lecture hall the reification of human beings in factory and office." The role of reason is transformed: "Reason serves as a universal tool for the fabrication of all other tools." Its "old ambition to be purely an instrument of purposes has finally been fulfilled." Now, "[t]he exclusivity of logical laws stems from this obdurate adherence to function and ultimately from the compulsive character of self-preservation." Capitalist modes of production thus crucially influenced modes of thought, conviction, and persuasion. In the political and social context, "nature as true self-preservation is thereby unleashed, in the individual as in the collective fate of crisis and war" (23). As for Hobbes, the principle of self-preservation reigns in modern society, leading inevitably and imminently to endless crises and wars.

Horkheimer and Adorno argue that "the control of internal and external nature has been made the absolute purpose of life" (24). In this period when "self-preservation has been finally automated, reason is dismissed by those who, as controllers of production, have taken over its inheritance and fear it in the disinherited" (24–25). Thus, the flight from reason is a central mark of modern capitalist society. Given that the "essence of enlightenment is the choice between alternatives, and the inescapability of this choice is that of power" (25), the "instruments of power" are "language, weapons, and finally machines" (29). The authors summarize their gloomy poetic vision of the close connection of barbarism to the nature and meaning of modern bourgeois society:

> Human beings have always had to choose between their subjugation to nature and its subjugation to the self. With the spread of bourgeois commodity economy the dark horizon of

myth is illuminated by the sun of calculating reason, beneath whose icy rays the seeds of *the new barbarism* are germinating. Under the compulsion of power, human labor has always led away from myth and, under power, has always fallen back under its spell. (25, emphasis added)

To support their conclusions about the flight from reason and the social control of nature, the authors analyze the Homeric tale of Odysseus and the Sirens, which reveals the "intertwinement of myth, power, and labor" (25). In it, Odysseus and his companions sail by the island of the lovely Sirens on their return to Ithaca. As instructed by the witch Circe, Odysseus plugs his men's ears with beeswax and has them bind him to the mast. He alone hears the Sirens' seductive song, promising to reveal the future but luring the hapless listener toward shipwreck.[87] He begs to be released from his fetters, but his faithful men only bind him tighter. For the authors, this tale reveals "a precise correlation" between "cultural heritage and enforced work . . . both are founded on the inescapable compulsion toward the social control of nature." Odysseus's outwitting of the Sirens is "a prescient allegory of the dialectic of enlightenment. Just as the capacity to be represented is the measure of power, the mightiest person being the one who can be represented in the most functions, so it is also the vehicle of both progress and regression" (27). In this reading, Odysseus "is represented in the sphere of work." "As owner," in contrast to his sailors, the workers, "he cannot give way to the lure of self-abandonment," while his "companions, despite their closeness to things, cannot enjoy their work because it is performed under compulsion, in despair, with their senses forcibly stopped." When "[t]he servant is subjugated in body and soul, the master regresses. No system of domination has so far been able to escape this price" (27). More specifically, modern "humanity, whose skills and knowledge become differentiated with the division of labor, is thereby forced back to more primitive anthropological stages, since, with the technical facilitation of existence, the continuation of domination demands the fixation of instincts by greater repression" (27–28). Instead of progress, the traditional hallmark of enlightenment, humanity is doomed to regression since "[a]daptation to the power of progress furthers the progress of power, constantly renewing the degenerations which prove

---

87. For a very interesting essay on the negative power of music, see Alex Ross, "When Music Is Violence," *The New Yorker*, July 4, 2016, 65–69, esp. 69.

successful progress, not failed progress, to be its own antithesis. *The curse of irresistible progress is irresistible regression*" (28, emphasis added). The enlightenment of progress totally nullifies the progress of enlightenment.

Capitalism shattered enlightened humanist ideas and paved the way for the return to myth. Instead of enlightened progress, the authors see repression and regression for the individual, society, and the means of production. "The calamity is not that individuals have fallen behind society or its material production" but that the "machinery of control" in which "technical and social tendencies . . . converge" results "in the total encompassing of human beings." In the context of power and domination, the hallmark of modern society, "[m]ind becomes in reality the instrument of power and self-mastery for which bourgeois philosophy has always mistaken it" (28).

Enlightenment and capitalist economy led to "the transformation of the world into industry" (29). As an important consequence, "thought is repudiated by the rulers themselves as mere ideology." For example, in Nazi Germany, "[i]t is a telltale manifestation of the bad conscience of the cliques in whom economic necessity is finally embodied that its revelations, from the 'intuitions' of the *Führer* to the 'dynamic worldview,' no longer acknowledge their own atrocities as necessary consequences of logical regularities." The Nazis' "mythological lies about 'mission' and 'fate,'" which replaced "earlier bourgeois apologetics," do not even "express a complete untruth: it is no longer the objective laws of the market which govern the actions of industrialists and drive humanity toward catastrophe" (30). Those who witnessed the horrors of the first half of the twentieth century were betrayed by Enlightenment protocols for progress. *Dialectic of Enlightenment* is therefore inextricable from the shock of Nazism and fascism; without the ideological context of Nazi Germany, the work is unintelligible.

In the world of capital and industry, the authors emphasize, "the power of the system over human beings increases with every step they take away from the power of nature" and "denounces the reason of the reasonable society as obsolete" (30–31). No wonder "enlightened humanity is losing itself" and cannot be saved "by a thinking which, as an instrument of power, has to choose between command and obedience." Ironically, "[i]n the mastery of nature, without which mind does not exist, enslavement to nature persists. By modestly confessing itself to be power and thus being taken back into nature, mind rids itself of every claim to mastery which had enslaved it to nature" (31). Although "[e]ach advance of civilization has renewed not only mastery but also the prospect of its alleviation," enlightened thinking blocks our ability to see it. (32).

Toward the end of this introductory chapter, Horkheimer and Adorno turn their hard criticism against positivism, claiming "Enlightenment in its bourgeois form had given itself up to the positivist moment long before Turgot and d'Alembert," (32) by which they mean well before the eighteenth century.[88] Positivism is a philosophy of science according to which *positive facts*—information derived from sensory experience and interpreted through logical or mathematical methods—are the exclusive source of all authoritative knowledge, and that truth resides only in knowledge so derived. Since the data are culled from sensory experience, or empirical evidence, positivism is based on empiricism. In holding that every rationally justifiable assertion can be verified through experimental, logical, or mathematical proof, it rejects metaphysics and theism.

Horkheimer and Adorno see it as a grave threat to truth because "[i]t was never immune to confusing freedom with the business of self-preservation. The suspension of concept, whether done in the name of progress or of culture, which had both long since formed a secret alliance against truth, gave free rein to the lie." The surrender of Enlightenment thought to positivism at the expense of metaphysics blurred the distinction between truth and lie; because the positivist world "merely verified recorded evidence and preserved thought, debased to the achievement of great minds, as a kind of superannuated headline, the lie was no longer distinguishable from a truth neutralized as cultural heritage." If Bacon led the Enlightenment astray with his nature-enslaving science, the positivists formed an "alliance against truth" and "gave free rein to the lie" (32).

The dialectic of enlightenment debunks the Enlightenment: "By sacrificing thought, which in its reified form as mathematics, machinery, organization, avenges itself on a humanity forgetful of it, enlightenment forfeited its own realization" (33). Thought was the soul of the Enlightenment, yet when it succumbed to "blind power" and domination—"nature understood by masterful science"—it became irrational myth. The authors argue that the "fault lies in a social context which induces blindness," though they continuously acknowledge and stress "the false absolute, the principle of blind power" (33). In modern capitalist society, "Bacon's utopia, in which 'we should command nature in action,' has been fulfilled on a telluric scale, the essence of the compulsion which he ascribed to

---

88. Anne-Robert-Jacques Turgot (1727–1781) was a French economist and financial reformer under Louis XV and Louis XVI, and Jean-Baptiste le Rond d'Alembert (1717–1783) was a French mathematician, physicist, philosopher, and music theorist who, with Denis Diderot, edited the *Encyclopedia*.

unmastered nature is becoming apparent. It was power itself" (33–34). In the end, for Horkheimer and Adorno, power and only power defined the modern political, social, and economic condition. No one since Hobbes had portrayed human society in such gloomy, dark, inhumane terms; except for power—subjugation and domination—people have nothing to strive for. As such, the book is a great commentary on the world's existential condition in 1942 when Nazism and fascism seemed invincible. Ironically, like Spengler, Horkheimer and Adorno presented history as the inevitable decline of human power, autonomy, and freedom.

However, they also saw hope in a dialectic turn that might expose the grand "deception" of enlightenment: "Knowledge, in which, for Bacon, 'the sovereignty of man' unquestionably lay hidden, can now devote itself to dissolving that power. But in face of this possibility enlightenment, in the service of the present, is turning itself into an outright deception of the masses" (34). *Dialectic of Enlightenment* sets out to advance the humanist cause by separating thought from power.

Odysseus: Myth and Enlightenment

> It is a yearning for the homeland which sets in motion the adventures by which subjectivity, the prehistory of which is narrated in the *Odyssey*, escapes the primeval world.
>
> —Horkheimer and Adorno, *Dialectic of Enlightenment*, 1944

In their second chapter, Horkheimer and Adorno elaborate on their earlier discussion, claiming that "[j]ust as the story of the Sirens illustrates the intertwinement of myth and rational labor, the *Odyssey* as a whole bears witness to the dialectic of enlightenment" (35).[89] The story should be counted as "bourgeois prehistory" (46), and we should identify the dialectic of enlightenment not only with Francis Bacon and the early modern Enlightenment period, but in the classical Homeric epics, which, as Nietzsche perceived, present the first clear example of the "ambivalent relationship of enlightenment to power" (36).

Following the traditional views of Homer's epic, Horkheimer and Adorno admit that in its "oldest stratum," the *Odyssey* "shows clear links

---

89. For an analysis of the second chapter of *Dialectic of Enlightenment*, see James I. Porter, "Odysseus and the Wandering Jew: The Dialectic of Jewish Enlightenment in Adorno and Horkheimer," *Cultural Critique* 74 (Winter 2010): 200–13.

to myth" in that "the adventures are drawn from popular tradition." However, "as the Homeric spirit takes over and 'organizes' the myths, it comes into contradiction with them." Hence, the "familiar equation of epic and myth," which Auerbach draws in the first chapter of *Mimesis*,[90] "proves wholly misleading when subjected to philosophical critique." For "the two concepts diverge," distinguishing "two phases of an historical process." They impute to Homer "a universality of language" that, in contrast, for example, to Auerbach's contention that his poems are based on a well-defined social hierarchy,[91] "*disintegrates the hierarchical order of society through the exoteric form of its depiction, even and especially when it glorifies that order*" (35, emphasis added).

"The celebration of the wrath of Achilles and the wanderings of Odysseus is already a nostalgic stylization of what can no longer be celebrated." Although most literary critics see Daniel Defoe's *Robinson Crusoe* as the prototype of the bourgeois individual,[92] the authors boldly argue that "the hero of the adventures turns out to be *the prototype of the bourgeois individual*, whose concept originates in the unwavering self-assertion of which the protagonist driven to wander the earth is the primeval model" (35, emphasis added). In contrast to Auerbach's identification of Homeric poems with myths and the barbaric age,[93] Horkheimer and Adorno claim that until Homer, "true humanity has flourished only in conjunction with the barbaric element" (59), but his epics reflect "a world charged with meaning" that "reveals itself as an achievement of *classifying reason, which destroys myth by virtue of the same rational order which is used to reflect it*" (35–36, emphasis added). "The Promised Land for Odysseus is not the archaic realm of images"; rather, with him, "the power of myth, transposed into mental forms, survives only as imagination" (59).

Horkheimer and Adorno argue that Nietzsche first advanced "[u]nderstanding of the element of bourgeois enlightenment in Homer." He was among the few after Hegel who "recognized the dialectic of enlightenment" (36), or the relationship of enlightenment to power, in early works such as *The Birth of Tragedy* (1872) and *Philosophy in the Tragic Age of the Greeks* (1873). On the one hand, according to Nietzsche, the "'task of enlightenment'" is to "show up the pompous behavior of princes and states-

---

90. Auerbach, "Odysseus' Scar," 3–23.

91. Ibid., 3–23.

92. See, for example, Watt, *Rise of the Novel*.

93. See Zakai, *Erich Auerbach and the Crisis of German Philology*, 96–105.

men as a deliberate lie.' " On the other, "enlightenment had always been a means employed by 'great artists of government' (Confucius in China, the Roman Empire, Napoleon, the Papacy . . .). . . . The self-deception of the masses . . . is highly advantageous: making people small and governable is hailed as 'progress'!" Nietzsche remained of two minds about these terms: "whereas he perceived in enlightenment both the universal movement of sovereign mind, whose supreme exponent he believed himself to be, and a 'nihilistic,' life-denying power, only the second moment was taken over by his pre-fascist followers and perverted into ideology" (36). Modern German politics thus powerfully determined Horkheimer and Adorno's reading of Homer's poems (and Nietzsche). Since the fascist reading of Homer aims "to liquidate enlightenment," its "earliest traces" particularly "threaten to unleash the process" that "the bad conscience of present-day devotees of the archaic . . . seek to hold back" (37).

In German thought, any recognition of "Homer's antimythological, enlightened character, his opposition to chthonic mythology, remains untrue because limited." Its adoration of Homer is based on an idolization of myth perceived as "naked force." In other words, in Germany,

> [t]he alleged authenticity of the archaic, with its *principle of blood and sacrifice*, is already tainted by the devious bad consciousness of power characteristic of the *'national regeneration'* today, which uses primeval times for self-advertising. The original myth itself contains the moment of mendacity which triumphs in *the fraudulent myth of fascism* and which the latter imputes to enlightenment. (37, emphases added)

Nazi admiration of Greek culture is of course only part of the general German Graecophilia, or adoration of Greek and classical culture. In 1822, Hegel noted that, for the Germans, "Athens" is the "most worthy fatherland of a cultural people," and this delusion achieved its apotheosis in Leni Riefenstahl's propaganda film *Olympia*.[94] Here, we find evidence that *Dialectic of Enlightenment* is intended as a grand commentary on the horrors of Nazi Germany.

---

94. Georg Wilhelm Friedrich Hegel, *Lectures on the Philosophy of World History*, ed. and trans. R. F. Brown and P. C. Hodgson (Oxford: Clarendon Press, 2011), 73. On German Graecophilia, see Suzanne L. Marchand, *Down from Olympus: Archaeology and Philhellenism in Germany, 1750–1970* (Princeton: Princeton University Press, 1996).

Despite the Nazis' use and abuse of Homer, the authors continue, "no work bears more eloquent witness to the intertwinement of enlightenment and myth than that of Homer, the basic text of European civilization" (37). More to the point in terms of their overall thesis, "[m]yths are precipitated in the different strata of Homer's subject matter; but at the same time the reporting of them, the unity imposed on the diffuse legends, *traces the path of the subject's flight from the mythical powers*" (37, emphasis added). Odysseus's "peregrinations from Troy to Ithaca trace the path of the self through myths," and the "primeval world is secularized as the space he measures out." For example, the hero's adventures "bestow names on each of these places, and the names give rise to a rational overview of space" (38).

Auerbach claims that Homer's poems contain "*only legend, 'make-believe.'*"[95] The authors of *Dialectic of Enlightenment* argue that Odysseus is "the man who has thus come of age" because he does not believe in the truth of "the myths" nor "that sea and earth" are "actually populated by demons." In psychological terms, his adventures "are dangerous temptations deflecting the self from the path of its logic" (38). In physical terms, the "implacable nature that he now commands . . . triumphs on his return home as the implacable judge, avenging the heritage of the very powers he has escaped" (38–39). Ultimately, "[t]he faculty by which the self survives adventures, throwing itself away in order to preserve itself, is cunning." Equipped with this mental power, "Odysseus outwits the natural deities" (39).

His story has many ramifications for the dialectic of enlightenment. First, the authors count it as "bourgeois prehistory" (46). Second, he "discovered in words what in fully developed bourgeois society is called *formalism*: their perennial ability to designate is bought at the cost of distancing themselves from any particular content which fulfills them, so that they refer from a distance to all possible contents." From "the formalism of mythical names and the statutes, which, indifferent like nature, seek to rule over human beings and history, emerges nominalism, the prototype of bourgeois thinking" (47, emphasis original), which holds that universal essences or general ideas do not exist. Third, Odysseus's adventures reveal the "irrationality of reason" as "precipitated in cunning," namely, "the adaptation of bourgeois reason to any unreason which confronts it as a stronger power" (48). Ultimately, "the lone voyager armed with cunning is already *homo oeconomicus*." The reason is clear: "the *Odyssey* is already a Robinsonade," or one of the many imitations that followed this highly successful work. "Both these prototypical shipwrecked sailors

---

95. Auerbach, *Mimesis*, 13, emphasis added.

make their weakness—that of the individual who breaks away from the collective—their social strength. Abandoned to the vagaries of the waves, helplessly cut off, they are forced by their isolation into a ruthless pursuit of their atomistic interest." Both Odysseus and Robinson Crusoe "embody the principle of the capitalist economy," and "[t]heir powerlessness in face of nature already functions as the ideology for their social predominance" (48).

Horkheimer and Adorno give priority to Homer over Defoe to show the deep historical origins of "the conflict between enlightenment and myth" (56). If, for Cassirer and Auerbach, Homer's epics belong to the realm of myth, then for Horkheimer and Adorno, they contain the germs of the dialectic of enlightenment. Their first chapter may begin with Francis Bacon and the elision of enlightenment, science, and achieving power over nature, but in the second chapter, they push these origins back. At its end, they discuss the nature and meaning of "homeland," reflecting their own yearning as exiles and the misappropriation of the concept by the Nazis:

> It is a yearning for the homeland which sets in motion the adventures by which subjectivity, the prehistory of which is narrated in the *Odyssey*, escapes the primeval world. The fact that—*despite the fascist lies to the contrary—the concept of homeland is opposed to myth* constitutes the innermost paradox of epic. Precipitated in the epic is the memory of an historical age in which nomadism gave way to settlement, the precondition of any homeland. (60, emphasis added)

"Homeland and nature . . . had first to be wrested from myth." They intrinsically reflect "a state of having escaped" (61) from culturally sanctioned concepts to concrete human interactions. Time and again, we can see how the innovative rereading of Horkheimer and Adorno, Auerbach, Mann, and Cassirer were spurred by the brutish political certainties of their times.

Enlightenment and Morality

> Reason is the agency of calculating thought, which arranges the world for the purposes of self-preservation and recognizes no function other than that of working on the object as mere sense material in order to make it the material of subjugation.
>
> —Horkheimer and Adorno, *Dialectic of Enlightenment*, 1944

"Excursus II: Juliette or Enlightenment and Morality" deals with the Age of Reason and Enlightenment.[96] Cassirer argued that the Enlightenment adopted the Stoic "conception of the *fundamental equality of men*,"[97] epitomized by Thomas Jefferson's Declaration of Independence (1776), which stipulated: "We hold these truths to be self-evident; that all men are created equal; that they are endowed by their Creator with certain unalienable rights; that among these are life, liberty, and the pursuit of happiness." Only to secure these rights, Jefferson posits, "governments are instituted among men, deriving their just powers from the consent of the governed." Cassirer called these assertions "the language of the Stoic philosophy," expressing "the essence of men and the very character of human reason." The basis of the US Declaration of Independence and, later, the French Declaration of the Rights of Man and the Citizen (Déclaration des droits de l'homme et du citoyen, 1789) was "the intellectual Declaration of Independence that we find in the theoreticians of the seventeenth century," when "reason had first declared its power and its claim to rule the social life of man. It had emancipated itself from the guardianship of theological thought; it could stand on its own." He argued that with the revival of Stoic philosophy, "the theory of the natural right of man was no longer an abstract ethical doctrine but one of the mainsprings of political action."[98]

Nothing of this glorious vision can be found in *Dialectic of Enlightenment*. In their second excursus, the authors deal with two groups: "the *somber writers* of the early bourgeois period, such as Machiavelli, Hobbes, and Mandeville, who spoke up for the egoism of the self, thereby recognized society as the destructive principle and denounced harmony" (71, emphasis added), and "[t]he *dark writers* of the bourgeoisie," like the Marquis de Sade and Friedrich Wilhelm Nietzsche, who "unlike its apologists, did not seek to avert the consequences of the Enlightenment with harmonistic doctrines" (92, emphasis added). In Horkheimer and Adorno's hands, enlightenment is dire, dark, duplicitous, marked by egoism and a perpetual state of war—all against all, dog-eat-dog. Bacon saw in enlightenment "the form of knowledge which most ably deals with the facts, most effectively assists the subject in mastering nature" (65). Accordingly, argued

---

96. For an overview of the period, see Avihu Zakai, "The Age of Enlightenment," in *Cambridge Companion to Jonathan Edwards*, ed. Stephen Stein (New York: Cambridge University Press, 2006), 80–99; and Zakai, *Jonathan Edwards's Philosophy of Nature*.

97. Cassirer, *Myth of the State*, 100, emphasis original.

98. Ibid., 167–68.

the champions of Critical Theory, the "system's principles are those of *self-preservation*" (65, emphasis added). Knowledge is predicated on egoism in the enlightenment worldview: "Self-preservation is the constitutive principle of science, the soul of the table of categories, even if, as in Kant, it has to be deduced idealistically" (68).

Enlightenment is inextricable from the rise of science and the triumph of the capitalist, industrial market economy, the basis of bourgeois society. "The market economy it unleashed was at once the prevailing form of reason and the power which *ruined reason*" (70, emphasis added). They attribute to Kant the idea that "reason is the agency of calculating thought, which arranges the world for the purposes of *self-preservation* and recognizes no function other than that of working on the object as mere sense material in order to make it the material of *subjugation*" (65, emphasis added). Instead of liberty, reason led to manipulation, domination, oppression, enslavement, both of nature and human beings. It became an essential tool of domination in modern industrial society, in which "[e]verything—including the individual human being, not to mention the animal—becomes a repeatable, replaceable process, a mere example of the conceptual models of the system" (65).

In 1784, Immanuel Kant (1724–1804) coined the famous dictum: "Enlightenment is mankind's exit from its self-incurred immaturity. Immaturity is the inability to make use of one's own understanding without the guidance of another . . . *Sapere Aude!* [Dare to know] Have the courage to use your own understanding! That is the motto of enlightenment."[99] From the gloomy perspective of Nazism and fascism, Horkheimer and Adorno find the root of "Kantian optimism" in "a horror of relapsing into barbarism." Instead of Kantian "respect and reciprocal love," now "fascism, which by its iron discipline relieves its peoples of the burden of moral feelings, no longer needs to observe any discipline" (67). Likewise, Kant's categorical imperative—"Act only according to that maxim whereby you can at the same time will that it should become a universal law"[100]—was discredited by fascism, which "treats human beings as things, centers of modes of behavior," and has no difficulty making such treatment a universal rule. In the past, "rulers sought to shield the bourgeois world from the flood of naked violence, which now has broken over Europe" (67). Under these assumptions, the authors draw an essential and inextricable

---

99. Kant, "What Is Enlightenment?," 58.

100. Immanuel Kant, *Grounding for the Metaphysics of Morals*, 1785, trans. James W. Ellington (Indianapolis: Hackett, 1993), 30.

link between Kant and Nietzsche: "From Kant's *Critique* [*of Pure Reason*, 1781] to Nietzsche's *Genealogy of Morals* [1887], the hand of philosophy had traced the writing on the wall" (68).

They single out an avatar, who "put that writing into practice, in all its details"—the Marquis de Sade, whose work reflects "the bourgeois subject freed from all tutelage" (68). *Juliette, or Vice Amply Rewarded* was published in 1797–1801, accompanied by the earlier *Nouvelle Justine, or The Misfortunes of Virtue* (1791). While Justine, Juliette's sister, is a virtuous woman, who consequently encounters nothing but despair and abuse, Juliette is an amoral nymphomaniac murderer, who is successful and happy. The novel follows a pattern of violently pornographic scenes followed by long treatises on a broad range of philosophical topics, including theology, morality, aesthetics, and naturalism. Sade "erected an early monument" to the "totalitarian trust-masters," or "[t]he conspiracy of rulers against peoples, implemented by relentless organization," which "finds the Enlightenment spirit since Machiavelli and Hobbes no less compliant than the bourgeois republic." For them, "human beings become mere material," and, after "the brief interlude of liberalism in which the bourgeois kept one another in check, *power is revealing itself as archaic terror in a fascistically rationalized form*" (68, emphasis added). In *Justine*, Sade has the Prince of Francavilla say that once "the people" were "freed from the fear of a future Hell," they would "abandon themselves to anything" (68–69). "Take away its god from the people you wish to subjugate," he pronounces, "and you will demoralize it." The confusing use of *it* for the people, not the god, exposes his ideology. *It* is nothing with a claim on his conscience. "As long as it has no other god than yours, you will always be its master" (70).

The gloomy vision of society in Sade's *Juliette* is based in part on the "market economy." Over time, "the development of the economic system in which the control of the economic apparatus by private groups creates a division between human beings, self-preservation, although treated by reason as identical, had become the reified drive of each individual citizen and proved to be a destructive natural force no longer distinguishable from self-destruction." Kant's "Pure reason became unreason" because it was "as immune to errors as it was devoid of content." In economic and political terms, "[f]or those at the top, *shrewd self-preservation means the fascist struggle for power*" (71, emphasis added).

The authors find the transformation from reason to power to the destruction of humanist values evident in Sade's works. For him, "enlightenment was not so much an intellectual as a social phenomenon," and "[h]is work lays bare the mythological nature of the principles on which civilization was based after the demise of religion: those of the Decalogue, of paternal authority, of property" (90). While "Justine, the virtuous sister, is a martyr to the moral law," Juliette "draws the conclusion the bourgeoisie sought to avoid: she demonizes Catholicism as the latest mythology, and with it civilization as a whole." Sacrilege replaces sacrament: "intellectual pleasure in regression, *amor intellectualis diaboli*, the joy of defeating civilization with its own weapons." Juliette "wields the instruments of rational thought with consummate skill" (74). Her "*credo* is science. She abominates any veneration which cannot be shown to be rational," such as "belief in God and his dead son, obedience to the Ten Commandments," and so forth. Her "specific passion" is "the conversion of what is condemned without scientific proof into something to be striven for, and of what is respected without proof into an object of revulsion, the transvaluation of values, the 'courage to do the forbidden'" (76).

The same is the case with Nietzsche: "Once the objective order of nature has been dismissed as prejudice and myth, nature is no more than a mass of material." He recognizes no law and no power over him, but to the extent that "the understanding . . . recognizes any law of life, it is that of the stronger." His "doctrine" holds that "the weak are guilty . . . since they use cunning to circumvent the natural law," and he "hates and abominates" Christianity, the religion that calls the meek blessed and bequeaths them the earth, "no less than Sade" does. In *Genealogy of Morals*, he argues:

> . . . the strong are allowed to injure the weak, since, to act in this way, they must only use the gifts they have received. The strong individual does not, like the weak, disguise himself with a character other than his own. He merely expresses in action what he has received from nature. Everything which follows from that is therefore natural: his expression, his violence, his cruelties, his tyrannies, his injustices . . . (78)

The ramifications for fascism are very clear: "By elevating the cult of strength to a world-historical doctrine, German fascism took it to its absurd conclusion" (79). From Enlightenment's myth of power, through Sade's abomination of the rational, and Nietzsche's cult of strength, the road was opened for the rise and triumph of fascism and Nazism. This intellectual development, the authors lament, reveals "the story of thought as an instrument of power" (92).

In "their blackest book," Horkheimer and Adorno joined with "the black writers of the bourgeoisie," such as the Marquis de Sade and Nietzsche, "to conceptualize the Enlightenment's process of self-destruction. On their analysis, it is no longer possible to place hope in the liberating force of Enlightenment."[101] They too "did not pretend that formalistic reason had a closer affinity to morality than to immorality" (92) and are quick to mention that with fascism, "power has come fully into its own" (93). No one before had portrayed the Enlightenment in such desperately antihumanistic terms, yet this black description is only prologue to the next chapter.

Enlightenment as Mass Deception

> Technical rationality today is the rationality of domination. It is the compulsive character of a society alienated from itself.
>
> —Horkheimer and Adorno, *Dialectic of Enlightenment*, 1944

> In Fascism radio becomes the universal mouthpiece of the *Führer*; in the loudspeakers on the street his voice merges with the howl of sirens proclaiming panic, from which modern propaganda is hard to distinguish in any case.
>
> —Horkheimer and Adorno, *Dialectic of Enlightenment*, 1944

Chapter 4, "The Culture Industry: Enlightenment as Mass Deception," deals with modern capitalist mass culture, the entertainment industry, "especially cinema, radio, jazz, and magazines" (105), as well as advertisement, which provides clear evidence of the inherent "rationality of domination" (95). The myth of enlightenment, the quest for power, domination, and subjugation, is evident in the monopolistic transformation of the human condition and society as a whole. Based on Marxist historical materialism, the view that modes of production influence modes of thought, the authors meticulously examine the various spheres of the culture industry, claiming that they debase the human condition and lead to barbarism.

Their harsh criticism sees inextricable connections between "Donald Duck in the cartoons and the unfortunate victim in real life" who both "receive their beatings so that the spectators can accustom themselves to theirs" (110). Similarly, "[f]un is a medicinal bath which the entertainment industry never ceases to prescribe"; as "the instrument for cheating happiness" (112), laughter leads to the "flight from the everyday world"

---

101. Habermas, *Philosophical Discourse of Modernity*, 106.

(113). The problem is not that "the culture industry serves up amusement but that it spoils the fun by its business-minded attachment to the ideological clichés of the culture which is liquidating itself." In masking its motives, in disguising "the bunch of keys of capitalist reason" as "the bells on the fool's cap," and using a kiss to market lipstick, "the culture industry is corrupt" (114).

With their rise, big business, trusts, and corporations used modern technology to acquire more power and influence over the masses. In the nineteenth-century United States, the robber barons, people like Andrew Carnegie, John D. Rockefeller, and Cornelius Vanderbilt, acquired their fortunes by controlling "steel, petroleum, electricity, chemicals" and transportation by ruthless means (95). However, technology began to gain power over capitalist society at large. The culture industry not only "entrenches itself" but began "producing, controlling, disciplining" the "needs of consumers" (115). More specifically, "[t]echnical rationality today is *the rationality of domination*. It is the compulsive character of a society alienated from itself" (95, emphasis added). With the aid of new technology, "the obscure subjective intentions of board chairmen," who replaced the robber barons, dictate social norms and desires (96).

Horkheimer and Adorno believed that the myth of power and domination is an integral part of barbarism. The culture industry's delivery of mass deception thus signals a return to barbarism. This chapter, more than any other, reflects their American experience, and their criticism of American modern culture leads to some astonishing conclusions, such as their criticism of jazz and films. In their eyes, no corner of society is immune to the inhuman intent of the culture industry or the struggle for power and domination; hence, they cannot allow any notion of a public sphere where individuals can freely identify and discuss societal problems and influence political action. In modern capitalist society, this enlightened liberal social sphere, the public sphere, is ruled by competing economic interests and considerations. In contrast, Habermas envisioned a public sphere that served as a counterweight to political authority and took place in face-to-face discussions in coffee houses, cafés, and public squares as well as in letters, books, drama, and art.[102]

Based on their Marxist modes of thought and persuasion, Horkheimer and Adorno argue that "the basis on which technology is gaining power over society is the power of those whose economic position in

---

102. See Jürgen Habermas, *The Structural Transformation of the Public Sphere: An Inquiry into a Category of Bourgeois Society* (Cambridge: Polity Press, 1989 [1962]).

society is strongest." The characteristics of "technological rationality" are "standardization and mass production," and it "sacrifices what once distinguished the logic of the work from that of society." They cite "the step from telephone to radio": the first "liberally permitted the participant to play the role of subject," while the second "democratically makes everyone equally into listeners," restricting "them in *authoritarian fashion* to the same programs" (95, emphasis added) or, at any rate, indistinguishable programs. The same can be said about cinema, magazines, and advertising. Technology serves the power of economic groups, leading *ipso facto* to domination and subjugation.

Reinhold Niebuhr (1892–1971), the famous American Protestant theologian, raised the same harsh criticism of capitalist society. Among his most influential books are *Moral Man and Immoral Society* (1932) and *The Nature and Destiny of Man* (1943). His exposure to the problems of industrialism as a pastor in Detroit led him to denounce Henry Ford: "Henry Ford is America," he wrote.[103] He expressed his aversion to the unbridled greed and lack of social responsibility displayed by wealthy magnates:

> What a civilization this is! Naïve gentlemen with a genius for mechanics suddenly become the arbiters over the lives and fortunes of hundreds and thousands. Their moral pretensions are credulously accepted at full value. No one bothers to ask whether an industry which can maintain a cash reserve of a quarter of a billion ought not make some provision for its unemployed.[104]

The main difference between these two critiques of capitalism is point of view, Niebuhr's is theological; Horkheimer and Adorno's is sociological. However, the latter take distinctly idiosyncratic positions, arguing, for example, that to "impress the omnipotence of capital on the hearts of expropriated job candidates as the power of their true master is the purpose of all films, regardless of the plot selected by the production directors" (98). They point to Nazi Germany, where "even the most carefree films of democracy were overhung already by the graveyard stillness of dictatorship" (99).

They believed the "whole world is passed through the filter of the

---

103. Richard W. Fox, *Reinhold Niebuhr: A Biography* (San Francisco: Harper & Row, 1985), 95–96. See also Zakai, "The Irony of American History."

104. Reinhold Niebuhr, *Leaves from the Notebook of a Tamed Cynic* (Cleveland: Meridian, 1957 [1929]), 123.

culture industry" (99) with profound implications for the human condition: film "debars the spectator from thinking," and through it, "[t]he power of industrial society is imprinted on people once and for all." In "[e]ach single manifestation . . . the culture industry inescapably reproduces human beings as what the whole has made them. And all its agents, from the producer to the women's organizations, are on the alert to ensure that the simple reproduction of mind does not lead on to the expansion of mind" (100).

They believe the predominance of "mechanical reproducibility" is reflected in jazz: "the jazz arranger excludes any phrase which does not exactly fit the jargon. If he jazzes up Mozart, he changes the music not only where it is too difficult or serious but also where the melody is merely harmonized differently" (101). Through the media of films and jazz, the industry culture or the culture industry dictates an "insatiable uniformity," a "unified standard of value," where "the identity of all industrial cultural products" is realized in "a mocking fulfillment of Wagner's dream of the total art work" (97). The overt "paradox of routine travestied as nature is detectable in every utterance of the culture industry, and in many is quite blatant." For example, "[a] jazz musician who has to play a piece of serious music, Beethoven's simplest minuet, involuntarily syncopates, and condescends to start on the beat only with a superior smile" (101).

Modern industry's means of production, assembly line automatization and mechanization, or "the universal victory of the rhythm of mechanical production and reproduction" (106–07), crucially influenced uniformity and standardization in the culture industry, leading to "stylized barbarism" (101), "[a]esthetic barbarism" (104), "the negation of style" (102), or "the aesthetic equivalent of power," reflecting "obedience to the social hierarchy" (103). It is defined by exclusion: "[o]nly what has been industrialized, rigorously subsumed, is fully adequate to this concept of culture." Since the modes of action and production determine the modes of conviction and persuasion,

> [o]nly by subordinating all branches of intellectual production equally to the single purpose of imposing on the senses of human beings, from the time they leave the factory in the evening to the time they clock on in the morning, the imprint of the work routine which they must sustain throughout the day, does this culture mockingly fulfill the notion of a unified culture which the philosophers of the individual personality held out against mass culture. (104)

The barbarization of modern culture cannot be separated from the barbarization of modern capitalist society. The authors argue that "[n]ot for nothing did the system of the culture industry originate in the liberal industrial countries, just as all its characteristic media, especially cinema, radio, jazz, and magazines, also triumph there" (104–05). Where some see progress, they see decadence, decay.

Based on the Marxist view of history, according to which the material conditions of a society's modes of production determine its organization and development, the authors define the culture industry as "entertainment business" whose "control of consumers is mediated by entertainment." Its "tendencies . . . are turned into the flesh and blood of the public by the social process" and "reinforced by the survival of the market in the industry" (108). For example, "the captains of the film industry" look only to "box-office success," so "[t]heir ideology is business" (108–09). They impose it by creating an "[e]ntertainment [that] is the prolongation of work . . . sought by those who want to escape the mechanized labor process so that they can cope with it again." These benighted workers do not see that "the only escape from the work process in factory and office is through adaptation to it in leisure time," which renders "all entertainment" an "incurable sickness" (109).

Horkheimer and Adorno have nothing good to say about the culture industry. Behind it lurk selfish capitalist interests. Even "cartoon and stunt films . . . merely confirm *the victory of technological reason over truth.*" In these films, "[t]he quantity of organized amusement is converted into the quality of organized cruelty." The "enjoyment of the violence done to the film character turns into violence against the spectator." Based on violence and cruelty, films are no longer "the world of dream" but rather reflect the hard and harsh conditions of modern life and society (110, emphasis added).

Given modern capitalist society's inhuman nature, it is clear that "the bloated entertainment apparatus does not make life more worthy of human beings." Instead, "the culture industry endlessly cheats its consumers out of what it endlessly promises" (111). Paradoxically, it may promote its productions as a "flight from the everyday world," but, in fact, "[e]ntertainment fosters the resignation which seeks to forget itself in entertainment" (113). For men educated in the prestigious citadels of European and German high culture, the American "fusion of culture and entertainment is brought about . . . not only by the debasement of culture but equally by the compulsory intellectualization of amusement" (114). "Amusement itself becomes an ideal, taking the place of the higher values it eradicates" (115).

The culture industry is immanent in bourgeois enlightenment, exhibiting the same quest for power, domination, and subjugation in "producing, controlling, disciplining" the "needs of consumers." Since "the need for entertainment was largely created by industry," business and entertainment are closely aligned: "To be entertained means to be in agreement. Entertainment makes itself possible only by insulating itself from the totality of the social process" (115). More specifically, it prevents "thinking as negation," contributing to the "advance of stupidity" (116). In the capitalist "age of universal advertisement," "the culture industry makes itself the irrefutable prophet of the existing order" (118), celebrating, for example, "the triumph of the giant corporation over entrepreneurial initiative. . . . The fight is waged against an enemy who has already been defeated, the thinking subject" (120). They find the close relationship between power and domination in jazz: "Existence in late capitalism is a permanent rite of initiation. Everyone must show that they identify wholeheartedly with the power which beats them. This is inherent in the principle of syncopation in jazz, which mocks the act of stumbling while elevating it to the norm" (124).

The result of such inhuman power and domination, uniformity and conformity, signaled the end of thinking and personal identity, hence, the end of tragedy: "Today tragedy has been dissipated in the void of the false identity of society and subject, the horror of which is still just fleetingly visible in the vacuous semblance of the tragic." Its "liquidation . . . confirms the abolition of the individual" (124). Singularity is not possible when the "standardized mode of production of the culture industry" makes "the individual illusory in its products." Individuals are "tolerated only as far as their wholehearted identity with the universal is beyond question. From the standardized improvisation in jazz to the original film personality who must have a lock of hair straying over her eyes so that she may be identified as such, pseudoindividuality reigns" (124-25). An example of "uniform identity" may be found in "Yale locks which differ by fractions of a millimeter." From uniformity and conformity, the road to fascism and Nazism is short: "The citizens whose lives are split between business and private life, their private life between ostentation and intimacy, their intimacy between the sullen community of marriage and the bitter solace of being entirely alone, at odds with themselves and with everyone, are virtually already Nazis" (125).

Radio reveals how modern technology assists in the creation of totalitarianism. "In fascism radio becomes the universal mouthpiece of the *Führer*; in the loudspeakers on the street his voice merges with the howl of sirens proclaiming panic, from which modern propaganda is hard to distinguish in any case." A comparison with the Protestant Reformation is revealing: "The National Socialists knew that broadcasting gave their cause stature as the printing press did to the Reformation." They ascribe "[t]he

Führer's metaphysical charisma, invented by the sociology of religion," to the "omnipresence of his radio addresses, which demonically parodies that of the divine spirit." Yes, "the *Führer*'s address is . . . a lie," but the radio infers "the human word as absolute, the false commandment." The radio permits Hitler himself to command "both the holocaust and the supply of trash" (129).

Based on their historical materialism, Horkheimer and Adorno argue that since culture is a commodity, "it merges with the advertisement. The more meaningless the latter appears under monopoly, the more omnipotent culture becomes." Power and domination are integral to advertising, "which performed a social service in orienting the buyer in the market." As "the free market is coming to an end, those in control of the system are entrenching themselves in advertising" (131), and like the other spheres of the culture industry, it is absorbed by fascism and Nazism: "Advertising becomes simply the art with which Goebbels presciently equated it, *l'art pour l'art*, advertising for advertising's sake, the pure representation of social power" (132).

The union of advertising with the culture industry, technologically and economically, reveals how modes of production influenced modes of thought and behavior or how new modes of persuasion led to new modes of action and conduct. "In both, the same thing appears in countless places, and the mechanical repetition of the same culture product is already that of the same propaganda slogan. In both, under the dictate of effectiveness, technique is becoming psychotechnique, *a procedure for manipulating human beings*" (133).

Language is critical, as advertisement transforms "words . . . from substantial carriers of meaning to signs devoid of qualities." Its usage reveals how the "*demythologization of language*, as an element of the total process of enlightenment, *reverts to magic*" (133, emphasis added). For example, "the name of a homeland," to which "magic most readily attached, is today undergoing a chemical change. It is being transformed into arbitrary, manipulable designations." Likewise, "[i]f the German fascists launch a word like 'intolerable' [*Untragbar*] over the loudspeakers one day, the whole nation is saying 'intolerable' the next. . . . The blind and rapidly spreading repetition of designated words links advertising to the totalitarian slogan" (134–35). In Nazi Germany, the "violence done to words" is most clear: "in any word one can distinguish how far it has been disfigured by the fascist 'folk' community" (135).

In concluding this chapter, the authors claim that the culture industry leads to a flight from reason, humanism, civilization, and democracy.

"Today the culture industry has taken over the civilizing inheritance of the frontier and entrepreneurial democracy" because it allows "the freedom to choose an ideology, which always reflects economic coercion." Although the effects are evident in many spheres, the success of advertising is their prime example: "personality means hardly more than dazzling white teeth and freedom from body odor and emotions." The unmistakable triumph of advertising in the culture industry is demonstrated by "the compulsive imitation by consumers of cultural commodities, which, at the same time, they recognize as false" (135–36). Civilization has become an antihumanization process.

The Jewish Question— The Epitome of *Dialectic of Enlightenment*

> Only the liberating of thought from power, the abolition of violence, could realize the idea which has been unrealized until now: that the Jew is a human being. This would be a step away from the anti-Semitic society, which drives both Jews and others into sickness, and toward the human one. Such a step would fulfill the fascist lie by contradicting it: the Jewish question would indeed prove the turning point of history.
>
> —Horkheimer and Adorno, *Dialectic of Enlightenment*, 1944

The last chapter of *Dialectic of Enlightenment*, "Elements of Anti-Semitism: Limits of Enlightenment," should be read along with other attempts by German-speaking intellectuals who fled Nazi Germany, among them Mann, Cassirer, Auerbach, Arendt, and others, to provide an apology for, or defense and justification of, Jewish thought and culture against Nazi racism and anti-Semitism; they all turned their disciplines to the task. Except for Mann, they all belonged to what George L. Mosse called "German Jews beyond Judaism," people who searched "for a personal identity beyond religion and nationality."[105] The trauma of Nazism, of forced exile and the rising knowledge of Holocaust atrocities, transformed their views, and in their writings, they came to the defense of Judaism directly or indirectly.

Various approaches were available to them, each reflecting the centrality they attached to specific concerns. Cassirer and Auerbach never

---

105. Mosse, *German Jews beyond Judaism*, 2.

tackled anti-Semitism directly but point to the importance of Jewish thought and culture to Western civilization. Auerbach's goal in "Figura" (1938) and *Mimesis: The Representation of Reality in Western Literature* (1946) was to reject the chauvinist, racist, and anti-Semitic premises of Aryan philology, based on *völkisch* mysticism and Nazi historiography, which eliminated the Hebrew Bible, or Old Testament, from German *Kultur* and *Volksgeist*, in particular, and Western civilization in general. Immediately after the 1933 Nazi Revolution, when "nationalist anti-Semitism" led by "blood communities" (144) began its murderous attack on Jews, Auerbach began accumulating evidence and arguing with singular erudition that the Old Testament, not classical Greek myth, is the origin of Western culture's representation of reality. Scripture leads "from distant legend and its figural interpretation into everyday contemporary reality,"[106] while the premises of Aryan philology and culture lead from legend to flight from reality—*Schwärmerei*. The former respects the individual's perceptions and experiences, while the latter dismisses when it does not condemn them.

Likewise, Ernst Cassirer concluded his essay "Judaism and the Modern Political Myth" (1944) with an apology for Jewish life and thought:

> What the *modern Jew* had to defend in this combat [against Nazism] was not only his physical existence or the preservation of the Jewish race. Much more was at stake. *We had to represent all those ethical ideals that had been brought into being by Judaism and found their way into general human culture, into the life of all civilized nations.*[107]

Elsewhere he claimed, exactly as Auerbach did in the first chapter of *Mimesis*, "Odysseus' Scar," that "the Nazis based their power upon historical social myths," while "the Jews have always shown little inclination for mythical thought."[108] In *An Essay on Man* (1944), he provided a strong defense of Jewish beliefs and praised the Old Testament as one source of humanism, freedom, and the rise of the ethical standpoint of religious consciousness, stressing that "the great prophets of Israel no longer spoke merely to their

---

106. Auerbach, *Mimesis*, 159.

107. Cassirer, "Judaism and the Modern Political Myth," 241, emphasis added.

108. Dimitri Gawronsky, "Cassirer: His Life and His Works," in *The Philosophy of Ernst Cassirer*, ed. Paul A. Schilpp (Evanston: The Library of Living Philosophers, 1949), 33.

nations. Their God was a god of Justice and His message was not restricted to a special group." The ultimate message of this "prophetic religion" was "its ethical meaning."[109]

Thomas Mann's defense of Jewish life and thought can be seen in his address, "The Theme of the Joseph Novels," delivered at the Library of Congress in Washington, DC, on November 17, 1942. He informed the audience that "some people were inclined to regard *Joseph and His Brothers,*" his four-part novel written over the course of sixteen years, from 1926 to 1943, "as a Jewish book, even merely a novel for the Jews." He agreed; "the selection of the old testamental subject was certainly no mere accident" because of "the growing vulgar anti-Semitism which is an essential part of the Fascist mob-myth, and which commits the brutish denial of the fact that *Judaism and Hellenism are the two principal pillars upon which our occidental civilization rests.*" Hence, he declared: "To write a novel of the Jewish spirit was timely, just because it seems untimely."[110]

In contrast, Hannah Arendt looked at anti-Semitism head on, devoting the first chapter of *The Origins of Totalitarianism* (1951) to "Antisemitism" and the "Jewish Question." Likewise, the authors of *Dialectic of Enlightenment* devoted its last chapter to these problems, which revealed the central significance of the "ambivalent relationship of enlightenment to power" (36). Examined in these terms, they boldly claimed that "[o]nly the liberation of thought from power, the abolition of violence, could realize the idea which has been unrealized until now: that the Jew is a human being." In the transformation from an anti-Semitic to a human society, "the Jewish question would indeed prove the turning-point of history" (165).

They first address Judaism in chapter 3, where they praise it for leading to the flight from myth: "The demise of idolatry follows necessarily from the ban on mythology pronounced by Jewish monotheism" (89). Auerbach makes the same contention, claiming that in contrast to myth, "legend," and "make-believe," the hallmarks of the Homeric style, the Old Testament revealed the "development of the concept of the historically becoming," which is the great contribution of its realism, or "the Jewish-Israelitish realm of reality," to Western culture and history.[111] (However, Horkheimer and Adorno present a different valuation of Homeric myth, as we saw earlier, making it hard to know how they value the Jewish "ban.")

---

109. Cassirer, *Essay on Man*, 103.

110. Mann, "The Theme of the Joseph Novels," 11–12, emphasis added. See also Kurzke, *Thomas Mann*, 414.

111. Auerbach, *Mimesis*, 14–16, 23.

They reserve their fullest, most systematic apology for Jewish culture and thought for the last chapter, "Elements of Anti-Semitism: Limits of Enlightenment." Like Auerbach and Cassirer, Horkheimer and Adorno believe Jewish culture and thought were crucial for the civilizing process that abandoned myth and embraced rationalist thought. They reiterate much of Mann, Auerbach, and Cassirer's arguments in defense of Judaism; they accept and defend its universal humanist message as a crucial contribution to European civilization. For example, they argue that its prohibitions were a vehicle for enlightenment and progress because religious sacrifice became rational. Most important for our concerns here, they saw the "Jewish Question" and anti-Semitism as an embodiment of the dialectical intertwining of enlightenment and power, or the myth of power.

The last chapter of *Dialectic of Enlightenment* begins with an important distinction: "Anti-Semitism today is for some a question affecting human destiny and for others a mere pretext. For the fascists, the Jews are not a minority but the antirace," so for fascists, "on their extermination the world's happiness depends." Against this view, the liberal conception holds that "the Jews, free of national or racial features, form a group through religious belief and tradition and nothing else." The authors deem both views "true and false at the same time." The first announces the truth that the Jews "are branded as absolute evil by absolute evil" (137), "[b]ut by assuming the unity of humanity to have been already realized in principle, the liberal thesis serves as an apology for the existing order." It reflects "[t]he dialectical intertwinement of enlightenment and power, the dual relationship of progress to both cruelty and liberation, which has been brought home to the Jews no less by the great exponents of enlightenment than by democratic popular movements" and "manifests itself in the makeup of the assimilated Jews themselves" (138). More specifically,

> [t]he enlightened self-control with which adapted Jews effaced within themselves the painful scars of domination by others, a kind of second circumcision, made them forsake their own dilapidated community and wholeheartedly embrace the life of the modern bourgeoisie, which was already advancing ineluctably toward a reversion to pure oppression and reorganization into an exclusively racial entity.

Hence, "[r]ace today is the self-assertion of the bourgeois individual, integrated into the barbaric collective." The basis of this radical position is that the "harmonious society to which the liberal Jews declared their allegiance has finally been granted to them in the form of the national community"

(138), yet, given that twentieth-century nationalist states and communities in Europe turned to racism, "[t]he persecution of the Jews, like any other persecution, cannot be separated from that [political] order" (139). "Bourgeois anti-Semitism" is inseparable from capitalism since it "has a specific economic purpose: to conceal domination of production" (142).

Even dialectical materialism will acknowledge that the phenomenon of anti-Semitism is not so simple. As "a malady so deeply embedded in civilization," no "plausibly rational, economic, and political explanations" can "appease it, since rationality itself, through its link to power, is submerged in the same malady." Anti-Semitism is closely associated with the human condition since its "behavior is unleashed in situations in which blinded people, deprived of subjectivity, are let loose as subjects." It is "a well-rehearsed pattern, indeed, *a ritual of civilization, and the pogroms are the true ritual murders.* They demonstrate the impotence of what might have restrained them—reflection, meaning, ultimately truth" (139-40, emphasis added).

As the chapter progresses, the authors' apology for Jewish life and thought intensifies and becomes more and more apparent.[112] "Christianity is . . . a regression beyond Judaism." While in the latter, God "demands what he is owed and settles accounts with the defaulter," Christianity stresses "the moment of grace, although that, too, is contained in Judaism, in God's covenant with men and in the Messianic promise" (145). (Judaism is a national religion while Christianity is a transnational religion.) As Auerbach held, Judaism is *"religion without myth"* and, hence, a vehicle for enlightenment and progress (165, emphasis added). Further, Christianity is a transnational religion, while "pre-Christian Judaism was hardly separable from national life, from collective self-preservation." To define their religious community, the Jews reshaped "the heathen ritual of sacrifice," which "not only took place in worship and in the mind but determined the form of the labor process," making it rational. Here lies the crucial role of taboo[113] in Jewish modes of conduct: "The taboo is transformed into

---

112. An excellent analysis of the last chapter of *Dialectic of Enlightenment*, especially in terms of its apology for, and defense of, Jewish thought and culture, can be found in Rabinbach, "Cunning of Unreason," esp. 184-98. See also, Porter, "Odysseus and the Wandering Jew."

113. Horkheimer and Adorno as well as Cassirer were greatly influenced in their analysis of the taboo by Sigmund Freud's *Totem and Taboo: Resemblances between the Mental Lives of Savages and Neurotics* (1913), in which he applies psychoanalysis to the fields of archaeology, anthropology, and the study of religion.

the rational organization of the work process. It regulates administration in war and peace, sowing and harvesting, food preparation and slaughter. Although the rules may not arise from rational reflection, rationality arises from them" (146). In the context of Jewish modes of thought and action, taboo is the turning point away from magic and myth toward rationality. The Jews "converted taboos into maxims of civilization while the others were still enmeshed in magic" (153).

Cassirer too argued that the Jews broke away from taboos. In "the prophetic books of the Old Testament we find an entirely new direction of thought and feeling" with regard to a "taboo system" that clearly broke away "from all former mythical conceptions" of reality. "Now, to seek for purity or impurity in an object, in a material thing, has become impossible. Even human actions, as such, are no longer regarded as pure and impure. The only purity that has a religious significance and dignity is purity of the heart."[114] Cassirer accordingly linked Judaism to other "higher ethical religions," which inaugurated "a new positive ideal of human freedom" in contrast to the "taboo system" based on "fear" and "passive obedience":

> All the higher ethical religions—the religion of the prophets of Israel, Zoroastrianism, Christianity—set themselves a common task. *They relieve the intolerable burden of the taboo system, but they detect, on the other hand, a more profound sense of religious obligation that instead of being a restriction or compulsion is the expression of a new positive ideal of human freedom.*[115]

For Cassirer, the break with taboo signals a new freedom to think about strictures. For Horkheimer and Adorno, taboo signals a civilizing process in which society triumphs over nature. "The Jews themselves, over the millennia, have played their part in this. . . . The Jews appeared to have successfully achieved what Christianity had attempted in vain: the disempowerment of magic by means of its own strength," and they did it "without relapsing through symbols into mythology." Hence, "they were the first to subdue in themselves the susceptibility to the lure of base instincts, the urge toward the beast and the earth, the worship of images." Nazi Germany brutally attacked the ramifications of this major cultural transformation and civilizing process; since the Jews "invented

---

114. Cassirer, *Essay on Man*, 107.
115. Ibid., 108, emphasis added.

the concept of the kosher, they are persecuted as swine. The anti-Semites appoint themselves executors of the Old Testament: they see to it that the Jews, having eaten of the Tree of Knowledge, unto dust shall return" (153).

These important distinctions should be seen in light of Nazi and fascist culture, which signaled the returned to magic, myth, and worship of images: the goal of "the fascist cult of formulae, the ritualized discipline, the uniforms, and the whole allegedly irrational apparatus, is to make possible mimetic behavior." Their "death's heads and masquerades, the barbaric drumming, the monotonous repetition of words and gestures, are so many organized imitations of magical practice." Here we find "[t]he *Führer*, with his ham-actor's facial expressions and the hysterical charisma turned on with a switch, lead[ing] the dance. In his performance he acts out by proxy and in effigy what is denied to everyone else in reality. Hitler can gesticulate as a clown, Mussolini risk false notes like a provincial tenor, Goebbels talks as glibly as the Jewish agent whose murder he is recommending" (152), but for the Jews in Nazi Germany, no matter their true character, "their image, that of the defeated, has characteristics which must make totalitarian rule their mortal enemy: happiness without power, reward without work, a homeland without frontiers, *religion without myth*" (165–6). The Nazis and fascists hate them because "they secretly covet" these conditions. In contrast to the Nazi culture of hate, paranoia, and bigotry, "[r]econciliation is Judaism's highest concept, and expectation its whole meaning," while the Nazi's "paranoid reaction stems from the incapacity for expectation." In light of their theme—the dialectical intertwinement of enlightenment and power—the authors claim that "[t]he *anti-Semites are realizing their negative absolute through power, by transforming the world into the hell they have always taken it to be*" (165).

The marrow of *Dialectic of Enlightenment* is the contention that the overall humanization process, based on flight from myth, power, and domination, and a turn toward rationalism, is inextricable from the "Jewish Question." The Jewish question and that of anti-Semitism are inextricable from history and as such from the general issue of the dialectic of enlightenment:

> Only the *liberating of thought from power*, the abolition of violence, could realize the idea which has been unrealized until now: *that the Jew is a human being*. This would be a step away from the anti-Semitic society, which drives both Jews and others into sickness, and toward the human one. Such a step would fulfill the fascist lie by contradicting it: *the Jewish*

question would indeed prove the turning point of history. (165, emphasis added)

This contention is the litmus test of history; the rejection of anti-Semitism and racism would signal a major historical and intellectual transformation.

The reform of society is a precondition for any possible solution of the Jewish question; abolishing the quest for power and control inherent in enlightenment will *ipso facto* transform attitudes toward the Jews and lead to a more just society. Horkheimer and Adorno provide an important modification of Marx's dictum—"the emancipation of the Jews is the emancipation of mankind from Judaism"[116]—claiming rather that emancipation from enlightenment's myth of power will emancipate the Jews and everyone else. Marx emphasized "the emancipation of mankind from Judaism," while Horkheimer and Adorno stressed the emancipation of society from power and dominance. Until that glorious time comes, and the Jewish question is solved, the authors are quick to warn that, at present, with World War II raging, the "dialectic of enlightenment is culminating objectively in madness" (169). They conclude: "Enlightenment itself, having mastered itself and assumed its own power, could break through the limits of enlightenment" (172).

Dialectic of Enlightenment ends with an important statement about the centrality of the Jewish question to history. Solving it is a crucial indicator of the transfer from the unjust to the just society. Hannah Arendt gives it similar importance in beginning *The Origins of Totalitarianism* with a long chapter on "Antisemitism": "Only the horror of the final catastrophe made the 'Jewish question' so prominent in our everyday political life." She finds that "the birth and growth of modern anti-Semitism has been accompanied by and interconnected with Jewish assimilation."[117] In her view, anti-Semitism is inseparable from totalitarianism's "absolute evil" and

---

116. See https://en.wikipedia.org/wiki/On_the_Jewish_Question. Marx wrote his 1844 essay, "On the Jewish Question," in reply to Bruno Bauer's book *The Jewish Question* (1843), which argues that Jews can achieve political emancipation only if they relinquish their particular religious consciousness. The required secular state, he assumes, leaves no "space" for social identities, such as religion. Marx contradicted Bauer's view that the nature of the Jewish religion prevented Judaism's assimilation. Instead, he focused on the specific social and economic role of Jews in Europe, which he thought was lost when capitalism, the material basis for Judaism, assimilated European societies as a whole.

117. Arendt, *Origins of Totalitarianism*, 3, 7.

its "attempt at global conquest and total domination."[118] Horkheimer and Adorno end their study of "the dialectical intertwinement of enlightenment and power" with anti-Semitism as a litmus test: when anti-Semitism is eradicated, enlightenment will have finally achieved a truthful insight—no human beings are demons or gods but pawns of power. In both cases, exiled German Jewish intellectuals constructed their answers, not only to the horrors and barbarism of Nazism, but also to their existential human condition as Jews. Only Horkheimer and Adorno offer a solution to the Jewish question as true heirs of Marx.

Epilogue

As the horrors and atrocities of the Holocaust became increasingly clear, two German Jewish exiles living in the United States provided an apology for the Jewish people. If we compare it to other examples in history, then Augustine's *The City of God* comes immediately to mind. It was written as an apology for the Christian faith when the Christians and Christianity were blamed for the Fall of Rome; the last chapter of *Dialectic of Enlightenment* was written during the destruction of European Jewry, and its authors strove, exactly like the Doctor of Grace, to provide explanations to vicissitudes of time and history. Augustine wrote *The City of God* to explain Alaric's conquest of Rome in terms of the premises of sacred, ecclesiastical history,[119] comforting his fellow Christians in Carthage: "Citizens of Jerusalem . . . you do not belong here [earth], you belong somewhere else."[120] Their existential state in the world is that of "resident strangers" or "resident aliens."[121] In contrast, Horkheimer and Adorno see the Jews' portion and destiny as integral to the long history of "the dialectical intertwinement of enlightenment and power." Augustine pointed to heaven as the true place for Christians; Horkheimer and Adorno define the conditions for remediating Jewish alienation on earth.

Ultimately, the various explanations of the Doctor of Grace and the great champions of Critical Theory were not aimed to supply a simple

---

118. Ibid., viii.

119. On the nature and meaning of sacred, ecclesiastical history as a unique mode of historical thought and Augustine's singular contribution to it, see Zakai and Mali, "Time, History and Eschatology."

120. Brown, "Saint Augustine," 11.

121. Brown, *Augustine of Hippo*, 313–14.

remedy to current disasters but rather to explain the terrible historical situation Christianity faced in the fifth century and European Jews faced in the twentieth century within a well-defined, coherent philosophy of history, either sacred, ecclesiastical history or Marxist dialectical materialism. The success of these two works clearly shows that these authors' unique historical and philosophical explanations deeply touched the imagination of their readers.

Conclusion

Exile, Trauma, and Interpretation

> Nobody who lived in Germany in the twenties and early thirties could escape politics.
>
> —Felix Gilbert, *A European Past: Memoirs 1905–1945*, 1998

> This time [in exile] . . . in this work of my old age . . . I knew what I was setting out to do and what task I was imposing upon myself: to write nothing less than the novel [*Doctor Faustus*] of my era, disguised as the story of an artist's life.
>
> —Thomas Mann, *Story of a Novel: The Genesis of Doctor Faustus*, 1949

At thirteen, the Austrian Jewish economic and social historian Sidney Pollard (1925–1998) witnessed the 1938 Austrian *Anschluss*.[1] His family was forced to leave a spacious apartment in Vienna and move "to a one-room flat in the ghetto of Leopoldstadt." His father lost his income, and on his way to school, Pollard "saw the horror of the notorious 'scrubbing,' as well-dressed, middle-age [Jewish] people were on their knees in the street, forced to clear the pavements, with toothbrushes and other unsuitable gear, of the painted election slogans, surrounded by jeering crowds."[2]

---

1. For a description of the occupation and annexation of Austria into Nazi Germany and the tragic fate of its Jews, see Edmund de Wall, *The Hare with the Amber Eyes: A Family's Century of Art and Loss* (New York: Farrar, Straus and Giroux, 2010), chaps. 24–26; and Anne-Marie O'Connor, *The Lady in Gold: The Extraordinary Tale of Gustav Klimt's Masterpiece, Portrait of Adele Bloch-Bauer* (New York: Knopf, 2012).

2. Sidney Pollard, "In Search of a Social Purpose," in *Out of the Third Reich: Refugee Historians in Post-War Britain*, ed. Peter Alter (London: I. B. Tauris, 1998), 197.

Later that year, Pollard was sent to England in a *Kindertransport*[3] and, when age permitted, volunteered for army service: "Unlike my British fellow soldiers who were conscripted to fight a conventional war against an enemy state, at least in the early stage, for me *it was to fight pure brutal barbarous evil which had wrecked my life and threatened to destroy civilization as I know it*."[4] Likewise, the famous French Jewish historian Marc Bloch (1886-1944), cofounder of the highly influential Annales School of French social history, joined the French Resistance in 1942 in "a world assailed by the most appalling barbarism"[5] and died fighting in 1944. Modes of thought and modes of action, modes of conviction and modes of conduct were closely intertwined in Pollard and Bloch's lives. As Pollard remembered: "We were highly politicized—not perhaps surprisingly since politics had wrenched our lives out of their course—and tended to be contemptuous of the philistines who did not think politics the most important thing in their lives."[6]

German nationalism, Nazism, and fascism "wrenched" the lives of the five exiled intellectuals I have discussed in this book—Thomas Mann, Ernst Cassirer, Erich Auerbach, Max Horkheimer, and Theodor Adorno—"out of their course." In response, they marshalled history, philosophy, politics, and literature in the fight against those who stood against the best of European civilization.

The authors discussed here did not join the British army or the French Resistance movement to fight Nazi barbarism. They rejected Stefan Zweig's radical rejection or surrender by suicide and took up their pens to fight the Nazi sword. As Adorno wrote: "*the only home truly available*" to exiles, "*though fragile and vulnerable, is in writing.*"[7] Out of their various sad ordeals and exilic agonies, they constructed Western humanist civilization's retort, wielding its supple language and vast erudition against Nazism and fascism's slobbering threats. They all began their works in 1942, the year of Stalingrad, and shared "a general conviction that *Stalingrad* signifies a

---

3. On this sad experience, see W. G. Sebald, *Austerlitz* (London: Hamish Hamilton, 2001), and *The Emigrants* (London: Harvill, 1996). On life in Nazi Germany during the 1930s, see Irmgard Keun, *Nect Mitternach (After Midnight)*, 1937 (London: Melville House, 2011).

4. Pollard, "In Search of a Social Purpose," 197, 200, emphasis added.

5. Marc Bloch, *Strange Defeat: A Statement of Evidence Written in 1940* (New York: Octagon, 1969 [1949]), 177-78.

6. Pollard, "In Search of a Social Purpose," 198.

7. Adorno quoted in Said, *Reflections on Exile*, 184, emphasis added.

turning-point in the war."[8] Taken as a whole, their works constituted an important chapter in modern intellectual history.

The underlying premise behind this study is that an extraordinary historical crisis led to the creation of a unique and important body of work. Thomas Mann's *Doctor Faustus* (1947), Ernst Cassirer's *The Myth of the State* (1946), Erich Auerbach's *Mimesis* (1946), and Max Horkheimer and Theodor W. Adorno's *Dialectic of Enlightenment* (1944) testify to the flame that intellectuals who fled Nazi Germany carried into exile to keep humanism, dignity, and liberty alive amid darkness and death. They had nothing but their nimble and educated minds, their deep memories, and their sharp pens to fight against the evils of their time.

Their struggle was not unique in the annals of Western history. Augustine's *The City of God* and Dante's *Divine Comedy* bear the scars of their authors' sad, devastating historical experience. In the same vein, the four works analyzed here were not written by Ivory Tower scholars, disconnected from the practical concerns of everyday life. To the contrary, their works were first and foremost polemic, a highly politicized *Kulturkampf* against Nazism and fascism. They cannot be separated from the dark age in which they were written; they are inseparable from their authors' endangered existential condition and the death of the world as they knew it. Mann's novel is a grand politicization of literature, using a cultural archetype to figure the evils of Nazi barbarism in his continuous struggle to wake his people up. Cassirer politicized the whole history of Western thought, tracing what he had once seen as the decline of myth before reason through its resurgence. Auerbach's is an awe-inspiring politicization of philology, using the whole course of Western literature to emphasize the rise and predominance of the rational representation of reality against mythology and the obfuscations of elite privilege. Horkheimer and Adorno politicized sociology and philosophy, showing that the tendency to subordinate the truth to power did not start with fascism but with the Enlightenment and capitalist, bourgeois society. To fully understand these works, we must unveil the goal each author set for himself in writing, while explaining the authors' common space of experience and horizon of expectations. I analyzed these four works together because it is the best way to fully comprehend the shared agonies and horror of their time—more specifically, the crisis/turning point of 1942—and their common reaction. All rejected the chauvinist, racist, anti-Semitic premises of *völkisch* mysticism and Nazi historiography, which sought to eliminate the

---

8. Evans, *Third Reich at War*, 421, emphasis original.

Hebrew Bible, or Old Testament, from German *Kultur* and *Volksgeist* in particular and Western humanist culture and *civilization* in general and then to eliminate the Jews, which would include these writers and those dear to them. From this perspective, their works reanimated the history of ideas and their lives refuted all imputations of inferiority. I have written elsewhere about one of them (*Erich Auerbach and the Crisis of German Philology*, 2016) and several of them in other contexts (David Weinstein and Avihu Zakai, *Jewish Exiles and European Thought in the Shadow of the Third Reich: Baron, Popper, Strauss, Auerbach*, 2017), but my intent here was to reflect the wide variety of their attacks and to capture their common spirit. Only by examining their shared experience can we understand the unique form and content of their works. The mission these exiled intellectuals took upon themselves in the crucial year of 1942 was nothing less than the rescue of Western humanist civilization.

Traditionally, scholars have treated these four books by German-speaking exiles as models of academic endeavor in their particular disciplines. However, each testifies, often directly, to the author's experience and his "rage against the dying of the light."[9] The comparative approach provides an overarching view of these important testimonies in modern intellectual history. All these works were based on shared traumatic experiences in Nazi Germany prior to emigration, a common traumatic exilic displacement after emigration, and finally, common *Kulturkampf* against Nazi barbarism. The testimonies of many are more reliable and more powerful than the limited witness of one. Hence, despite their differences in terms of disciplines, genres, themes, and approaches, these writers all followed Sir William Blackstone, the English jurist and judge, who wrote in his *Commentaries on the Laws of England* (1765–1769), "*Scribere est agere*" (to write is to act).

Viewing the works discussed here as testimonies, we must note that their authors rarely spoke about their hard life in Nazi Germany before emigration or, later, about the hardship of their life in exile: "With very few exceptions, memoirs, including those of scholars who eventually arrived in America, keep strangely silent about any incident of harassment suffered before an escape was managed, and identifying the specific events that crystallized a refugee's decision to leave Germany often is next to

---

9. Dylan Thomas, "Do Not Go Gentle Into That Good Night," *The Poems of Dylan Thomas* (New York: New Directions, 1952).

impossible."[10] Their writings and letters offer only scattered glimpses of their ordeals before and after exile. Historian and fellow exile from Nazi Germany Hans Baron wrote dryly of his "agitated" life marked by "war, exile, migration, and repeated changes of the language."[11] This troubled life provided him—and the other exiles—a tremendous sense of mission as revealed in his masterpiece, also begun in 1942, *The Crisis of the Early Italian Renaissance: Civic Humanism and Republican Liberty in an Age of Classicism and Tyranny* (1955).[12] In this celebrated book, he raised the torch of humanism, republicanism, liberty, and freedom against Nazi totalitarianism and flatly denied the claim by German nationalist and chauvinist historians that "[h]umanism north of the Alps, and in particular in Germany, developed from a native, late medieval background essentially independent of any—at least any salutary—influence from the south," namely, Italy.[13] In 1972, he conceded, "I began to interpret some basic aspects of the early-Renaissance conflicts on the eve of the nascent Quattrocento state-system *in this light,*" when, "between 1935 and 1955 the 'sfide' [challenges] of varying 'totalitarianisms' to the older European traditions largely determined the political and intellectual climate."[14]

Baron provided a vivid picture of persecution, migration, and exile: "Who could have thought that one's own national comrades (*Volksgenossen*), with which one thought oneself united for life, could take away future, and people (*Volk*), and fatherland, and all that was considered sacred. This experience is now reserved to us, Jews." He lamented that he and other German Jews like him had considered themselves "not Zionists at all, but

---

10. Michael H. Kater, "Refugee Historians in America: Preemigration Germany to 1939," in *An Interrupted Past: German-Speaking Refugee Historians in the United States after 1933*, ed. Hartmut Lehmann and James J. Sheehan (Cambridge: Cambridge University Press, 1991), 77.

11. "The Course of My Studies in Florentine Humanism," *In Search of Florentine Civic Humanism: Essays on the Transition from Medieval to Modern Thought*, 2 vols. (Princeton: Princeton University Press, 1988), 1:182.

12. Hans Baron, *The Crisis of the Early Italian Renaissance* (Princeton: Princeton University Press, 1966). On Baron's life and work, see Weinstein and Zakai, *Jewish Exiles and European Thought*.

13. Baron, "Course of My Studies," 183.

14. Baron to Renzo Pecchioli, June 12, 1971, cited in Kay Schiller, "Hans Baron's Humanism," *Storia della storiografia* 34 (1998): 85.

rather real Germans." Now pondering the prospect of exile for the first time following the Nazi Revolution of 1933, he grieved that life in Germany "under the Swastika flag"[15] and dominated by racism and anti-Semitism "was enough to make him want to withdraw from the world."[16] At a "time when so many gods have proved to be empty," Baron bemoaned in July 1933, he finally realized that we have to "fight our way abroad," namely, to go into exile, as he did in 1935.[17] In September, he continued, "It hurts so much to leave home with so many memories of human inadequacies."[18] Compare Walter Benjamin's words: "In 1932, when I was abroad, it began to be clear to me that I would soon have to bid a long, perhaps lasting farewell to the city of my birth," Berlin.[19] Auerbach wrote to Benjamin in 1937 about "the horrifying inauthenticity of 'Bluebopropaganda,'" eliding *Blut und Boden*, blood and soil, the Nazi criteria for defining "Germanness."[20]

Again, we have only glimpses of the devastated and threatening situation in which some of these exiles found themselves with the triumph of the Wehrmacht in the early 1940s. Ernst Cassirer's wife Toni described the context and conditions in Sweden, where he wrote "the fourth volume of *The Problem of Knowledge* (*Philosophy, Science, and History since Hegel*, 1950)"[21] prior to their emigration to the United States in 1941. She said, "unbelievable as it may seem the whole book was composed between July 9th and November 26th 1940." The reason for such urgency? "Belgium, France, and Holland were overrun, Norway and Denmark were occupied, and *we never knew whether Hitler would appear the next day in Sweden.*"[22]

---

15. Baron to Walter Goetz, March 23, 1933, cited in Anthony Molho, "Hans Baron's Crisis," in *Florence and Beyond: Culture, Society and Politics in Renaissance Italy*, ed. David S. Peterson and Daniel E. Bornstein (Toronto: Center for Reformation and Renaissance Studies, 2008), 78.

16. Molho, "Hans Baron's Crisis," 78.

17. Baron to Goetz, July 11, 1933, cited in Molho, "Hans Baron's Crisis," 79.

18. Baron to Goetz, September 26, 1933, cited in ibid.

19. Walter Benjamin, *Berlin Childhood around 1900* (Cambridge: Harvard University Press, 2006), viii.

20. Auerbach to Benjamin, January 3, 1937, in Elsky, Vialon, and Stein, "Scholarship," 751.

21. Lofts and Calcagno, "Translators' Introduction," xvi.

22. Toni Cassirer, quoted in Charles Hendel, "Preface," in Ernst Cassirer, *The Problem of Knowledge: Philosophy, Science, and History since Hegel*, trans. William H. Woglom and Charles W. Hendel (New Haven: Yale University Press, 1950), ix, emphasis added.

Likewise, Auerbach began writing *Mimesis* in May 1942 in Istanbul. To what extent was he aware of the Wehrmacht's critical threats in Russia at the Battle of Stalingrad and North Africa in the Battle of El Alamein? In a letter written in summer 1946, he describes in his aloof, reserved way some of the deep fears and anxieties he was suffering in 1942: "Things have gone well for us *against all odds*. The *new order* [Nazi German army] *did not reach these straits; that really says it all*. We have lived in our apartment and *suffered* nothing but small discomfort and fear: *until the end of [19]42 it looked very bad*, but then the clouds gradually withdrew."[23]

These authors in exile took up their pens in 1942 to hold up a mirror to the Nazis' dark, barbaric face. Exile pushed them and allowed them to defend European humanist civilization against fascist barbarism in no uncertain terms. Apart from Mann, all of them were German-speaking Jewish *Bildungsbürgertum* and therefore dedicated to keeping alive the humanist ideals of *Bildung*, Renaissance humanism, and Enlightenment. German nationalism, Nazism, and fascism ruined—sought to extinguish—their lives and surely extinguished the lives of people they cherished. Given that Nazism "had wrenched" their lives "out of their course," they variously marshalled history, politics, and literature to combat those who stood against the moral values of European civilization: "The humanist ideals of *Bildung* and the Enlightenment lived on, even under the Nazis," wrote the German-born American historian George L. Mosse:

> Among liberals and left-wing intellectuals, the flame was kept alive from exile; whether it continued to burn inside Germany is more difficult to determine. But it was the German Jewish *Bildungsbürgertum* [middle-class cultured intellectuals] which, more than any other single group, preserved Germany's better self across dictatorship, war, holocaust, and defeat.[24]

The works of the five exiled intellectuals analyzed here give clear proof and vivid testimony of this assertion.

The German Jewish exiled historian Fritz Stern likewise claimed that German Jewish intellectuals preserved the best of German culture from exile: when "Germany turned into a monstrous tyranny, we became the *guardians of German history*; from 1933 to 1945, German history was

---

23. Auerbach to Dr. Martin Hellweg, June 22, 1946, in Elsky, Vialon, and Stern, "Scholarship," 757, emphasis added.

24. Mosse, *German Jews beyond Judaism*, 82.

being written here [USA] and in England or not at all."[25] Arthur Rosenberg (1889–1943), another German Jewish exiled historian, similarly observed: "Someday it will be seen that there was no active and critical historical research [in Germany] after 1933, that it indeed could not have existed, and that therefore *the critical historical scholarship of Germany had survived solely in emigration*."[26] This sense of great historical mission wove trauma, exile, and interpretation inextricably together.

Exile is a traumatic experience. Life in exile entailed tremendous hardship. As the political theorist Judith N. Shklar wrote: "It is not easy to generalize about exiles, nor do they lend themselves to abstraction. Yet exile is a common experience and so searing that it should invite reflection. No experience is more fundamental, and not one has been used metaphorically more seriously."[27] Adorno wrote that "every intellectual in emigration, without exception, is damaged" (*Jeder Intellektuelle in der Emigration, ohne alle Ausnahme, ist beschädigt*).[28] Another exile from Nazi Germany, the philosopher Karl Löwith (1897–1973), explained: "Even those who can find a new homeland and obtain citizenship rights in another country will take a large part of their life to heal this breach, and indeed, even more so if they took their Germanness for granted and perceived themselves as German before Hitler."[29] Thomas Mann, who lived in California during the war, wrote to Adorno about his agonizing exilic experience: for exiles, "homeland . . . has become foreign," and "here in the foreign land that has become home we cannot help feeling we are in the wrong place, something which robs our own existence of a certain moral authority."[30] The trauma of persecution and exilic displacement raised the urge to provide meaning and significance to this ordeal.

---

25. Fritz Stern, "German History in America, 1884–1984," *Central European History* 19 (June 1986): 132, emphasis added.

26. Arthur Rosenberg, cited in Winfried Schulze, "German Historiography from 1930s to the 1950s," in *Paths of Continuity: Central European Historiography from the 1930s to the 1950s*, ed. Hartmut Lehmann and James Van Horn Melton (Cambridge: Cambridge University Press, 2003), 29, emphasis added.

27. Judith N. Shklar, *Political Thought and Political Thinkers*, ed. Stanley Hoffmann (Chicago: Chicago University Press, 1998), 57.

28. Theodor W. Adorno, *Minima Moralia: Reflexionen aus dem beschädigten Leben* (Frankfurt am Main: Suhrkamp, 2007), 32.

29. Karl Löwith, *My Life in Germany Before and After 1933: A Report* (Urbana: University of Illinois Press, 1994), 144.

30. Mann to Adorno, January 9, 1950, in Adorno and Mann, *Correspondence, 1943–1955*, 41.

"Modern Western culture is in large part the work of exiles, émigrés, refugees," Edward Said wrote.[31] According to Said, who knew firsthand, exile is above all "life led outside habitual order"; it "is like death but without death's ultimate mercy, it has torn millions of people from the nourishment of tradition, family, and geography."[32] Hence, "exile's predicament" is "as close as we come in the modern era to tragedy."[33] At Yale University during the 1950s, Auerbach told Geoffrey Hartman a sad "anecdote of a concert violinist, a refugee like himself, who complained that in America his violin emitted a different tone."[34] Indeed, many exiles lived "a life in translation." Exiles crossed "from one meaning of *Übersetzung* [translation] to the other, from one *Übersetzung* to another *Übersetzung*."[35] In the words of George Steiner, it "seems proper that those who create art in a civilization of quasi-barbarism, which has made so many homeless, should themselves be poets unhoused and wanderers across language."[36]

The lives of the five intellectual exiles I deal with turned upside down with the Nazi Revolution, forcing them to flee. They all could have written what Löwith wrote about the new German barbarism: "The German solution to the Jewish question is in principle only the most overt aspect of barbarity, which sanctions every brutality in the service of a monstrous state." Löwith believed pessimistically that having been "confronted with this dehumanization of the human being, mere humanism [was] incapable of raising even one effective protest,"[37] yet many thought otherwise; they dedicated their lives in exile to exploring the causes of the trauma that not only ruined their lives but was eroding Western humanist civilization as a whole. By doing so, they waged *Kulturkampf* and eventually won the day.

---

31. Said, *Reflections on Exile*, 173.

32. Ibid., 186.

33. Ibid., 174, 183.

34. Hartman, *Scholar's Tale*, 169.

35. Seyhan, "German Academic Exiles in Istanbul," 286.

36. Quoted in Said, *Reflections on Exile*, 174.

37. Löwith, *My Life*, 147. Deep pessimism ruled Löwith's thought: "The problem of history as a whole is unanswerable within its own perspective. Historical processes as such do not bear the least evidence of a comprehensive and ultimate meaning. History as such has no outcome. There never has been and never will be an immanent solution to the problem of history, for man's historical experience is one of steady failure. . . . *The world is still as it was in the time of Alaric; only our means of opposing and destruction (as well as of reconstruction) are considerably improved and are adorned with hypocrisy*" (*Meaning in History*, 191, emphasis added).

I use a contextualized approach rather than textualism to illuminate the authors' common space of experience and horizon of expectations. Hans Baron defined this approach: "Unless we know exactly when, where and under what conditions a work was written . . . we cannot judge the author's intention" or "the relationship of his work to the actual life of his time."[38] Georg Lukács, the Hungarian Marxist philosopher, aesthetician, literary historian, and critic, emphasized the contextualized approach over pure textualism, when he wrote that it "would be possible to consider his study" *The Theory of the Novel* (1920) "simply in itself," but, "I believe that in looking back over the history of almost five decades [since its first publication] *it is worthwhile to describe the mode in which the work was written because this will facilitate a proper understanding of it.*"[39] The historical context is essential to any understanding of the content and form of the works analyzed here.

Text and context are inextricable, never more so than in works begun in the year 1942, the year of Stalingrad, the nadir of European humanist civilization. Horrifying events demand radical questions and answers. Mann found it imperative to revive a horrifying old German tale to reveal the "secret union of the German spirit with the Demonic."[40] Cassirer examined "radical change in the form of political thought" in his times, "the appearance of a new power: the power of mythical thought."[41] Auerbach revealed the source of the rational representation of reality and human dignity in Western literature against Aryan racist philology and Nazi historiography, which claimed that the "Old Testament as a book of religious instruction must be abolished once and for all" in an effort to "end the unsuccessful attempts of the last one-and-a-half millennia to make us all spiritual Jews."[42] Horkheimer and Adorno's goal was to reveal why humanity was sinking into "a new kind of barbarism" and to demonstrate a cultural progress turned "into its opposite."[43] Engulfed in the

---

38. Baron, *From Petrarch to Leonardo Bruni*, 2.

39. Lukács, *Theory of the Novel*, 12, emphasis added. The quote is taken from the preface of 1962.

40. Mann, "Germany and the Germans," May 29, 1945, in *Thomas Mann's Addresses*, 51.

41. Cassirer, *Myth of the State*, 3.

42. Rosenberg, *Myth of the Twentieth Century* (1930), quoted in Head, "Nazi Quest," 69.

43. Horkheimer and Adorno, *Dialectic of Enlightenment*, xiv, xiii.

vacillations of time and history, the writers discussed here were trying to cope with the tragedy by providing countermyths, accounts, explanations, rationalizations. Given the crucial importance of the mythical turn in Nazi Germany, they all deal with myth in their works. Mann provided a unique rendering of modern German history in the mythical figure of Faustus. Cassirer provided a singular history of political thought from the decline of myth in Greek philosophy to its rise and eventual triumph in Nazism and fascism. Auerbach struggled against the Aryan appropriation of Greek myth and emphasized rather rational, realistic representation stemming from the Old Testament. Horkheimer and Adorno strove to show that Enlightenment was based on a myth of domination, observing, "Myth is already enlightenment, and enlightenment reverts to mythology."[44]

The contextual approach also determines the structure of my book. In the first chapter and the last, I explore the darkest works begun in 1942 to illuminate the despair of that time. They reflect the deepest pessimism as well as sheer determinism; *Doctor Faustus* rests on the predetermined frame of an old German tale that snakes through the national literature, moving from a covenant with Satan to a predestined destruction and annihilation, which is seen as the cornerstone of modern German history from the Protestant Reformation to Nazi barbarism; *Dialectic of Enlightenment* revives Hobbes's dark vision of human society as "a war of all against all" and "Spinoza's proposition: 'the endeavor of preserving oneself is the first and only basis of virtue,' " which "contains the true maxim of all Western civilization" as cornerstones of the modern culture industry.[45] In both works, human life is controlled and directed by inhuman, impersonal laws: Satan's apocalypse and eschatology for Mann and the view that the material conditions of modes of production determine society's organization and development for Horkheimer and Adorno. I begin with the horrifying German tale and conclude with a frightening picture of modern capitalist life.

In contrast, Cassirer and Auerbach provide a more traditional humanist, enlightened description of the history of Western politics and literature, respectively, despite their deep pessimism about the decline and fall of Western humanist civilization. Both begin with the triumph of reason over myth in Greek philosophy and the Old Testament, respectively, yet both followed Oswald Spengler's vision of the "Decline of the West" in political philosophy and literature, respectively. I placed them in the middle of my book because they both portray history as the progress of

---

44. Ibid., xviii.
45. Ibid., 22.

humanism until blindsided by its decline in the early twentieth century, which witnessed the rise of the myth of the state and the dissolution of realism into subjectivism. Both defend the humanist values of Western civilization, despite the Nazi avalanche and while acknowledging their decline and fall in the early twentieth century.

The merit of this structure is that it exposes the persistent, deep trauma caused by Nazi barbarism and forced exile. As they strove to construct plausible, sometimes idiosyncratic, interpretations in their own disciplines of what caused the decline of Western civilization, these five exiles were forced to question their worldviews, their scholarship, their careers. They were all critics and could criticize themselves with ruthless acuity. Their deep pessimism looks sharply down at modern history as an abyss. Another intellectual exile, Erich Neumann (1905–1960), a German Jewish psychologist, philosopher, and student of Carl Jung, expressed a similar view in his book *Depth Psychology and a New Ethic* (1963):

> The modern world has witnessed a dramatic breakthrough of the dark, negative forces of human nature. The 'old ethic,' which pursued an illusory perfection by repressing the dark side, has lost its power to deal with contemporary problems. Neumann was convinced that the deadliest peril now confronting humanity lay in the 'scapegoat' psychology associated with the old ethic. We are in the grip of this psychology when we project our own dark shadow onto an individual or group identified as our 'enemy,' failing to see it in ourselves. The only effective alternative to this dangerous shadow projection is shadow recognition, acknowledgement, and integration into the totality of the self. Wholeness, not perfection, is the goal of the new ethic.[46]

The works written in 1942 offer small solace for the vicissitudes of history's grief and agony; did their authors feel psychologically impelled to set the record straight by arguing down the specious, debased logic of Nazism and fascism? Their portion was that of *Paradise Lost*; like John Milton, they wrote about the paths that led to the decline and fall of their beloved humanist Western civilization. Unlike Milton, none of them dared to write or perhaps to conceive of a *Paradise Regained*. In an Old Testament simile,

---

46. Erich Neumann, *Depth Psychology and a New Ethic* (London: Hodder & Stoughton, 1969), book's cover.

they struggled like Jacob with the Angel of History and would not let him go until he blessed them.

Mann's novel and Horkheimer and Adorno's study clearly differ from the other works for another important reason. Their desperate darkness deterred people from reading them. Many colleagues and friends told me they had never read *Doctor Faustus* or *Dialectic of Enlightenment*, especially the latter, which I find it the most painful of those I study. The contextualized approach may help to unveil the trauma scarring these works and elevate the authors' problematical choices in structure, discourse, and viewpoint for clearer analysis. Are they writing in a secret language for initiates only? Were their own language and culture so compromised that they had to parody or reformulate them? Deeply scarred by the unprecedented political trauma of their times, these writers revisited an older form, the apologia, to defend and justify a Western humanist civilization that would outlast the Nazi "Thousand-Year Reich." The French economist and futurist Bertrand de Jouvenel (1903–1987) wrote: "There is tyranny in the womb of every utopia"; for Horkheimer and Adorno, in the Enlightenment as much as in the Nazi dystopia.[47]

Mann's protagonist, the composer Adrian Leverkühn, dies on August 25, 1940, but "[i]n those days Germany, a hectic flush on its cheeks, was reeling at the height of its savage triumphs, about to win the world on the strength of the pact that it was intended to keep and signed with its blood."[48] Thus ends *Doctor Faustus* with a grand politicization of literature. Likewise, Horkheimer and Adorno concluded their study with the contention: "Only the *liberating of thought from power*, the abolition of violence, could realize the idea which has been unrealized until now: *that the Jew is a human being*." This step will show, they believed, that "*the Jewish question would indeed prove the turning point of history*."[49]

Context is crucial to the understanding of any text. It explains why all the writers I deal with politicized their respective disciplines. Löwith wrote that he was "apolitical before 1933, and had lived accordingly," yet "under the spell of National Socialist terror," he felt "forced to preserve a tradition" that overtly opposed German "barbarism."[50] Especially for many

---

47. See Akash Kapur, "Couldn't Be Better: The Return of the Utopians," *The New Yorker*, October 3, 2016, 66.

48. Mann, *Doctor Faustus*, 534.

49. Horkheimer and Adorno, *Dialectic of Enlightenment*, 165.

50. Löwith quoted in Reinhart Koselleck, "Foreword," in Löwith, *My Life in Germany*, xiii.

German-speaking Jewish intellectuals driven into exile, "the textual space of past ages was not only an object of scholarly inquiry but also source of consolation for the drama of the present."[51] This observation applies to the writers and works I deal with.

Finally, despite their dire pessimism, the books analyzed here aimed at salvation. Cassirer and Auerbach implied that only freedom from myth enables rational politics, realism, and serious representation of, and respect for, ordinary human life. By raising Western humanist values as a mirror to show the ugliness of Nazi barbarism, they provided a model to be emulated. Mann and Horkheimer and Adorno went so far as to offer the possibility of future salvation, but only by radically reexamining a past model that caused the present calamity. At the end of *Doctor Faustus*, after Adrian has gone mad, his mother comes to see him: "She came . . . her white hair pulled back tight, determined to fetch her lost child back to his childhood. At their first meeting, Adrian lay trembling for a long while on the breasts of this woman."[52] The image brings to mind Michelangelo's *Pietà*. The devil's curse, that Leverkühn be permitted no love, proves wrong. The dialectic of the *Dialectic of Enlightenment* makes room for hope and possible salvation at the end, albeit in a very strange, dialectic way. The authors claim, "Enlightenment itself, having mastered itself and assumed its own power, could break through the limits of enlightenment"[53] and, further, emancipate the Jews and, hence, everyone else.

The authors of the four works discussed here lived through an age of extremes and horrifying, absolute sinfulness; their interpretations in their respective disciplines bear the tragic mark. If they politicized history, reading and interpreting their chosen subject through a lens darkened by their experiences, they were not alone. "Nobody who lived in Germany in the twenties and early thirties could escape politics"[54] because "life at that time" was "very much politicized,"[55] wrote the German-born American historian Felix Gilbert (1905–1991). The writers and works I analyze in this study

---

51. Schiller, "Paul Oskar Kristeller," 126.

52. Mann, *Doctor Faustus*, 532.

53. Horkheimer and Adorno, *Dialectic of Enlightenment*, 172.

54. Felix Gilbert, *A European Past: Memoirs 1905–1945* (New York: Norton, 1998), 77.

55. Gilbert, "The Historical Seminar of the University of Berlin in the Twenties," in *An Interrupted Past: German-Speaking Refugee Historians in the United States after 1933*, ed. Hartmut Lehmann and James J. Sheehan (Cambridge: Cambridge University Press, 1991), 69.

are clear proof. Memories of persecution, exile, and the horrors of war and barbarism prevented most of them from returning to Germany after the war; only Horkheimer and Adorno returned, perhaps understandable from their obtuse observations of US culture. Even Thomas Mann preferred to resettle in Switzerland. Cassirer and Auerbach moved to the United States and died there. "The Age of Catastrophe" left its indelible mark on their lives as it did on Hannah Arendt, Leo Strauss, and Hans Baron, to name only a few who chose to stay in America. The books they started in 1942 have resonated since in modern intellectual history, no small feat for those who survived the Nazi avalanche. Having witnessed "the gruesome spectacle of a world bursting asunder,"[56] they could not remain passive spectators. They burned to explain what went wrong, not only with their personal lives or their beloved Germany, but with the foundations, values, and visions of Western humanist civilization as a whole.

Eventually, the works I deal with, which struggled against Nazism by exposing its inherent barbarism and antihumanism, profoundly changed the content and form of modern intellectual history; Mann transformed the field of German literature by exposing the "secret union of the German spirit with the Demonic"; Cassirer's work revealed the important power of the myth in shaping the menace of Nazi antihumanist political and social thought; Auerbach's study crucially influenced the fields of literary history, literary criticism, and comparative literature; finally, the work of Horkheimer and Adorno is undoubtedly the most influential publication of the Frankfurt School of Critical Theory and profoundly inspired the New Left of the 1960s and 1970s.

---

56. Klaus Mann, *Turning Point*, 356–57.

Bibliography

Abromeit, John. *Max Horkheimer and the Foundations of the Frankfurt School*. New York: Cambridge University Press, 2011.
Adorno, Theodor W. *Letters to His Parents: 1939–1951*. Cambridge: Polity, 2006.
———. *Negative Dialectics*. New York: Seabury Press, 1973.
———. *Minima Moralia: Reflexionen aus dem beschädigten Leben*. Frankfurt am Main: Suhrkamp, 2007.
———. *The Stars Down to Earth*. Ed. Stephen Crook. London: Routledge, 1994.
Adorno, Theodor W., and Walter Benjamin. *Theodor W. Adorno and Walter Benjamin: The Complete Correspondence, 1928–1940*. Ed. Henri Lonitz, trans. N. Walker. Cambridge: Harvard University Press, 1999.
Adorno, Theodor W., and Thomas Mann, *Theodor Adorno and Thomas Mann: Correspondence, 1943–1955*. Ed. C. Gödde and T. Sprecher. Cambridge: Polity, 2006.
Alter, Peter, ed. *Out of the Third Reich: Refugee Historians in Post-War Britain*. London: I. B. Tauris, 1998.
Altmann, Alexander, ed. *Between East and West: Essays Dedicated to the Memory of Bela Horovitz*. London: East West Library, 1958.
American Jewish Committee. *The Jews in Nazi Germany: A Handbook of Facts Regarding Their Present Situation*. New York: American Jewish Committee, 1935.
Améry, Jean. *At the Mind's Limits: Contemplations by a Survivor on Auschwitz and Its Realities*, 1966. Trans. S. Rosenfeld and S. P. Rosenfeld. Bloomington: Indiana University Press, 1980.
———. "On the Necessity and Impossibility of Being a Jew," 1966. In *At the Mind's Limits: Contemplations by a Survivor on Auschwitz and Its Realities*, 85–89.
Angress-Klüger, Ruth. "Jewish Characters in Thomas Mann's Fiction." In *Horizonte: Festschrift für Herbert Lehner zum 65. Geburstag*, ed. H. Mundt et al., 161–72. Tübingen: Niemeyer, 1990.
Ankersmit, Frank R. *History and Tropology: The Rise and the Fall of Metaphor*. Berkeley: University of California Press, 1994.

———. "Why Realism? Auerbach on the Representation of Reality." *Poetics Today* 20 (Spring 1999): 53–75.

Apter, Emily. "Comparative Exile: Competing Margins in the History of Comparative Literature." In *Comparative Literature in the Age of Multiculturalism*, ed. Charles Bernheimer, 86–96. Baltimore: Johns Hopkins University Press, 1995.

———. *The Translation Zone: A New Comparative Literature*. Princeton: Princeton University Press, 2006.

Arendt, Hannah. *Men in Dark Times*. New York: Harcourt, Brace & World, 1955.

———. *The Origins of Totalitarianism*. New York: A Harvest Book, 1976 [1951].

———. *The Portable Hannah Arendt*, ed. Peter Baehr. New York: Penguin, 2000.

———. "A Reply to Eric Voegelin," 1953. In Arendt, *The Portable Hannah Arendt*, 157–66.

Aristotle. *Aristotle: Poetics I*. Trans. Richard Janko. Indianapolis: Hackett, 1987.

———. *Aristotle's Theory of Poetry and the Fine Arts with a Critical Text and Translation of the Poetics*. Trans. Samuel H. Butcher. New York: Dover, 1951.

Arvidsson, Stefan. *Aryan Idols: Indo-European Mythology as Ideology and Science*. Chicago: University of Chicago Press, 2006 [2000].

Aschheim, Steven. *Culture and Catastrophe: German and Jewish Confrontations with National Socialism and Other Crises*. New York: New York University Press, 1996.

———. "German Jews Beyond *Bildung* and Liberalism: The Jewish Revival in the Weimar Republic." In Aschheim, *Culture and Catastrophe*, 31–44.

Atkinson, James B., and David Sices, eds. *Machiavelli and His Friends: Their Personal Correspondence*. DeKalb: Northern Illinois University Press, 1996.

Atkinson, Rick. *An Army at Dawn: The War in North Africa, 1942–1943*. New York: Henry Holt, 2002.

Auerbach, Erich. "Auerbach to Buber." January 12, 1957. National Library of Israel, Martin Buber Archive, ARH Ms. 350.

———. "Bibliography of the Writings of Erich Auerbach." In *Literary Language and the Challenge of Philology: The Legacy of Erich Auerbach*, ed. Seth Lerer, 395–405. Stanford: Stanford University Press, 1996.

———. "La Cour et la Ville," 1951. In Auerbach, *Scenes from the Drama of European Literature*, 133–79.

———. *Dante: Poet of the Secular World*, 1929. Trans. Ralph Manheim. New York: New York Review of Books, 2007.

———. *Dante: Poet of the Secular World*. Chicago: University of Chicago Press, 1961 [1929].

———. *Erich Auerbachs Briefe an Martin Hellweg, 1939–1950*. Ed. Martin Vialon. Tübingen: A. Francke Verlag, 1997.

———. "*Europäische Literatur und lateinisches Mittelalter* by Ernst Robert Curtius." *Modern Language Notes* 65 (1950): 348–51.

———. "Figura," 1938. In Auerbach, *Scenes from the Drama of European Literature*, 10–76.

———. *Introduction aux Etudes de Philology Romane*. Frankfurt am Main: Klostermann, 1949.

———. "Introduction: Purpose and Method." In Auerbach, *Literary Language and Its Public in Late Latin Antiquity and in the Middle Ages*, 5–24.
———. "Linguistics and Literary History: Essays in Stylistics by Leo Spitzer." *Comparative Literature* 1 (1949): 82–84.
———. *Literary Language and Its Public in Late Latin Antiquity and in the Middle Ages*. Trans. Ralph Manheim. Princeton: Princeton University Press, 1993 [1965].
———. *Mimesis: The Representation of Reality in Western Literature*. Princeton: Princeton University Press, 2003.
———. "Philology and *Weltliteratur*." *The Centennial Review* 13 (Winter 1969): 1–17.
———. *Scenes from the Drama of European Literature: Six Essays*. Gloucester: Peter Smith, 1973.
———. "Scholarship in the Times of Extremes: Letters of Erich Auerbach, 1933–46, on the Fiftieth Anniversary of His Death." *PMLA* 122 (January 2007): 742–62.
———. "Sermo Humilis." In Auerbach, *Literary Language and Its Public in Late Latin Antiquity and in the Middle Ages*, 25–81.
———. *Time, History, and Literature: Selected Essays of Erich Auerbach*. Ed. James I. Porter. Princeton: Princeton University Press, 2014.
———. "Vico and Aesthetic Historicism," 1949. In Auerbach, *Scenes from the Drama of European Literature*, 183–98.
———. "Vico's Contribution to Literary Criticism," 1958. In *Studza Philolopca et Litterariain Honorem L. Spitzer*, ed. Anna G. Hatcher and K. L. Selig, 31–37. Bern: Francke Verlag, 1958.
Bahr, Ehrhard. *Weimar on the Pacific: German Exile Culture in Los Angeles and the Crisis of Modernism*. Berkeley: University of California Press, 2007.
Bahti, Timothy. "Vico, Auerbach and Literary History." In *Vico: Past and Present*, ed. Giorgio Tagliacozzo, 99–114. Atlantic Highlands: Humanities Press, 1981.
Bance, Alan. "The Political Becomes Personal: *Disorder and Early Sorrow* and *Mario and the Magician*." In *The Cambridge Companion to Thomas Mann*, ed. Ritchie Robertson, 107–18. Cambridge: Cambridge University Press, 2001.
Barnes, Robin B. *Prophecy and Gnosis: Apocalypticism in the Wake of the Lutheran Reformation*. Redwood: Stanford University Press, 1988.
Barnett, Victoria. *For the Soul of the People: Protestant Protest against Hitler*. New York: Oxford University Press, 1992.
Baron, Hans. "The Course of My Studies in Florentine Humanism." In *In Search of Florentine Civic Humanism: Essays on the Transition from Medieval to Modern Thought*, 2 vols. Princeton: Princeton University Press, 1988, 1: 182–91.
———. *The Crisis of the Early Italian Renaissance: Civic Humanism and Republican Liberty in an Age of Classicism and Tyranny*. Princeton: Princeton University Press, 1966.
———. *From Petrarch to Leonardo Bruni: Studies in Humanistic and Political Literature*. Chicago: University of Chicago Press, 1968.
Bartlett, Robert. *The Making of Europe: Conquest, Colonization and Cultural Change, 950–1350*. Princeton: Princeton University Press, 1993.

Bein, A. "Modern Anti-Semitism and Its Place in the History of the Jewish Question." In Altmann, *Between East and West*, 164–93.
Beiser, F. C., ed. *The Cambridge Companion to Hegel*. Cambridge: Cambridge University Press, 1993.
Bendersky, Joseph W. *A Concise History of Nazi Germany*. Lanham: Rowman & Littlefield, 2013.
Benhabib, Seyla. "Autonomy as Mimetic Reconciliation." In Benhabib, *Critique, Norm, and Utopia*, 186–223.
———. *Critique, Norm, and Utopia: A Study of the Foundations of Critical Theory*. New York: Columbia University Press, 1986.
Benjamin, Walter. *Berlin Childhood around 1900*. Cambridge: Harvard University Press, 2006.
———. *The Correspondence of Walter Benjamin and Gershom Scholem, 1932–1940*. Ed. Gershom Scholem, trans. Gary Smith and Andre LeFevere, introduction by Anson Rabinbach. Cambridge: Harvard University Press, 1992.
———. *Illuminations*. Trans. Harry Zohn. New York: Schocken, 1969.
———. Letters to Auerbach in "Walter Benjamin and Erich Auerbach: Fragments of Correspondence." *Diacritics* 22 (Autumn–Winter 1992): 81–83.
———. "Theses on the Philosophy of History." In Benjamin, *Illuminations*, ed. Hannah Arendt, 245–55.
———. "Theses on the Philosophy of History." In Benjamin, *Illuminations*, trans. Harry Zohn, 253–64.
Bennett, Benjamin. "Magic and History: The Roots and Branches of Dr. Faustus." In *The Dark Side of Literacy: Literature and Learning Not to Read*. New York: Fordham University Press, 2008.
Bergen, Doris L. *Twisted Cross: The German Christian Movement in the Third Reich*. Chapel Hill: University of North Carolina Press, 1996.
Berger, Stefan. *The Search for Normality: National Identity and Historical Consciousness in Germany since 1800*. Oxford: Berghahn Books, 1997.
Berlin, Isaiah. "Corsi e Ricorsi." *Journal of Modern History* 50 (September 1978): 480–89.
———. *The Crooked Timber of Humanity: Chapters in the History of Ideas*. Ed. Henry Hardy. London: John Murray, 1990.
———. *The Hedgehog and the Fox: An Essay on Tolstoy's View of History*. London: Weidenfeld and Nicolson, 1953.
———. "A Note on Vico's Concept of Knowledge." In *Giambattista Vico: An International Symposium*, ed. Giorgio Tagliacozzo and Hayden White, 372–73. Baltimore: Johns Hopkins University Press, 1969.
Bermann, Sandra, and Michael Wood. *Nation, Language, and the Ethics of Translation*. Princeton: Princeton University Press, 2005.
Bernheimer, Charles, ed. *Comparative Literature in the Age of Multiculturalism*. Baltimore: Johns Hopkins University Press, 1995.
Beutin, Wolfgang, et al. *A History of German Literature: From the Beginning to the Present Day*. London: Routledge, 1993.

Bialas, W., and Rabinbach, A., eds. *Nazi Germany and the Humanities*. Oxford: Oneworld, 2007.
Birnbaum, Pierre. *Geography of Hope: Exile, the Enlightenment, Disassimilation*. Stanford: Stanford University Press, 2008.
Bishop, Paul. "The Intellectual World of Thomas Mann." In *Cambridge Companion to Thomas Mann*, ed. Ritchie Robertson, 36-41. Cambridge: Cambridge University Press, 2001.
Bloch, Marc. *Strange Defeat: A Statement of Evidence Written in 1940*. New York: Octagon, 1969 [1949].
Böhler, Britta. *The Decision*. Trans. Jeannette K. Ringold. Chicago: University of Chicago Press, 2015.
Bookbinder, Paul. *The Weimar Republic: The Republic of the Reasonable*. Manchester: Manchester University Press, 1996.
Bormuth, Matthias. "Meaning and Progress in History: Karl Löwith and Erich Auerbach." *Religions* 3 (2012): http://www.mdpi.com/journal/religions/special_issues/jewish-emigres/.
Bové, Paul A. *Intellectuals in Power: A Genealogy of Critical Humanism*. New York: Columbia University Press, 1986.
Bremmer, Jan N. "Erich Auerbach and His Mimesis." *Poetics Today* 20 (Spring 1999): 3-10.
Breslin, Charles. "Philosophy or Philology: Auerbach and Aesthetic Historicism." *Journal of the History of Ideas* 22 (July-September 1961): 369-81.
Brown, Peter. *Augustine of Hippo: A Biography*. Berkeley: University of California Press, 1969.
———. "Saint Augustine." In *Trends in Medieval Political Thought*, ed. B. Smalley, 1-21. Oxford: Oxford University Press, 1965.
Browning, Christopher. *Ordinary Men: Reserve Police Battalion 101 and the Final Solution in Poland*. New York: HarperCollins, 1992.
Brownlee, Kevin. "The Ideology of Periodization: *Mimesis* 10 and the Late Medieval Aesthetic." In *Literary History and the Challenge of Philology: The Legacy of Erich Auerbach*, ed. Seth Lerer, 156-78. Stanford: Stanford University Press, 1996.
Bryant, Edwin. *The Quest for the Origins of Vedic Culture: The Indo-Aryan Migration Debate*. Oxford: Oxford University Press, 2001.
Bultmann, Rudolf. *The History of the Synoptic Tradition*. Trans. J. Marsh. New York: Harper & Row 1963 [1921].
Burckhardt, Jacob. *The Civilization of the Renaissance in Italy*. New York: Dover, 2010 [1860].
Butcher, Samuel H. " 'Imitation' as an Aesthetic Term." In *Aristotle's Theory of Poetry and the Fine Arts with a Critical Text and Translation of the Poetics*, trans. S. H. Butcher, 121-62. New York: Dover, 1951.
Butler, Eliza Marian. *The Tyranny of Greece over Germany: A Study of the Influence Exercised by Greek Art and Poetry over the Great German Writers of the Eighteenth, Nineteenth, and Twentieth Centuries*. Boston: Beacon Press, 1958.

Butterfield, Herbert. *The Whig Interpretation of History*. New York: Norton, 1965 [1931].
Calder, William M., ed. *Werner Jaeger Reconsidered*. Atlanta: Scholars Press, 1992.
Calin, William. *The Twentieth-Century Humanist Critics: From Spitzer to Frye*. Toronto: University of Toronto Press, 2007.
Carey, Leo. "The Escape Artist: The Death and Life of Stefan Zweig." *The New Yorker*, August 27, 2012, 70–76.
Carlyle, Thomas. *On Heroes, Hero-Worship and the Heroic in History*. London: Chapman and Hall, 1893.
Cassirer, Ernst. *An Essay on Man: An Introduction to a Philosophy of Human Culture*. New Haven: Yale University Press, 1944.
———. "Judaism and the Modern Political Myth," 1944. In *Symbol, Myth, and Culture: Essays and Lectures of Ernst Cassirer, 1935–1945*, ed. Donald Philip Verene, 233–41. New Haven: Yale University Press, 1979.
———. *The Logic of Cultural Sciences: Five Studies*. New Haven: Yale University Press, 2000.
———. *The Logic of the Humanities*. New Haven: Yale University Press, 1961.
———. *The Myth of the State: A Portrait of the Disillusioned Philosopher*. New Haven: Yale University Press, 1961 [1946].
———. *Phenomenology of Knowledge*. New Haven: Yale University Press, 1958.
———. *The Philosophy of the Enlightenment*. Princeton: Princeton University Press, 1951 [1932].
———. *The Philosophy of Symbolic Forms*, vol. 1, *Language*. New Haven: Yale University Press, 1953.
———. *The Philosophy of Symbolic Forms*, vol. 2, *Mythical Thought*. New Haven: Yale University Press, 1955 [1925].
———. *The Problem of Knowledge: Philosophy, Science, and History since Hegel*. Trans. William H. Woglom and Charles W. Hendel. New Haven: Yale University Press, 1950.
———. *Symbol, Myth, and Culture: Essays and Lectures of Ernst Cassirer, 1935–1945*. Ed. Donald Philip Verene. New Haven: Yale University Press, 1979.
———. "The Technique of Our Modern Political Myths." In *Symbol, Myth, and Culture: Essays and Lectures of Ernst Cassirer, 1935–1945*, ed. Donald Philip Verene, 242–70. New Haven: Yale University Press, 1979.
———. *The Warburg Years (1919–1933): Essays on Language, Art, Myth, and Technology*. Trans. S. G. Lofts and A. Calcagno. New Haven: Yale University Press, 2013.
Catullus. *Catullus: The Shorter Poems*. Ed. and trans. John Godwin. Warminster: Aris & Philips, 1999.
Collingwood, R. G. *The New Leviathan: Or Man, Society, Civilization, and Barbarism*. Oxford: Clarendon 1991 [1942].
Confino, Alon. *A World without Jews: The Nazi Imagination from Persecution to Genocide*. New Haven: Yale University Press, 2014.
Coser, Lewis. *Refugee Scholars in America: Their Impact and Their Experiences*. New Haven: Yale University Press, 1984.

Costa-Lima, Luiz. "Auerbach and Literary History." In *Literary History and the Challenge of Philology: The Legacy of Erich Auerbach*, ed. Seth Lerer, 50–62. Stanford: Stanford University Press, 1996.
———. "Erich Auerbach: History and Metahistory." *New Literary History* 19 (Spring 1988): 467–99.
cummings, e. e. "The Bigness of Cannon." *XLI Poems*. New York: Dial Press, 1925.
Curthoys, Ned. *The Legacy of Liberal Judaism: Ernst Cassirer and Hannah Arendt's Hidden Conversation*. New York: Berghahn Books, 2013.
Curtius, Ernst Robert. *Deutscher Geist in Gefahr*. Stuttgart: Deutsche Verlags-Anstalt, 1932.
———. *Essays on European Literature*. Princeton: Princeton University Press, 1973.
———. *European Literature and the Latin Middle Ages*. Princeton: Princeton University Press, 1990 [1948].
———. "Die Lehre von den drei Stilen in Alertum und Mittelalter (zu Auerbach's *Mimesis*)" (The Teaching of the Three Styles in Antiquity and the Middle Ages (on Auerbach's *Mimesis*). *Romanische Forschungen* 64 (1952): 57–70.
Dante Alighieri. *The Divine Comedy of Dante Alighieri: Paradiso*. Trans. Allen Mandelbaum. Berkeley: University of California Press, 1982.
Damrosch, David. "Auerbach in Exile." *Comparative Literature* 47 (Spring 1995): 97–117.
DePietro, Thomas. "Literary Criticism as History: The Example of Auerbach's *Mimesis*." *Clio* 8 (1979): 377–87.
Descartes, René. *The Philosophical Writings of Descartes*, trans. John Cottingham, Robert Stoothoff, and Dugald Murdoch. 3 vols. Cambridge: Cambridge University Press, 1985.
De Wall, Edmund. *The Hare with the Amber Eyes: A Family's Century of Art and Loss*. New York: Farrar, Straus and Giroux, 2010.
Dierks, Manfred. "Thomas Mann's Late Politics." In *Companion to the Works of Thomas Mann*, ed. Hebert Lehnert and Eva Wessell, 203–20. Rochester: Camden House, 2004.
Dilthey, Wilhelm. *Das Erlebnis und die Dichtung. The Experience and the Poetry: Lessing, Goethe, Novalis, Hölderlin*. Leipzig: Teubner, 1914.
Docherty, Thomas. "Anti-Mimesis: The Historicity of Representation." *Forum for Modern Language Studies* 26 (1990): 272–81.
Doran, Robert. "Literary History and the Sublime in Erich Auerbach's *Mimesis*." *New Literary History* 38 (2007): 353–69.
Drida, Michael. "Introduction." In Auerbach, *Dante: Poet of the Secular World*, vii–xvii.
Dumbach, Annette, and Jud Newborn. *Sophie Scholl and the White Rose*. Oxford: Oneworld, 2006.
Edelstein, Ludwig. Review of *Mimesis*. *Modern Language Notes* 65 (June 1950): 426–31.
Ehrenburg, Ilya, and Vasily Grossman. *The Black Book: The Ruthless Murder of Jews by German-Fascist Invaders Throughout the Temporarily-Occupied Regions*

of the Soviet Union and in the Death Camps of Poland during the War of 1941–1945. Trans. John Glad and James S. Levine. New York: Holocaust Publications, 1981.

Eisenbaum, Pamela. "The Christian Canon and the Problem of Antisemitism." In *A Shadow of Glory: Reading the New Testament after the Holocaust*, ed. Tod Linafelt, 3–17. New York: Routledge, 2002.

Elon, Amos. *The Pity of It All: A History of the Jews in Germany, 1743–1933*. New York: Metropolitan Books, 2002.

Elsky, Martin. "Erich Auerbach's *Seltsamkeit*." In *Reading the Renaissance: Ideas and Idioms from Shakespeare to Milton*, ed. Mark Berley, 176–204. Pittsburgh: Duquesne University Press, 2003.

Elsky, Martin, Martin Vialon, and Robert Stein, eds. "Scholarship in Times of Extremes: Letters of Erich Auerbach, 1933–46, on the Fiftieth Anniversary of His Death." *PMLA* 122 (January 2007): 742–62.

Epstein, Joseph. "An Uncommon Reader: Erich Auerbach and the Understanding of Literature." *The Weekly Standard*, June 16, 2014. Web. June 20, 2014. http://www.weeklystandard.com/articles/uncommon-reader_794394.html.

Ericksen, Robert P. *Theologians under Hitler: Gerhard Kittel, Paul Althaus and Emanuel Hirsch*. New Haven: Yale University Press, 1985.

Evans, Arthur R., Jr. "Erich Auerbach as European Critic." *Romance Philology* 25 (1971): 193–215.

———. *On Four Modern Humanists: Hofmannsthal, Gundolf, Curtius, Kantorowicz*. Princeton: Princeton University Press, 1970.

Evans, Richard J. *The Third Reich at War, 1939–1945*. New York: Allen Lane, 2008.

Faulhaber, Cardinal Michael von. *Judaism, Christianity and Germany*. New York: Macmillan, 1934.

Fitzgerald, Robert. *Enlarging the Change: The Princeton Seminars in Literary Criticism 1949–1951*. Boston: Northeastern University Press, 1985.

Forstman, Jack. *Christian Faith in Dark Times: Theological Conflicts in the Shadow of Hitler*. Louisville: Westminster, 1992.

Fox, Richard W. *Reinhold Niebuhr: A Biography*. San Francisco: Harper & Row, 1985.

Freud, Sigmund. *Totem and Taboo: Resemblances Between the Mental Lives of Savages and Neurotics*. Amherst: Prometheus Books, 2000 [1913].

Friedlander, Eli. *Walter Benjamin: A Philosophical Portrait*. Cambridge: Harvard University Press, 2012.

Friedländer, Saul. *Nazi Germany and the Jews: The Years of Destruction, 1933–1939*. New York: HarperCollins, 1997.

———. *The Years of Extermination: Nazi Germany and the Jews, 1939–1945*. New York: HarperCollins, 2007.

Friedman, Matti. "70 years later, a handwritten note recalls the end of a literary life." http://www.haaretz.com/jewish-world/israeli-library-uploads-suicide-letter-of-jewish-writer-stefan-zweig-1.414312.

Friedman, Michael. "Ernst Cassirer." In *The Stanford Encyclopedia of Philosophy*, ed. Edward N. Zalta, Spring 2011. http://plato.stanford.edu/archives/spr2011/entries/cassirer/.

Fritzsche, Peter. *Life and Death in the Third Reich*. Cambridge: Harvard University Press, 2008.
Gay, Peter. *The Weimar Republic: The Outsider as Insider*. New York: Harper, 1968.
Geiger, Ido. *The Founding Act of Modern Ethical Life: Hegel's Critique of Kant's Moral and Political Philosophy*. Redwood City: Stanford University Press, 2007.
Gellrich, Jesse M. "*Figura*, Allegory, and the Question of History." In *Literary History and the Challenge of Philology: The Legacy of Erich Auerbach*, ed. Seth Lerer, 107–23. Stanford: Stanford University Press, 1996.
Gilbert, Felix. *A European Past: Memoirs 1905–1945*. New York: Norton, 1998.
———. "The Historical Seminar of the University of Berlin in the Twenties." In *An Interrupted Past: German-Speaking Refugee Historians in the United States after 1933*, ed. Hartmut Lehmann and James J. Sheehan, 67–71. Cambridge: Cambridge University Press, 1991.
Gimbel, Steven. *Einstein's Jewish Science: Physics at the Intersection of Politics and Religion*. Baltimore: Johns Hopkins University Press, 2012.
Gobineau, Joseph-Arthur de. *Gobineau: Selected Political Writings*. Ed. Michael D. Biddiss. London: Jonathan Cape, 1970.
———. *The Inequality of the Human Races*. New York: Howard Fertig, 1967.
———. *The Moral and Intellectual Diversity of Races*. New York: Garland, 1984.
Gordon, Peter E. *Continental Divide: Heidegger, Cassirer, Davos*. Cambridge: Harvard University Press, 2010.
———. "Heidegger in Black." *New York Review of Books*, October 9, 2014. http://www.nybooks.com/articles/archives/2014/oct/09/heidegger-in-black/.
Gouri, Haim. "And the Divisions—1942." *Haaretz Cultural and Literary Supplement*, February 24, 2017, 1. Hebrew.
Green, Geoffrey. *Literary Criticism and the Structure of History: Erich Auerbach and Leo Spitzer*. Lincoln: University of Nebraska Press, 1982.
Gumbrecht, Hans Ulrich. "'Pathos of the Earthly Progress': Erich Auerbach's Everydays." *Literary History and the Challenge of Philology: The Legacy of Erich Auerbach*, ed. Seth Lerer, 13–35. Stanford: Stanford University Press, 1996.
Gunkel, Hermann. *Creation and Chaos in the Primeval Era and the Eschaton: A Religio-Historical Study of Genesis 1 and Revelation 12*. Trans. K. W. Whitney, Jr. Grand Rapids: William B. Eerdmans, 2006 [1921].
———. *The Legends of Genesis*. Trans. W. H. Carruth. New York: Schocken, 1970 [1901].
Gurin, Waldmar. *Hitler and the Christians*. New York: Sheed & Ward, 1936.
Guttstadt, Curry. *Turkey, the Jews, and the Holocaust*. Cambridge: Cambridge University Press, 2009.
Haar, I., and Fahlbusch, M., eds. *German Scholars and Ethnic Cleansing, 1919–1945*. New York: Berghahn, 2005.
Habermas, Jürgen. "The Entwinement of Myth and Enlightenment: Max Horkheimer and Theodor Adorno." In *The Philosophical Discourse of Modernity*. Cambridge: MIT Press, 1990 [1987].
———. *The Philosophical Discourse of Modernity: Twelve Lectures*. Cambridge: MIT Press, 1987.

Hacohen, Malachi H. "Typology and the Holocaust: Erich Auerbach and Judeo-Christian Europe." *Religions* 3 (2012): http://www.mdpi.com/journal/religions/special_issues/jewish-emigres/.

Haffner, Sebastian. *Geschichte Eines Deutschen (The Story of a German)*. Stuttgart/München: Deutsche Verlags-Anstalt, 2000.

Hansson, Jonas, and Svante Nordin. *Ernst Cassirer: The Swedish Years*. Bern: Peter Lang, 2006.

Hardy, Henry, ed. *The Crooked Timber of Humanity: Chapters in the History of Ideas*. London: John Murray, 1990.

Harrington, A. "Ernst Troeltsch's Concept of Europe." *European Journal of Social Theory* 7 (2004): 479–98.

Hart, Thomas R. "Literature as Language: Auerbach, Spitzer and Jakobson." In *Literary History and the Challenge of Philology: The Legacy of Erich Auerbach*, ed. Seth Lerer, 227–42. Stanford: Stanford University Press, 1996.

Hartman, Geoffrey H. *A Scholar's Tale: Intellectual Journey of a Displaced Child of Europe*. New York: Fordham University Press, 2007.

———. "The Struggle for the Text." In *Midrash and Literature*, ed. Geoffrey H. Hartman and Sanford Budick, 3–18. New Haven: Yale University Press, 1986.

Hatzfeld, Helmut A. Review of *Mimesis*. *Romance Philology* 2 (1949): 333–35.

Head, Peter M. "The Nazi Quest for an Aryan Jesus." *Journal for the Study of the Historical Jesus* 2 (2004): 55–89.

Hegel, Georg Wilhelm Friedrich. *Aesthetics: Lectures on Fine Art*. 2 vols. Trans. T. M. Knox. Oxford: Clarendon Press, 1998.

———. *Encyclopedia of the Philosophical Sciences in Basic Outline: Part I: Science of Logic*, Trans. and ed. K. Brinkmann and D. O. Dahlstrom. Cambridge: Cambridge University Press, 2010.

———. *Hegel: The Letters*. Trans. Clark Butler and Christine Seiler. Bloomington: Indiana University Press, 2005.

———. *Hegel's Philosophy of Right*. Trans. T. M. Knox. Oxford: Clarendon Press, 1952.

———. *Introduction and Oriental Philosophy, Together with the Introduction from Other Series of These Lectures*, vol. 1, *Lectures on the History of Philosophy*. Trans. R. F. Brown and J. M. Stewart. Oxford: Clarendon Press, 2009 [1825–1826].

———. *Introduction to the Lectures on the History of Philosophy*. Trans. T. M. Knox and A. V. Miller. Oxford: Clarendon, 1985.

———. *Introduction: Reason in History. Lectures on the Philosophy of World History*. Trans. H. B. Nisbet. Cambridge: Cambridge University Press, 1975.

———. *Lectures on the Philosophy of World History*, vol. 1, *Manuscripts of the Introduction and the Lectures of 1822–1823*. Ed. and trans. R. F. Brown and P. C. Hodgson. Oxford: Oxford University Press, 2011.

———. *Outlines of the Philosophy of Right*. Trans. T. N. Knox. Oxford: Oxford University Press, 2008 [1821].

———. *Phenomenology of Spirit*. Trans. A. V. Miller. Oxford: Clarendon Press, 1977.

———. *Philosophy of History*. Trans. J. Sibree. New York: Dover, 1956.

———. *Philosophy of Mind.* Trans. A.V. Miller. Oxford: Clarendon, 1971.
———. *The Science of Logic.* Trans. and ed. George D. Giovanni. Cambridge: Cambridge University Press, 2010.
Helmreich, E. C. *The German Churches under Hitler.* Detroit: Wayne State University Press, 1979.
Hendel, Charles W. "Ernst Cassirer." In *The Philosophy of Ernst Cassirer,* ed. Paul A. Schilpp, 55–60. Evanston: The Library of Living Philosophers, 1949.
Helps, Arthur. "Preface." In Spengler, *The Decline of the West,* abridged edition, ed. Helmut Werner, xiii–xx. New York: Vintage, 1962.
Herf, Jeffrey, "Dialectic of Enlightenment Reconsidered." *New German Critique* 117 (Fall 2012): 81–89.
Heschel, Susannah. *The Aryan Jesus: Christian Theologians and the Bible in Nazi Germany.* Princeton: Princeton University Press, 2008.
———. "Nazifying Christian Theology: Walter Grundmann and the Institute for the Study and Eradication of Jewish Influence on German Church Life." *Church History* 63 (December 1994): 587–605.
———. "Reading Jesus as a Nazi." In *A Shadow of Glory: Reading the New Testament after the Holocaust,* ed. Tod Linafelt, 27–41. New York: Routledge, 2002.
———. "When Jesus was and Aryan." In *Betrayal: German Churches and the Holocaust.* Minneapolis: Fortress, 1999. 68–89.
Hinlicky, Paul R. *Before Auschwitz: What Christian Theology Must Learn from the Rise of Nazism.* Eugene: Cascade Books, 2013.
Hitler, Adolf. *Mein Kampf.* Boston: Houghton Mifflin, 1943.
Hobbes, Thomas. *De Cive (On the Citizen),* 1642.
———. *Leviathan or The Matter, Forme and Power of a Commonwealth Ecclesiastical and Civil,* 1651.
Hobsbawm, Eric. *The Age of Extremes: History of the World, 1914–1991.* New York: Pantheon, 1994.
Hodgson, Peter C. *Shapes of Freedom: Hegel's Philosophy of World History in Theological Perspective.* Oxford: Oxford University Press, 2012.
Holdheim, W. Wolfgang. "Auerbach's 'Mimesis': Aesthetic as Historical Understanding." *Clio* 10 (1981): 143–64.
———. "The Hermeneutic Significance of Auerbach's Ansatz." *New Literary History* 16 (Spring 1985): 627–31.
Holquist, Michael. "The Last European: Erich Auerbach as Precursor in the History of Cultural Criticism." *Modern Language Quarterly* 54 (September 1993): 371–91.
———. "The Place of Philology in an Age of World Literature." *Neohelicon* 38 (2011): 267–87.
Horkheimer, Max. *Between Philosophy and Social Sciences: Selected Early Writings.* Trans. G. F. Hunter and M. S. Kramer. Cambridge: MIT Press, 1993.
———. *Dawn and Decline: Notes 1926–1931 and 1950–1969.* New York: Seabury Press, 1978.
———. *Eclipse of Reason.* Oxford: Oxford University Press, 1947.

———. *A Life in Letters: Selected Correspondence.* Ed. and trans. M. R. Jacobson and E. M. Jacobson. Lincoln: University of Nebraska Press, 2007.

Horkheimer, Max, and Theodor W. Adorno. *Dialectic of Enlightenment: Philosophical Fragments.* Ed. Gunzelin Schmid Noerr and trans. Edmund Jephcott. Stanford: Stanford University Press, 2002 [1944].

Houlgate, Stephen. *An Introduction to Hegel: Freedom, Truth and History.* Oxford: Blackwell, 2005.

Igger, Georg G. *The German Conception of History: The National Tradition of Historical Thought from Herder to the Present.* Middleton: Wesleyan University Press, 1983 [1968].

———. "The German Professors in the Third Reich." *Central European History* 25 (1992): 445–50.

Jackman, Jarrell C. "Exiles in Paradise: German Émigrés in Southern California, 1933–1950." *Southern California Quarterly* 61 (Summer 1979): 183–205.

Jaeger, Werner. *Paideia: The Ideals of Greek Culture*, 3 vols. New York: Oxford University Press, 1962.

Jäger, Lorenz. *Adorno: A Political Biography.* New Haven: Yale University Press, 2004.

Jarvis, Simon. *Adorno: A Critical Introduction.* Cambridge: Polity Press, 2005.

Jay, Martin. *The Dialectical Imagination: A History of the Frankfurt School and the Institute of Social Research, 1923–1950.* Berkeley: University of California Press, 1996.

Jünger, Ernst. *Stahlgewittern, aus dem Tagebuch eines Stosstrufführers.* Berlin: E. S. Mittler & Sohn, 1920.

———. *Storm of Steel: From the Diary of a German Storm-Troop Officer on the Western Front.* Trans. Basil Creighton, intro. R. H. Mottram. Garden City: Doubleday, Doran & Company, 1929.

Jurdjevic, Mark. "Hedgehogs and Foxes: The Present and Future of Italian Renaissance Intellectual History." *Past and Present* 195 (May 2007): 241–68.

Kadir, Djelal. "Introduction: Comparative Touchstones of Literature." In Kadir, *Memos from the Besieged City*, 1–18.

———. *Memos from the Besieged City: Lifelines for Cultural Sustainability.* Stanford: Stanford University Press, 2011.

Kant, Immanuel. *Critique of Pure Reason.* Trans. and ed. Paul Guyer and Allen W. Wood. Cambridge: Cambridge University. Press, 1998.

———. *Critique of Pure Reason.* Prefaces and Introduction, 1787. http://staffweb.hkbu.edu.hk/p/cpr/prefs.html.

———. *Grounding for the Metaphysics of Morals*, 1785. Trans. James W. Ellington. Indianapolis: Hackett, 1993

———. "What Is Enlightenment," 1784. In *What Is Enlightenment? Eighteenth-Century Answers and Twentieth-Century Questions*, ed. James Schmidt. Berkeley: University of California Press, 1996.

Kater, Michael H. "Refugee Historians in America: Preemigration Germany to 1939." In *An Interrupted Past: German-Speaking Refugee Historians in the*

United States after 1933, ed. Hartmut Lehmann and James Sheehan, 73–93. Cambridge: Cambridge University Press, 1991.

Kaufmann, Walter. *Hegel: Reinterpretation, Texts, and Commentary*. Garden City: Doubleday, 1965.

Kazin, Alfred. "Erich Auerbach." *The American Scholar* (Summer 1965): 484.

Kelley, Louis G. "Auerbach, Erich." In *Encyclopedia of Contemporary Literary Theory: Approaches, Scholars, Terms*, ed. I. R. Makaryk, 233–26. Toronto: University of Toronto Press, 1993.

Kettler, David, and Gerhard Lauer, eds. *Exile, Science and Bildung: The Contested Legacies of German Emigre Intellectuals*. London: Palgrave Macmillan, 2005.

Keun, Irmgard. *Nect Mitternach (After Midnight)*. London: Melville House, 2011 [1937].

Kirsch, Adam. "Heidegger Was Really a Real Nazi." *Tablet Magazine*, September 26, 2016. http://www.tabletmag.com/jewish-arts-and-culture/books/214226/heidegger-was-really-a-real-nazi.

———. "The System: Two New Histories Show How the Nazi Concentration Camps Worked." *The New Yorker*, April 6, 2015, 77–81.

Kojève, Alexander. *Introduction to the Reading of Hegel*. New York: Basic Books, 1969 [1947].

Kontje, Todd. "Doctor Faustus and the Jewish Question." In Kontje, *Thomas Mann's World*, 168–73.

———. *Thomas Mann's World: Empire, Race, and the Jewish Question*. Ann Arbor: University of Michigan Press, 2011.

Konuk, Kader. *East West Mimesis: Auerbach in Turkey*. Stanford: Stanford University Press, 2010.

———. "Jewish-German Philologists in Turkish Exile: Leo Spitzer and Erich Auerbach." In *Exile and Otherness: New Approaches to the Experience of the Nazi Refugees*, ed. Alexander Stephan, 31–48. Oxford: Peter Lang, 2005.

Koselleck, Reinhart. "Foreword." In Löwith, *My Life in Germany Before and After 1933*. Urbana: University of Illinois Press, 1994 [1986]. ix–xvi.

Krois, John M. *Cassirer: Symbolic Forms and History*. New Haven: Yale University Press, 1987.

Krystal, Arthur. "The Book of Books: Erich Auerbach and the Making of *Mimesis*." *The New Yorker*, December 9, 2013, 83–88. Web. June 20, 2014. http://www.newyorker.com/magazine/2013/12/09/the-book-of-books.

Kulka, Otto Dov. *Landscapes of the Metropolis of Death: Reflections on Memory and Imagination*. London: Allan Lane, 2013.

Kurzke, Hermann. *Thomas Mann: Life as a Work of Art. A Biography*. Princeton: Princeton University Press, 2002 [1999].

Lambropoulos, Vassilis. *The Rise of Eurocentrism: Anatomy of Interpretation*. Princeton: Princeton University Press, 1993.

Landauer, Carl. "Auerbach's Performance and the American Academy, or How New Haven Stole the Idea of *Mimesis*." In *Literary History and the Challenge of*

Philology: The Legacy of Erich Auerbach, ed. Seth Lerer, 179–92. Stanford: Stanford University Press, 1996.

———. "'Mimesis' and Erich Auerbach's Self-Mythologizing." German Studies Review 11 (February 1988): 83–96.

Larmore, Charles. "The Secrets of Philosophy." The New Republic, July 3, 1989, 30–35.

Lehmann, Hartmut, and James Melton. Paths of Continuity: Central European Historiography from the 1930s to the 1950s. Cambridge: Cambridge University Press, 2003.

Lehmann, Hartmut, and James J. Sheehan, eds. An Interrupted Past: German-Speaking Refugee Historians in the United States after 1933. Cambridge: Cambridge University Press, 1991.

Lehnert, Herbert, and Eva Wessell, eds. A Companion to the Works of Thomas Mann. Rochester: Camden House, 2004.

Lerer, Seth, ed. Error and the Academic Self: The Scholarly Imagination, Medieval to Modern. New York: Columbia University Press, 2002.

———. Literary History and the Challenge of Philology: The Legacy of Erich Auerbach. Stanford: Stanford University Press, 1996.

———. "Philology and Criticism at Yale." Journal of Aesthetic Education 36 (Autumn 2002): 16–25.

Levin, Harry. "Two Romanisten in America: Spitzer and Auerbach." In The Intellectual Migration: Europe and America, ed. Donald Fleming and Bernard Bailyn, 463–84. Cambridge: Harvard University Press, 1969.

Levine, Emily. Dreamland of Humanists: Warburg, Cassirer, Panofsky, and the Hamburg School. Chicago: University of Chicago Press, 2013.

Linafelt, Tod, ed. A Shadow of Glory: Reading the New Testament after the Holocaust. New York: Routledge, 2002.

Littell, Jonathan. The Kindly Ones (Les Bienveillantes, 2006). New York: Harper, 2009.

Lofts, S. G. Ernst Cassirer: A "Repetition" of Modernity. Albany: State University of New York Press, 2000.

Lofts, S. G., and A. Calcagno. "Translators' Introduction." In Cassirer, The Warburg Years.

Lovejoy, Arthur. "The Meaning of Romanticism for the Historian of Ideas." Journal of the History of Ideas 2 (June 1941): 257–78.

———. "Reply to Professor Spitzer." Journal of the History of Ideas 5 (April 1944): 20–19.

Löwith, Karl. Meaning in History. Chicago: University of Chicago Press, 1949.

———. My Life in Germany Before and After 1933. Urbana: University of Illinois Press, 1994 [1986].

Luft, Sandra R. Vico's Uncanny Humanism: Reading the New Science between Modern and Postmodern. Ithaca: Cornell University Press, 2003.

Lukács, Georg. The Destruction of Reason. Atlantic Highlands: Humanities Press, 1981 [1962].

———. Studies in European Realism. New York: Grosset & Dunlap, 1964.

———. *The Theory of the Novel: A Historic-Philosophical Essay on the Forms of Great Epic Literature*. London: Merlin, 1971 [1920].
Lyman, Eugene W. "Ernst Troeltsch's Philosophy of History." *The Philosophical Review* 41 (September 1932): 443–65.
Machiavelli, Niccolò. *Machiavelli and His Friends: Their Personal Correspondence*. Ed. James B. Atkinson and David Sices. DeKalb: Northern Illinois University Press, 1996.
Man, John. *Attila the Hun: A Barbarian King and the Fall of Rome*. New York: Random House, 2006.
Mann, Klaus. *The Turning Point*. New York: L. B. Fischer, 1942.
Mann, Thomas. "A Brother." In *Death in Venice, Tonio Kröger, and Other Writings*. Ed. F. A. Lubich, 297–302. New York: Continuum, 1999.
———. "Bruder Hitler." *Esquire* 11, 3 (1939): http://larvatus.livejournal.com/291296.html.
———. *Doctor Faustus: The Life of the German Composer Adrian Leverkühn as Told by a Friend*. Trans. John E. Wood. New York: Vintage, 1999.
———. *Letters of Thomas Mann, 1889-1955*. Sel. and trans. Richard and Clara Winston. New York: Knopf, 1971.
———. *Mario and the Magician*. New York: Knopf, 1931.
———. *The Story of a Novel: The Genesis of Doctor Faustus*. New York: Knopf, 1961 [1949].
———. *The Tables of the Law*. Philadelphia: Paul Day Books, 2010 [1944].
———. *Thomas Mann: Death in Venice, Tonio Kröger, and Other Writings*. New York: Continuum, 1939.
———. *Thomas Mann's Addresses Delivered at the Library of Congress, 1942-1949*. Washington: Library of Congress, 1963.
———. *Thomas Mann's Addresses Delivered at the Library of Congress, 1942-1949*. Ed. Don Heinrich Tolzmann. Oxford and New York: Peter Lang, 2003.
———. "The Theme of the Joseph Novels," 1942. In *Thomas Mann's Addresses Delivered at the Library of Congress, 1942-1949*, 1–20. Washington: Library of Congress, 1963.
Mannheim, Karl. *Ideology and Utopia: An Introduction to the Sociology of Knowledge*. Trans. L. Wirth and E. Shils. New York: Harcourt Brace, 1955.
Marchand, Suzanne L. *Down from Olympus: Archaeology and Philhellenism in Germany, 1750-1970*. Princeton: Princeton University Press, 1996.
———. *German Orientalism in the Age of Empire: Religion, Race, and Scholarship*. New York: Cambridge University Press, 2009.
———. "Nazism, Orientalism and Humanism." In *Nazi Germany and the Humanities*, ed. W. Bialas and A. Rabinbach, 267–305. Oxford: Oneworld, 2007.
Marvell, Andrew. "An Horatian Ode upon Cromwell's Return from Ireland." www.bartleby.com/106/65.
———. "To His Coy Mistress," c. 1651–1652. http://www.poetryfoundation.org/poem/173954.

Matin, A. Michal. "'The Hun is at the Gate!': Historicizing Kipling's Militaristic Rhetoric." *Studies in the Novel* 31 (Winter 1999): 432–70.
Matheson, Peter, ed. *The Third Reich and the Christian Churches*. Grand Rapids: Eerdmans, 1981.
Matuschek, Oliver. *Three Lives: A Biography of Stefan Zweig*. London: Pushkin Press, 2011.
McLean, Roderick R. "Dreams of German Europe: Wilhelm II and the Treaty of Björkö of 1905." In *The Kaiser: New Research on Wilhelm II's Role in Imperial Germany*, ed. Annika Mombauer and Wilhelm Deist, 119–42. Cambridge: Cambridge University Press, 2003.
Megill, Allan. "Review: Why Was There a Crisis of Historicism." *History and Theory* 36 (October 1997): 429–416.
Meinecke, Friedrich. *Historicism: The Rise of a New Historical Outlook*. Trans. J. E. Anderson. London: Routledge & Kegan Paul, 1972 [1936].
Menand, Louis. "Practical Cat: How Eliot Became Eliot." *The New Yorker*, September 19, 2011. 76–83.
Menocal, María Rosa. *Shards of Love: Exile and the Origins of Lyric*. Durham: Duke University Press, 1994.
Molho, Anthony. "Hans Baron's Crisis." In *Florence and Beyond: Culture, Society and Politics in Renaissance Italy*, ed. David S. Peterson and Daniel E. Bornstein, 61–90. Toronto: Center for Reformation and Renaissance Studies, 2008.
Mombauer, Annika, and Wilhelm Deist, eds. *The Kaiser: New Research on Wilhelm II's Role in Imperial Germany*. Cambridge: Cambridge University Press, 2003.
Mommsen, Wolfgang J. "German Historiography during the Weimar Republic and the Émigré Historians." In *An Interrupted Past: German-Speaking Refugee Historians in the United States after 1933*, ed. Hartmut Lehmann and James J. Sheehan, 32–66. Cambridge: Cambridge University Press, 1991.
Morgan, Wendy. "Who Was Then the Gentleman? Social, Historical, and Linguistic Codes in the *Mystère d'Adam*." *Studies in Philology* (Spring 1982): 101–21.
Morgenthau, Hans. "*The Myth of the State* by Ernst Cassirer." *Ethics* 57 (January 1947):142.
Mosse, George L. *Confronting History—A Memoir*. Madison: Wisconsin University Press, 2000.
———. *The Crisis of German Ideology: Intellectual Origins of the Third Reich*. New York: Grosset & Dunlap, 1964.
———. *German Jews beyond Judaism*. Bloomington: Indiana University Press, 1985.
———, ed. *Nazi Culture: Intellectual, Cultural and Social Life in the Third Reich*. Madison: University of Wisconsin Press, 1966.
Moynahan, Gregory B. *Ernst Cassirer and the Critical Science of Germany, 1899–1919*. London: Anthem, 2013.
Mufti, Aamir R. "Auerbach in Istanbul: Edward Said, Secular Criticism, and the Question of Minority Culture." *Critical Inquiry* 25 (Autumn 1998): 95–125.
Muller, Jerry Z. *The Other God That Failed: Hans Freyer and the Deradicalization of German Conservatism*. Princeton: Princeton University Press, 1987.

Müller-Doohm, Stefan. *Adorno: A Biography.* Cambridge: Polity Press, 2005.
Mundt, Hannelore. *Understanding Thomas Mann.* Columbia: University of South Carolina Press, 2004.
Nelson, Lowry, Jr. "Erich Auerbach: Memoir of a Scholar." *Yale Review* 69 (1979–1980): 312–20.
———. "Erich Auerbach, 1892–1957." In *Medieval Scholarship: Biographical Studies on the Formation of a Discipline*, 3 vols., vol. 2, *Literature and Philology.* New York: Garland, 1998. 395–403.
Neumann, Erich. *Depth Psychology and a New Ethic.* London: Hodder & Stoughton, 1969.
Nichols, Stephen G. "Erich Auerbach: History, Literature and Jewish Philosophy." *Romanistisches Jahrbuch* 58 (2008): 166–85.
———. "Philology in Auerbach's Drama of Literary History." In *Literary History and the Challenge of Philology: The Legacy of Erich Auerbach*, ed. Seth Lerer, 63–77. Stanford: Stanford University Press, 1996.
Niebuhr, Reinhold. *Leaves from the Notebook of a Tamed Cynic.* Cleveland: Meridian 1957 [1929].
Norton, Amanda. "The One Who 'Taught Us How to Live on This Real Earth, without Any Conditions but Those of Life': Tracing the Influence of Michel de Montaigne on Erich Auerbach and *Mimesis*." *Monatshefte* (Winter 2008): 504–18.
Nova, Fritz, *Alfred Rosenberg: Nazi Theorist of the Holocaust.* New York: Hippocrene Books, 1986.
Nuttall, A. D. "Auerbach's *Mimesis*." *Essays in Criticism* 54 (2004): 60–74.
Oberman, Heiko A. *Luther: Man Between God and the Devil.* New Haven: Yale University Press, 1990.
O'Connor, Anne-Marie. *The Lady in Gold: The Extraordinary Tale of Gustav Klimt's Masterpiece, Portrait of Adele Bloch-Bauer.* New York: Knopf, 2012.
Olasky, Marvin. "If we lose the battle [Dietrich Bonhoeffer on living in totalitarian times]." http://www.freerepublic.com/focus/f-news/2549521/posts.
Olender, Maurice. *The Language of Paradise: Race, Religion, and Philology in the Nineteenth Century.* Trans. A. Goldhammer. Cambridge: Harvard University Press, 2008 [1989].
Pae, Hellmut. "The Scholar as Businessman." In *Out of the Third Reich: Refugee Historians in Post-War Britain*, ed. Peter Alter, 161–74. London: I. B. Tauris, 1998.
Paldiel, Mordecai. *Churches and the Holocaust: Unholy Teaching, Good Samaritans, and Reconciliation.* Jersey City: Ktav, 2006.
Pascal, Blaise. *Blaise Pascal: Pensées and Other Writings.* Trans. Honor Levi. Oxford: Oxford University Press, 1999.
Peterson, David S., and Daniel E. Bornstein, eds. *Florence and Beyond: Culture, Society and Politics in Renaissance Italy.* Toronto: Center for Reformation and Renaissance Studies, 2008.
Pinkard, Terry. *Hegel: A Biography.* Cambridge: Cambridge University Press, 2001.
———. *Hegel's Phenomenology: The Sociability of Reason.* Cambridge: Cambridge University Press, 1994.

Plato. *The Republic of Plato*. Trans. F. M. Cornford. New York: Oxford University Press, 1945.

Pocock, J. G. A. *The Machiavellian Moment: Florentine Political Thought and the Atlantic Republican Tradition*. Princeton: Princeton University Press, 2003 [1975].

Pois, Robert, ed. *Race and Race History and Other Essays by Alfred Rosenberg*. New York: Harper & Row, 1970.

Poliakov, Léon. *The Aryan Myth: A History of Racist and Nationalist Ideas in Europe*. New York: Barnes & Noble, 1974.

Pollard, Sidney. "In Search of a Social Purpose." In *Out of the Third Reich: Refugee Historians in Post-War Britain*, ed. Peter Alter, 195-217. London: I. B. Tauris, 1998.

Popper, Karl. *The Open Society and Its Enemies*. London and New York: Routledge, 2002 [1945].

———. *The Poverty of Historicism*. London and New York: Routledge, 1997 [1957].

———. *Unended Quest*. London and New York: Routledge, 2002 [1992].

Porter, James I. "Erich Auerbach and the Judaizing of Philology." *Critical Inquiry* 35 (Autumn 2008): 115-47.

———. "Odysseus and the Wandering Jew: The Dialectic of Jewish Enlightenment in Adorno and Horkheimer." *Cultural Critique* 74 (Winter 2010): 200-13.

Pound, Ezra. *Hugh Selwyn Mauberley: Life and Contacts*. New York: Ovid Press, 1920.

Rabinbach, Anson. "Between Apocalypse and Enlightenment: Benjamin, Bloch, and Modern German Messianism." In Rabinbach, *In the Shadow of Catastrophe*, 27-65.

———. *In the Shadow of Catastrophe: German Intellectuals between Apocalypse and Enlightenment*. Berkeley: University of California Press, 1997.

———. "The Cunning of Unreason: *Mimesis* and the Construction of Anti-Semitism in Horkheimer and Adorno's *Dialectic of Enlightenment*." In Rabinbach, *In the Shadow of Catastrophe*, 166-98.

———. "Why Were the Jews Sacrificed? The Place of Anti-Semitism in *Dialectic of Enlightenment*." *New German Critique* 81 (Autumn 2000): 49-64.

Ranke, Leopold von. "Universal Tendencies," 1833. In *Leopold von Ranke, The Secret of World History: Selected Writings on the Art and Science of History*, ed. Roger Wines, 121-64. New York: Fordham University Press, 1981.

Reed, T. J. "Mann and History." In *The Cambridge Companion to Thomas Mann*, ed. Ritchie Robertson, 1-19. Cambridge: Cambridge University Press, 2001.

———. *Thomas Mann: The Uses of Tradition*. Oxford: Clarendon Press, 1996 [1973].

Reiss, Hans. "Ernst Robert Curtius, 1886-1956: Some Reflections on the Occasion of the Fortieth Anniversary of His Death." *Modern Language Review* 91 (July 1996): 647-54.

Reitter, Paul. "Comparative Literature in Exile: Said and Auerbach." In *Exile and Otherness: New Approaches to the Experience of the Nazi Refugees*, ed. Alexander Stephan, 21-30. Oxford: Peter Lang, 2005.

Ringer, Fritz K. *The Decline of the German Mandarins: The German Academic Community, 1890-1933*. Cambridge: Harvard University Press, 1969.

Roberts, Andrew. *The Storm of War: A New History of the Second World War*. London: Allen Lane, 2009.
Robertson, Ritchie, ed. *Cambridge Companion to Thomas Mann*. Cambridge: Cambridge University Press, 2001.
Robinson, Armin L., ed. *The Ten Commandments: Ten Short Novels of Hitler's War Against the Moral Code*. New York: Simon & Schuster, 1943.
Rosenberg, Alfred. *Der Mythus des 20. Jahrhunderts. Eine Wertung der seelischgeistigen Gestaltenkämpfe unserer Zeit*. München: Hoheneichen-Verlag, 1930.
———. *Memoirs of Alfred Rosenberg*. Trans. E. Posselt. Chicago: Ziff-Davis, 1949.
———. *Myth of the Twentieth Century: An Evaluation of the Spiritual-Intellectual Confrontations of Our Age*. Newport Beach: Noontide Press, 1982.
———. *Race and Race History and Other Essays by Alfred Rosenberg*. Ed. R. Pois. New York: Harper & Row, 1970.
Rosenberg, Göran. *A Short Stop on the Road from Auschwitz*. Stockholm: Albert Bonniers Förlag, 2012.
Ross, Alex. "When Music Is Violence." *The New Yorker*, July 4, 2016, 65–69.
Rubanowic, Robert J. "Ernst Troeltsch's History of the Philosophy of History." *Journal of the History of Philosophy* 14 (January 1976): 79–95.
Said, Edward W. *Beginnings: Intention and Method*. New York: Basic Books, 1975.
———. "Erich Auerbach, Critic of the Earthly World." *Boundary 2* 31, 2 (2004): 550.
———. "Introduction to the Fiftieth Anniversary Edition of *Mimesis*." In Auerbach, *Mimesis*, ix–xxxii.
———. "Introduction: Secular Criticism." In Said, *The Word, The Text, and the Critic*, 1–30.
———, ed. *Literature and Society*. Baltimore: Johns Hopkins University Press, 1980.
———. *Nationalism, Colonialism, and Literature*. Minneapolis: Minnesota University Press, 1990.
———. *Reflections on Exile and Other Essays*. Cambridge: Harvard University Press, 2000.
———. *Representation of the Intellectual*. London: Vintage, 1994.
———. *The Word, The Text, and the Critic*. Cambridge: Harvard University Press, 1983.
Scaff, Susan von Rohr. "Doctor Faustus." In *The Cambridge Companion to Thomas Mann*, ed. Ritchie Robertson, 168–84. Cambridge: Cambridge University Press, 2001.
———. *History, Myth, and Music: Thomas Mann's Timely Fiction*. Rochester: Camden House, 1998.
Schaffer, Tom. "From Natural Religion to Natural Law: Rhetoric, Poetic, and Vico's Imaginative Universals." *Rhetorica: A Journal of the History of Rhetoric* 15 (Winter 1997): 41–51.
———. *Sensus Communis: Vico, Rhetoric, and the Limit of Relativism*. Durham: Duke University Press, 1990.
Schiller, Kay. "Hans Baron's Humanism." *Storia della storiografia* 34 (1998): 51–99.
———. "Paul Oskar Kristeller, Ernst Cassirer and the 'Humanistic Turn' in American Emigration." In *Exile, Science and Bildung: The Contested Legacies of German*

Emigre Intellectuals, ed. David Kettler and Gerhard Lauer, 125-38. London: Palgrave Macmillan, 2005.

Schilpp, Paul A., ed. *The Philosophy of Ernst Cassirer*. Evanston: The Library of Living Philosophers, 1949.

Scholder, Klaus. *A Requiem for Hitler and Other New Perspectives on the German Church Struggle*. London: SCM Press, 1988.

Schulin, Ernst. "German and American Historiography in the Nineteenth and Twentieth Centuries." In *An Interrupted Past: German-Speaking Refugee Historians in the United States after 1933*, ed. Hartmut Lehmann and James J. Sheehan, 8-31. Cambridge: Cambridge University Press, 1991.

Schulze, Winfried. "German Historiography from 1930s to the 1950s." In *Paths of Continuity: Central European Historiography from the 1930s to the 1950s*, ed. Hartmut Lehmann and James Melton, 19-42. Cambridge: Cambridge University Press, 2003.

Schmidt, James. "Mephistopels in Hollywood: Adorno, Mann, and Schoenberg." In *Cambridge Companion to Adorno*, ed. Tom Huhn, 148-80. Cambridge: Cambridge University Press, 2004.

Schweitzer, Albert. *The Quest for the Historical Jesus*. London: SCM Press, 2000 [1906].

Sebald, W. G. *Austerlitz*. London: Hamish Hamilton, 2001.

———. *The Emigrants*. London: Harvill, 1996.

Seyhan, Azade. "German Academic Exiles in Istanbul: Translation as the *Bildung* of the Other." In *Nation, Language, and the Ethics of Translation*, ed. Sandra Bermann and Michael Wood, 274-88. Princeton: Princeton University Press, 2005.

Shahar, Galili. "Auerbach's Scars: Judaism and the Question of Literature." *Jewish Quarterly Review* 101 (Fall 2011): 604-30.

Shaw, Brian J. "Reason, Nostalgia, and Eschatology in the Critical Theory of Max Horkheimer." *Journal of Politics* 47 (February 1985): 160-81.

Sheard, Eugene. "Foreword." In Sieg, *Germany's Prophet*, xi-xvii.

Shklar, Judith N. *Political Thought and Political Thinkers*. Ed. Stanley Hoffmann. Chicago: University of Chicago Press, 1998.

Sieg, Ulrich. *Paul de Lagarde und die Ursprünge des modernen Antisemitismus*. München: Carl Hanser Verlag, 2007.

———. *Germany's Prophet: Paul de Lagarde and the Origins of Modern Antisemitism*. Trans. Linda Ann Marianello. Waltham: Brandeis University Press, 2012.

———. *Paul de Lagarde und die Ursprünge des modernen Antisemitismus*. Munich: Carl Hanser Verlag, 2007.

Sims, Amy R. "Intellectuals in Crisis: Historians under Hitler." *The Virginia Quarterly Review* (Spring 1978): 262-246.

Skidelsky, Edward. *Ernst Cassirer: The Last Philosopher of Culture*. Princeton: Princeton University Press, 2008.

Snyder, Timothy. *Bloodlands: Europe between Hitler and Stalin*. New York: Basic Books, 2012.

———. "Hitler's World." *New York Review of Books*, September 24, 2015.
Solomon, R. C. "Hegel's Concept of 'Geist.'" *Review of Metaphysics* 23 (June 1970): 642–61.
———. *In the Spirit of Hegel: A Study of G. W. F. Hegel's Phenomenology of Spirit*. New York: Oxford University Press, 1983.
Spender, Stephen. *European Witness*. New York: Renal & Hitchcock, 1946.
Spengler, Oswald. *The Decline of the West*, abridged edition. Ed. Helmut Werner. New York: Vintage, 1962.
———. *The Decline of the West*. New York: Oxford University Press, 1926.
———. *The Decline of the West*. London: George Allen, 1934 [1918].
———. *Jahre der Entscheidung*. Munich: Beck, 1933.
Spitzer, Leo. *Geistesgeschichte* vs. History of Ideas as Allied to Hitlerism." *Journal of the History of Ideas* 5 (April 1944): 191–203.
———. *Linguistic and Literary History: Essays in Stylistics*. Princeton: Princeton University Press, 1948.
———. Review of Curtius, *Europäische Literatur und lateinisches Mittlelalter*, 1948. *American Journal of Philology* 70 (1949): 425–31.
Starn, Randolph. "Historians and 'Crisis.'" *Past and Present* 52 (1971): 3–22.
Steigmann-Gall, Richard. *The Holy Reich: Nazi Conception of Christianity, 1919–1945*. New York: Cambridge University Press, 2003.
Steinberg, Michael P. *Walter Benjamin and the Demands of History*. Ithaca: Cornell University Press, 1996.
Steinweis, Alan E. *Studying the Jews: Scholarly Antisemitism in Nazi Germany*. Cambridge: Harvard University Press, 2006.
Stephan, Alexander, ed. *Exile and Otherness: New Approaches to the Experience of the Nazi Refugees*. Oxford: Peter Lang, 2005.
Stern, Fritz. "German History in America, 1884–1984." *Central European History* 19 (June 1986): 131–63.
———. *The Politics of Cultural Despair: A Study in the Rise of the Germanic Ideology*. Berkeley and Los Angeles: University of California Press, 1961.
Stock, Brian. "Literary Realism in the Later Ancient Period." In *Literary History and the Challenge of Philology: The Legacy of Erich Auerbach*, ed. Seth Lerer, 143–55. Stanford: Stanford University Press, 1996.
———. "The Middle Ages as Subject and Object: Romantic Attitudes and Academic Medievalism." *New Literary History* 5 (Spring 1974): 531–32.
Tagliacozzo, Giorgio, ed. *Vico: Past and Present*. Atlantic Highlands: Humanities Press, 1981.
Tal, Uriel. *Christians and Jews in Germany: Religion, Politics, and Ideology in the Second Reich, 1870–1914*. Ithaca: Cornell University Press, 1975.
———. "The *Kulturkampf* and the Status of the Jews in Germany." In Tal, *Christians and Jews in Germany*, 81–20.
———. *Religion, Politics and Ideology in the Third Reich: Selected Essays*. London: Routledge, 2004.

Uhlig, Claus. "Auerbach's 'Hidden'? Theory of History." In *Literary History and the Challenge of Philology: The Legacy of Erich Auerbach*, ed. Seth Lerer, 36–49. Stanford: Stanford University Press, 1996.
Ullmann, Walter. "A Tale of Two Cultures." In *Out of the Third Reich: Refugee Historians in Post-War Britain*, ed. Peter Alter, 247–60. London: I. B. Tauris, 1998.
Vaget, Hans Rudolf. " 'German' Music and German Catastrophe: A Re-Reading of *Doktor Faustus*." In *A Companion to the Works of Thomas Mann*, ed. Herbert Lehnert and Eva Wessell, 221–44. Rochester: Camden House, 2004.
Verene, Donald P., ed. *Symbol, Myth, and Culture: Essays and Lectures of Ernst Cassirer, 1935–1945*. New Haven: Yale University Press, 1979.
Vernant, Jean-Pierre. "Foreword." In Olender, *Language of Paradise*, vii–xi.
Vico, Giambattista. *Giambattista Vico: An International Symposium*. Ed. Giorgio Tagliacozzo and Hayden White. Baltimore: Johns Hopkins University Press, 1969.
———. *The New Science of Giambattista Vico*, 1744 [1725]. Trans. T. G. Bergin and M. H. Fisch. Ithaca: Cornell University Press, 1968.
Viereck, Peter. *Metapolitics: From Wagner and the German Romantics to Hitler*. New York: Alfred A. Knopf, 1941.
Voegelin, Eric. *Race and State*. Trans. R. Hein. Baton Rouge: Louisiana State University Press, 1997 [1933].
Wallace, J. M. *Destiny His Choice: The Loyalism of Andrew Marvell*. Cambridge: Cambridge University Press, 1981.
Wallace, Robert M. *Hegel's Philosophy of Reality, Freedom, and God*. Cambridge: Cambridge University Press, 2005.
Wartenberg, Thomas E. "Hegel's Idealism: The Logic of Conceptuality." In *The Cambridge Companion to Hegel*, ed. F. C. Beiser, 102–29. Cambridge: Cambridge University Press, 1993.
Watt, Ian. *Rise of the Novel: Studies in Defoe, Richardson, and Fielding*. Berkeley: University of California Press, 1957.
Weinstein, David, and Avihu Zakai. "Exile and Interpretation: Popper's Re-invention of the History of European Political Thought." *Journal of Political Ideologies* 11 (June 2006): 185–209.
———. *Jewish Exiles and European Thought in the Shadow of the Third Reich: Baron, Popper, Strauss, Auerbach*. Cambridge: Cambridge University Press, 2017.
Weits, Eric D. *Weimar Germany: Promise and Tragedy*. Princeton: Princeton University Press, 2007.
Welch, Claude. *Protestant Thought in the Nineteenth Century*. 2 vols. New Haven: Yale University Press, 1972.
Wellek, René. "Auerbach and Vico." In *Vico: Past and Present*, ed. Giorgio Tagliacozzo, 85–96. Atlantic Highlands: Humanities Press, 1981.
———. "Erich Auerbach, 1892–1957." *Comparative Literature* 10 (1958): 93–94.
———. *A History of Modern Criticism: 1750–1950*, 8 vols. New Haven: Yale University Press, 1955–1992.

———. *A History of Modern Criticism: 1750–1950*, vol. 7: *German, Russian, and Eastern European Criticism, 1900–1950*. New Haven: Yale University Press, 1991.
———. "Leo Spitzer, 1887–1960." *Comparative Literature* 12 (Autumn 1960): 310–34.
———. "Review: Auerbach's Special Realism." *Kenyon Review* 16 (Spring 1954): 299–307.
Wells, Herbert George. *The War That Will End War*. Whitefish: Kessinger, 2009 [1914].
Wheatland, Thomas. *The Frankfurt School in Exile*. Minneapolis: University of Minnesota Press, 2009.
White, Donald O. "Werner Jaeger's 'Third Humanism' and the Crisis of Conservative Cultural Politics in Weimar Germany." In *Werner Jaeger Reconsidered*, ed. William M. Calder, 267–88. Atlanta: Scholars Press, 1992.
White, Hayden. "Auerbach's Literary History: Figural Causation and Modernist Historicism." In *Figural Realism: Studies in the Mimesis Effect*. Baltimore: Johns Hopkins University Press, 1999.
———. "Auerbach's Literary History: Figural Causation and Modernist Historicism." In *Literary History and the Challenge of Philology: The Legacy of Erich Auerbach*, ed. Seth Lerer, 124–42. Stanford: Stanford University Press, 1996.
Whitman, Walt. *Leaves of Grass*. Ed. W. Blodgett and S. Bradley. New York: New York University Press, 1965.
Wiggershaus, Rolf. *The Frankfurt School: Its History, Theories, and Political Significance*. Cambridge: MIT Press, 1995.
Wines, Roger, ed. *Leopold von Ranke, The Secret of World History: Selected Writings on the Art and Science of History*. New York: Fordham University Press, 1981.
Wolin, Richard. "Fascism and Hermeneutics: Gadamer and the Ambiguities of 'Inner Emigration.'" In *Nazi Germany and the Humanities*, ed. Wolfgang Bialas and Anson Rabinbach, 101–39. Oxford: Oneworld, 2007.
———. "National Socialism, World Jewry, and the History of Being: Heidegger's Black Notebooks." *Jewish Review of Books*, Summer 2014. http://jewishreviewofbooks.com/articles/993/national-socialism-world-jewry-and-the-history-of-being-heideggers-black-notebooks/.
———. *The Terms of Cultural Criticism: The Frankfurt School, Existentialism, Poststructuralism*. New York: Columbia University Press, 1992.
Wood, James, "Soul Cycle." *The New Yorker*, September 8, 2014, 78–82.
Wood, Michael. "Afterword." In Mann, *The Tables of the Law*, 114–20.
Wood, Thomas E., and M Jankowski. *Karski: How One Man Tried to Stop the Holocaust*. Hoboken: John Wiley & Sons, 1994.
Yovel, Yirmiyahu. *Hegel's Preface to the Phenomenology of Spirit*. Trans. Yirmiyahu Yovel. Princeton: Princeton University Press, 2005.
Zakai, Avihu. "The Age of Enlightenment." In *The Cambridge Companion to Jonathan Edwards*, ed. Stephen Stein, 80–99. New York: Cambridge University Press, 2006.

———. "Constructing and Representing Reality: Hegel and the Making of Erich Auerbach's *Mimesis*." *Digital Philology: A Journal of Medieval Cultures* 4, 1 (Spring 2015): 106–33.

———. *Erich Auerbach and the Crisis of German Philology: An Apologia for the Western Judeo-Christian Humanist Tradition in an Age of Peril, Tyranny, and Barbarism*. Tel Aviv: Hakibbutz Hameuchad, 2016. Hebrew.

———. *Erich Auerbach and the Crisis of German Philology: The Humanist Tradition in Peril*. Dordrecht: Springer, 2016.

———. "Exile and Criticism: Edward Said's Interpretation of Erich Auerbach." *Society* 57 (2015): 275–82.

———. "Exile and Criticism: On Edward Said's Use and Abuse of Erich Auerbach's Works." In *Catharsis*, 129–51. Jerusalem: Carmel Publishing House, 2014. Hebrew.

———. *Exile and Kingdom: History and Apocalypse in the Puritan Migration to America*. Cambridge: Cambridge University Press, 1992.

———. "The Irony of American History: Reinhold Niebuhr and the American Experience." *La Revue LISA/ LISA e-journal*, World War II Thematic dossier, 2008, 1–21. http://www.unicaen.fr/mrsh/lisa/publicationsGb.php?p=2&numId=1&it=inTheWar.

———. "Jonathan Edwards, the Enlightenment, and the Formation of Protestant Tradition in America." In *The Creation of the British Atlantic World*, ed. Elizabeth Mancke and Carole Shammas, 182–208. Baltimore: Johns Hopkins University Press, 2005.

———. *Jonathan Edwards's Philosophy of Nature: The Re-Enchantment of the World in the Age of Scientific Reasoning*. London: T&T Clark, 2010.

———. *Jonathan Edwards's Philosophy of History: The Re-Enchantment of the World in the Age of Enlightenment*. Princeton: Princeton University Press, 2003.

———. "Philology and Racism." *Haaretz*, April 12, 2012. Hebrew.

———. "The Poetics of History and the Destiny of Israel: The Role of the Jews in English Apocalyptic Thought during the Sixteenth and Seventeenth Centuries." *The Journal of Jewish Thought and Philosophy* 5 (1996): 313–350.

———. "Professor of Exile: Edward Said's Misreading of Erich Auerbach." *Moment Magazine*, August 14, 2014. http://www.momentmag.com/edward-said-erich-auerbach/.

———. "Reformation, History, and Eschatology in English Protestantism." *History and Theory* 16 (October 1987): 300–18.

Zakai, Avihu, and Anya Mali. "Time, History and Eschatology: Ecclesiastical History from Eusebius to Augustine." *The Journal of Religious History* 17 (December 1993): 393–417.

Zakai, Avihu, and David Weinstein. "Erich Auerbach and His 'Figura': An *Apologia* for the Old Testament in an Age of Aryan Philology." *Religions* 3 (2012): 320–38. http://www.mdpi.com/journal/religions/special_issues/jewish-emigres/ Web. 20 June 2014. http://www.mdpi.com/2077-1444/3/2/320.

---. "Exile and Interpretation: Popper's Re-Invention of the History of European Political Thought." *Journal of Political Ideologies* 11 (June 2006): 185-209.

---. "Exile and Interpretation: Popper's Re-Invention of the History of European Political Thought." *Zmanim* (Winter 2008): 14-27. Hebrew.

---. "'Figura' and *Mimesis* in Cultural War: Erich Auerbach's Struggle against Aryan Philology." *Atmol* 242 (November 2015): 19-22. Hebrew.

Zimmerer, Jürgen. "Annihilation in Africa: The 'Race War' in German Southwest Africa, 1904-1908, and Its Significance for a Global History of Genocide." *GHI Bulletin* 37 (Fall 2005): 51-57.

Ziolkowski, Jan M. "Bibliography of the Writings of Erich Auerbach." In Auerbach, *Literary Language and Its Public in Late Antiquity and in the Middle Ages*, 395-405.

---. "Foreword." In Auerbach, *Literary Language and Its Public in Late Antiquity and in the Middle Ages*, ix-xxxix.

Zweig, Stefan. *The World of Yesterday: An Autobiography*. London: Cassell, 1943 [1942].

Index

Abraham, 205
Achilles, 282
Adam and Eve, 44
Advertisement, 283, 290, 292, 295–97
Adorno, Theodor, 5–9, 11, 14–15,
   17, 19–21, 25, 29–31, 84–85, 88,
   90, 104, 155–56, 161, 174, 180,
   203, 220, 237, 243–306, 308–9,
   314, 316–17, 319, 321; and crisis
   mode of historical thought, 7,
   10, 250, 259; and Thomas Mann,
   257, 314
   Against Epistemology, 257
   Authoritarian Personality, 254
   Dialectic of Enlightenment, 5–7,
   9, 11, 14, 84, 90, 155, 161, 174,
   220, 243–306, 309, 317, 319–20;
   concept of enlightenment,
   272–81; content and form,
   264–72; Enlightenment and
   morality, 285–90; enlightenment
   as mass deception, 290–97;
   historical context, 257–64; the
   Jewish question as the epitome
   of dialectic of enlightenment,
   297–305; Odysseus, myth and
   enlightenment, 281–90
   In Search of Wagner, 257
   *Minima Moralita: Reflections from
   Damaged Life*, 254
   On the Philosophy of Modern Music,
   30
   Prisms, 257

Aesthetic historicism, 179, 210, 229
Aestheticism and barbarism, 66–67, 69
Aesthetics, 17–18, 68, 86, 99, 109, 254,
   288
Agape, 77
Age of Catastrophe, 1–22, 40, 89, 164,
   178, 249, 259, 321
Age of Reason and Enlightenment,
   131–35, 274
Alexandria, 4, 219
All Souls College, 96
Allegory, 5, 226, 278
Améry, Jean, 212
   "On the Necessity and Impossibility
   of Being a Jew," 212
Angel of history, 7, 164, 246, 319
Annales School, 3, 308
Ansatzpunkt (point of departure), 175,
   183, 192, 216, 226, 228
Anti-Semitism, 12–15, 35–36, 38, 97,
   108, 110, 119, 124, 171, 190, 197,
   200–3, 208, 214, 245, 256–57,
   264, 271, 297–305, 312
Apocalypse, 23–82, 218, 317
Apologia, 6, 13, 167, 174, 178–79, 196,
   220, 319
Apter, Emily, 236
Aquinas, Thomas, 45, 168, 187
   Summa Theologica, 45
Arendt, Hannah, 2, 237, 247, 259, 297,
   299, 321
   The Origins of Totalitarianism, 299,
   304

Aryan philology, 8, 13–14, 84, 108, 167–242, 247, 298; and the elimination of the Old Testament, 196–211
Aryanism, 87, 99, 124, 197, 201, 222, 231
Athenian democracy, 123
Attila (king of the Huns), 57
Atlantic Republican Tradition, 126
Auerbach, Erich, 3, 5–6, 8–11, 247, 250–52, 258, 263, 265, 269, 271, 282, 284–85, 297–98, 299–301, 308–10, 312–13, 315–17, 320–21; apologetic moment, 215–20; Aryan philology and the elimination of the Old Testament, 196–211; and the crisis mode of historical thought, 7, 10; epiphany in Istanbul, 215–20; exile, interpretation, and alienation, 236–42; and Goethean humanism, 183; and historicism humanism, 183; it's personal, 211–15; knowing the enemy, 169–78; life, time, and world, 187–96; and Marxism, 19; *Mimesis'* form and content, 225–32; *Mimesis'* method and approach, 232–36; philology and history, 178–85; philology and ideology, 185–87; philology, teleology, and historicist humanism, 220–25; and rational representation of reality, ix, 8, 167–242, socialist, Marxist approach, 20, 45, 75, 84–85, 87, 90, 104, 106, 107–8, 111–12, 115, 121, 146, 153, 161, 163–65; and *Weltliteratur*, 183
Dante: Poet of the Secular World, 186–87, 190, 211
"Epilegomena to *Mimesis*," 215, 221, 238
"Figura," 108, 168, 171–76, 177–78, 180, 182–83, 186–87, 191–92, 196, 213, 216, 221, 226–28, 231–32, 235, 238, 240, 298
Literary Language & Its Public in Late Latin Antiquity and in the Middle Ages, 170, 229
Mimesis: The Representation of Reality on Western Literature, 5–6, 8–11, 13, 17–20, 84–85, 90, 99, 106–8, 111, 119, 121, 153, 165, 167–243, 247, 250–52, 258, 265, 281–82, 298–99, 309, 313
"Philology and *Weltliteratur*," 239–41
"Sermo Humilis," 224
The Technique of the Early Renaissance Novelle in Italy and France, 189
"Vico and Aesthetic Historism," 179, 210
"Vico's Contribution to Literary Criticism," 225
Augustine, St., 6, 124, 148, 168, 172, 174–75, 240, 251, 258, 305, 309
City of God, 6, 174, 251, 305, 309
Auschwitz, 73–74
Australia, 2
Austria, 163, 193, 260, 307
Austrian Anschluss, 307

Bacon, Francis, 269, 273; utopia of, 280–81, 285–86, 291
In Praise of Knowledge, 273
Baden School of Neo-Kantianism, 82
Baku, 4, 219
Balzac, Honoré de, 234
Barbaric turn, 56, 66, 68, 275
Baron, Hans, 5, 15, 84, 90, 104, 108, 112, 115, 126, 163–65, 179, 187, 202, 220, 225, 237, 239, 258, 265, 310–12, 321
The Crisis of the Early Italian Renaissance, 84, 90, 115, 165, 220, 258, 265, 311
Barth, Karl, 251
Beatrice, 46, 77

Bebel August, 58
Hunnen-Briefe (Letters from the Huns), 58
Beckmann, Max, 216
Beethoven, Ludwig van, 30, 52, 76, 293
Fidelio, 76
Ninth Symphony, 52, 76
Bekennende Kirche (Confessional Church), 208
Belgium, rape of, 58
Benjamin, Walter, 7-8, 10, 16, 19-20, 164-65, 189, 213-16, 246, 249-51, 254-55, 259-60, 262, 265, 312; and Golgotha of hope, 8; suicide of, 260
"Angel of History," 7, 164, 246, 319
Berlin Childhood around 1900, 213
"Theses on the Philosophy of History," 7, 164, 246, 250, 262
Berg, Alban, 30, 255
Berlin, 15, 24, 32, 68, 70, 76, 91-94, 98-99, 109, 151, 188-89, 196, 202-3, 213, 215, 312
Berlin, Isaiah, 98-99
Bildungsbürgertum (cultured middle-class intellectuals), 66
Black Sea, 63
Blackstone, William, 1, 5, 310
Commentaries on the Laws of England, 1765-1769, 1, 5, 310
Bloch, Ernst, 3, 251, 254, 308
Bluebopropaganda, 10, 215, 312
Blumenberg, Hans, 115
Blutsgemeinschaft (Community in Blood), 15
Blut und Boden (blood and soil), 6, 10, 15, 67, 69, 87, 206, 215, 312
Book of Revelation (Apocalypse), 42, 49
Brazil, 1, 39, 220
Brecht, Bertolt, 31
Buber, Martin, 233
Buchenwald, 52, 72-74, 79
Bund Deutscher Mädel (girls' Nazi youth organization), 55

Burckhardt, Jakob, 170, 185, 239

Calin, William, 173
Casablanca Conference, 39
Cambridge School of Political Thought, 125-26
Camus, Albert, 3
Capitalism, 50, 244-97, 301
Carnegie, Andrew, 291
Carlyle, Thomas, 131-41, 153; against Enlightenment, 138-39; great men, 138-41; and hero worship, 131-41; and "March of Fascism," 140
On Heroes, Hero Worship, and the Heroic in History, 137
Carpe diem, (seize the day), 218
Cassirer, Ernst, 2, 5-6, 8-12, 14, 16-21, 83-166; age of reason and Enlightenment, 131-35; and Carlyle, 137-41; and crisis mode of historical thought, 7, 10, 89, 104, 108, 116, 164; early life and works, 90-97; Enlightenment and its enemies, 97-100; exile and interpretation, 101-5; and Gobineau, 141-44; and Hegel, 145-52; and Heidegger, 151, 159-60, 162, 165, 173, 188, 316-17, 320-21; and idealistic philosophy of sciences, 92; and Judaism, 106-8; and Machiavelli, 125-30; medieval theory of the state, 123-25; modern political myth, 152-63, 195, 220, 237, 250, 259, 263, 278, 269, 275-76, 285-86, 297-98, 300, 302, 308; new driving force, 105-13; Plato's legal state, 117-23; and Rosenberg, 135-37; and Spengler, 162; sudden convulsions, 86-90; the whole flight of humanity, 113-23
The Case of Jacques Rousseau, 94
Descartes's Critique of Mathematics and Natural Scientific Knowledge, 91

Cassirer, Ernst *(continued)*
  Determinism and Indeterminism in Modern Physics, 96
  "Die Verfassung des Deutschen Reichs," 98
  Einstein's Theory of Relativity, 93
  Essay on Man, 12, 104, 107, 298
  Freedom and Form: Studies of German Intellectual History, 93
  (ed.) *Immanuel Kants Werke*, 91
  The Individual and the Cosmos in Renaissance Philosophy, 93
  "Judaism and the Modern Political Myth," 13, 108, 298
  Language and Myth, 94
  (ed.) *Leibniz' Philosophische Werke*, 91
  The Logic of the Humanities, 94
  The Myth of the State, 5, 10, 83–166, 195, 220, 247, 250, 252, 265, 271, 273, 309
  Philosophy of Symbolic Forms, 94
  Philosophy of the Enlightenment, 94–95, 97–100, 105
  The Platonic Renaissance in England, 93
  The Problem of Knowledge in the Philosophy and Science of Modern Times, 92
  The Problem of Knowledge: Philosophy, Science, and History since Hegel, 96, 312
  Substance and Function, 93
  "The Technique of Our Modern Political Myths," 83
  "Tragedy of Culture," 102
Cassirer, Toni, 91, 102–3, 105, 312
Caucasus, 3, 219
Cesare Borgia, 129–130
Chamberlain, Houston Stewart, 24, 135–36, 181, 200–2, 206, 211
  The Foundations of the Nineteenth Century, 135, 200–1

Chaplin, Charlie, 67
  The Great Dictator, 67
Charles I, King of England, 217
Chauvinism, 7–8, 26, 35–36, 63, 67, 69, 90, 99, 108, 171, 298, 309, 311
Christ, 14, 67, 75, 186, 203, 205, 208–9, 216–18, 224, 234, 240
Cicero, 125
Cinema, 5, 290–94
Circe, witch-goddess, 85, 155, 278
Cohen, Hermann, 91–92, 98, 106, 114
Collingwood, R. G., 2, 7, 89, 178, 259
  The New Leviathan: or Man, Society, Civilization, and Barbarism, 7, 220, 253
Columbia University, 3, 96, 249, 253
Concentration camps, 8–9, 28, 44, 73, 75, 173, 274
Congress of Victory (*Reichsparteitag des Sieges*), 211
Congreve, William, 61
Community of Blood and Fate, 7, 69, 88, 203
Congreve, William, 62
Columbia University, 3, 249, 253
Copernicus, Nicolaus, 15, 95, 128, 142–44, 157, 184, 197
Corneille, Pierre, 224
Crimea, 3, 39, 219
Crisis of German ideology, 9, 115, 155, 161
Crisis of German philology, 167–242, 310
Crisis history, 10, 164, 250
Crisis mode of historical thought, 7, 10–11, 15, 89, 164, 250, 259, 164–65
Croce, Benedetto, 170, 189
  The Philosophy of Giambattista Vico, 189
Cromwell, Oliver, 138, 140, 217–18,
  Lord Protector, 217

Culture industry, 256, 270, 290–91, 203–7, 317
Curtius, Ernst Robert, 170, 182, 185, 237–38
  European Literature and the Latin Middle Ages, 229, 238

Dante Alighieri, 6, 18, 41, 44, 59–60, 71, 138, 140, 168, 177, 186–87, 190–92, 196, 211, 229, 233, 235; as *il Sommo Poeta* (the Supreme Poet)
  The Divine Comedy of Dante Alighieri, 6, 44–47, 77, 111, 165, 230, 309
  Inferno, 44–45, 50, 60, 136, 172
  Purgatory, 46, 60
Dantean moment, 41
Dark writers of the Enlightenment, 286
Decline of the West, 9, 11, 106, 158, 317
Defoe, Daniel, 282, 285
  Robinson Crusoe, 282, 285
Delitzsch, Friedrich, 206
  The Great Deception, 206
Descartes, René, 91, 131, 174
Devil, 5, 16, 28–30, 41–44; pact with Hitler, 41, 46–63, 72, 77–81, 122, 126–27, 210, 243, 320
Devilization of German state and society, 13, 110
Dialectic Marxism, 20, 147
Dialectical materialism, 19, 301, 306
Deutsche Christen, 202, 204
Devil, 127
De Wall, Edmund, 307
  The Hare with the Amber Eyes: A Family's Century of Art and Loss, 307
Dinter, Artur, 206
  The Sin against the Blood, 206
Donets, 3, 219

Dostoevsky, Fyodor, 36
Dürer, Albrecht, 49–50, 72, 79
  Apocalypsis cum Figuris, 49–50
  Knight, Death and the Devil, 50, 72

Ebert, Friedrich, 65
Egypt, 3–4, 36, 40, 219
Eiser, Hans, 257
Einstein, Albert, 97
El Alamein, battle of, 3–4, 40, 168, 219, 313
Elective aversions, 15–21
Elective affinities, 8–15
English Civil War(s), 217
Enlightenment, 8–9; and enslavement of nature, 9, 269, 273–74, 279, 287; and mythic terror, 17, 85, 276; and universalism, 134
Enslavement of nature, 9, 269, 273–74, 279, 284
Epiphany in Istanbul, 196, 215–20
Eschatology, 23–82, 84, 327
Esmeralda, 46
Evangelical Lutheran Church, 197, 207
Evans, Arthur H., 170, 185
Exile and alienation, 240–41
Exile and interpretation, 6, 101–5, 307–22
Exiles, émigrés, refugees, 180, 315
Exile, trauma, and interpretation, 307–21

Fairfax, Mary, 217
Fairfax, Thomas, 217
Fall of Rome, 174, 251, 305
Faulhaber, Cardinal Michael von, 205–7
  Judaism, Christianity and Germany, 205–7
Faust (Faustus), 5, 8, 11, 23–82, 84, 86, 90, 127, 164–65, 210, 212, 220, 231, 243, 247, 250–52, 257–58, 263, 266, 271–76, 307, 309, 317, 319–20

Faustus, Johannes, 42
Faustian moment, 41
Faustus Tale, 27, 54, 76
Feuchtwanger, Lion, 31
Fichte, Johann Gottlieb, 16, 114, 127, 129, 137
Figural interpretation of history, 13, 75, 111, 168, 186, 192, 222, 235
Figural realism, 235
Films, 257, 291–94
Flaubert, Gustave, 237–38
Flight from reason, 7, 9, 11, 32, 51, 73, 97, 154, 156, 210, 221–22, 246, 253, 257, 277–78, 296
Florentine civic humanism, 126
Ford, Henry, 292
Formalism, 284–85
Fortress Europe, 27, 48, 63, 78
Franco-Prussian War, 57
Frankfurt, 19–20, 42, 70–71, 88, 98, 156, 214, 245, 247–49, 253–55, 257, 265
Frankfurt School of Critical Theory, 19, 88, 247, 254, 268, 321
"Freedom Movement," 72
Friedrich Wilhelm University, 93
French classicists, 224–25
Freud, Sigmund, 248, 254
Friedländer, Saul, 169
The Years of Extermination: Nazi Germany and the Jews, 1939–1945, 169
French Realism, 230
French realists, 234–35
French Revolution, 149, 151
Fritsch, Theodor, 206
The False God, 206
Fromm, Erich, 156, 253, 255, 268–69
Escape from Freedom, 156, 253
Fuchs, Traugott, 192

Galileo Galilei, 131
Gasset, José Ortega y, 269

Geist, 24, 175, 240, 260
Genesis, book of, 169, 189, 216, 233
Genghis Khan, 195
George, Stefan, 91
German barbarism, 63, 315
German catastrophe, 26–27, 52, 56, 64, 69
German culture as a precursor to Nazism, 65–71
German ideology, 9, 115, 155, 161
German historicism, 15, 85, 127, against Enlightenment, 131–35
German pact with the Devil, 28, 46–49, 51, 53, 63, 80
German will to legend, 66, 72, 174
Gilbert, Felix, 307, 320
Gilson, Étienne, 124
Gobineau, Count Joseph Arthur de, 114–15, 137, 141–45, 153; and Aryan race, 141–45; as second Copernicus, 144; and the totalitarian race, 141–45
On the Inequality of the Human Races, 142–45
Godesberg Declaration, 197, 207–8
Goebbels, Joseph, 193, 296, 303
Goethe, Johann Wolfgang von, 20, 24, 41, 43, 51, 55; and "Goethean humanism," 183; and Weimar Classicism (*Weimarer Klassik*), 73, 77–78, 94, 134, 137; and *Weltliteratur*, 183, 239
The Awakening of Epimenides, 55
Faust, 41, 43, 77–79
Goethe University Frankfurt, 20, 214–15, 255, 265
"Goethean humanism," 183
Goethean moment, 41
George, Stefan, 91
Gordon, Peter E., 160
Gothenburg, Sweden, 96, 101, 150, 161
Gotthelf, Jeremias, 43

Graecophilia, 283
Greek Philosophy, 105, 114–23, 163, 317
Gregory of Tours, Bishop and historian, 224
Grotius, Hugo, 129
Grünberg, Carl, 248
Grundmann, Walter, 197, 200, 208–9

Habermas, Jürgen, 243, 265–66, 291
  The Philosophical Discourse of Modernity, 243
Halle, 49
Hamburg, 93, 96, 98, 206
Hartman, Geoffrey H., 19, 185, 191, 236, 315
  A Scholar's Tale: Intellectual Journey of a Displaced Child of Europe, 179
Hegel, Georg Wilhelm Friedrich, 15–20, 96, 102, 106, 111, 114–15; and absolutism, 148; and Auerbach, 17–18; and Cassirer, 18, 85; Hegelian view of history, 102–3; and historical determinism, 103; and historicism, 16, 85, 146; and Machiavelli, 127, 129, 132, 139, 141, 145–52, 169, 182, 221, 230, 240, 244–47, 251, 254, 260, 262, 268, 282–83; and Marx and Lenin, 147; and Napoleon, 67, 137, 149; and Popper, 18, 85, 145–46; and Strauss, 18–19; "The real is rational and rational is real," 19, 106; and totalitarianism, 16, 85, 145; and worship of state, 142–52
  Aesthetics: Lectures on Fine Art, 18
  Hegel's Philosophy of Right, 147–48
  Phenomenology of Spirit, 142, 147
  Philosophy of History, 142, 148, 151
  Philosophy of Right, 147–48

Hegelian metaphysics, 146
Hegelianism, 146
Heidegger, Martin, 6, 96, 159–62; and Cassirer, 151, 159–60, 162, 165, 173, 188, 316–17, 320–21; Davos debate, 160; fatalism, passivity, and pessimism, 160, 165, 173; *Geworfenheit* (thrown into the stream of time and history), 160
  Being and Time, 159
Heimat (homeland), 6, 87, 242
Hindenburg, Paul von, 47
Hellenism, 12, 37, 299
Heraclitus of Ephesus, 6, 190
Herder, Johann Gottfried, 16, 127, 134, 173, 183, 199
  Letters for the Advancement of Humanity, 127
Herero and Namaqua genocides, 47
Herodotus, 121
Hesiod, 121–22
Historia calamitatum, 1, 89, 259, 272
Historical materialism, 248, 270, 290, 296
Historically becoming, 111, 299
Historicism, 15–17, 19, 20, 85, 127–28, 142–52, 179, 183–84, 190, 210, 222, 224–25, 229, 235–36, 239; as Copernican Revolution, 184
Historicist philology, 182
History science of reality, 221, 239
Hitler, Adolf, 24, 26–27, 32, 34, 35–36, 38, 41, 44, 48, 54–55, 59, 96–97, 102, 105, 111–13, 135–37, 141, 173, 190, 193, 195, 204–5, 211, 249, 258, 262, 275, 296, 303, 312, 314
  Mein Kampf, 136, 202
Hitler-Jugend, 35
Hobbes, Thomas, 20, 129, 281; *Bellum omnium contra omnes* (each against all), law of the jungle,

Hobbes, Thomas *(continued)*
  244, 265; self-preservation, 277, 281, 286; "a war of all against all," 266
  Leviathan, 244, 288, 317
Hobsbawm, Eric, 1, 40, 164, 259
  The Age of Extremes: History of the World, 1914–1991, 1, 40, 164, 259
Höhe, Daniel Zur, 67–68
Holborn, Hajo, 104, 116, 147
Holocaust, 9, 12–13, 123, 263, 274, 296–97, 305, 313
Holquist, Michael, 220
Homer, 9, 36, 111, 121–22, 169, 223, 225, 227, 230, 232–33, 237, 242, 264, 266, 278, 281–85, 299
  Odyssey, 9, 85, 89, 96, 155–56, 165, 167, 186, 232, 256, 267, 270, 281, 284–85
Horkheimer, Max, 5–9, 11, 14–15, 17, 19–21, 25, 29–31, 84–85, 88, 90, 104, 155–56, 161, 174, 180, 203, 220, 237, 243–306, 308–9, 314, 316–17, 319, 321
  Dialectic of Enlightenment, 5–7, 9, 11, 14, 84, 90, 155, 161, 174, 220; concept of enlightenment, 272–81; content and form, 264–72; Enlightenment and morality, 285–90; enlightenment as mass deception, 290–97; historical context, 257–64; the Jewish question the epitome of dialectic of enlightenment, 243–306, 309, 317, 319–20; Odysseus, myth and enlightenment, 281–90
  Eclipse of Reason, 248, 252–53, 264, 266
Hossenfelder, Joachim (Bishop of Berlin), 203
Hugh of St. Victor, 241–42
Humanism, 12, 38, 51–52, 60, 66, 68, 73, 79, 101, 105, 107, 126, 173, 180, 183–84, 187, 190, 195, 202, 220, 223–25, 239–41, 274, 296, 298, 309, 311, 313, 315, 318, 321
Humanist philology, 225
Huns, 57–58
Huxley, Aldous, 269
Hynkel, Adenoid, 67

Idealism, 92, 126
Ideology of periodization, 229
Idiosyncratic interpretation, 131, 183, 222, 225, 237, 318
Indo-European hypothesis, 197–202
Indo-European language, 197
Indo-Germanische, 197
Inferno, 44–45, 50, 60, 136, 172
Institute for Social Research (Institut für Sozialforschung), 19, 88, 245, 248, 253, 255–57, 262, 265, 274
Institute for the Study and Eradication of the Jewish Influence on German Church Life, 208
Istanbul, 3, 111, 153, 165, 168, 191–92, 196, 214–17, 215–20, 240, 242, 313; Auerbach's epiphany in, 215–20
Ithaca, 278, 284

Jaspers, K. H., 269
Jay, Martin, 249
Jazz, 290–95
Jefferson, Thomas, 132
Jena, battle of, 149
Jerusalem, 49, 60, 97, 175, 240, 305
Jesus, 199–209, 215, 262
Jews, emancipation of, 15, 304
Jews, extermination of, 13, 110
Jewish-Israelitish realm of reality, 9, 299
Jewish question, 297–306
John of Patmos, Saint, 50–51
Jones, William, 197
Joyce, James, 8, 11, 169
  Ulysses, 153, 186, 232

Judaeo-Christian depravity, 201
Judeo-Christian humanist tradition, 15, 167, 174–75, 178, 187, 197–98, 216, 225–26, 229–31
Judaism, 12–15, 37–38, 106–13, 168, 197, 200, 204–9, 297, 300–4, 313
Jung, Carl, 318
Jünger, Ernst, 68; aesthetic of industrial war, 68
Strom and Steel, 109

Kant, Immanuel, 17, 86, 91–92, 93, 95, 98, 103, 115, 184, 239, 270, 287–88; Copernican Revolution of, 95 184
Critique of Pure Reason, 288
Karski, Jan, 263
Kazin, Alfred, 167
Kingdom of God, 50–51, 200, 217–18
Kingdom of Satan, 50
Kipling, Rudyard, 58
"The Hun is at the gate," 58
Kharkov, 3, 219
Kramer, Heinrich, 42
Malleus Maleficarum (Hammer of the Witches), 42
Krause, Reinhold, 203–4
Kridwiss, Sixtus, 66–68
Kristallnacht (Night of Broken Glass), 193–94, 208
Kulturgeschichte, 170, 185
Kulturkampf, 4, 7–8, 21, 46, 51, 79, 84, 86, 90, 118, 161, 163–64, 177, 183, 238, 247, 271, 309–10, 315
Kursk, battle of, 59, 147
Kurzke, Hermann, 80

Lagarde, Paul de, 24, 199–200
Landauer, Carl, 236
Lang, Fritz, 257
Law of the jungle, 113, 244, 277
Lawrence, D. H., 66, 174
Letter from Germany, 66, 174
Lenin, Vladimir, 20, 147

Levels of style, 222, 226, 228, 234
Leverkühn, Adrian, 41, 44, 48, 59, 60, 69, 70, 78, 81, 212, 319; as a hero of his times, 53; as an ideal figure, 53; illness, 67; pact with the devil, 59; as son of Hell, 52, 54, 77
Apocalypsis cum Figuris, 28, 49–50, 52, 54, 65–71, 76
The Lamentation of Dr. Faustus, 30, 52, 76
Levin, Harry, 237
Locke, John, 129, 133
Lommatzsch, Erhard, 189
Löns, Hermann, 72
Der Wehrwolf (Warwolf), 72
Löwith, Karl, 2, 314, 319
Lucifer, 42, 44, 60
Lukács, Georg, 2, 40, 66, 174, 195, 259, 316
The Theory of the Novel, 316
Luther, Martin, 8, 10, 23, 28, 50, 79, 138, 140, 197, 199, 203, 207–9
Lutheran Church, 23, 197, 207
Lutheran Reformation, 197, 209

Macaulay, Thomas Babington, 126
Critical, Historical and Miscellaneous Essays, 126
Machiavelli, Niccolò, 16, 86, 114, 125–30; Copernican Revolution, and Cesare Borgia, 129; devilization of, 127; as an incarnation of the devil, 127; and medieval political thought, 128; as Mephistopheles, 127; and modern secular state, 134; new art of politics, 130; new science of politics, 128; 'original sin,' 126; and Plato, 130; and political realism, 127; revolution of, 125, 128; and secularization, 128; separating of ethics and politics, 148, 149–50, 152; separating politics from morality, 146; and totalitarian state, 126

Machiavelli, Niccolò *(continued)*
  First Ten Books of Titus Livy (Discorsi), 129, 165, 192, 265, 286, 288
  The Prince, 16, 127, 129–30
Machiavellian moment, 129
Machiavellian revolution, 126
Machiavellianism, 16, 114, 126–27, 129
Magazines, 290, 292, 294
Mahler, Gustav, 30
Mandeville, Bernard, 265, 286
Mann, Johann Heinrich, 23
Mann, Heinrich, 23
Mann, Kalus, 1, 39–40
  The Turning Point, 1
Mann, Monica, 31
Mann, Thomas, 5; and Adorno, 257, 269, 285, 297, 299–300, 308–9, 313–14, 316–17, 319–21; and Alfred Rosenberg, 135–37, 169, 173, 191, 195, 210; apocalyptic reading of German history, 7–8; and barbarization of German culture, 9–10, 12, 14, 20–21, 23–82; and crisis mode of historical thought, 7, 10; criticism of Fascism and Nazism, 32–37, 104, 127; as Der Kaiser, 29; exile and literary mission, 29–32
  Buddenbrooks, 24
  Doctor Faustus, 5, 10, 23–82; the barbarization of German culture, 65–71; Faustus reckoning and German abomination, 77–81, 84, 86, 90, 164–65, 212, 220, 247, 250, 252, 257–58, 263, 266, 271, 276, 309; history: time and place," 47–48; literary antecedents, 41–47; peculiar intertwining of time's course, 61–66; Satan's apocalypse, 71–77
  "Appeal to Reason," 24, 32
  "Bruder Hitler, 195–96
  Death in Venice, 24
  "Ein Appell an die Vernunft" ("An Appeal to Reason"), 24
  "Goethe und Tolstoi," 24
  Joseph and His Brothers, 12, 36–37, 299
  Joseph the Provider, 36–37
  "Little Mr. Friedmannm," 23
  The Magic Mountain, 24, 68
  Mario and the Magician, 32–34
  Reflections of an Unpolitical man, 24
  Simplicissimus, 23
  The Tables of the Law, 37–41
  "The Theme of the Joseph Novels," 299
  "Von deutscher Republik" ("The German Republic"), 24
Marburg University, 91, 190, 212–14
Marburg School of Neo-Kantianism, 91–92, 94, 114
Marcellinus, Ammianus, 223–24
  Res Gestae, 223
Marcuse, Herbert, 254–55
Marlow, Christopher, 28, 42–43
  Doctor Faustus, 28
  The Tragical History of the Life and Death of Doctor Faustus, 42
Marquis de Sade, 256, 265, 286, 288–89
  Juliette, 288
  Justin, 288–89
Marx, Karl, 15–16, 19–20, 86, 145, 147, 246–49, 254, 265, 267, 269–70, 291, 294, 304–5, 316
Marxism, 19, 203, 244
Marxist dialectic, 147, 245, 262, 306
Marvell, Andrew, 217–19
  "An Horatian Ode upon Cromwell's Return from Ireland," 217
  "To His Coy Mistress," 217–18
Meinecke, Friedrich, 15–16, 127
Mein Kampf, 136, 202
Meister Eckhart, 135
Melita Maschmann, 55

Menocal, María Rosa, 167
  Shards of Love: Exile and the Origins of Lyric, 167
Mephistopheles, 27–28, 42, 127
Midway (Battle of), 3, 168, 219
Migration Age, 258
Millennium, 109, 157
Milton, John, 41, 44, 217–18, 318
  Paradise Lost, 41, 44, 318
  Paradise Regained, 318
Miltonian moment, 41
Modern Realism, 222, 233–34
Molière (Jean-Baptiste Poquelin), 224–25
Monteverdi, 76
  L'Arianna, 76
Montgomery, Bernard Law, 39
Moses, 37
Mosse, George L., 12, 108, 297, 313
Müller, Ludwig (Reich's Bishop), 204
Munich, 23, 55, 62, 66, 71, 77, 98, 114, 188, 205, 215, 248
Munich university, 248
Mussolini, Benito, 33, 141
Myth of the blood, 12, 15, 109, 252
Mythology, 6, 14, 17, 85, 87, 93, 122; and Enlightenment, 317; Greek, 155, 199, 256, 268, 270, 274–75, 289, 299, 302, 309; Norse, 136, 172; and philosophy, 134; Scandinavian, 138
Mythology of blood, folk, and homeland (*Heimat*), 6

Namibia, 47
Namibian War, 47
Napoléon Bonaparte, v, 67, 138, 149, 151, 283
National Socialism, 24, 32, 42, 69, 72, 87, 108, 141, 146, 153, 158, 203, 208, 220, 252–53, 276
Natural rights, 131–35
Nazi barbarism, 4–5, 7, 8–11, 17, 21, 23, 30, 36–39, 42, 50, 54, 56, 61, 63, 66–67, 69–70, 85, 90, 108, 142, 152, 159, 161, 164, 169, 172–74, 178–80, 192, 217, 220, 225, 243, 246, 250–53, 257, 262–63, 271–72, 275, 277–78, 287, 290, 291, 293, 305, 308–10, 310, 315–21
Nazi culture, 108, 169, 247, 303
Nazi historiography, 8, 13, 36, 54, 90, 108, 182, 208, 309, 316
Nazi mythology, 105, 118
Nazi propaganda, 17
Nazi racialist propaganda, 10, 67
Nazi Revolution, 13, 24, 36, 48, 70, 88, 97, 105, 110, 155, 165, 175, 253, 298, 312, 315
Nazi tyranny and barbarism, 108
Neo-Kantianism, 91, 94, 115
Neumann, Erich, 318
  Depth Psychology, 318
Newton, Isaac, 102, 144
Nicholas of Cusa, 92
Niebuhr, Reinhold, 21, 241, 292
  Moral Man and Immoral Society, 292
Niemöller, Martin, 163
Nietzsche, Friedrich, 24, 91, 261, 265, 270, among the dark writers of the Enlightenment, 270, 281–83, 286, 288–89
  The Birth of Tragedy, 282
  Genealogy of Morals, 288
  Philosophy in the Tragic Age of the Greeks, 282
Neumann, Franz, 220, 253
  Behemoth: The Structure and Practice of National Socialism, 220, 253
Neumark, Fritz, 214
New Testament, 13, 75, 111, 168, 187, 200, 204, 208–9
Noah's Ark, 218
Norse mythology, 136, 172; Odin, 138
Nuremberg, 72, 193, 211

Nuremberg, 72, 193
Nuremberg Laws, 212
Nurse myths, 57

Odessa, battle of, 63
Odysseus, 9, 85, 106-7, 155, 165, 182, 232-33, 264, 266-67, 270, 278, 281-85; as prototype of the bourgeois individual, 282, 298, 301
Odysseus' Scar, 9, 106-7, 109, 233, 298
Odyssey, 9, 85, 89, 96, 155-56, 165, 167, 232-33, 256, 267, 270, 281-85
Old Testament, 6, 8-9, 12, 13-14, 36, 75, 107-8, 111, 121, 167, 168, 171-74, 185-87, 193, 196, 198, 200, 202-9, 211, 227, 242, 298-99, 302-3, 310, 316-18

Pacific Palisades, 25, 252, 256
Palestrina, 23, 59, 62
Pandora Box, 274
Panzer Army Africa (Panzerarmee Afrika), 4, 219
Paradiso, 45
Pascal, Blaise, 174-75
  Pensées, 174
Patton, George, 72-73
Paul, Saint, 14, 168, 200, 204-5, 238
Paulus, Friedrich, 3, 219
Persia, 4, 113, 197, 219
Peter, Saint, 215, 223
Peter Valvomeres, 235
Petronius, 237
Philology, 8, 13-14, 84, 108, 167-242, 247, 298
Philology and history, 178-75
Philology and ideology, 185-87
Philology and Weltliteratur, 239-42
Pietà, 77, 320
Plato, and Legal State, 9, 114-24; and Hegel, 20, 140, 147; and Machiavelli, 86, 130; and Marx, 16, 20, 140; and Popper, 85; and rational theory of state, 111, 124-26, 130, 140, 153, 161-62, 226; and Socrates, 119-22
The Republic of Plato, 119, 124, 226, 233
Timaeus, 122
Platonic eternal ideas, 226
Platonic ideal state, 124
Platonic moment, 120
Pocock, J. G. A., 126
Poliakov, Léon, 198
Politics of presentation and representation, 221-22
Pollard, Sidney, 307-8
Popper, Karl, 16, 18-20, 84; and Cassirer, 85, 103; and Hegel, 145-46, 161, 164, 179, 187, 225, 310; and Hegelian historical determinism, 103, 104, 119-21; and Plato, 85; and Strauss, 128
The Open Society and Its Enemies, 145-46, 163
The Poverty of Historicism, 145-46
Positivism, 280-81
Pre-Socratic philosophers, 9, 118
Princeton seminar, 237-39
Propaganda, 10, 17, 27, 55, 65, 67, 111, 193, 206, 215-17, 257, 264, 283, 290, 295-96, 312
Protestant Reformation, 9, 27, 49-50, 75, 131, 263, 295, 317
Proust, Marcel, 8, 11, 169
Prussia, 20, 57, 147, 149, 151-52, 159, 179, 188-89
Prussian State Library in Berlin, 189
Pufendorf, Samuel von, 129, 133
Purim, 111-12
Purgatorio, 45
Puritan Revolution, 217-18

Rabelais, François, 242

Index / 361

Racial anthropology, 198
Racine, Jean, 225, 231
Radio, 25, 35-36, 40, 56, 141, 270, 290, 292, 294-96
Ranke, Leopold von, 6
Rathenau, Walther, 24
Rational representation of reality, ix, 8, 167-242
Realism, 9, 11, 16, 18, 127, 167-242, 299, 318, 320
Realism, modern, 222, 233-34
Reichstag, 47, 58, 76, 88, 249
Renaissance, 15, 60, 68, 84, 90, 93, 95, 115, 128, 131, 165, 189, 202, 211, 220, 234, 239, 258, 265, 311, 313
Renaissance Humanism, 68, 313
Representation of reality, 5, 8-10, 13, 107, 121, 176, 216, 221-22, 227-28, 230, 233-35, 251, 298, 309, 316
Riefenstahl, Leni, 173, 283
  Olympia, 173, 283
Riker, Heinrich John, 92
Ritter, Gerhard, 57
  Machtstaat und Utopia (National Power and Utopia), 57
Rockefeller, John D., 291
Roman Empire, 14, 57, 240, 251, 283
Romance philology, 178, 188-90, 196
Romantic Movement, 88, 98, 114, 133
Romanticism, 99-100, 126, 129, 132-34, 209; against Enlightenment, 100
Rommel, Erwin, 4, 39, 219
Rosenberg, Alfred, 109, 135-37, 153, 172, 201-2, 252
  The Myth of the Twentieth Century: An Evaluation of the Spiritual-Intellectual Confrontations of Our Age, 109, 135, 137, 153, 172, 201, 252
  Volkischer Beobachter (Populist Observer), 135
Rosenberg, Arthur, 314

Rosenzweig, Franz, 251
  The Star of Redemption, 251
Rothacker, Erich, 212
Rousseau, Jean-Jacques, 95, 129, 138
Russia, 3-4, 20, 39-40, 58-59, 63-64, 70, 72, 90, 147, 219, 313

Sack of Rome, 2, 240, 258
Said, Edward W., 180, 191, 315
Sanskrit, 197, 199
Satan, Satanism, 7, 10, 13, 23, 26-29, 37, 40-42, 44-46, 48-52, 54, 59-72, 75-76, 78-80, 86, 110, 127, 317
Satanic apocalypse and eschatology, 27, 40, 42, 49, 51, 62, 67, 71-77
Satanic prophecy, 27, 70-77
Schelling, Friedrich Wilhelm Joseph, 134; philosophy of mythology, 134
Schiller, Friedrich, 52; and Goethe, 73; and Weimar Classicism (*Weimarer Klassik*), 73, 76
  "Ode to Joy" ("Ode an die Freude"), 52, 76
Schweitzer, Albert, 101, 150
Scholem, Betty, 97
Scholem, Gershom, 20, 97, 251
Schopenhauer, Arthur, 24, 67
  The World as Will and Representation, 67
Self preservation, 20, 244, 266, 276-77, 285, 287-88, 301
Seneca, 125
Separation of styles, 222, 235
Sermo gravis, 222
Sermo humilis, 222, 224
Sermo remisus, 222
Sermo remisus et humilis, 222
Sermo sublimis, 222
Sevastopol, 3, 219
Shakespeare, William, 138, 140, 231
Sirens, 85, 156, 267, 278, 281, 290, 295
Skidelsky, Edward, 90

Shklar, Judith, 314
Skinner, Quentin, 126
Socrates, 119–20, 122
Sodom and Gomorrah, 65
Space of experience and horizon of expectations, 309, 316
Span, Othmar, 98
Spender, Stephen, 2, 89, 178, 259
Spengler, Oswald, 6, 106, 136, 151, 157–62; fatalism, 157–59; and Heidegger, 160, 162, 162, 169, 209, 275–76; philosophy of pessimism, 158
  Decline of the West, 106, 136, 157–59, 169, 266, 275, 317
  The Duties of German Youth, 159
  The Hour of Decision, 152, 159, 179
Spies, Johann, 42
Spinoza, Baruch, 21, 147, 244, 276, 317
Spitzer, Leo, 170, 180–83, 192, 226; philological circle, 181
  Anti-Chamberlain, 181
Stalingrad, battle of, 4, 37, 40, 58–59, 90, 100, 147, 168, 219, 243, 261, 263, 308, 313, 316
Standardization and uniformity of culture, 242, 276, 292–93
Steiner, George, 192, 315
Stendhal (Marie-Henri Beyle), 187, 234
Stern, Fritz, 313
Stoic ideas, 17, 85, 100, 114, 124–25, 144, 268, 286; revival of, 131–33
Stoic philosophers, 114–15, 125–26, 132, 286
Stoicism, 124, 131
Strauss, Leo, and totalitarianism, 16; and Hegel, 18, 84, 93, 128; and Popper, 128, 179, 225, 237, 310, 321
  Natural Right and History, 84
Student uprising in Munich, 55
Sweden, 96–97, 101–2, 118, 312
Switzerland, 25, 32, 195, 321

Syphilis, 46, 52

Taboo, 301–3
Tacitus, Publius Cornelius, 224
Technology, 271, 277, 291–92, 295
Teutonic peoples, 135
Thirty Years' War, 72
Thousand-Year Reich, 6, 71, 105, 109, 157, 216, 319
Tillich, Paul, 255
Time and eternity, 217–20
Tobruk, 4, 219
Tolstoy, Leo, 36
Totalitarianism, 8, 16, 20, 84–85, 87, 104, 121, 128, 137, 144–45, 252, 259, 271, 274, 295, 299, 304, 311
Tragedy, 32, 45, 51, 54, 102, 191, 222, 234–35, 259, 295, 315, 317
Trauma, 5–6, 12, 21, 101, 139, 252, 268, 297, 307–20
Treblinka, 212
Troeltsch, Ernst, 92
Troy, 284
Turkey, 3, 186, 191–92, 215, 219, 238
Turning-point, 3, 7, 10–11, 14–15, 17, 54, 58–59, 114–15, 124–25, 127, 134, 138, 150, 164, 175, 216, 226–28, 234–35, 250–51, 258, 264, 273, 297, 302, 304, 299, 309, 319
Typology, 75–76, 238

Ulysses, 153, 167, 186, 232
University of Bonn, 25
University of Frankfurt, 88, 247–48, 253, 255
University of Gothenburg, 96, 161
University of Hamburg, 93, 96
University of Marburg, 190, 212–13
University of Princeton, 25, 136, 152, 196, 237
University of Vienna, 248

Value judgment, 223–24
Vanderbilt, Cornelius, 291

Vico, Giambattista, 169, 173, 179, 183, 184, 189, 210, 213, 221, 225, 228–29, 239
  The New Science of Giambattista Vico, 189
Virgil (Publius Vergilius Maro), 46
Vogler, Georg, 67
Volk and Führer, 33
Völkisch historiography, 84
Völkisch ideology, 72
Völkisch mysticism, 8, 13, 172, 247, 298, 309
Volksgeist (national spirit), 15, 167, 173, 298, 310
Volksseele (ethnic soul), 15
Voltaire, François-Marie Arouet, 17; style in propaganda, 17
Voronezh, 3, 219
Vossler, Karl, 170, 191

Wagner, Richard, 24, 32, 52, 135, 257, 293
  Ring of the Nibelung, 52
  Tristan und Isolde, 52
  The Twilight of the Gods, 52
Warburg Library for Science and Culture, 93, 103
Wartburg, 60, 208
Weber, Max, 50
  The Protestant Ethic and the Spirit of Capitalism, 50
"We, the Dead, Accuse," 73–74
Weimarer Klassik, 52, 73
Weimar Republic, 5, 24, 32, 47, 52, 57, 65–66, 72, 87–88, 93, 97–99, 117, 173–74, 189, 210–11, 240, 275

Wellek, René, 153, 170, 175, 183, 222, 242
Wells, H. G., 62
Weltliteratur, 183, 187, 230, 239–42
Western humanist civilization, 3, 11, 151, 153, 196, 261, 283, 268, 308, 310, 315, 317, 319, 321
White Rose, 55–56
Whitman, Walt, 237
Wilhelm II, Kaiser, 57, 255
Wilhelmine Germany, 57, 188
Windebland, Wilhelm, 92
Wittenberg, 60
Woolf, Virginia, 8, 11, 169, 223, 232
  To the Lighthouse, 232
Woltmann, Ludwig, 211
  The Teutons and the Renaissance in Italy, 211
World War I, 24, 36, 58, 61, 64–65, 68, 93, 97, 136, 154, 172, 188, 209–10, 248, 251; "the war that will end war," 61
World War II, 2–3, 7, 11, 21, 35, 39, 46, 48, 51, 64, 69, 70, 89–90, 97, 103, 118, 153–54, 161, 169, 178, 194, 199, 213, 215, 219, 236, 238, 240, 242, 249, 253, 259, 260, 263, 271, 304
Wulf, Harm, 72

Yale University, 19, 87, 89, 96, 102, 153, 173, 191, 196, 242, 295, 315

Zola, Émile, 237
Zweig, Stefan, 1, 4, 39, 220, 308

www.ingramcontent.com/pod-product-compliance
Lightning Source LLC
Chambersburg PA
CBHW030126240426
43672CB00005B/40